A History
Leek

Images of Bygone Leek

Ray Poole

DEDICATION

The late George Lovenbury, George Bowyer, Colin Parrack and Beryl Johnson did much to collect, record and preserve items of Leek's history, and I am grateful to them. In many ways the book is dedicated to their memory

ACKNOWLEDGEMENTS

Someone once said, "I have put my sickle into other mens' corn". In compiling this book I found it necessary to do just that, and there are many people, individuals and groups, whose work and resources have been tapped, and to whom thanks are due. I am always grateful to my former employer, the late Fred Hill, whose insight in producing 'Leek News' during the 1920s and 30s has provided many pages of material and much inspiration. I have drawn upon the fine collection of the late Stuart Hobson, and thanks are expressed to Mrs Barbara Hobson. Other main sources for information and material have included the Leek and District Historical Society collection, the Robert Cartwright collection, the Leek and Moorlands Historical Trust, Leek Library, the County Record Office Stafford, Leek Post and Times, Leek and District Field Club, Leek Cricket Club and the Brindley Mill. Individuals who have helped are numerous, and many may have done so without knowing. I therefore list the following: John White (who kindly loaned his fine copy of Slagg's 1862 map of Leek and other items), Rev. Michael Fisher, Geoffrey Fisher, Basil Jeuda, Harold Bode, Basil Turner, Michael Drynan, John Felthouse and John Newall. Robert Milner is always a constant and reliable source of information.

I must also thank Paul Anderton and the late Alan Jeffrey, whose local history classes have always been a source of inspiration. Finally the alphabetical listing of the names of the Napoleonic French prisoners on page 26 was the result of many hours of painstaking work by Joan Bennett, Colin Parrack, Cathryn Walton and myself for the Leek Historical Trust exhibition, and subsequent publication, *French Connections*.

And a special word of thanks to my wife, whose patience endures my shortcomings and tolerates piles of paper and files in places where they should not be.

CHURNET VALLEY BOOKS

6 Stanley Street, Leek, Staffordshire.ST13 5HG 01538 399033

www.thebookshopleek.co.uk

ISBN 1 897949 73 1

CONTENTS

LEEK OLD TOWN HALL

It was in the upper room of the old Town Hall, illustrated above, that the business of the Leek Savings Bank (see accompanying article) was conducted from 1823 to 1853.

Built about 1806 at the fork of Sheep Market and Stanley Street, it stood till 1872, when it was condemned to be taken down and was sold to Mr. J. Flower, who used much of the material in the building of Portland House.

The basement comprised of two cells in which delinquents were at one time temporarily imprisoned. Originally the ground floor was an open shelter, but later was enclosed with windows, &c., as shown in the illustration, and used as a news room. The top room was used for any public business connected with the town.

INTRODUCTION

Leek is an example of a traditional country market town that became a mill town with the advent of the silk and textile industry. It is essentially a Victorian town, for this was the era of its greatest growth. Its inhabitants are, and always have been, pragmatic, as gritty as the moorland countryside which surrounds the town, and as tenacious as the rocks which dominate so much of the local landscape.

The thread of Leek's history, like the thread in a piece of its famous woven silk, has produced an intricate pattern, with many colours of light and shade. Its characters and personalities have blended into the rich pattern of its past, and left their mark in the shaping of the age in which they lived. This book is dedicated to their memory.

The object of this portrait of bygone Leek is to recapture and record some aspects of the town's history, and a few of the events and activities which involved the lives of its citizens, in forming its intangible but nontheless real character.

This book basically follows the structure of my earlier book, Yesterday's Town, Leek, published by Barracuda Books in 1989, and now out of print. This has been entirely revised and substantially re-written in the light of knowledge gained in the twelve years or so since its publication. Subsequent research, by a number of individuals and groups, has enabled me to make considerable corrections and add new material. In particular, there is a new section - Part One - which picks up certain images from that long period of Leek's history from the time of the Domesday Book to the dawn of the Victorian age.

But the story of Leek did not end there. The full history of 20th century Leek is waiting to be told, but as a small step in this direction, Part Three contains brief sketches of the urban growth and municipal development of Leek between the two world wars.

Inevitably, since this book is the work of an individual, the picture presented is a personal, even idiosyncratic one. In responding to the challenge I have tried to hold a mirror to the past to reflect a few images of bygone times. Much has had to be omitted, and there will no doubt be errors, so the image will not be faultless. There is no reference to the period before 1066, and I have dealt with the years 1066-1837 in the short first section, Part One. Any errors and omissions are entirely mine; I take sole responsibility for them.

Ray Poole, Leek, 2001.

IMAGES OF BYGONE LEEK: PART ONE
BEFORE THE VICTORIAN ERA

CHURCH OF ST. EDWARD THE CONFESSOR.

St Edward's Church (from an old print)

Cucking a Scold in the Churnet.

From Sleigh's History of Leek 1883

LEEK 1066-1837

WRITTEN HISTORY IS RATHER LIKE weaving on the loom of time. It can never reveal the whole pattern, nor can it show the entire picture; it can only reflect, on the surface, the images produced by the underlying thread. There is therefore a great danger that such history might then become just a sterile catalogue of dull recorded facts, the stones and wood, the bricks and mortar, the nuts and bolts of history, as it were, when it is the ideas those images generate that are more important. The history of a community is shaped by its language, personalities, creative movements and, perhaps above all, renewal, for if the process of renewal ceases, we perish, or become the mere fossilized remains of a bygone age, a sarcophagus of buried time.

Philip James Bailey, an early Victorian poet, in his long poem entitled 'Festus', said: "We live in deeds, not years; in thoughts, not breaths; In feelings, not figures on a dial."

Figures on a dial are usually static, the hand of history moves onwards, passing over those images, motivated by the movement of the changing times. The march of history, therefore, never ceases; it is a constant process of renewal. Across the years the images change. The camp, the croft, the manor and the castle yield to the mill, the factory and the finance houses of modern times.

The development of machinery, the advance of technology, the growth of commerce and the evolution of transport have transformed the old conditions of life, and brought wealth and influence to some towns previously obscure and unheard of, and thus it is with Leek.

To encapsulate a thousand years or so of Leek's history is beyond the scope and purpose of this or any single book. Nevertheless, the centuries before the Victorian Era are not lost or barren, and we can call up certain images from those years to serve as milestones along the way.

Call up an image of the DOMESDAY BOOK..........

William of Normandy conquered England in 1066 and was crowned King. Twenty years later he ordered a full statistical survey of England's population and resources, and this first census was completed in 1086.

The entry for Leek in the Domesday Book says: "The King holds Lec, Earl Algar held it". Algar was the son of Leofric, Duke of Mercia. It comprised one hide and land for twelve ploughs. A hide was generally reckoned as a basis for tax assessment, an area which could be ploughed in one year with one plough and a team of eight oxen. The population was stated as 15 villagers and 13 smallholders with six ploughs.

It is interesting to compare the status of Leek in those early days with that of its neighbouring Staffordshire Moorlands towns, Cheadle having one caracute of land (caracute = hide), and Biddulph one hide and land for three ploughs.

Communities were grouped in legal and administrative areas, known as 'Hundreds', within the county. The meaning of the term is obscure. Some authorities state that the area would originally have included 100 families, whilst others favour 100 hides of land. Leek and Cheadle were in the Totmonslow Hundred, and Biddulph in the Hundred of Pirehill. These old names are still used in relation to the structure of Magistrates' Courts areas.

Call up a image of the ABBEY OF DIEULACRES..........

Its soaring columns and arches rising above the low-lying mists in the upper reaches of the valley of the River Churnet, to the north of the town. This large and important Cistercian monastery played a significant role in the economic and religious life of the town from its foundation in 1214AD to its dissolution under King Henry VIII in 1538.

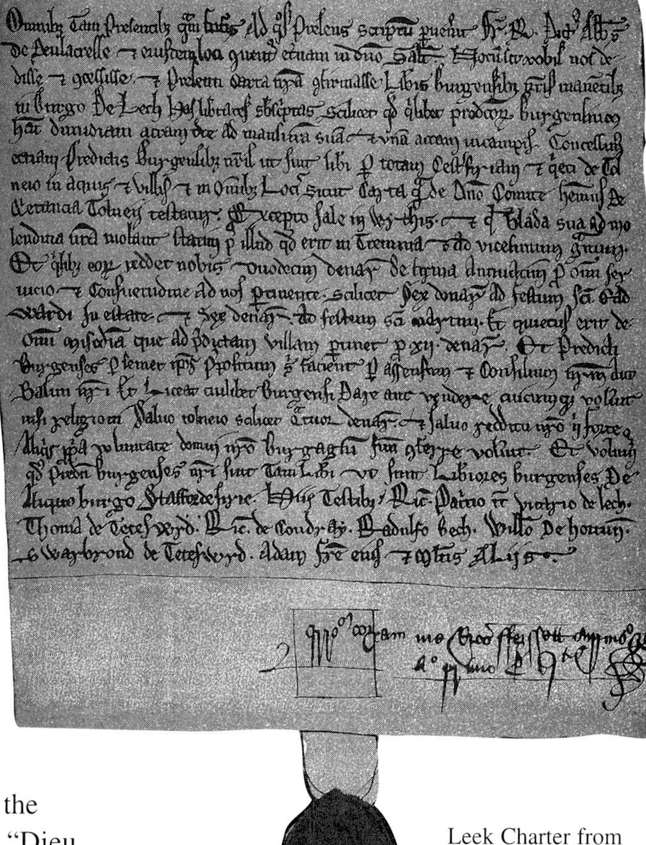

Leek Charter from Sleigh's History of Leek

King William handed Leek to his nephew, Hugh Lupus, 1st Earl of Chester. His descendent, Ranulph de Blundeville, 6th Earl of Chester, and a man of considerable power, founded Dieulacres Abbey in unusual circumstances. His grandfather had earlier established an abbey at Poulton, near Chester, which existed in fear of agitation from the Welsh. Ranulph, the grandson, the story goes, was told in a dream by his grandfather to up stocks at Poulton and establish a new Cistercian abbey at Cholpesdale, near Leek. When the younger Ranulph told his wife of the dream she was alleged to have remarked "Dieu l'encres" (God grant the increase and make it prosper), and thus the name of Dieulacres was formed.

Agriculture and wool were the mainstays of the economy and the subsequent wealth generated by the Abbey of Dieulacres. The abbey possessed granges at Swythamley, Birchall, Westwood, Roche Grange, Foker, Easing and New Grange as well as other land and farms within the township of Leek and Lowe. Two water mills were operated by the abbey, and the fishponds, or stews, for the monks' essential supplies of fresh fish were located at Pool End.

The abbot and monks of Dieulacres exerted a great influence over the religious life of Leek. The advowson, or right to appoint a vicar, was lodged with the abbey until the Dissolution of the Monasteries under King Henry VIII. The names of the long line of Vicars of Leek is known since the Abbey records provided them.

Life at the Abbey did not always run smoothly. Disputes occurred from time to time, and matters were complicated by the dependent chapeleries at Horton, Cheddleton and Ipstones, but the abbey vigorously defended its rights, the abbot usually being a very powerful (and not always scrupulously honest) figure. Some abbots felt it necessary to keep bands of armed retainers. In 1379 Abbot William de Lichfield was charged as an accessory to the murder of John Warton of Leek. There was a great riot

Above: Abbey seals from Sleigh's History of Leek

Bottom right:
Masonry and stone coffin lid preserved in
gable end of a farm barn

Below: Round window in St Edward's Church

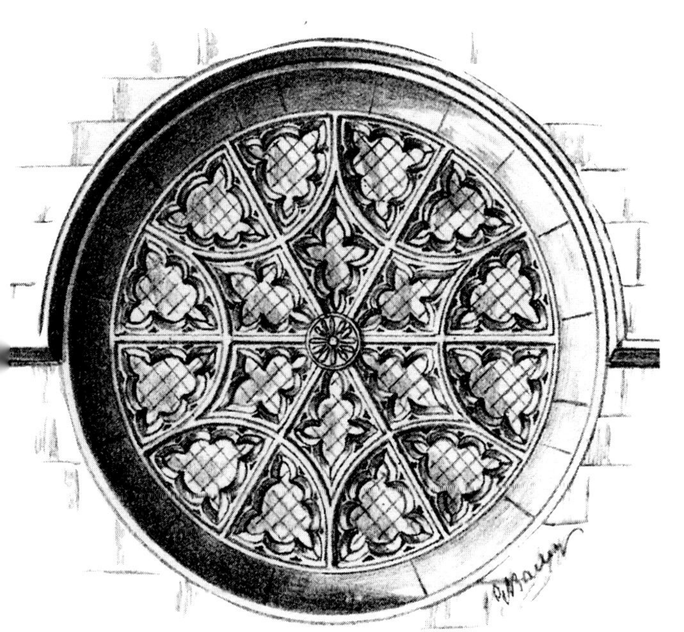

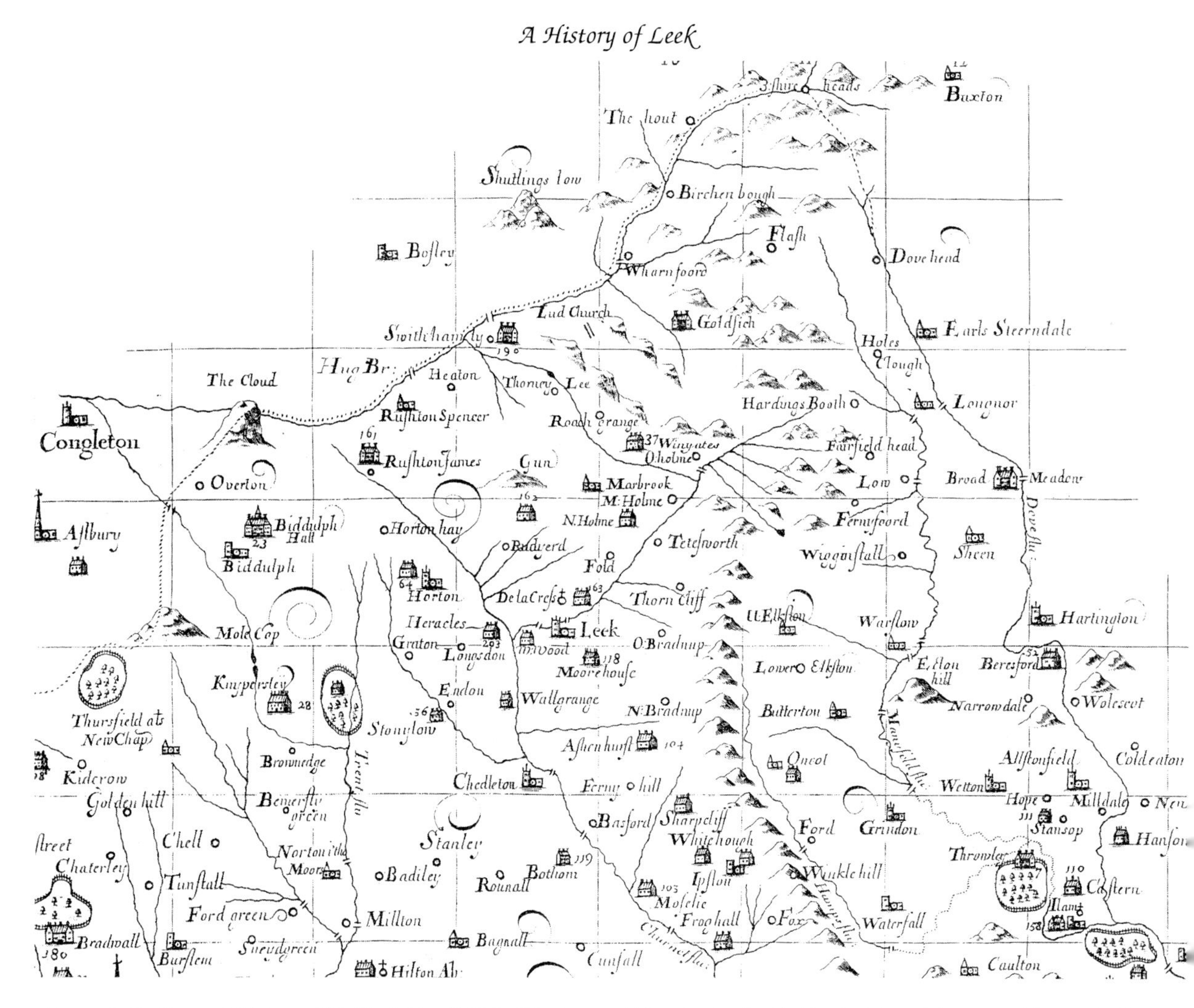

From Plot's *Natural History of Staffordshire* (1686), Dieulacres Abbey in the fertile flood plain of the upper Churnet Valley

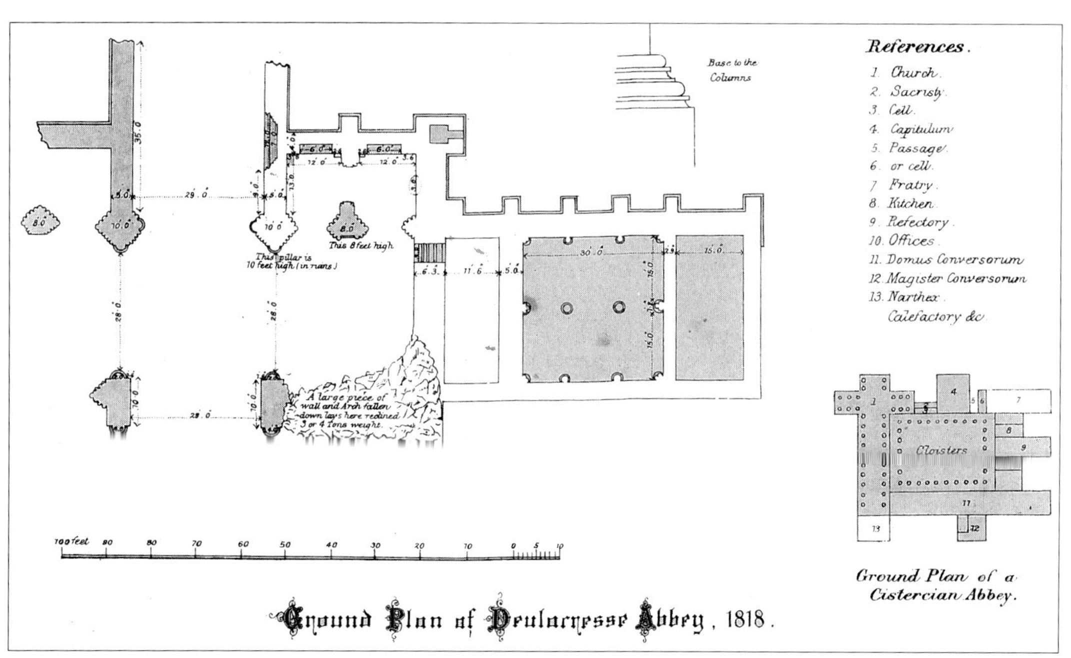

From Sleigh's History of Leek

in Leek in 1516 when Abbot William Albyn enlisted armed forces to prevent the arrest of a number of wrongdoers accused of murder.

The Abbot at the time of the Dissolution in 1538 was Thomas Whitney, who tried unsuccessfully to retain some of the abbey's assets. The abbey was subsequently demolished, the site virtually becoming a building materials supply yard, for much of the fabric was used in other buildings in the area, and around Abbey Farm. (Please note that there is no public access to the site.)

Call up an image of the MARKET CROSS..........

The stone cross in Leek Market Place is a true market cross. However, it has been moved to several different sites since it was first erected in the Market Place, possibly as early as the 13th Century, when the Market Charter was granted in 1208, and each move coincided with a significant phase in Leek's history.

Its first move from its original position took place in 1806, when the little building that became Leek's original town hall was built on that same spot. This marked an important step in the local government of the town, for it was in this building that the Leek Improvement Commissioners held their meetings, together with the magistrates. Here the affairs of the town were debated, and law and order were dispensed. At first the ground floor was used on market days by the market folk, who found it cold and cramped, and later, when windows were put in, it served as a reading room and the office of the Leek Savings Bank. In 1872 the trustees of the Leek Town Lands decided that it was inadequate for the needs of the growing town. It was then sold for £85 to Joseph Flower, demolished, and some of the masonry used in other buildings, notably Portland House (now also demolished).

Leek's Market Cross was in the cemetery between 1858 and 1986

In 1806, then, the Market Cross was moved for the first time to a new site at Cornhill, on a sharp rise of land near the turnpike road, looking towards Cheddleton Heath, around which, from 1857, the cemetery would develop. Indeed, it was this development which brought about its next move, for the dominant vantage point it had occupied was chosen for the erection of the Gothic style Cemetery Chapel by the architect William Sugden in 1858. A short move of a mere few hundred yards to the south-west was the new site of the cross, on a pathway, and here it remained for over 100 years, as the cemetery developed around it.

The cross was finally moved back into the Market Place in 1986 as part of a pedestrianisation scheme in the lower Market Place and upper Derby Street area, and it now stands but a few yards from its original site!

Miller's Olde Leeke (1890) quotes an article from the Leek Times of September 23rd 1871, which says:

> *One of the Abbots of Dieu-la-cresse erected it as a badge of the mutual dependence of the town on the Abbey; and also, perhaps, of the Abbey on the market. And at its foot, every week, one of the monks, or their bailiff, attended to take the tolls.*

It is clear that, as the market prospered, a good deal of trading, bartering and haggling would be carried on around the foot of the cross. It was always the prerogative of the Lord of the Manor or his agents to collect the market tolls at the cross.

Another old custom, recalled by Miller, was that of publishing the banns of marriage at the Market Cross. He cites, as evidence, the Leek Parish Register:

> *The bands (sic) of marriage between Robert Fernihough, carpenter, of the parish of Ipstones, and Ellen Smith, of ye same place, were duly published at ye Market Cross, at Leek, in ye county of Stafford thre (sic) several times on July 15th, 22nd, and 29th, 1657, and were marryed Sept. 15th, 1657.*

The Market Cross in its present location surrounded by busy market stalls

Call up a image of the ENGLISH CIVIL WAR..........

It is perhaps surprising that this major event in the nation's history had relatively little impact on Leek itself. However, with such a wide conflict sweeping through the land, Leek did not escape entirely, though the area never saw a major battle. Leek and the Moorlands, generally speaking, sided with Parliament, and any attempt at Royalist infiltration was promptly dispatched. However, a Royalist garrison was eventually established at Leek, and there was also one at Biddulph.

The area supplied men for service in the troop of parliamentary soldiers known as the Moorlanders, and a garrison was set up in Leek. These local men would no doubt take part in the attacks on Stafford by the Moorlanders. In 1644 Colonel Sir John Bowyer of Knypersley was appointed governor of Leek. As elsewhere throughout the land, the war would divide families, setting brother against brother.

The Trafford headstone in Leek churchyard

A story from the time of the Civil War recounts an incident in which a Royalist named William Trafford, who died at Swythamley in 1697, saved himself from attack by a group of Cromwell's men by passing himself off as a rustic idiot, and answering "Now thus" to their questioning, whilst continuing with his threshing work. Thinking they had apprehended a bucolic simpleton, they left him alone. His headstone in Leek churchyard carries the inscription "Now thus".

Call up an image of THOMAS PARKER..........

Thomas Parker senior was a lawyer in Leek during the 17th Century. In 1666 his son was born, also called Thomas, after his father. At the time the Parker family was living in a stone-built house at the northern end of the Market Place, which is now fronted by the old shops between Foxlowe and the Vicarage, where Church Street joins the Market Place. Young Thomas followed his father into the legal profession, became a distinguished barrister, and was later appointed Queen's Counsel. He was knighted in 1705, and was appointed Lord Chief Justice in 1710. In 1716 he was created Baron of Macclesfield, and in 1718 was raised to the exalted position of Lord Chancellor of England. His final accolade came in 1721, when he became the first Earl of Macclesfield.

He earned the nickname of 'Silver-tongued Parker', and the reason for this became apparent when, in 1725, he was impeached on charges of mal-practice and corruption, put on trial before his peers and was found guilty. He was removed from office, and fined £30,000 for his crimes, a debt that was ultimately discharged in full.

He was Lord of the Manor of Leek, and his lasting memorial in the town is the Old Leek Grammar School on Clerk Bank, which he founded in 1723. He died in Soho Square, London, on April 28th 1732 at the age of 66.

There is an interesting side-light on the life of Lord Chancellor Parker - a possible link with the East India Company. In 1720 Parker's daughter Elizabeth married William Heathcote, MP for Buckingham, who was created a Baronet in 1733. He was the eldest son of Samuel Heathcote of Hackney, a director of the New East India Company. Other members of the Heathcote family also became directors. It was a custom that ships owned by the company were named after leading political figures of the day. Between 1716 and 1779 there were four ships named 'Heathcote', and in service between 1735 and 1739 a ship named 'Macclesfield'. This does not prove that Parker himself was involved with the company, but it identifies him with one of the most important East India families of the day.

Above, Thomas Parker and right, the tablet over the door of the old Leek Grammar School.

Below: The old Grammar School (centre) with the Maude Institute to the left and the driveway to Mount Pleasant Methodist Church on the right.

Call up an image of CHARLES EDWARD STEWART..........

Bonnie Prince Charlie, the Young Pretender, has often been accorded inflated status in Leek's history. Nevertheless, it is important that his brief and fleeting impact be recorded. Leek was just one of the many towns the rebel Highlanders passed through in 1745, when the Prince led his rebellious march south in an abortive attempt to seize the English throne. Always in pursuit was the King's Army, led by the Duke of Cumberland and General Wade.

The picture of a handsome young prince marching boldly into town at the head of his tartan-clad army is over-romanticised. These Scotsmen were rebels, and some were reluctant rebels. They had been on the march for over a month, travelling over rough countryside, often sleeping in the open air, and this was December, the depth of a bleak Moorland winter. The wild moorland area from Macclesfield to Ashbourne through Leek was an inhospitable place, a wilderness of despair for many of the Scots. The rebels, bearing the ravages of their arduous journey, were passing through unknown and hostile territory. Apart from the Prince's chosen favourites, the Stuarts, Camerons and McDonalds, they would be a cold, footsore, mud-bespattered lot, straggled out over a wide expanse of countryside, in constant fear of pursuit and ambush. They would certainly be hungry, and would no doubt be seeking warmth and sustenance wherever they could find it. The impact that this unruly mob would make on the town of Leek, in their brief stay, must have been quite considerable. The Jacobite Rebellion reached Leek on Tuesday, December 3rd, 1745.

The actual whereabouts of the Prince himself are shrouded in mystery. Contemporary sources present a confusing picture, and, whilst there is much hearsay and verbal tradition, hard evidence is very sparse. The Duke of Cumberland was leading a campaign of manoeuvre and counter-manoeuvre, his tactics being to anticipate the movement of the rebels, and endeavour to be one jump ahead of them, as this contemporary report from the Derby Mercury shows:

Stafford, December 4th 1745

H.R.H. the Duke of Cumberland is just returned with the Army under his command, which was assembled at Stone by four in the morning yesterday, upon positive Advices of the Rebels marching by Congleton. H.R.H.'s Van guard was in motion towards Newcastle, when advice came that the Rebels were gone from Leek and Ashbourne, and it was thereupon resolved to march the Army as soon as possible to Northampton, in order to intercept them in their march towards the South. The Van guard will be at Northampton on Friday night.

This report makes no mention of Bonnie Prince Charlie himself, and L. Eardley Simpson, in his book *Derby and the '45* offers the suggestion that...

....it may be doubted whether Charles slept at Leek at all on his way to Derby, the other story being that he resumed the march the same day, and spent the night at Ashbourne Hall. The stay in Leek was a brief one, however, though it is stated that some of the men took the chance of getting their swords sharpened and of having a little musket practice.

Another contemporary newspaper, The Caledonian Mercury, published in Edinburgh, carried regular reports 'from the field', usually in the form of letters:

Derby, Dec. 3. A Party of the Rebels are at Ashbourn, 15 miles from hence, and the Remainder at Leek. The former demanded Billets for 3000 Men. An Express is sent to give Notice to the Duke of Cumberland.

The same journal published the following extract from a letter from Ford Green, Staffordshire, dated December 4:

The Town of Leek was last night vastly filled with a Multitude of Ruffians, being the main Body of the Rebels, with their Baggage and Cannon, which are said to be fourteen or sixteen Pieces. All along as they have travelled, they take all the Horses, Saddles, Bridles, Boots, Armour, or any thing else they can carry off. They pretend to pay for what they have, and give a Penny for a Night's Eating; and for what they plunder, some of them will give something, as Sixpence for an Horse, and so presume to say they have paid for him. From the House in which the young Prince, as they call him, lodged at Leek, were taken things of great Value. Some Rebels have Saddles, some ride with an Halter, and some without either Saddle or Bridle.

This is one of the few direct references to the Prince himself, and, whilst the word 'lodged' implies the provision of temporary accommodation, it does not prove that he spent the night in Leek. However, this is in line with the usual practice throughout the Prince's journeyings, for, in order to protect those who gave him shelter, very rarely is any mention made of the houses in which he lodged.

History goes on to record that, having reached Derby, the Jacobite Rebellion foundered, and the Rebels began their long retreat. A meeting was held at which it became clear that Cumberland's army had out-manoeuvred them, and would be waiting for them at Leicester as they continued their march south. This army could not be beaten without sustaining heavy losses, and, even then, Wade's and other forces would await the weakened rebels as they neared London. There was no alternative but to retreat, and on December 9th the rebels were back in Leek. The Caledonian Mercury records the event:

Dec. 9. The Rebels were at Ashbourn on Saturday Morning, and went to Leek that night. Before they left Ashbourn they shot two Men, one of whom died on the Spot. They have taken all the Horses they could lay their Hands upon, and have plundered and done great Damage.......

By an Express just arrived from Leek there is an Account that 1000 of the Rebels marched last night from thence for Macclesfield. There is even less evidence of the actual lodgings of the much-saddened Bonnie Prince Charlie on the retreat, and the people of Leek would no doubt be glad to see the back of them, for, as the Derby Mercury commented, "we hear that they do more mischief now in the Country than when they came".

Events, short in duration, but of some significance in the history of Leek.

An artist's impression of the Scottish rebels

Call up an image of JAMES BRINDLEY..........

If Bonnie Prince Charlie made no permanent mark on the history of 18th Century Leek, then James Brindley most certainly did. Brindley was a pioneer figure amongst the great civil engineers of the past 200 years; indeed, in many respects he was way ahead of his time, and his influence on the industrial history of the nation was immense.

James Brindley was born in 1716 at Tunstead, Wormhill, Derbyshire, the eldest of the seven children of James and Susanna Brindley. His home was a small cottage, long demolished, that became known as Brindley's Croft. A memorial tablet on the site bears the words:

HERE STOOD THE COTTAGE IN WHICH JAMES BRINDLEY WAS BORN OF HUMBLE BIRTH, HE BECAME FAMOUS AS THE PIONEER BUILDER OF THE GREAT CANALS OF ENGLAND.

When Brindley was ten years old the family moved to a farm at Lowe Hill, Leek, where he grew up, and took an early interest in mills and milling.

In 1733, at the age of 17, he was apprenticed to Abraham Bennett, wheelwright and millwright of Sutton, near Macclesfield. Here he gained much practical experience, and in 1742 he moved back to Leek to set up in business on his own account as a millwright, with a workshop in Mill Street. Thus was launched a career that would change the face of England for ever.

His many natural talents and skills in the field of civil engineering led to him being dubbed 'Schemer' Brindley. He was soon involved in work in the Potteries, where trade was expanding, and both the pottery and the mining industries employed his services. This brought him into contact with such figures as Josiah Wedgwood and Earl Gower of Trentham, as well as numerous other industrialists who were calling for mills and steam engines.

It was Earl Gower who commissioned Brindley to carry out the initial survey for the Trent and Mersey Canal, to link Liverpool with the Potteries. His canal building activities then came to the notice of the Duke of Bridgewater, brother-in-law of Earl Gower, who had envisaged a canal from Worsley to Manchester. Thus James Brindley became the engineer and surveyor of the Bridgewater Canal, in addition to the Trent and Mersey, which ultimately linked the Mersey with the Humber - the West coast with the East coast - when it became known as the Grand Trunk.

Other canal companies then enlisted Brindley's services, such was his fame, and the ensuing complex of waterways ultimately linked the Mersey, the Trent, the Severn and the Thames - Brindley's great 'Grand Cross' canal system. Brindley moved from Leek to Newchapel. He had married Anne, daughter of John Henshall in 1765, and taken up residence at Turnhurst Hall.

Deeply involved with James Brindley were the brothers John and Thomas Gilbert, 18th Century Staffordshire entrepreneurs with many industrial and commercial interests. It was Gilbert's interest in the limestone quarries at Caldon Low which led to the construction of the Caldon Branch of the Trent and Mersey Canal from Etruria to Froghall in 1777, a branch of which would, much later, put Leek on the canal map.

Alas, it was his work on the Caldon Canal that led to Brindley's death. In 1772 he had been surveying the route in the Ipstones area, working in a typical Moorlands downpour. He got thoroughly soaked, and was given a bed in a local inn, which happened to be damp. His severe chill aggravated his diabetes, and he became very ill. He never recovered, and died on 27 September, 1772, aged 56. He was buried at Newchapel.

Brindley's lasting memorial in Leek is, of course, the water-powered cornmill on the River

Churnet, at the junction of Abbey Green Road with Mill Street. Evidence of Brindley's involvement in the mill is attributed to a stone in the wall on the first floor which bears the inscription 'TI 1752 JB'. Brindley constructed a large, curved weir to divert the water from the river to power an undershot weir, 16 feet in diameter. The Brindley Mill was a working cornmill through to the 1940s. The front section was demolished as part of a scheme for widening the road at the bottom of Mill street in the late 1940s. The mill became derelict, and was rescued in the 1970s, when it was reconstructed and refurbished. Restoration work was completed by a trust, which now runs the site as a working museum, which is open to the public at certain times during the spring and summer.

The Brindley Mill before the front section was demolished for road widening

PEDIGREE OF BRINDLEY AND WILLIAMSON.

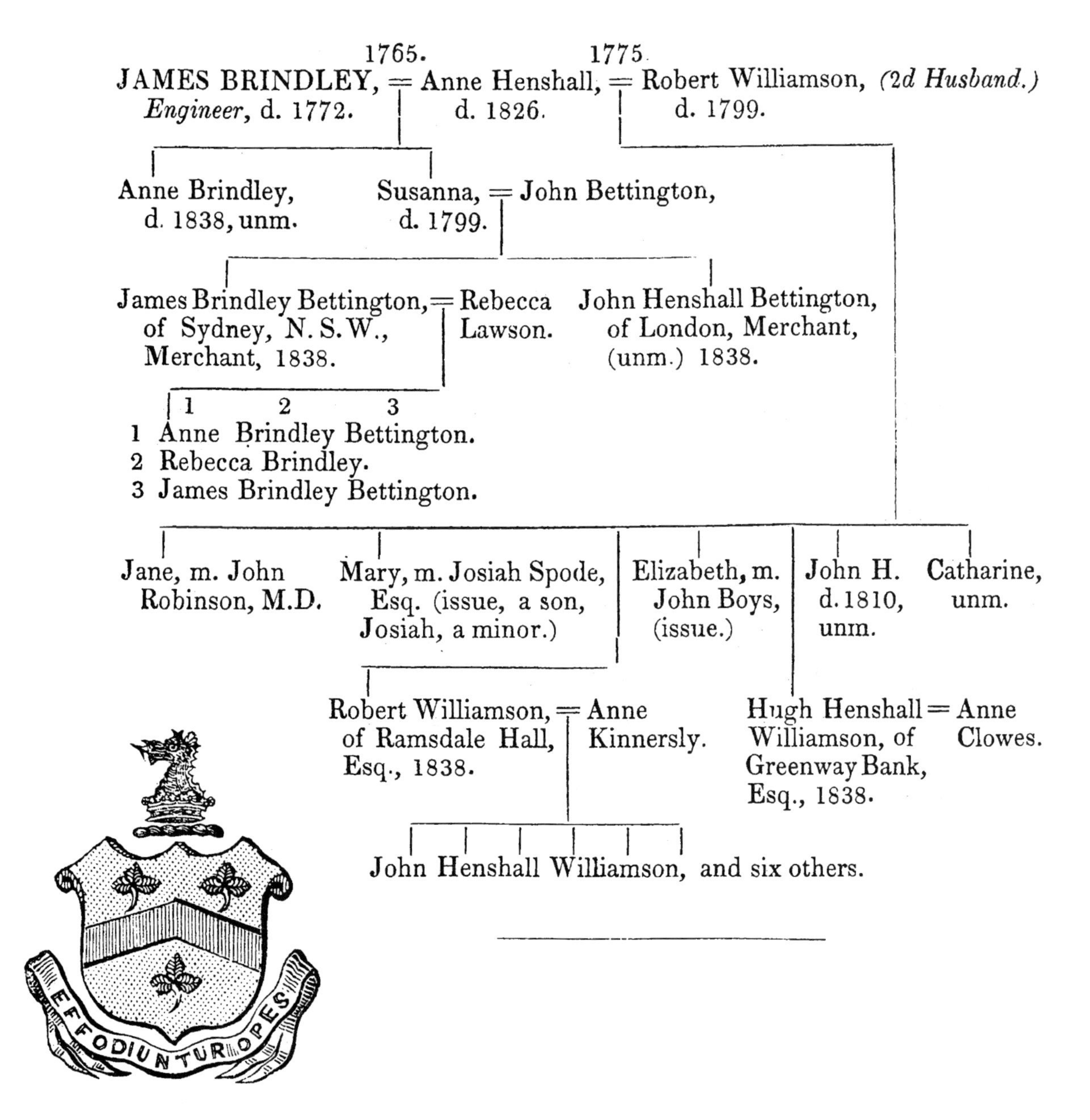
1765. 1775.
JAMES BRINDLEY, = Anne Henshall, = Robert Williamson, *(2d Husband.)*
Engineer, d. 1772. d. 1826. d. 1799.

Anne Brindley, d. 1838, unm.
Susanna, = John Bettington, d. 1799.

James Brindley Bettington, = Rebecca Lawson.
of Sydney, N. S. W., Merchant, 1838.
John Henshall Bettington, of London, Merchant, (unm.) 1838.

1 Anne Brindley Bettington.
2 Rebecca Brindley.
3 James Brindley Bettington.

Jane, m. John Robinson, M.D.
Mary, m. Josiah Spode, Esq. (issue, a son, Josiah, a minor.)
Elizabeth, m. John Boys, (issue.)
John H. d. 1810, unm.
Catharine, unm.

Robert Williamson, = Anne Kinnersly.
of Ramsdale Hall, Esq., 1838.
Hugh Henshall = Anne Clowes.
Williamson, of Greenway Bank, Esq., 1838.

John Henshall Williamson, and six others.

(ARMS OF WILLIAMSON). *Or*—a chevron between three trefoils slipped, *gules*.
Crest—out of a ducal coronet, *gules*, a dragon's head, *or*.

From John Ward's History of Stoke on Trent (1843)

Call up an image of the NAPOLEONIC WARS..........

When Napoleon was rampant in Europe in the early 1800s large numbers of French prisoners from the Napoleonic Wars were sent to England. Some were held in Chatham and Portsmouth, others in the larger city prisons, like Bristol and Plymouth. Norman Cross, a prison near Peterborough, acted as a large 'clearing house' for prisoners. Thousands of prisoners of war passed through these established prisons before being sent on to various inland parole towns, far away from the sea, as a deterrent to escape. Leek was one such town, as were Ashbourne and Lichfield.

At that time, Leek was still a quiet, rural market town, almost isolated from the rest of the country in its moorland location. This, of course, was one reason for its choice as a parole town. The silk industry was still in its infancy, and the outside world had made very little impact on the town. Foreigners would hardly ever be seen in the streets, and one can imagine the effect that the influx of scores of red blooded young Frenchmen would have on this rural community, uprooted as they were from their homes and families, and from their service and social life.

Parole prisoners were usually officers of the army or navy, often with their servants, as well as men of other ranks. The men on parole in Leek were captured either in the Peninsular campaign or the expedition to Flushing, while others were taken off ships in the English Channel or on their way home from San Domingo.

Over 340 prisoners passed through the parole station at Leek between 1803 and 1814, by which time most of them had returned to France.

They were billeted in various houses in the town, mainly around St. Edward's Church, Spout Street (now St. Edward Street), Derby Street, Spooners Lane (now Broad Street), Mill Street and Clerk Bank. They were under the supervision of a Parole Agent, and were allowed a certain amount of freedom, to fraternise with the Leek townsfolk. However, they were subject to a strict discipline, and had to attend a muster twice a week. Nevertheless, those officers who were Freemasons were able to form a lodge and chapter in Leek in 1810-11. The officers also gave enthusiastic support to the various groups of travelling theatricals that visited the town from time to time.

Perhaps the most notable prisoner to be held in Leek was General Jean Baptiste Brunet who was captured at San Domingo in 1803. He arrived in Leek on 12 June 1804, with his Adjutant General, Charles le Fevre, his aide-de-camp Captain Frederick Deguilly and his servants, one of whom was Jean Vatel.

General Brunet had a distinguished military record. He served with the army in San Domingo, with General Rochambeau, who was a prisoner in Ashbourne. Here he was involved in the capture of the Negro leader, Toussaint L'Ouverture.

Toussaint L'Ouverture achieved fame as the leader of a massive black slave revolt in Haiti against the European white powers - Spanish, British and French. Once in power, Toussaint L'Ouverture set up far-reaching economic reforms in a draft constitution for his nation, aimed at prosperity for all. This did not sit well with Napoleon Bonaparte who could not tolerate the idea of a slave ruling the rich colony of Haiti, and the largest invasion fleet in French history set out to depose the upstart Toussaint, the co-called 'Black Napoleon'.

Rochambeau was appointed chief of the French army on Haiti, and General Brunet was ordered to work a subterfuge in a plot to capture the rebel black leader. Brunet wrote a false letter, couched in flowery terms, to Toussaint, inviting him to meet Brunet to discuss certain important matters that could not be conducted in writing. Toussaint was naturally suspicious, but was hoodwinked into thinking that the French really needed him, and he was anxious to find out what the propositions were.

Having thus lured Toussaint to a meeting, Brunet excused himself before the discussions began, and immediately a group of soldiers burst into the room to arrest Toussaint. Brunet then took charge of the captured black leader, and transferred him to a French frigate for transportation. Toussaint's health broke down, and he died in captivity in 1803. It was during this year that General Brunet was captured and brought to Leek. Among other high-ranking officers were Colonel Felix (also taken at San Domingo), Lt Col Pinguet and Lt Col Fremont (captured at Martinique), naval captains Garron, Bigot, Aregnandeau, and Lefebure, Lt Col Farras (of 113 Regiment) and Col Neraud (belonging to the army of San Domingo).

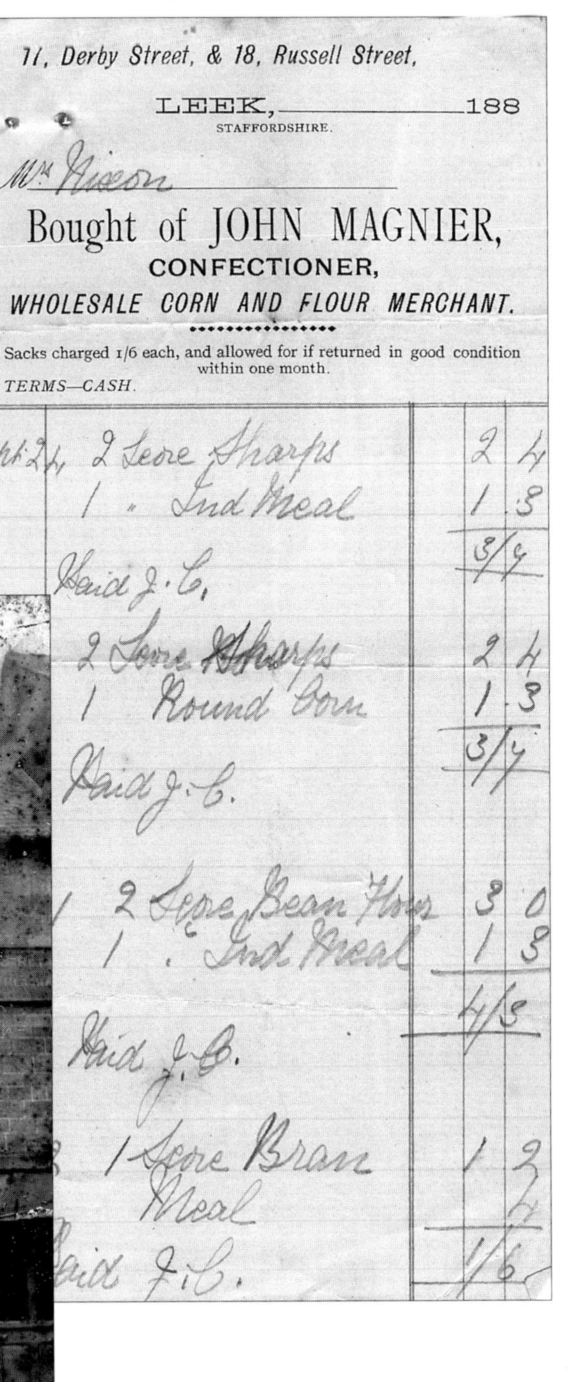

17, Derby Street, & 18, Russell Street,

LEEK, ________ 188
STAFFORDSHIRE.

Mr Nixon

Bought of JOHN MAGNIER,
CONFECTIONER,
WHOLESALE CORN AND FLOUR MERCHANT.

Sacks charged 1/6 each, and allowed for if returned in good condition within one month.

TERMS—CASH.

Sept 24	2 Score Sharps	2	4
	1 " Ind Meal	1	3
		3/7	
	Paid J. C.		
	2 Score Sharps	2	4
	1 Round Corn	1	3
		3/7	
	Paid J. C.		
	2 Score Bean Flour	3	0
	1 " Ind Meal	1	3
		4/3	
	Paid J. C.		
	1 Score Bran	1	2
	Meal		4
		1/6	
	Paid J. C.		

Peter Magnier, a descendant of Pierre Louis Magnier, is seen here at the door of his shop, 17 Derby Street.

Names such as Boucher, Gallant, Monstey, Nourrie, Ducrozs, Virot, Labeaute, Aminoff, Mishon and Millou were also prominent among the officers. There were also a number of surgeons, naval and military, and several boys.

Among other ranks were names like Martin, Baillet, Blanchard, Devilliers, Leduc, Laroche, Lahonton, Picard, and Robin.

The first name in the General Entry Book of French Prisoners of War on Parole at Leek is that of J. Piedagnel, a naval ensign, and the last name (No 346) is I. Poiteoin (of 113 Regiment). Joseph Julien Piedagnel was an accomplished marine artist who had an adventurous life. Two of his pen and wash pictures of naval scenes are in the National Maritime Museum.

The degree of freedom available to the prisoners is reflected in the number of men who married local girls and settled in Leek. A member of the French aristocracy, Louis François Achille Perier, Comte de Salvert, had three children by Ellen Goostrey, whom he eventually married. Other marriages between French prisoners and local girls were as follows:

Jacques François Neau and Mary Lees
Jean Choque and Jane Ball
Adrien Jausserand and Sarah Hanley
Jean Toufflet and Agnes Lowndes
François Gheysele and Sarah Lowe
J.M. Duclezeau and Hannah Ashton
Jean Baptiste François Mien and Frances Smith
Jean Vatel and Sarah Spilsbury
Jean Baptiste Deslisle and Harriett Sheldon
Pierre Louis Magnier and Ann Thompson
Alexander Gay and (1) Julia and (2) Sophy

Some of the men who married lived in Leek for many years and were traders. An army Secretary of Administration, Pierre Louis Magnier. who was captured at Flushing, married Ann Thompson and became a baker and flour dealer, eventually with a shop at 17 Derby Street. Later descendents of Magnier were in the motor business, also operating motor charabancs.

Jean Baptiste François Mien, an army servant, was captured at San Domingo in 1804. He married Frances Smith, and died in Leek in 1870, aged 84, and was buried in Mount Pleasant chapel graveyard. On 21 January 1793, when he was a boy of seven, he is reputed to have witnessed the execution of Louis XVI.

François Neau, a privateer officer on the merchant vessel Perseverance, married Mary Lees, daughter of Matthew Lees of the Duke of York. He had a small shop in Derby Street where he sold straw hats, ivory and bone fancy articles and handicrafts made by the French prisoners. His widow lived on in Derby Street for many years, in a thatched white cottage, where she made excellent toffee. Neau returned to France in 1814, leaving his wife and family in Leek, and, in spite of promises, never returned and never offered any financial support to his family.

Alexander Gay, a seaman, married a daughter of Thomas Beard of The Hole (Ball Haye Road), and lived in Leek until he died in 1850, age 65.

Many of the prisoners were skilled artists and craftsmen, and spent the long hours of their captivity producing pictures, drawings, trinket boxes, pieces of fretwork, marquetry, scrimshaw work and bone and ivory articles.

Some of the prisoners who died in Leek are buried in the lower part of St Edward's churchyard.

They are as follows:

Jean Baptiste Nillot, died 9 June 1811, age 43
Joseph Debcc, died 2 September 1811, age 34
Charles Luneaud, died 4 March 1812, age 70
Captain Decourbes, shot in a duel at Ballington by Captain Robert, 17 October 1812, age 29.
Charles Blanchard, died 13 March 1805.

This explains why that area to the north of St. Edward's Church is traditionally referred to locally as 'Petty France', ie Little France. Also buried in the churchyard is Emma, the four-year-old daughter of François and Mary Neau, who died on 8 February 1810.

It is a pity that more is not known about this fascinating period of Leek's past. It is clear that there are still descendants of the French prisoners living in the town, and it may well be that some local residents possess some of the articles in bone, ivory and wood which were made by the prisoners during their long leisure hours in Leek. Many of these items, such as combs, small household items, trinkets and boxes, were sold at the little shop in Derby Street owned by Jacques François Neau and his wife, Mary.

As a result of the joint efforts of the Leek and Moorlands Historical Trust and the Moorlands Towns Partnership, a fine Memorial to the prisoners has been erected in the Garden of Remembrance to the north of St. Edward's Church, near to the graves of some of the prisoners.

The Memorial was inaugurated on March 26, 1996 by the Baron Gourgaud, President of the Foundation 'Le Souvenir Napolonien' in Paris. The ceremony was witnessed bt Rear-Admiral de Kersauson, Military and Naval Attache at the French Embassy, London, with Vice-Admiral Lucas, representing the Foundation 'Le Souvenir Français', London, accompanied by his Standard-bearer, M. Malvoisin. Also in attendance at the ceremony were Col. German, Vice-Lieutenant of Staffordshire, civic leaders and representatives of the Royal British Legion. The Memorial can be visited at any time.

Thus did some of the major movements in the nation's long history sweep over and around Leek, shaping the nature and character of the town and its people, as these few images have served to illustrate. But the greatest period of the town's development was yet to come, as the Victorian era dawned, heralding a time of great growth, expansion and progress for the town. The wealthy silk manufacturers became the new elite of Leek, and from their position of power, secure in their big houses, were able to exert a great influence over the town, dominating local government, trade associations and societies. That this was an influence for the general good is perhaps a testimony to their integrity, for many of the new institutions established during the latter half of the nineteenth century were aimed at the education and enlightenment of all - always providing, of course, that they had the desire, the means and the ability to avail themselves of them. The social life of Leek during those Victorian and Edwardian years was certainly enterprising and vigorous in many aspects, as the following chapters will show.

No. 6.

H. R. MAGNIER,

CYCLE & MOTOR DEPOT,

Ball Haye Street,

Garage
SILK STREET. . . LEEK, STAFFS.

CARS FOR HIRE.

DISTRICT AGENT FOR
Darracq, Humber & Rover Cars.
Royal Enfield, Sunbeam, Rover Cycles,
etc.

Telegrams:—"Magnier, Leek." Telephone, No. 72.

Dunlop, Michelin, and Continental Motor Tyres stocked.

For. Mr Roland Taylor.

Oct 1908	Reenamelling & Plating Cycle New Palmer Cover fitted New Pedals Rubber Chain Blocks & Shoes, Handles, Overhauling etc	£3.3..
	...el 2/6 New Brake Spring 6	3
		2
	... fitted ...e & Block for Brake & Adj.	1
		£3..10

...d June 15th/09

J. Magnier

Telephone No. 78.

Arthur J. Magnier

MOTOR COACH TOURS

Comfortable & Reliable

Through the **FINEST SCENERY**
in STAFFORDSHIRE
and DERBYSHIRE

This page: Items of business stationery used by members of the Magnier family. The surname has survived in the area for several generations.

Following two pages:

1. A page from the General Entry Book for the French prisoners at Leek.

2. The list of names in the General entry Book

Current Number.	Name of Prize.	When taken.	Whether Man of War, Privateer, or Merchant Vessel.	Prisoners' Names.
241	Flushing	1809 15 Aug	Land	Thos Dupuy
	"	"	"	Ad. Billiard
	"	"	"	J.B. Nolliot
	"	"	"	Jean Langle
245	"	"	"	J Bt Roußet
	No 77.	1809. 15 May	Gun Boat	P.G. Jn Beyrinck
	No 27.	1809. 20 March	Do	Mich. Cordona
		1809. 27 Jany	An American Brig	Alexa Chasteau
	Taken On Shore	12th Sept 1808	at Samana	Ed Nerac
250	La Venus	30 Nov. "	Merchant Vessel	Claude Hauzer
	La Centinelle	16th May 1807	Schooner	Pierre Notin
	Flushing Hospital	15th Aug 1809	Land	Ant. Bourbousieur
	"	"	"	Ae J Derly
	La Fortune	5th Nov. 1807	Privateer	B Boutin
255	Le Pheaton	26 Mar. 1806	Brig of War	Alexa Gay
	L'Aventurier	2nd June 1803	M. V.	Louis Duclos
	Venus	1st July "	"	Henry Le Comte
Thus far entered in General Entry Book T.I.				
	Martinique	24 Feb 1809	Land	Louis Jos. Froliart
	Flushing	15th Aug 1811	"	J.B. Deliguy
260	Chasseure	31 Decr 1810	French Privateer	Gilbt Laforet

A page from the general entry book of French prisoners of war, on parole at Leek

Aiguier 222
Aldebouriere 140 D
Alexandre 299
Alexandre 321 D
Allaire 180
Aminoff 162 D
Andrejean 34 D
Antoine 336
Aregnandeau 150 R
Arnouts 31 D
Aubert 74
Auguste 146 D
Auzon 168 R
Ayercant 68
Bagot 78 D
Bagot 212
Baillet 19
Barnetch 118 D
Barri 136 D
Bastard 92 D
Baudry 29
Bauyn 319
Bayou 288
Bayou 302
Bazin 73 D
Benelot 110 D
Benolt 307
Bequin 225
Berge 194
Bernard 50 R
Bernardeau 104
Berthault 23
Berthault 262
Bertien 312
Bessere 152 D
Beyrinck 246
Bigot 75
Bigot 323
Billiard 242
Blanchard 38 D
Blanchet 128 Dd
Bonfils 297
Bonnaire 308
Boucher 149 D
Boucher 190
Bourbousieur 252
Bourdonnaye 127
Bourgioine 310
Bouteiller 46 R
Boutin 79
Boutin 155
Boutin 254 D
Boyer 52 R
Brayer 8
Bridault 63 D
Broutin 237
Brunet 143
Cailliez 49 D
Calmel 206 R
Calvy 119 D
Carret 158
Carron 304 D
Castle 295
Cazabon 40 D
Cernay 76 D
Chadard 334
Chanoine 274
Charpentier 30
Charriere 199 R

Chasle 230
Chasteau 248 D
Chauvin 41 D
Chenon 36
Chevalier 82
Chevalier 164
Chilion 300
Choquet 89
Chosal 6 R
Cire 108 D
Coger 326
Colin 95 R
Collinet 21
Connor 98
Cordona 247 D
Courcy 120 D
Cousin 2 R
David 261
Davoux 116
De Albe 193 R
Debec 24 Dd
Debulelth 167
Decoubas 215
Dedouit 60 D
Deflere 286
Deguilly 145
Delange 289
Delavel 58 R
Delibeau 231 D
Deliguy 259
Delon 39
Demandot 111 D
Demesen 157
Depontier 99
Derly 253 D
Desessarts 53 R
Deshauteurs 223
Desilles 38
DesLisle 22
Destibichio 166
Destibechio 169
Devilliers 17 D
Dobreurnsky 239
Dorguellly 51
Douall 81
Dousinaque 61
Douver 4
Dreivet 337 D
Dubois 133 D
Ducamp 165 R
Duclezeau 122 D
Duclos 256
Ducross 57 D
Ducrozs 129 R
Duffer 233
Dulsac 273
Dumontier 54 D
Dumoulin 77 R
Dupeyre 338
Duplais 18
Dupont 292
Dupy 241
de Salvert 141
de St Just 213
Faure 335
Favord 294
Fayolle 9 D
Felix 123 D
Feutry 236

Flagelle 35 R
Fort 153 Dd
Fremont 221 R
Frohart 258 D
Gadobert 154 D
Gallais 278
Gallant 188
Garron 72 D
Gary 28 R
Gatteblee 277
Gaudin 64 D
Gay 44 E
Gay 255
Gayhard 327
Genovine 316
Gheysele 5
Giron 109 D
Givone 69 R
Godinot 283
Goracci 311
Goyhence 181
Grandjean 348
Grandville 202 R
Grielen 131
Grimard 102 R
Grimard 163
Guigurd 132
Guillebow 279
Guirard 320
Gunille 197
Gyselinx 175 D
Happey 159 D
Hardouin 91
Hauzer 250 D
Hebert 107
Herecalle 83 D
Heron 32
Herzog 332
Hinet 224 R
Hobarre 191
Homo 208 D
Hoquart 96 R
Hostis 103
Huitaud 298
Jausserand 101
Jazoron 207 D
Jores 138
Joubert 329
Jourdan 59
Joyeuse 25
Jube 271
Juglan 14 R
Kergariou 176 D
Knell 11
L'ange 90 D
Labeaute 130
Laforet 260
Lagentiere 226
Lahonton 37 Dd
Lair 68 D
Lamps 343 D
Landrien 268
Langle 244
Laprade 340
Lapyere 234
Larea 80
Laroche 85 Dd
Laroche 135 Dd
Latouche 114 R

Lauga 86 D
Launay 184
Lauraine 67 R
Le Barbier 331
Le Bas 177 D
Le Blanc 105 D
Le Blond 198
Le Clerce 10 R
Le Clere 182
Le Clerk 124 D
Le Comte 257
Le Fauve 55
Le Febvre 187
Le Fevre 97 D
Le Fevre 144
Le Mers 200
Le Minihy 214
Le Peltier 134 R
Le Sage 66 D
Le Sourd 7 D
Le Sourd 174
Lebaufranchet 269
Leclerq 272
Leduc 303
Lefebure 342
Lefeore 282
Lemonier 183 D
Lelotfre 344
Lepriere 13 R
Leterriere 341
L'Hotte 115 D
Lianard 240
Lourde 192
Luneaud 27
Magniere 227
Maires 189 D
Malecorne 88 R
Marescoe 106
Margalihan 142
Marmier 216
Marmier 218
Martin 113 D
Martin 285
Mas 305
Masset 210 R
Mathiew 263
Maupillier 26 R
Mazard 291
Melani 317
Menant 217
Merle 267
Mespoulet 121 R
Mien 160
Millou 186 R
Mishon 185
Monstey 62 D
Monucret 205
Moulin 94 D
Nanny 309
Nappy 318
Nau 71
Neeschouve 211
Nerac 249 R
Neraud 139 D
Nially 219 R
Nielly 15 D
Ningelgon 209
Nolliot 243 Dd
Nontonnet 203

Notin 251 D
Nourrie 117
Obet 201 R
Olivier 264
Orsaneau 170
Parroni 315
Pensier 42 R
Percy 70 D
Perrot 100
Peyrotte 151 D
Picard 45 D
Picard 204
Pichevin 179
Piedagnel 1
Pierregeuse 333
Pineschi 314
Pinguet 220
Poiteoin 346
Pommie 173 R
Porter 238
Pousseur 276 D
Preugou 196
Regalan 301
Richelle 16 D
Rivoat 339
Robert 280
Robin 93
Roesseu 235
Roger 12
Romain 322
Rouault 125 D
Rouge 161
Rousset 245
Sallo 87 D
Salluneuve 324
Saluce 265 D
Sampson 148 D
Saravella 266
Sarobe 33 D
Saudre 84 R
Sauque 290
Serriere 112 D
Servant 293
Serve 275
Sire 171 D
Sire 172 D
Soldani 313
Souville 56 R
Tanre 328
Tarras 306
Tessier 126 D
Texier 137 Dd
Thoinnet 296
Thoisy 47 D
Thuret 178 R
Touflet 33
Vacossin 284 D
Vanivintershoven 270
Vankosten 228
Vatel 147
Vaussanger 40 D
Vavassieur 232
Verdeil 20 R
Verhulst 229
Viauld 195
Victor 325 D
Vincenot 330
Virot 281
Vivien 156
Yvon 287

THE NAMES OF THE FRENCH PRISONERS IN ALPHABETICAL ORDER

The numbers are the prisoner's number in the General Entry Book.

D = Discharged R = Ran E = Exchanged Dd = Died

The graves of the French prisoners who died in Leek are found in the lower section of St Edward's churchyard - of which it might be said "there is some corner of an English field that is forever France".

Right, the gravestone of Emma, the 4 year old daughter of François and Mary Neau, is located near the path alongside the Vicarage in St Edward's churchyard

The grave of Joseph Debec, Captain of "La Sophie", who died in Leek, September 2nd 1811.

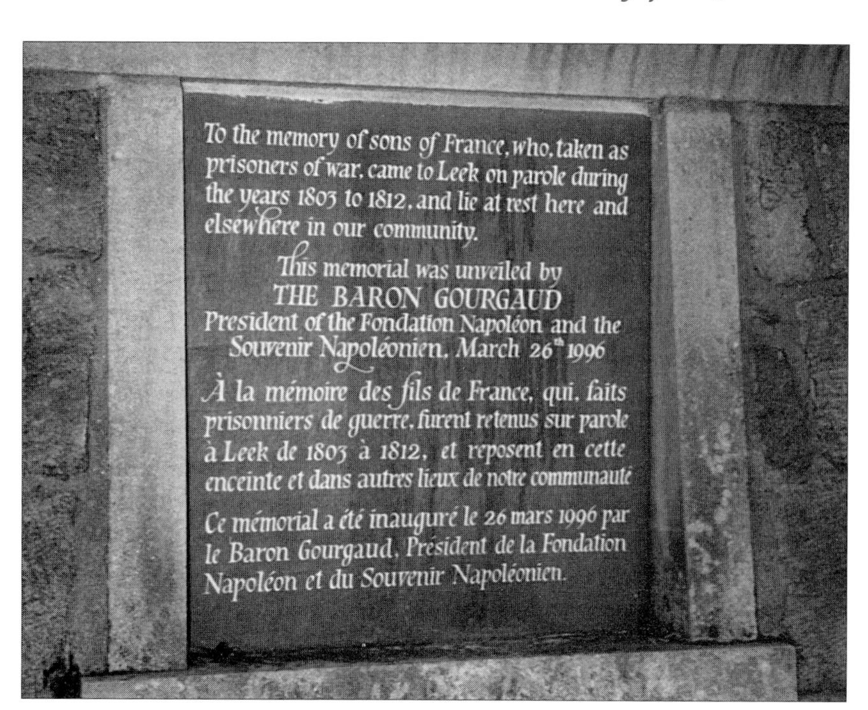

The tablet on the Memorial in St Edward's churchyard, which was unveiled by the Baron Gourgaud on March 26th 1996.

Below, ancient cross remains and the early round window, St Edward's church. These windows are believed to date from the time of Dieulacres Abbey.

Leek has some interesting crosses. This ancient saxon cross, which still stands in St. Edward's churchyard, is much older than the Market Cross.

Old Westwood (from Sleigh's History of Leek)

Leek from Ladderedge, from an old print

VICTORIAN AND EDWARDIAN LEEK

Derby Street

St. Edward Street

INTRODUCTION

WHAT WAS LEEK LIKE IN THE NINETEENTH CENTURY?

IT IS A QUESTION OFTEN ASKED by many people for a variety of reasons - the student, engaged on a local history study project; the visitor, who sees the town as it is today and wonders about the past; the new resident, who only knows the Leek of today and speculates on what made it so; the older resident, whose memory has perhaps faded or become erased by the changing scene; the nostalgia-seeker, who just loves Victoriana and ephemera from the past; the local historian, anxious to make a record of the past for the benefit of future generations, or the conservationist, wishing to preserve and conserve all that is good from yesterday's town.

There are several ways of recording local history. Oral history, word-of-mouth, is always interesting, but subject to the fallibility of human memory and, though local anecdotes, legends and folk tales are fine in their place, they have a tendency to bristle with errors and hearsay.

Written history is, of course, the ideal but, in order to be authoritative, it must be backed by painstaking research and a close study of documentary evidence and original source material.

Then there is pictorial history, a visual record of a town's past seen through the lens of a camera. Every town has its professional and amateur photographers, its local newspaper and, over the years, its various series of local picture postcard views. Leek is no exception to this rule, and it is from these various sources that this portrait of bygone Leek is made.

It does not pretend to be definitive; its only claim to authority is that it is the work of an amateur historian. Most of the pictures and material which follow have been selected to present an impression of Victorian and Edwardian Leek, and to illustrate its growth and development during those years.

Leek is essentially a Victorian town. As we have seen, the elements which made it so were present long before those years. But by far the greatest period of Leek's commercial and industrial development, its growth and prosperity, came during the middle and later Victorian years. The silk and textile industry began to flourish, the old-established mills enjoyed great prosperity, and more were founded. This led to an increase in population, and all these trends had a substantial influence on the town and its people.

The image of Leek as a developing Victorian town is brought into focus in a comparison of three town maps, sections of which are reproduced here. Firstly, the Leek of 1838, in the map copied in 1899 by R Ewan and included in Miller's Olde Leeke Vol 2 (1900). Secondly, the map of Leek produced in 1862 by Charles Slagg, Town Surveyor at that time, under the Leek Improvement Commissioners. Thirdly, the Leek of 1879, one of the earliest, very detailed large-scale Ordnance Survey maps of the town.

THE 1838 MAP OF LEEK

By 1838 the basic road pattern of the town was already laid out, following the Medieval pattern. The main roads passing through Leek were old-established highways, some of them having been turnpiked in the late 18th Century, but many of the streets were as yet undeveloped. The old terraced housing along Mill Street is clearly shown, and the streets around the Market Place and town centre are developed, for this was largely the extent of pre-Victorian Leek, but the northern, western and southern areas of the town (now largely housing estates) are shown as open fields. An interesting feature of this map is the naming of the owners of the land over which the town would later be developed.

To the east, in the area bounded by Buxton Road. Osborne Street, Ashbourne Road (then London Road) and Ball Haye Street, sparse development is shown. A number of mills are marked, these being mainly the pioneers in the local silk industry, with dye works strategically placed near the River Churnet.

The terraced houses along King Street, Albion Street and London Street are mainly the old weavers' cottages, characterised by their attic work-rooms, where the long weaving looms would be set up. These were known locally as 'shades', and they were well-established by 1838, a cottage industry unique to the silk trade.

Certain streets are shown with their original names, notably: Spout Street (now St Edward Street); Custard Street (now Stanley Street); Canal Street (now Broad Street); Workhouse Street (now Brook Street); and London Road (now Ashbourne Road).

Thus, the 1838 map reveals much information about early Victorian Leek, and is a valuable aid in assessing the growth of the town from that time. R. Ewan made a facsimile of the map some 60 years later - the only variations being a slightly different letter style and the omission of relief hachuring to show the hilly areas.

CHARLES SLAGG'S MAP OF 1862

Charles Slagg was appointed Town Surveyor to the Leek Improvement Commissioners on 17th November 1857. He served for about five years, and towards the end of his period in office he produced his Plan of the Town and Environs of Leek, which reflects the growth of the town at that time. He was able to show the railway and a number of new streets mainly on the fringe of the old town, but the basic street pattern of the earlier map can still be seen.

Slagg's map shows a large area of open land lying between London Street and the present Ashbourne Road, where an extensive scheme of infill housing would see the construction of Southbank Street, Fynney Street, Shoobridge Street, Leonard Street, Cromwell Terrace, Livingstone Street, Talbot Street, Moorhouse Street, Wood Street and Grosvenor Street - terraced houses of style and quality for all classes of the growing population. This area of land was owned mainly by Mrs Shoobridge and Mr James Nixon.

To the north of Derby Street, the Ford Street and Bath Street area was awaiting development when Slagg drew up his map. On the western side of the town, land off Canal Street, owned by Hugh Sleigh, was designated for Hartington Street, Hugo Street and Dampier Street. Off Britannia Street, Chorley Street and Gladstone Street would be constructed on the late T. Atkinson's land, and further west, Grove Street and Westwood Grove would stretch out over open land owned by the Earl of Macclesfield. Slagg was also able to include the railway, the gas works and the cattle market at the junction of Ashbourne Road with Derby Street.

AN EARLY ORDNANCE SURVEY MAP

Some ten years later, in the 1870s, the Ordnance Survey was busily engaged in surveying work for their new large-scale maps. This work had been finally authorised in 1863 when, after much discussion and changes of policy, the Ordnance Survey finally adopted the 6 inch and 25 inch scales as being most suitable for large-scale maps of Great Britain.

The maps were produced for urban areas, to meet the growing demand from municipal authorities, county, district and parish councils whose engineers and surveyors were engaged in the laying-out of buildings and in lighting, power, water and drainage schemes. However, until 1892, certain town maps were also published on much larger scales, and Leek is fortunate to have been provided with maps on the scale of 1:500, approximately 10 feet to 1 mile, or more precisely, 127 inches to the mile.

Leek thus had a set of accurate maps presenting a detailed picture of the streets and buildings of the Victorian town a bird's-eye view, as it were, laid out as a precise and accurate plan. The vast amount of fine detail depicted is of great interest to the historian, for we can distinguish buildings now demolished or altered, street lines that have changed, and the vast gardens and ornamental grounds behind some of the more fashionable houses around the town centre, where many of the town's leading citizens lived. Great areas such as these have now been commercially developed, and their former glory lost forever.

These splendid late-Victorian maps also show the layout, location and size of the churches, schools, inns and other public buildings, with the textile mills spread widely around the town, thus illustrating the importance of this industry to the economy of Leek.

SOME IMAGES OF VICTORIAN AND EDWARDIAN LEEK

The quaint little building which served as Leek's Town Hall stood at the south-west corner of the Market Place, at the junction of Stanley Street (formerly Custard Street) and Sheepmarket. Built in 1806, it served the town as a public building in several ways. The business of the Leek Savings Bank was conducted here between 1823 and 1853. The old town hall is an image of the local government of the day, for here the Leek Improvement Commissioners, met in the upper room, which also served as a magistrates' court. The basement contained two cells, where felons were locked up. At first, the ground floor was open, and used by the market traders, but was later enclosed by windows, when it became a newsroom. In 1872 the building was deemed inadequate for the needs of the growing town and, following a meeting of the Leek Town Land Trustees, it was sold to Mr Joseph Flower for £85. He used much of the masonry to build Portland House, formerly in Rosebank Street, and now also demolished.

Just across the road stood the Old Black's Head Inn, at the southern end of the Market Place. Here, in 1775, the early Methodists held meetings in a room above the stable in the inn yard. The room, known as the Club Room, continued in use until 1785, when the first chapel was built on the Mount Pleasant site. John Wesley visited Leek on five occasions: 23 March, 1772, 24 July, 1774, 30 March, 1782, 23 May, 1784, and 5 April, 1788, two of the visits being made when the Black's Head room was in use, and the fifth and final visit after the new chapel, Mount Pleasant, had been opened. The room was also used for a period by the Congregationalists.

The new Black's Head, built on the site in the 1850s, was a fine example of the early work of William Sugden, architect. It later became the Alexandra Club, before being converted to a shop, now Woolworths. The new shopfront has completely altered the ground floor, but the upper storeys are still virtually intact, and are typical of the work of Leek's Victorian architects, Sugden & Son.

William Sugden, a Yorkshireman from Keighley, came to Leek in 1849 to supervise the building of the stations on the Churnet Valley Line of the North Staffordshire Railway. He settled in the town, and set up in business as an architect. His son, Larner, was born in Leek in 1850, and when his education was complete he joined his father in the firm, forming a very effective and successful partnership which left its mark in the provision of many fine Victorian buildings in the town.

However, the Sugdens were not successful in winning the contract for the new Butter Market, planned for the Market Place. This was awarded a competitor, Thomas Brealey, and this well-proportioned building, with its market hall to the rear, gave the market traders the opportunity to have permanent indoor stalls. It has also been used for a variety of public gatherings (including boxing matches) over the years, "If wet, in the Butter Market" being a familiar appendage to advertisements for outdoor functions! In Edwardian times, the Market Hall fulfilled a social need, when the poor children of the town were able to obtain a hot meal there.

Another feature of the Market Place was the Challinor Fountain, on the site of the old town hall. This was presented to the town on 9 December, 1876, by Mr William Challinor, a local solicitor. The highly regarded work of Joseph Durham RA, it was exhibited at the Royal Academy in London, where it was seen by Mr Challinor, who purchased it to present to the town to commemorate the securing of a water supply from the springs at Upperhulme. It was moved to Brough Park in 1924, when the park was opened to the public, where it remained until its reinstatement on the site of the new Staffordshire Moorlands District Council offices at Moorlands House in Stockwell Street.

The piety of the Victorian era is indicated by the strength of the churches, most of which were generously supported by the professional families and the silk manufacturers, enabling large and impressive church buildings to be erected or enlarged. All Saints' Church was built in 1887 to the design of Richard Norman Shaw, the famous and influential Victorian architect. This highly-regarded church has a spacious interior, with a low clerestory and a rather squat central tower. Joseph Challinor and Hugh Sleigh were generous benefactors, and the builders were James Heath of Endon. The chancel painting and panelling is by Gerald Horsley, the Gothic style pulpit and reredos are attributed to Letharby, and some of the stained glass is by Morris and Co. The church has a number of examples of the work of the Leek School of Needlework, the enterprise, encouraged and inspired by William Morris, of Mrs Thomas Wardle and her circle of needlewomen.

The Church of St. Edward the Confessor, standing on an elevated site near the Market Place, is a building of mixed styles and periods of architecture. The church commissioned George Edmund Street to rebuild the chancel in 1885. It is significant that Leek was able to employ the services of nationally eminent Victorian architects, like Street and Shaw. It was the wealth generated by the silk industry that made this possible.

The Victorian Decorated Gothic style St. Luke's Church, completed in 1864, was the work of London architects, F. and H. Francis. Again, the silk industry was a great benefactor. There are memorials to Andrew Jukes Worthington and others to the Challinor and Chell families. These well-attended Anglican churches were able to support full-time clergy and curates, and day and Sunday schools were established, as well mission churches. The Congregationalists, formerly Presbyterians, had been meeting for worship in Derby Street since 1683, first in the loft of a stable, then in two houses, on the site of which a small, purpose-built chapel was erected. This was replaced by the new church of 1863. In 1717 the church had 250 members. A division occurred amongst them in 1833, when a break away group worshipped firstly in the Methodists' old room in the Black's Head stable, and later in their own building in Union Street. This building was later to become the Temperance Hall, then a skating rink. For some time used by the Salvation Army, and ended its days as the Majestic Cinema.

The two bodies of Congregationalists were re-united in 1856 under the ministry of Rev J. Hankinson, and the new Congregational Church, Trinity Church, as it is now, was erected in Derby

Street, on the site of the old chapel, in 1863 by Sugden and Son, the Leek architects. Built in the decorated Gothic style, of local Hollington stone, the spire stands 130 feet above street level.

The original Roman Catholic chapel stood at the corner of Fountain Street and Portland Street. It was built in 1828 by a Cheadle builder named Higgs at a cost of £700. The priest was Father Jeffries, a friend of Mrs Henry Bermingham. The chapel remained in use until 1864, when the Roman Catholics moved to a new church in King Street, before the present St Mary's Church, architect A. Vicars, was built in 1887, when the King Street building became the Parish Hall. The priest at the time was Rev Alfred M. Sperling, a well-loved figure whose services were rewarded in 1916 by his appointment to the dignity of Private Chamberlain to His Holiness the Pope.

Mount Pleasant Methodist Chapel was typical of the free-church architecture of its time, with a large gallery round three sides, massive organ, with choir stalls in front and central pulpit. The first chapel was built on the site in 1785, later to be converted into a house for the minister. The new building was opened on 14 July 1811, at a cost of £4,156, and was improved and enlarged, with a new organ, in 1853 for £700. It was demolished in 1980 and the site was developed for sheltered housing.

Pioneering work in the Sunday School movement, which had its small beginnings in 1797, was centred at Mount Pleasant, and later at West Street School, originally built in 1815, where a day school was established in 1855. The school was greatly extended by Sugden in 1881.

Brunswick Methodist Church, built in 1856 in Market Street, was another example of the Victorian Gothic style of the architecture of William Sugden. It was enlarged and improved in 1890. Brunswick was able to support a day school in Regent Street, which had extensive additions in 1880. Brunswick was demolished in 1977.

Mill Street Chapel and Ragged School was built in 1870, serving this heavily-populated area of the town. It closed in 1990. The old chapel at Ball Haye Green was opened in 1846, with a Sunday School. This was replaced by a new chapel in Milk Street in 1894. These chapels were all Wesleyan, and in addition there was a Primitive Methodist Chapel in Fountain Street, and a Methodist New Connexion, Bethesda, on the corner of Ball Haye Street and Queen Street.

Just above the chapel at Ball Haye Green stands 'Club Row', and example of an early move towards what eventually became the building society movement. Here, a group of local people 'clubbed' together to save money on a regular basis to buy their own terraced cottages. This idea later became regularised when, at No. 15 Stockwell Street, the offices of the Leek and Moorlands Building Society were first established on a permanent basis in May 1856, largely through the efforts of William and James Challinor, in conjunction with Thomas Shaw, who was then managing clerk, and became the first secretary of the new society. The very first Leek Building Society, however, was launched as early as 1824 with terms for borrowers under the proposition: *A house for £80 to be paid for by monthly instalments of One Pound One Shilling for six years.*

Health and welfare became a priority, as the population of Leek steadily increased. The Cottage Hospital (Alsop Memorial Hospital) dates from 1870, and is another Sugden building. The original portion of the hospital was built in memory of Mr James Alsop JP by his widow, Mrs A. E. Alsop, on a site given by John and Robert Alsop, his nephews. Additional land was subsequently purchased out of money given by the late Miss Carr and the late John Robinson Esq and others, so that by 1908 the site area was much larger than originally. It was the gift of a legacy of £1,000 by the late Miss Elizabeth Flint which enabled the trustees to consider building a new wing as an extension to the original hospital. The trustees of her will, J. Challinor, T. A. Argles and H. R. Sleigh, judiciously adminstered the legacy to enable the endowment of a bed, to be called the Elizabeth Flint Memorial Bed. In addition, gifts were made by the family of the late Sir Thomas Wardle and W. H. Rider Esq. Isaac Heath, a member of the General and Building Committees, gave money to provide the Isaac Heath Lift, and Miss Agnes Carr-Smith endowed the female ward with beds and equipment. A general appeal was launched by the Trustees, which brought a generous response from Leek people, notably George Davenport, John Hall, R.S. Milner, Arthur Nicholson, the late Mrs Robinson (Westwood), Rev A. E. Robinson and other leading citizens and manufacturers, producing a total of £1,411. The new wing was formally opened by Mr T. Argles of Milnthorpe, Westmorland, formerly of Haregate Hall, on Monday, 12 July 1909.

The town had a number of substantial residences for the gentry of the day. The earliest deed of Ball Haye Hall is reputed to date back to Elizabethan times, granted by Sir Ralph Bagnall to Henry Davenport, who died in 1680 at the age of 93. Ball Haye Hall was rebuilt about 1797, using stone from Upperhulme. The estate came on the market in 1853, by a court order, and was sold, together with 42 acres of land, for 5,150 to Joshua and John Brough. For a number of years the Hall was occupied by the Worthington family, followed by John Hall, JP for 45 years. The stone entrance porch with four Corinthian columns and fluted carved stone dado led to an impressive interior where there was a mixture of ancient and modern. Most rooms had old grates dating back to the early 18th century, and, in the drawing room, an Adam design mantlepiece with fine scroll work, beading and carved figure plaques. Many of the rooms overlooking the Park were impressive, with old oak beams, panelled walnut doors and old stone paving. The intention in the 1930s was that the Hall should become Leek's hospital. To this end, carnivals were held to raise money, but the project never materialised and, after being used for military purposes during the Second World War, the hall became residential council flats, before being demolished.

Other major residences for the gentry of Leek included Haregate Hall, Pickwood Hall, Woodcroft Hall, Westwood Hall and Highfield Hall. Haregate Hall, described as a "quaint Dutch-looking house", was the home of Toft Chorley, last survivor of the main line of the Chorley family. During the 1880-90s it belonged to Ernest Andrew Worthington, JP, silk manufacturer, followed by Thomas Atkinson Argles, JP.

Pickwood is approached by a drive off the Ashbourne Road. In Victorian times it was the home of William Challinor, who was born there on 10th March 1821. The house later passed to his son, William Edward Challinor. The family were solicitors, with offices in a Georgian building in Derby Street.

Pickwood is a fine house, built mainly of red brick with stone facings and a fine, heavy doorway. It stands on the south-eastern edge of Leek, commanding a splendid view, beyond its terraced lawns and gardens, over a deep valley towards Ballington Wood. A small brook runs down the valley from Lowe Hill, to join the stream near the Lady of the Dale Well, where the entrance to the old drive to Pickwood from the south was located. During the occupation of the Challinor family the house underwent many changes. An extra wing was added, some of the work being done by Sugden, the Leek architect.

Westwood Hall stands to the west of Leek, on level ground above the valley of the River Churnet. It was substantially rebuilt in the Elizabethan style by John Davenport in the early 19th Century. Davenport was born in Leek, but had a pottery business in Longton. The hall was described in White's Directory of 1834 as a neat mansion with extensive plantations and pleasure grounds. It was further enlarged in 1851, when the clock tower and great hall were added. The house has extensive stables and a coach house, and a splendid gazebo stands in the wooded and lawned grounds. In 1868 Westwood

Hall became the residence of John Robinson, and it remained in the family until 1908. The next owner was the Pottery manufacturer, H.L. Johnson. The hall was later bought by Staffordshire County Council and opened as Westwood Hall Girls' High School in 1921.

Highfield Hall, was a substantial 18th Century country residence built of red brick with stone facings and leaded light windows, with a slated and lead roof surmounted by a handsome weathervane. Its imposing portico was supported on two circular stone pillars. The hall stood in attractive grounds about 580 feet above sea level, with a pleasant south-west aspect. It was approached from the main Leek to Macclesfield road by a carriage drive lined with rhodedendrons, shrubs and trees, leading to a broad, open forecourt.

The hall had a large glass conservatory, and sun loggia, and extensive stables were attached to the Home Farm, approached by the back drive leading from Bridge End. The pleasure grounds surrounding the hall had wide sweeping lawns, rose gardens, flower beds and a charming rock garden. The grounds extended to over five acres, and included many fine shrubs and trees.

The entire Highfield Hall Estate comprised about 364 acres in all. In addition to the hall and its pleasure grounds, the estate included two dairy farms, the Home Farm and Highfield Stud Farm, numerous fields, and five small residences, including the picturesque Entrance Lodge at the end of the drive.

Kelly's Post Office Directory of 1868 states: *Highfield Park was taken on a lease for seven years by a party of gentlemen, who formed a committee for the purpose of forming a recreation ground: it is situated about 1 mile from the town, and a charge of 1d is made for admittance to the grounds. A small grandstand has been erected here, it being the new course for Leek Races. Bowling, croquet, swings, archery, dancing, athletic sports and occasional fetes render it the favourite resort of all parties.*

Athletic sports were held regularly, and a dance at Highfield Hall usually followed the sports. The 'Staffordshire Advertiser' of 27th April 1867, reporting on the athletics, said: *The committee have worked with great zeal, being determined to ascertain if, under a spirited management, a 'Belle Vue' would pay in Leek.*

In 1870 Highfield Hall was purchased by Edwin Cliffe Glover, of a wealthy Potteries family engaged in brewing, mining and ironworking, mainly in the Longton area. He purchased the estate from the representatives of the previous owners, Mrs Sarah Fowler and her sons, Matthew and Joshua Gaunt. Like the Gaunts, he was a strong supporter of the Cricket Club, being a Vice President. He allowed the club the free use of the ground, and thus Leek Cricket Club had its first permanent home at Highfield.

Glover died in 1886, after which Arthur Nicholson (later Sir Arthur) took up residence, and continued to allow the Cricket Club free use of the ground. Sir Arthur Nicholson was a keen breeder of shire horses, a passion which he shared with King George V. Consequently, when the King and Queen Mary visited Leek on 23rd April 1913 to visit the factory of Brough, Nicholson and Hall Ltd., it was natural that the royal party should also visit Highfield Hall, where Sir Arthur's prize shire horses were viewed with interest.

Woodcroft Hall was another silk manufacturers' residence, standing on the higher ground above the old gas works, off Newcastle road. New housing in recent years has completely obliterated all visible signs of it, but it was an imposing building in its day. Local architects Sugden and Son designed ambitious enlargements and improvements for it, but it was eventually demolished. In the 1880s it was the residence of Henry Davenport, followed by William Prince, who had a silk mill in Bath Street. Marcus Prince, a member of the Leek Amateur Operatic Society, was listed as the owner in 1904.

With the help of these images and other visual records of Leek's past, old maps and old photographs, and with a little imagination, it is possible to recapture some of the sights and sounds of yesterday's town. Imagine for instance, the sight of the workmen erecting the cross on the high spire of St Mary's Roman Catholic Church in 1887, or the stonemasons working high above Derby Street on the spire of the new Congregational Church in 1863. And what a splendid sight the large copper dome capping the tower of the Nicholson Institute would be when newly-erected in 1884, under the supervision of William and Larner Sugden, Leek's Victorian architects. At the time of writing, October 2001, the building has recently undergone extensive repair and renewal work, and the copper dome can again be seen in its former glory. No doubt the passing of time, the ravages of the local climate, and atmospheric pollution will again create a coating of verdigris to turn the dome green again, but for a time we are able to see it as our Victorian forebears saw it, and perhaps we may relate more closely to those personalities and events which were the making of Victorian and Edwardian Leek.

The Nicholson Institute with its large copper dome was erected in 1884
and remains an architectural feature of the Town to this day.

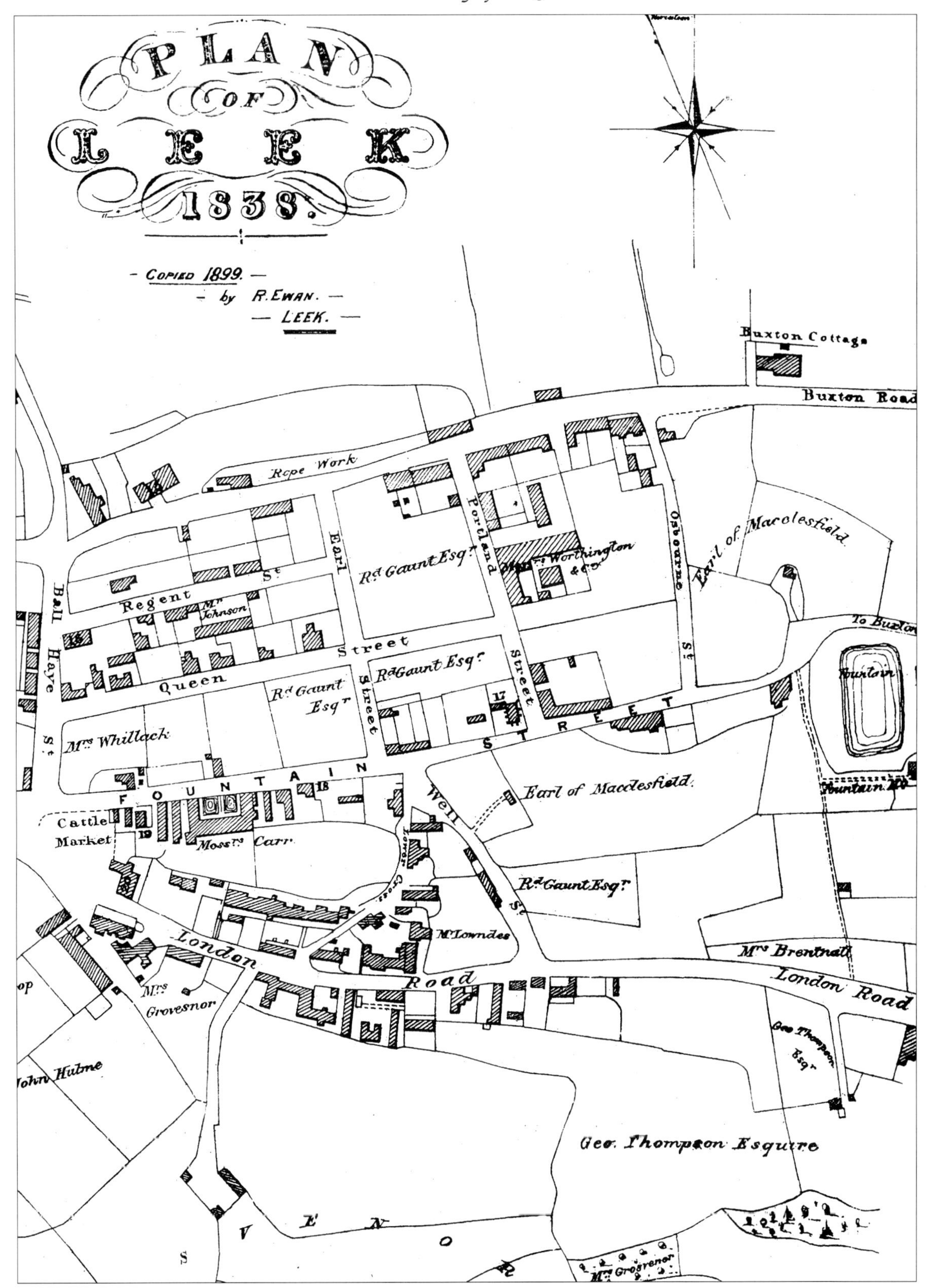

This section of the 1838 map shows the area between Fountain Street and London Road (now Ashbourne Road) where the factories of Brough, Nicholson and Hall would be developed. St Luke's church is not yet built. Note the rope works on Buxton Road.

The town centre as shown on the 1838 map. Note the old names of some of the streets: Canal (Broad) Street, Spout (St. Edward) Street, Custard (Stanley) Street. The warren of properties behind the Market Place and the extensive grounds of some of the properties in Spout Street and Derby Street are clearly shown.

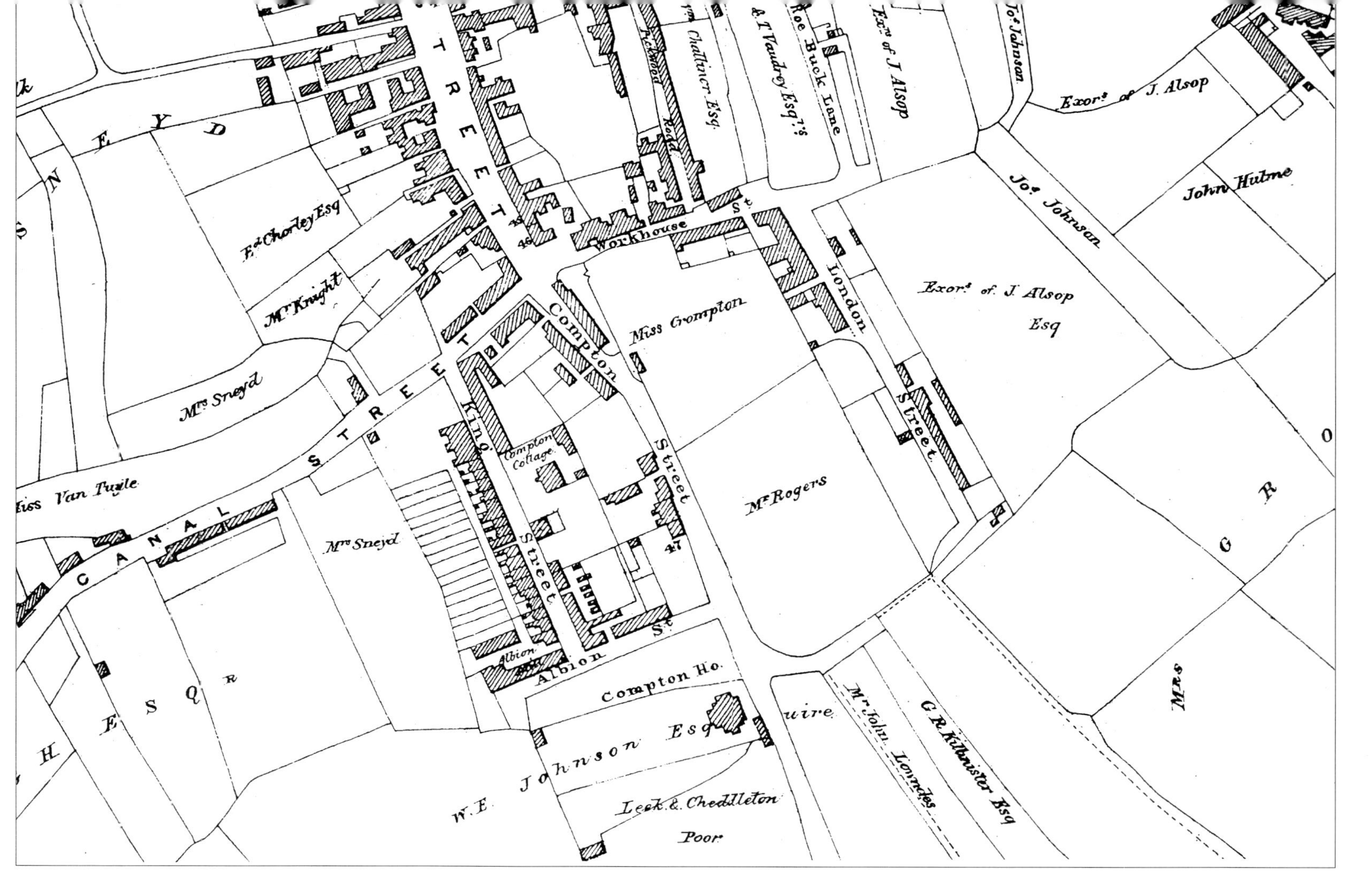

In the later years of the 19th century this area was developed extensively. Streets in the large area bounded by Workhouse (now Brook) Street and Haywood Street, Ashbourne Road, Southbank Street and Compton would fill out this large area in which London Street, with its silk weavers' houses, remains as the oldest street.

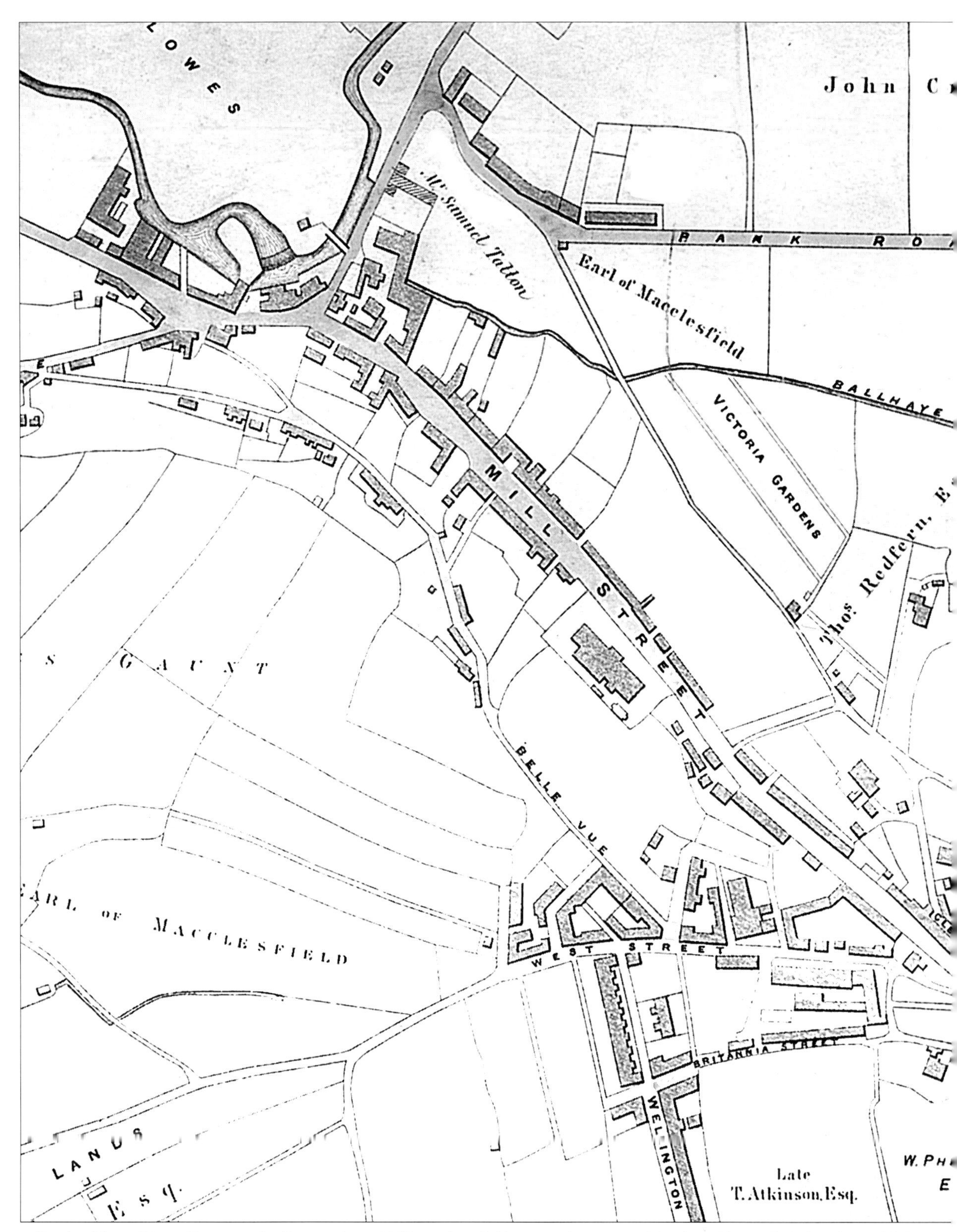

Charles Slagg, Town Surveyor for 5 years from 1857 produced this very clear map of Leek. This section showing Mill Street and the West End, shows the weir of the Brindley Water Mill, the Big Mill on Mill Street and the large open area where streets would soon be developed. Slagg's map is dated 1862.

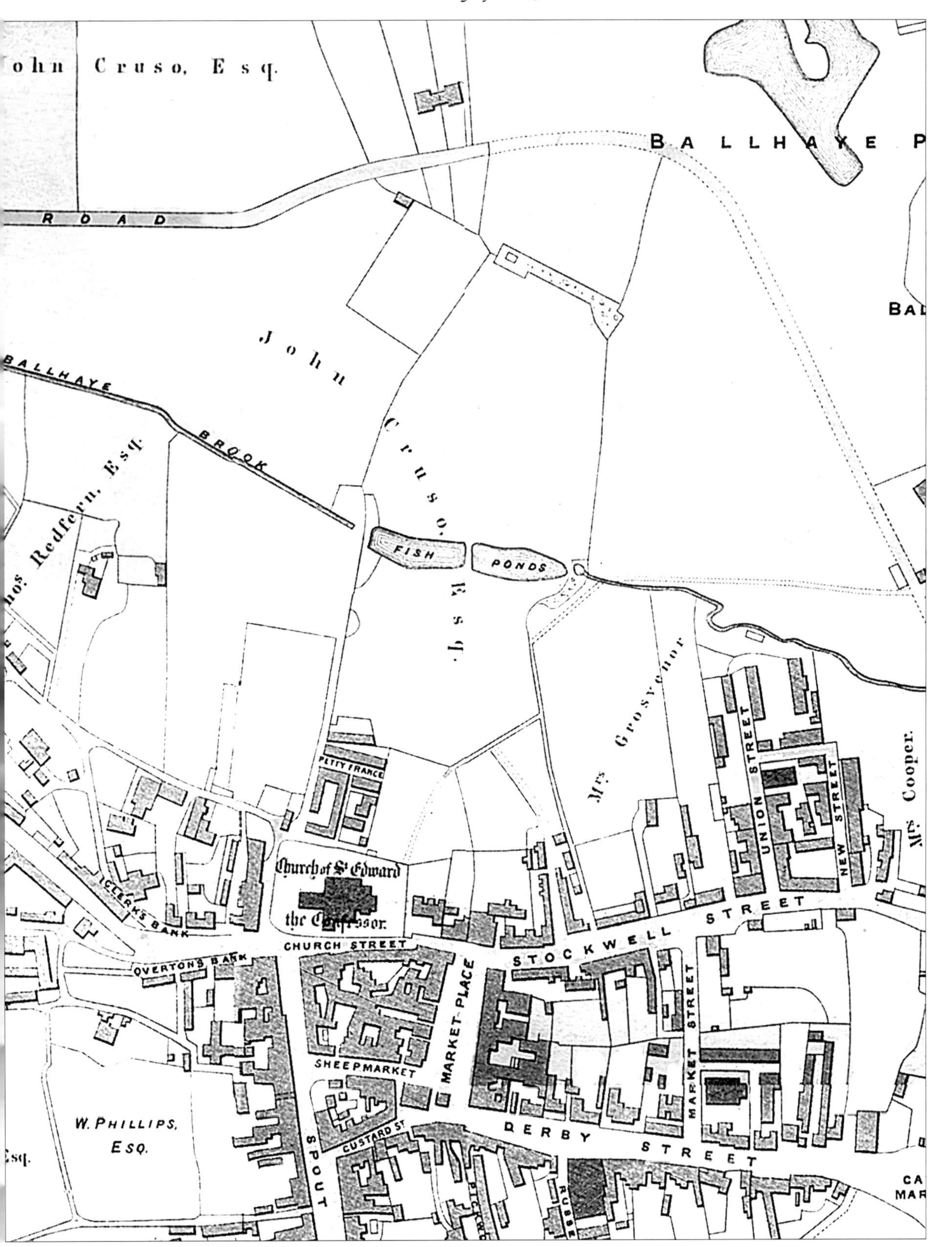

This area to the north of the Market Place shows the extensive land owned by John Cruso, Solicitor, of Foxlowe. Mrs Grosvenor also owned land and property off Stockwell Street. The line of Park Road is shown, with Ball Haye Park top right

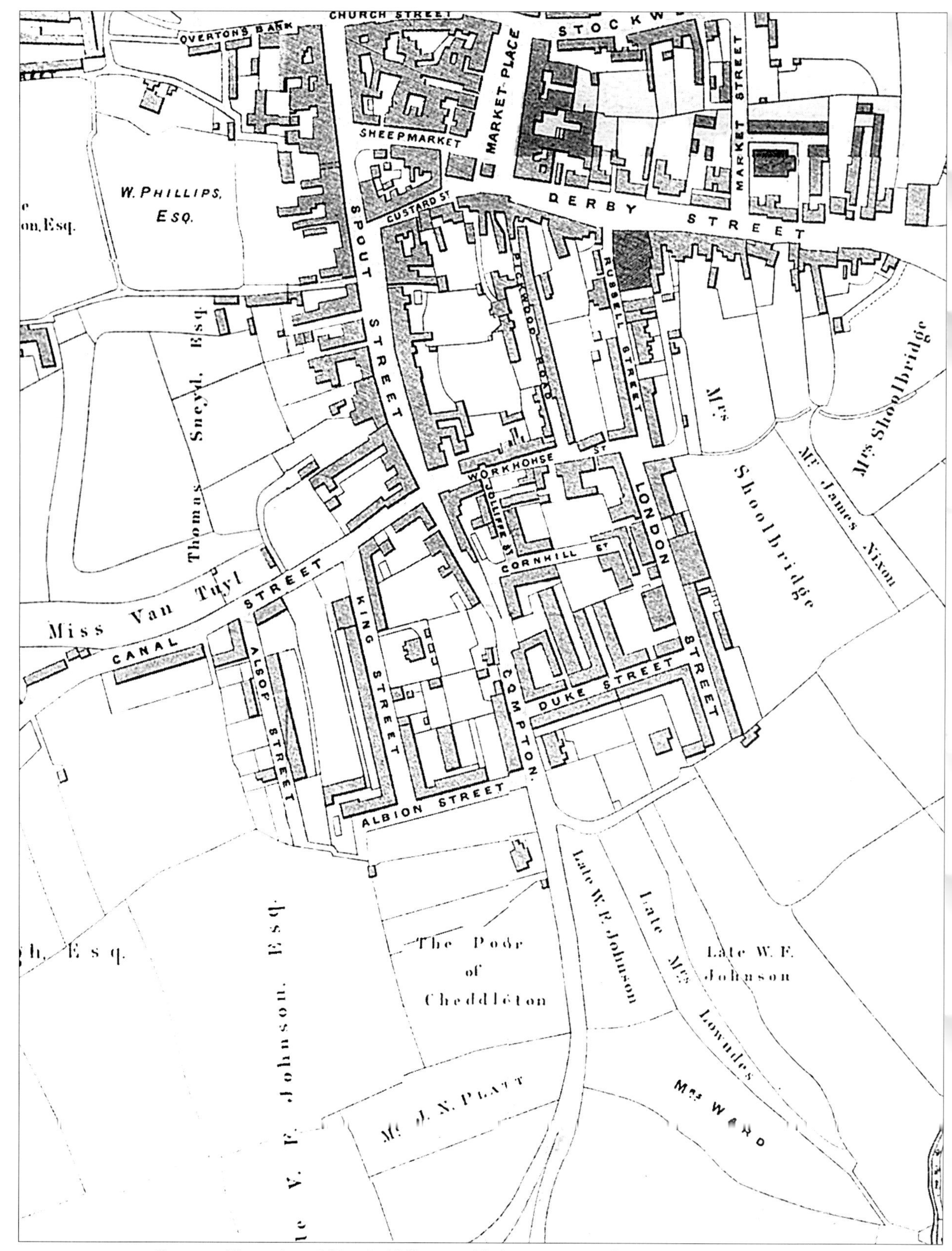

Compare this section of Slagg's 1862 map with the same area of the 1838 map on page 41.
The old street names have not yet been changed.

Significant developments have taken place by 1862, when this area is compared with the 1838 map on pages 40 and 41. The construction of Haywood Street and Southbank Street, with neighbouring streets, would soon take place.

The road up to Ball Haye Green is shown on this section of Slagg's 1862 map. The open area of land, owned by Miss Gaunt is awaiting development. This is now the Prince Street area.

Slagg's 1862 map (20% larger) here shows the new St. Luke's church, further factory developments on Brough, Nicholson and Hall's site, and the Cattle Market still occupying the open space at the bottom of Derby Street.

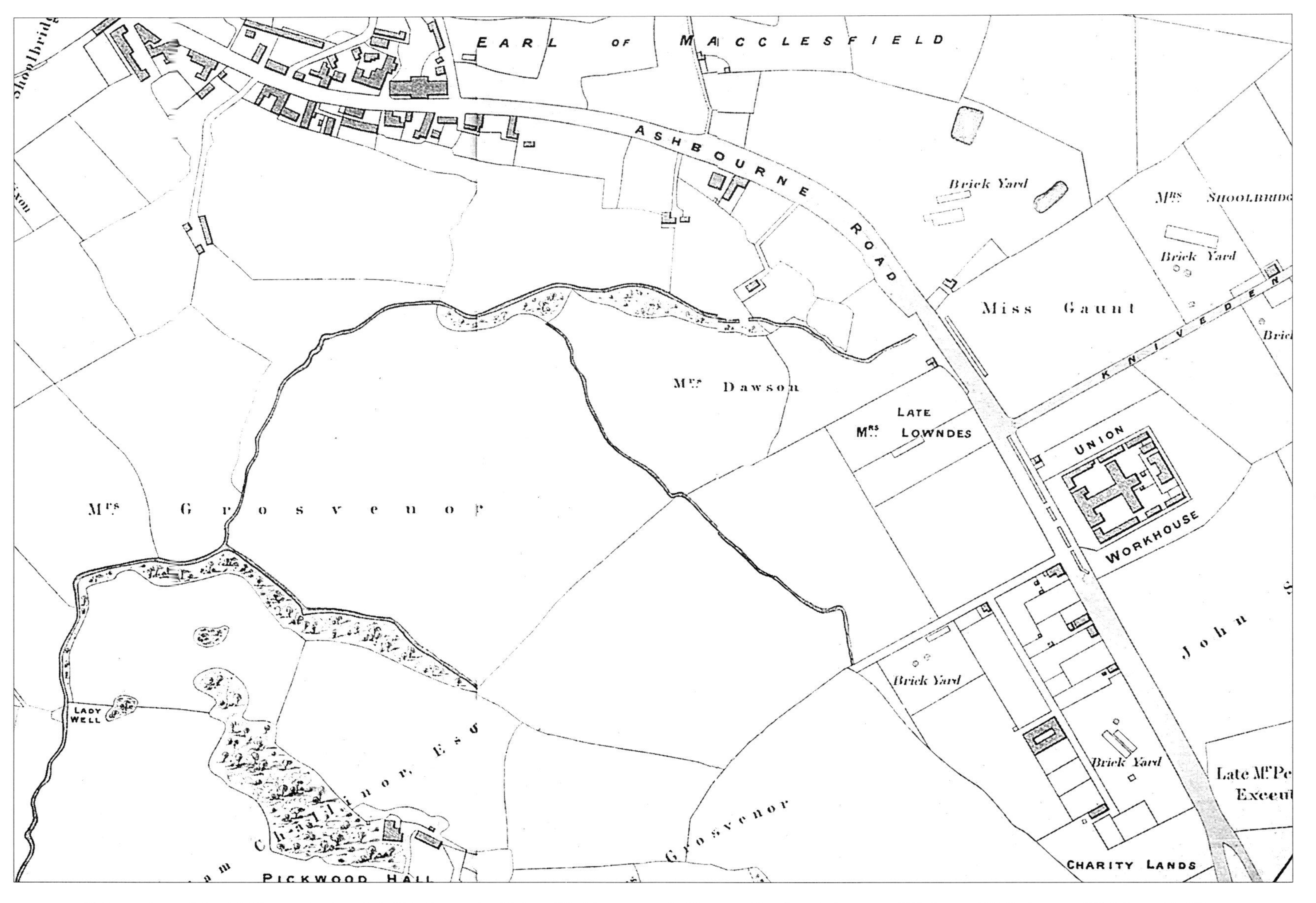

This section of the 1862 map (reduced 20%) shows the Union Workhouse on Ashbourne Road and the site of Pickwood Hall, home of William Challinor.

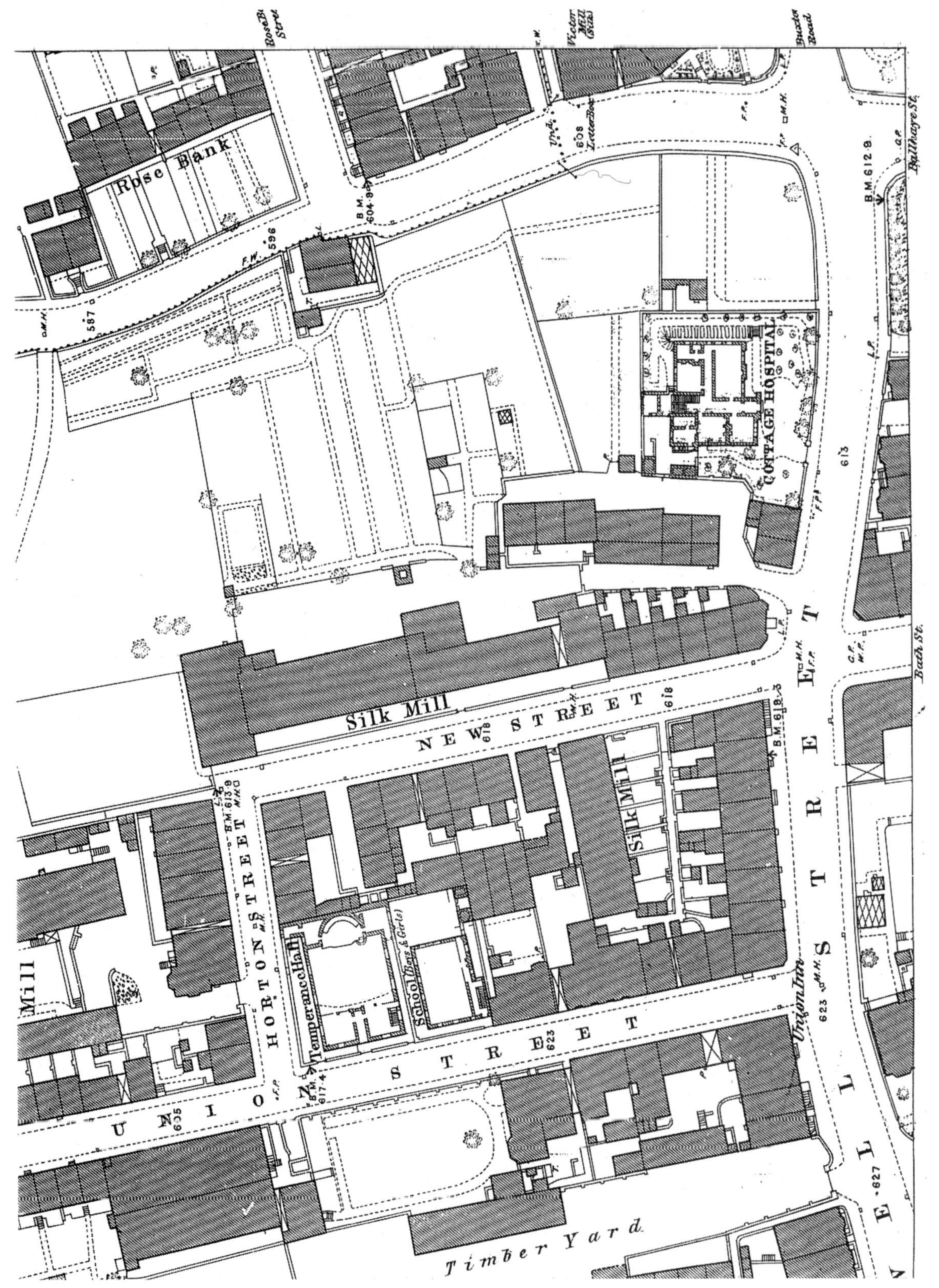

From the 1879 Ordnance Survey map, Stockwell Street to Rosebank. The Cottage Hospital and a number of Mills are shown, and the Temperance Hall in Union Street.

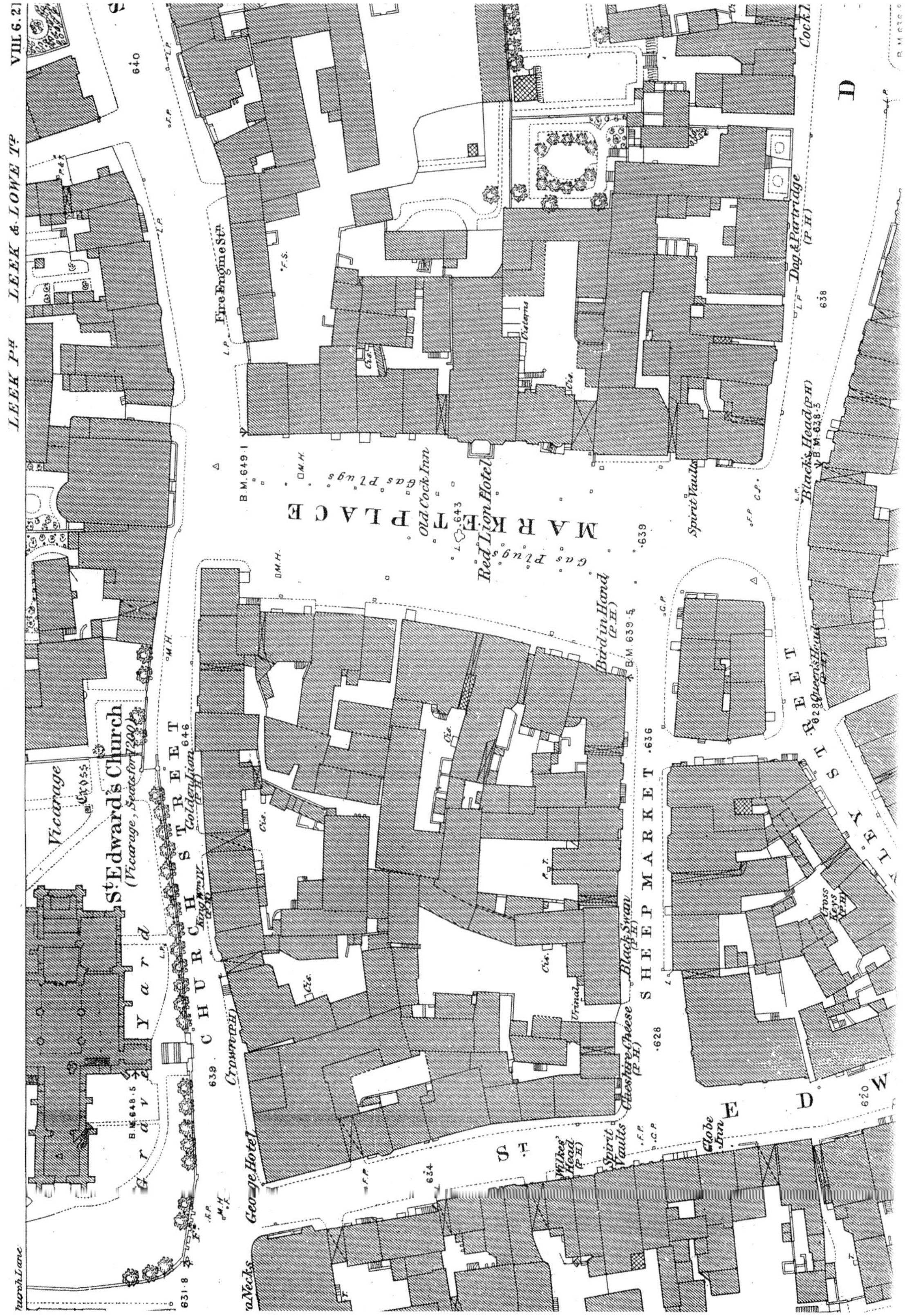

From the 1879 Ordnance Survey map, the area around the Market Place. The many inns in the area, particularly along Church Street, are a reminder of the days of stagecoach travel.

The eastern end of Derby St, Congregational Church to the Public Baths, and the new layout of the Smithfield Market, Haywood St. Note the large gardens behind the Derby Street properties.

Part of the Town centre off Derby Street to the North. Two Methodist churches and the Regent Street school are shown. A large silk mill stands in Bath Street.

In this composite photograph, the camera of W.H. Nithsdale has captured the rainy scene at the opening of Belle Vue Road on 13th September 1906.

The old Black's Head, Market Place. The early Methodists met in a room above the stables at the rear. Six cottages with attic weaving sheds also stood in the lane behind the inn.

Derby Street, showing the Roebuck and, on the right, the old Congregational Chapel, replaced by the present Sugden building in 1863 (now Trinity Church).

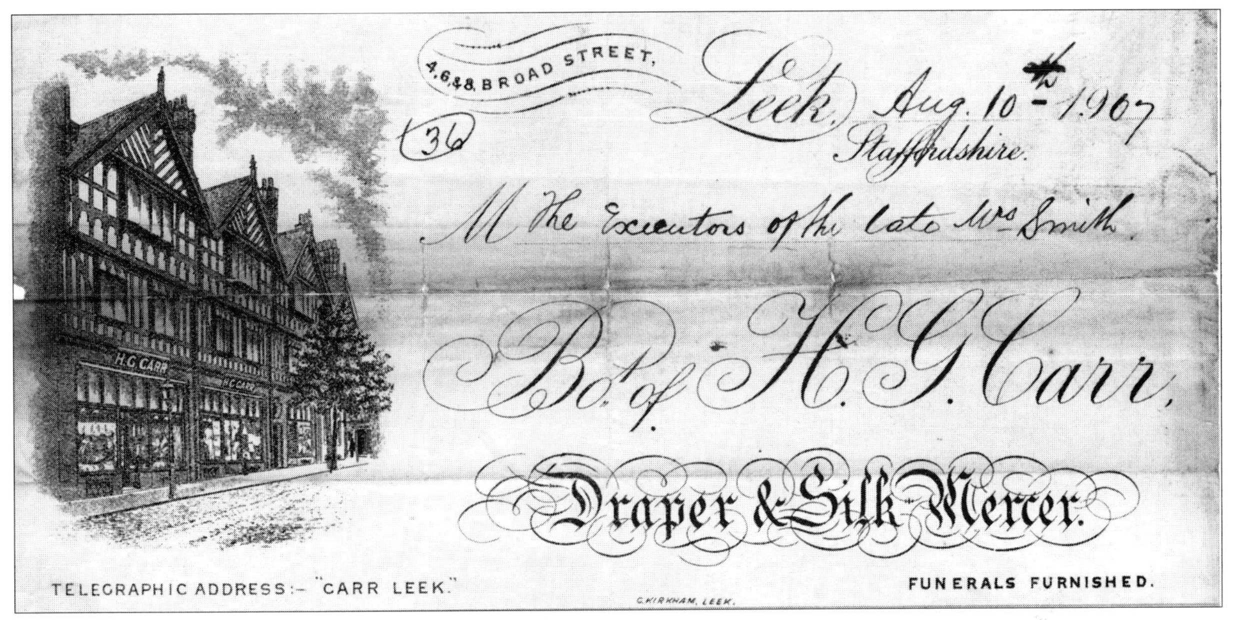

4, 6 & 8, BROAD STREET,

(36)

Leek, Aug. 10th 1907
Staffordshire.

M The Executors of the late Mrs Smith.

Bot. of H. G. Carr,

Draper & Silk Mercer.

TELEGRAPHIC ADDRESS:- "CARR LEEK."

C.KIRKHAM, LEEK.

FUNERALS FURNISHED.

Above:
The bill-head shows the fine block of Tudor-style architecture in present day Broad Street. It was built by the architect James Gosling-Smith for Henry Bermingham, silk manufacturer.

Illustration of the late Mr Deakin's Cooperage, once a familiar landmark in Derby Street. The late Mr and Mrs Deakin are seen standing in the foreground. These premises are now occupied by Messrs Hunters.

Caption and picture from Leek News 1927

The offices of the Leek Building Society, 15 Stockwell street, founded 1856. The Society later moved into Stockwell House, a little further down the street, becoming Leek & Moorlands Building Society. This was rebuilt as a new Chief Office in 1931. After a succession of mergers and name changes, including a long period as the Leek and Westbourne Building Society, the name was streamlined to the Britannia Building Society in 1975. It is now one of the largest building societies in the Country.

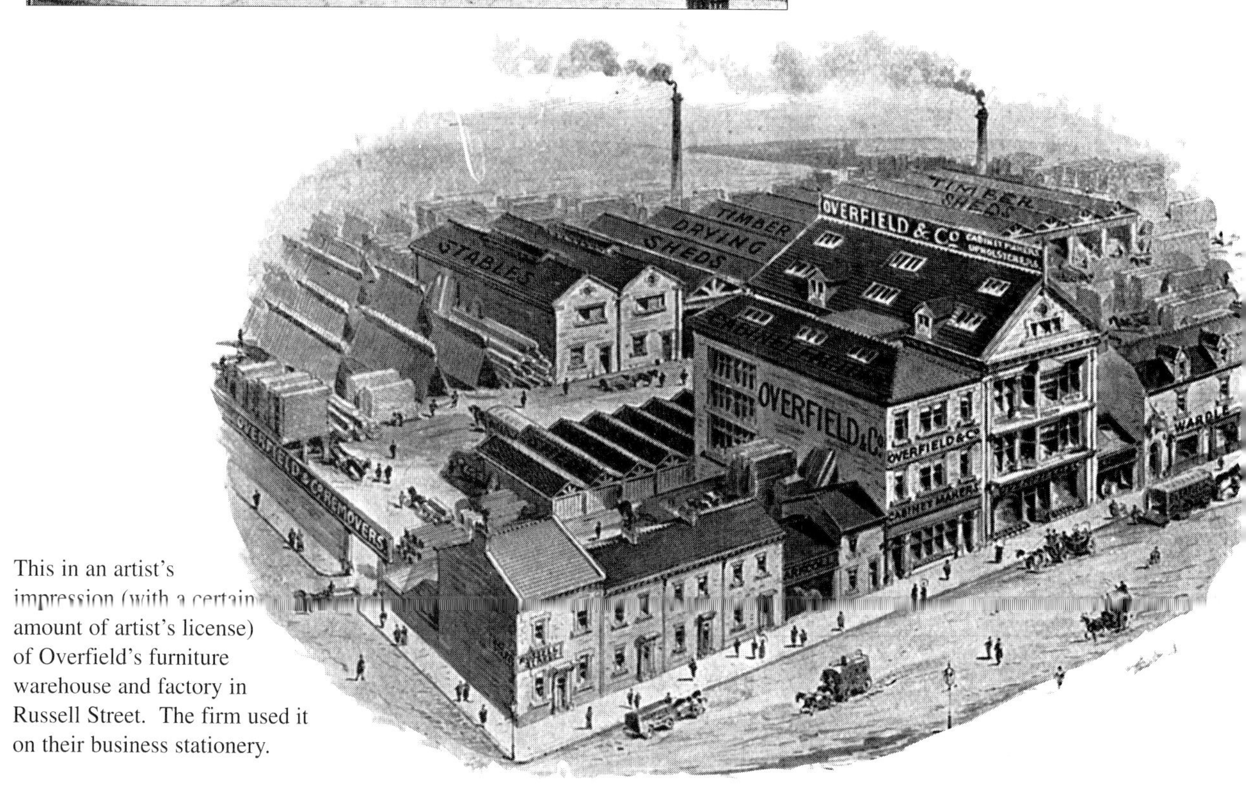

This in an artist's impression (with a certain amount of artist's license) of Overfield's furniture warehouse and factory in Russell Street. The firm used it on their business stationery.

The L.U.D.C. Gas Department showroom is on the left, with the Public Baths on the corner of Bath Street. The little shops on the corner of Ball Haye Street are then seen, and on the right-hand side of Fountain Street the small spire of the Primitive Methodist Chapel, with the factory of Brough, Nicholson & Hall in the distance. The small building to the right was a public weighing machine.

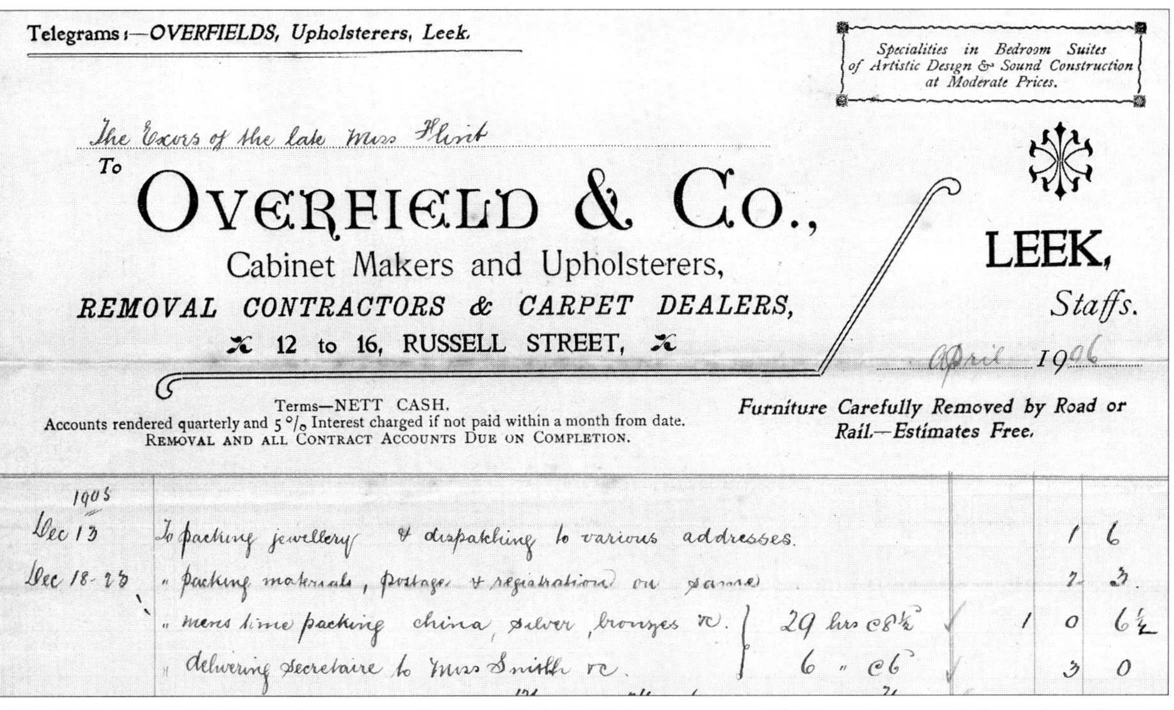

Telegrams:—OVERFIELDS, Upholsterers, Leek.

Specialities in Bedroom Suites of Artistic Design & Sound Construction at Moderate Prices.

The Excrs of the late Miss Flint

To

OVERFIELD & Co.,

Cabinet Makers and Upholsterers,

REMOVAL CONTRACTORS & CARPET DEALERS,

12 to 16, RUSSELL STREET,

LEEK, *Staffs.*

April 1906

Terms—NETT CASH.
Accounts rendered quarterly and 5 % Interest charged if not paid within a month from date.
REMOVAL AND ALL CONTRACT ACCOUNTS DUE ON COMPLETION.

Furniture Carefully Removed by Road or Rail.—Estimates Free.

1905						
Dec 13	To packing jewellery & dispatching to various addresses.				1	6
Dec 18-23	" packing materials, postage & registration on same				2	3
	" mens time packing china, silver, bronzes &c.	29 hrs @ 8½		1	0	6½
	" delivering Secretaire to Miss Smith &c.	6 " @ 6			3	0

Overfield's billhead indicates the many services provided by this large concern. Their warehouse and showroom in Russell Street was a late Sugden building. It later became the offices of the Co-operative Society.

Two traders of Victorian Leek - their business stationery can be seen on the page opposite.

Hambletons sold musical instruments and cycles from their shop at 10 Sheepmarket.

E. Green, grocer and cheese factor, moved from this site just across the road to High Street about 1901, when this street was constructed. The shop later became Pickford's grocers.

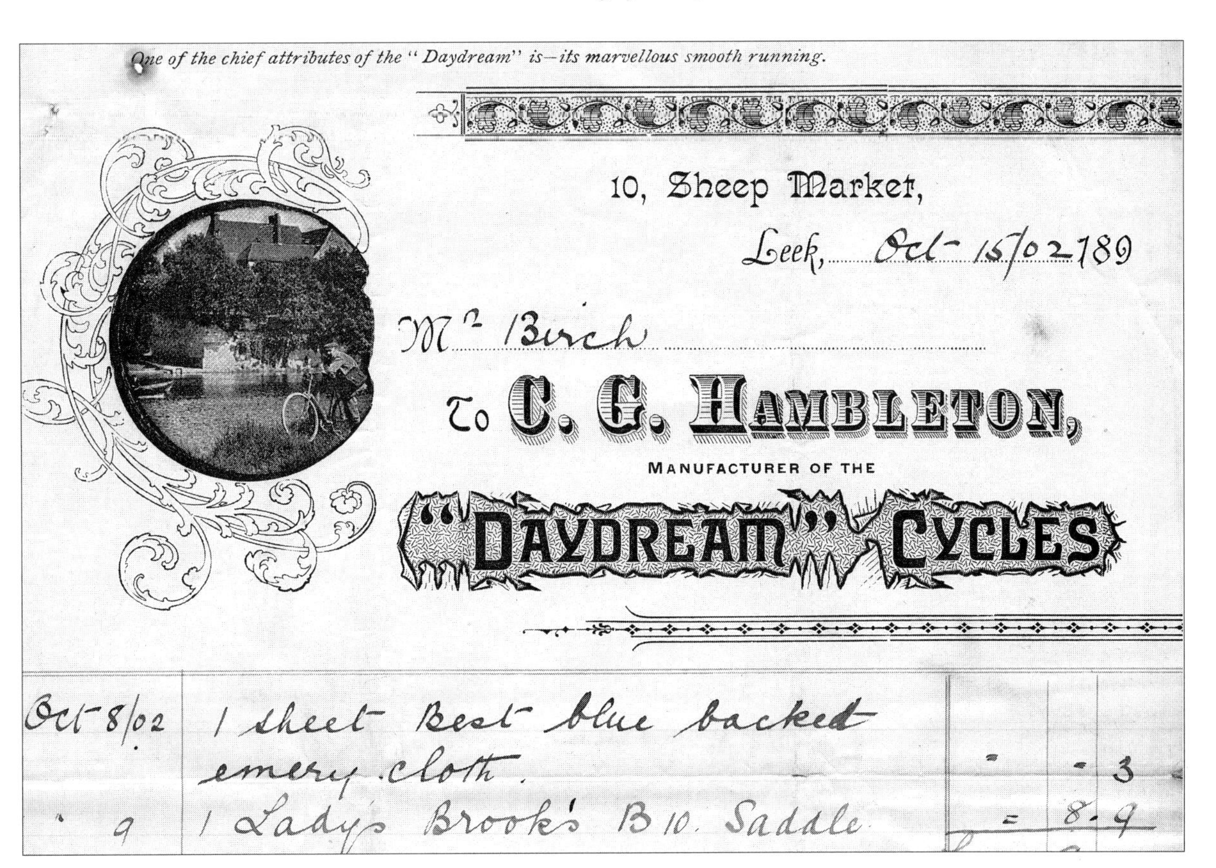

One of the chief attributes of the "Daydream" is—its marvellous smooth running.

10, Sheep Market,

Leek, Oct 15/02 189

Mr Birch

To C. G. HAMBLETON,

MANUFACTURER OF THE

"DAYDREAM" CYCLES

Oct 8/02	1 sheet Best blue backed emery cloth.	-	-	3
9	1 Lady's Brook's B10. Saddle	-	8	9

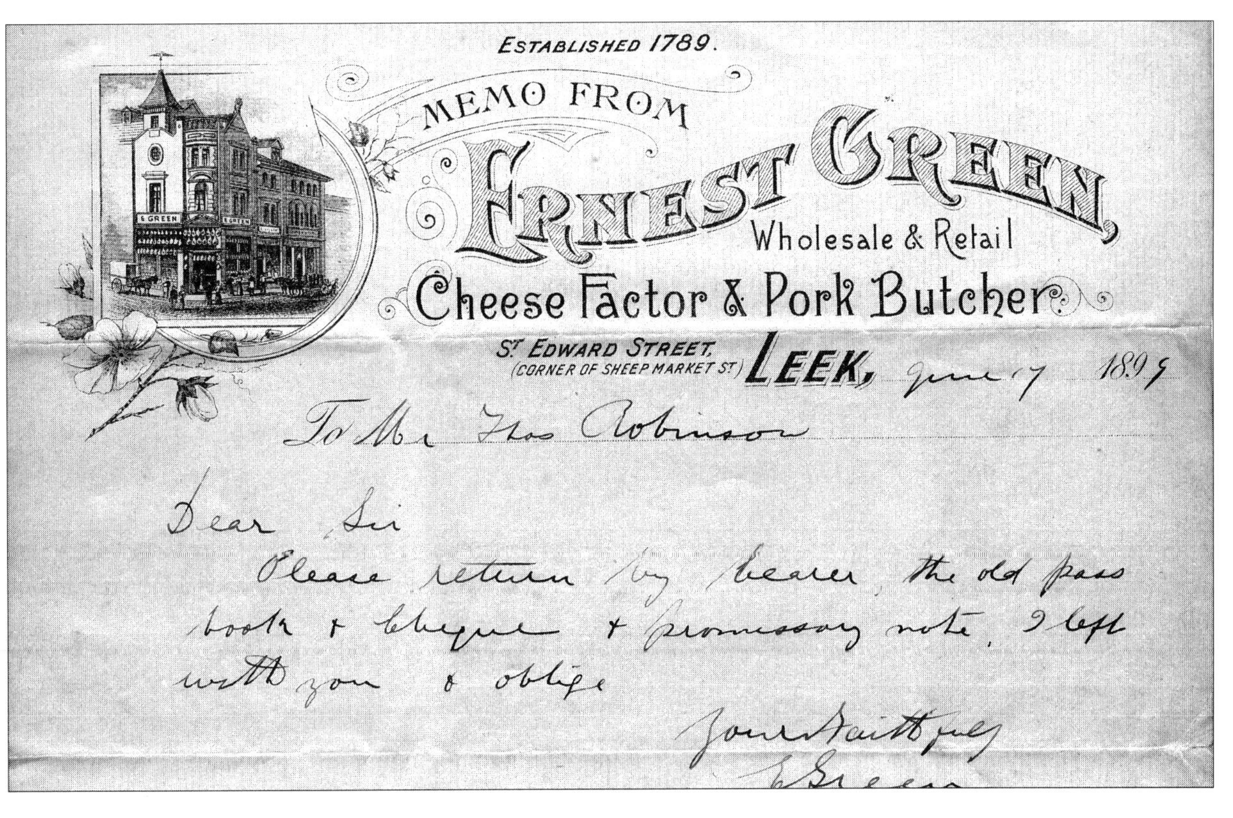

ESTABLISHED 1789.

MEMO FROM

ERNEST GREEN

Wholesale & Retail

Cheese Factor & Pork Butcher.

St EDWARD STREET,
(CORNER OF SHEEP MARKET ST)

LEEK, June 7 1899

To Mr Thos Robinson

Dear Sir

Please return by bearer the old pass book & cheque & promissory note, I left with you & oblige

Yours faithfully

E Green

The stable yard at the rear of the Red Lion Hotel.

Salter and Salter was an old established boot and shoe shop in St. Edward Street.
See letter head opposite, showing that it was a branch shop.

No. 30 Branch,

Leek, Nov 4 1893

Mrs Prince (dec)

Bought of SALTER & SALTER,

WHOLESALE and RETAIL BOOT and SHOE MANUFACTURERS,

TANNERS & CURRIERS

Terms Cash ; No Abatement.

Oxford Mills, Park Lane, Leeds.

THE RED LION.
Commercial and Family Hotel,
LEEK.
BILLIARDS.
POSTING.
Proprietor - - - HARRY SWIFT.
OMNIBUS MEETS EVERY TRAIN.

Below: Salter's shop is seen on the right of this photograph, just behind the gas lamp. The street surface of St Edward Street is stone setts, as were many Leek streets at the time.

The original Roman Catholic Chapel, Fountain Street.

Right: An artist's impression of the main entrance to Mount Pleasant Methodist Church which was opened on July 14th 1811.
The original 1785 chapel, which was converted into a house for the minister, lies beyond the main building, as seen in the picture below.

Below: Mount Pleasant House, formerly the Chapel, where the Sunday School was held.

Mount Pleasant House, formerly the Chapel in which Wesley preached and the School was held.
Thos. T. Blaylock 97-

RULES

OF THE LEEK WESLEYAN METHODIST

SUNDAY SCHOOL.

FIRST.—The Scholars must all come clean washed and combed, at Nine o'Clock in the Morning, and half-past One at Noon.

SECOND.—They are not to go out if they can possibly avoid it; nor at all until the change has taken place. When they go they must take a permit from the Teacher.

THIRD.—Not one word must be spoken in School Hours to any body but the Teacher. No looking off books, or getting lessons aloud are permitted.

FOURTH.—The Girls are not to walk with their pattens on in the School.

FIFTH.—Those who write, must shew every line as they write it to their Teacher before they begin upon another.

SIXTH.—If a Scholar neglect coming to School, or sending a reasonable excuse for not coming two Sundays together, such Scholar's name will be liable to be crossed out of the List.

SEVENTH.—Those who are not present when the names are called over, will be marked for late attendance.

EIGHTH.—If a Scholar be convicted of cursing, or swearing, or quarreling, or wilful lying, or calling nick-names, or using indecent language, they shall be admonished for the first offence, punished for the second, and excluded for the third.

NINTH.—If a Scholar be found guilty of a misdemeanor which may not be here particularly specified, and the offence is considered of so capital a sort as to require exemplary punishment, he shall be forthwith expelled from the School.

TENTH.—When the Scholars are dismissed they must go straight home without loitering in the Streets, and if any be seen running, jumping, or playing at any play or game, or in other respects misbehaving themselves, they will be treated as in the 8th Rule.

ELEVENTH.—Those Scholars who can read the Bible, and repeat the Wesleyan Catechism No. 1, will be taught to write (providing their own paper.) and those who have made a proficiency in reading and writing, and whose good conduct recommends them to notice, may learn accounts on Saturday Evening's.

TWELFTH.—When the Children go to Chapel they must walk regularly, two and two along the Street, neither thronging or pushing each other, nor speaking one word from the time they leave the School to the time they come out of Chapel; they must go reverently and quietly to their seats, not striding over the forms, or pushing to get places. They must sit, stand and kneel always with the Congregation. They are not to go out of Chapel during the Service on any pretence whatever: and if either by word or action they disturb those who are near them, their names will be taken down that they may be reported for bad behaviour when they come to School again.

TO THE TEACHERS.

It is your business to see that the above Rules are observed by all the Children under your particular inspection—to avoid as much as possible all corporal punishment—to report offenders when you think it necessary to the Visitor, and to read and enforce these Rules in your Class regularly once a month.

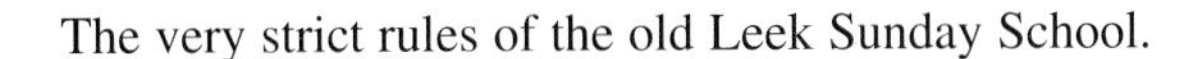

W. M. HILLIARD, PRINTER, MARKET-PLACE, LEEK.

The very strict rules of the old Leek Sunday School.

An artist's impression of Brunswick Methodist Church, Market Street, another Sugden building in the Victorian Gothic style.

Below:
The Maude Institute and the old Leek Grammar School, founded by the Earl of Macclesfield.

The Maude Institute is dedicated to the memory of the former Vicar of St. Edward's Church, Rev. C.B. Maude.

The Challinor Fountain on its original site in the Market Place. It was presented to the Town by William Challinor to mark the bringing to Leek of a water supply from the Springs at Upperhulme. This highly regarded work by the sculptor Joseph Durham, R.A. was exhibited at the Royal Academy in London where it was purchased by Challinor. It spent many years in Brough Park and was finally returned to the Town Centre in the 1980s when it was positioned outside the new Staffordshire Moorlands Council Offices.

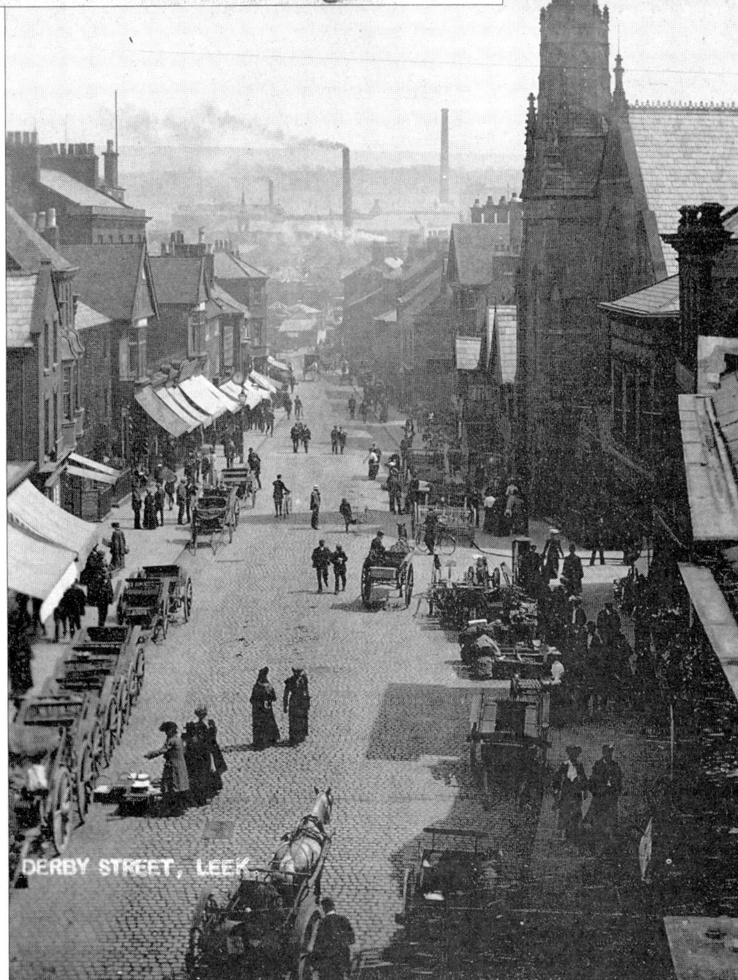

Derby Street in the days before the motor car. The Gothic spire of Sugden's Congregational Church is seen on the right.

Two scenes in the Market Place, about 1900. Horse-drawn delivery waggons are in evidence, and the old wooden stalls are seen attracting shoppers

The picture of Mill Street shows the tall terraced houses, built with their backs into the rock face. Sugden's Big Mill is seen in the distance. The Police Station once stood at the top left-hand corner, below the present West Street W.M. Club.

Mill Street, carrying the main road from Macclesfield into Leek, was constructed in the late 18th century, when the road was turnpiked. Before that time the route to Macclesfield went alongside the church.

St. Edward's Church, rebuilt after a fire of 1297. The tower is 14th century, the South Porch c.1670, and the arch 1634. The chancel is Victorian, 1865-67, the work of the architect G.E. Street.

All Saints Church. Richard Norman Shaw was the renowned architect of this Anglican church, built in 1887, in the Perpendicular and Renaissance styles. The church has a central tower and a low clerestory. The chancel decorations are by Horsley. Letharby designed the Reredos, and the stained glass windows are mostly by Morris and Co.

The large mill on the right is California Mill, with a small dyeworks in front. Up the hill, to the left the workers' terraced houses in Horton Street can be seen. To the right is the works of Spilsbury and Co. and on the extreme left, the larger factory of Clemesha Bros and Birch, destroyed by fire in 1965.

Leek's Victorian firemen are seen here with their old fire engine. The Secretary of the brigade for many years was Robert Farrow(1822-1906), Leek's long serving Sanitary Inspector. He settled inLeek in 1847, working as a tallow chandler and was appointed Sanitary Inspector by the Improvement Commissioners in 1867. Amongst many other things he was responsible for the annual report of death and diseases. He is seen here standing on the far right, with full beard.

St Edward's Church bells ready to be re-hung in December 1907. The group comprises, left to right: A. Rider, F. Turner, E. Sherratt Jun, F. Walwyn, J. Rider, A.E. Ridgway (conductor), E. Sherratt Senr, J. Newall, A. Abbott, M. Carding (church warden), Rev R.D. Stamer, Vicar of Leek.

JUNE, 1898.

Dr. Jim McClew
Mr. C. T. Gwynne
Mrs. C. T. Gwynne
Mrs. Wm. Tatton
An Assistant of Dr. Burnett's
Dr. J. J. Ritchie
Dr. R. Burnett
Mrs. J. M. Johnson

Mrs. Underwood
Dr. J. M. Johnson
Mr. W. Tipper
Dr. John McClew
Mrs. John McClew
Mrs P. J. Worthington
Capt. Smith
Mr. John Hall

Miss McRobie
Mr. Arthur H. Shaw
Mr. Wm. Tatton
The Rev. T. H. B. Fearon
Mr. Henry Salt
Miss Salt
Mr. Thomas Shaw
Mr. William Carr

Dr. A. Somerville
Miss Shaw
Mr. Isaac Heath

Mr. R. S. Milner
Mrs. Sumerling
Mr. Joseph Challinor
Miss Rayner

Mr. Sumerling
Mr. R. Farrow
Mr. S. Blades
Mrs. John Hall
Mrs. B. B. Nixon
Mrs. E. Gailey
Miss Robinson
Mrs. Fearon

Mr. John Robinson
Miss Carr
Sir Thomas Wardle
Mrs. Arthur Shaw
Mrs. S. Gibson
Mrs. Sugden
Mrs. Cartwright
Mrs. S. Blades.

THE above group was taken at the Cottage Hospital on the **7th July, 1898**, when an influencial gathering assembled to witness **the dedication of a piece of ground to the north side of the Hospital.**

Miss Carr, who performed the ceremony, can be seen in the **centre of the group.** On her right is the late **Mr. John Robinson, of Westwood**, and on her left (standing) is Mr. William Carr—two very generous benefactors to whom Leek owes much.

The land then dedicated was comprised of three lots. The first lot contained 487 square yards and was purchased for £150 4s. 0d., of which Miss Carr gave £33 8s. 7d., the balance being raised by subscriptions. The second piece, which cost £77 14s. 0d., was purchased and given to the Hospital by Mr. John Robinson, who also defrayed the cost (£44 10s. 0d.) of the West fence. The third plot was purchased for £95 0s. 0d. and given by Mr. William Carr.

It is a particularly interesting group in which can be seen many who were prominent in the public life of the town at the end of last century.

From Leek News, this gathering of Leek worthies, professional and business people, epitomises the great wealth in the town, amongst the upper classes.

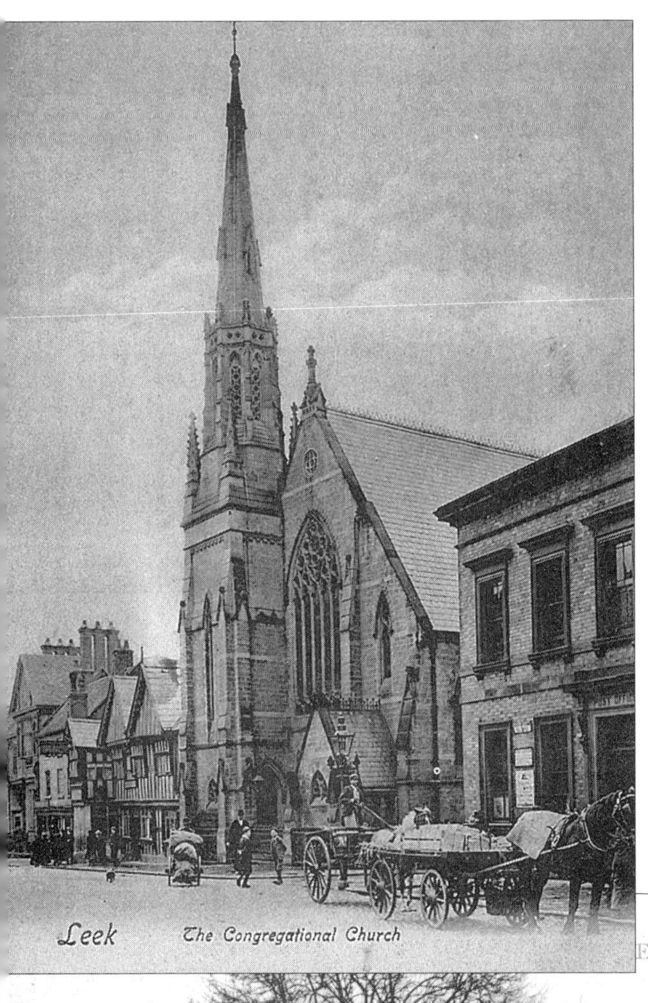

Sugden buildings in Leek.
Left, the Congregational Church (1863),
below, the Cottage Hospital (1870).
The hospital was built in memory of James
Alsop, J.P. It was enlarged in 1908, on
additional land to the right.

(See LEEK NEWS cutting opposite)

The interior of Mount Pleasant Methodist Church.
The style is typical of its day - gallery around three sides, full pipe organ, choir seats and large elevated pulpit.
The first chapel was built on this site in 1785, later converted into a house for the minister. A new chapel was opened in 1811, and considerably enlarged, with a new organ in 1853 - the building and organ are shown in this picture.

The 1806 Town Hall, which stood at the south end of the Market Place, at the junction of Stanley Street (then Custard Street) and Sheepmarket.
The Leek Improvement Commissioners met in the upper room, which also served as the Magistrates' Court.
The ground floor became a Reading Room and the office of the Leek Savings Bank.

St Luke's Church, Cawdry House and the old Cattle Market site - from a sketch of 1894.

Ball Haye Hall

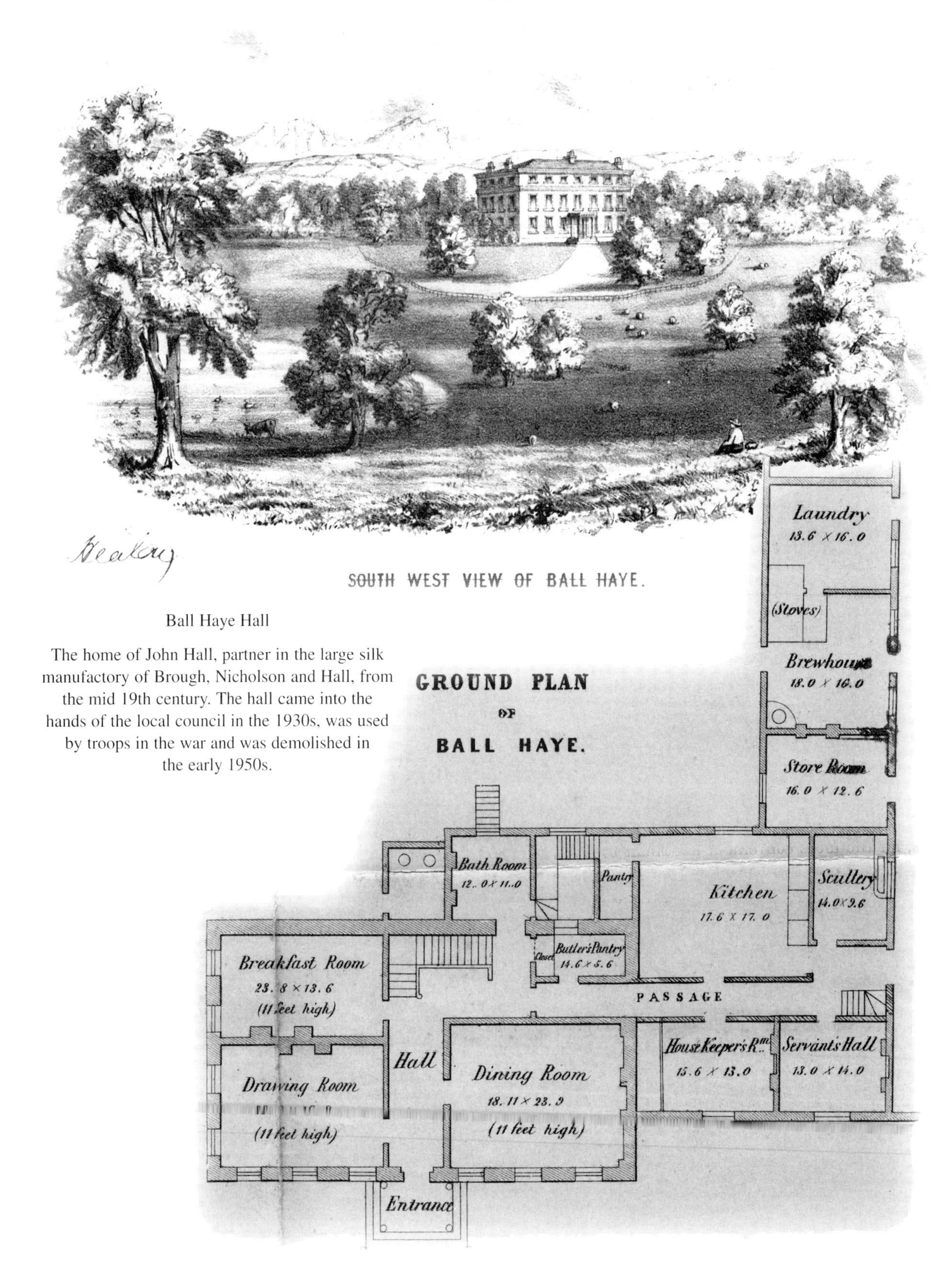

Ball Haye Hall

The home of John Hall, partner in the large silk manufactory of Brough, Nicholson and Hall, from the mid 19th century. The hall came into the hands of the local council in the 1930s, was used by troops in the war and was demolished in the early 1950s.

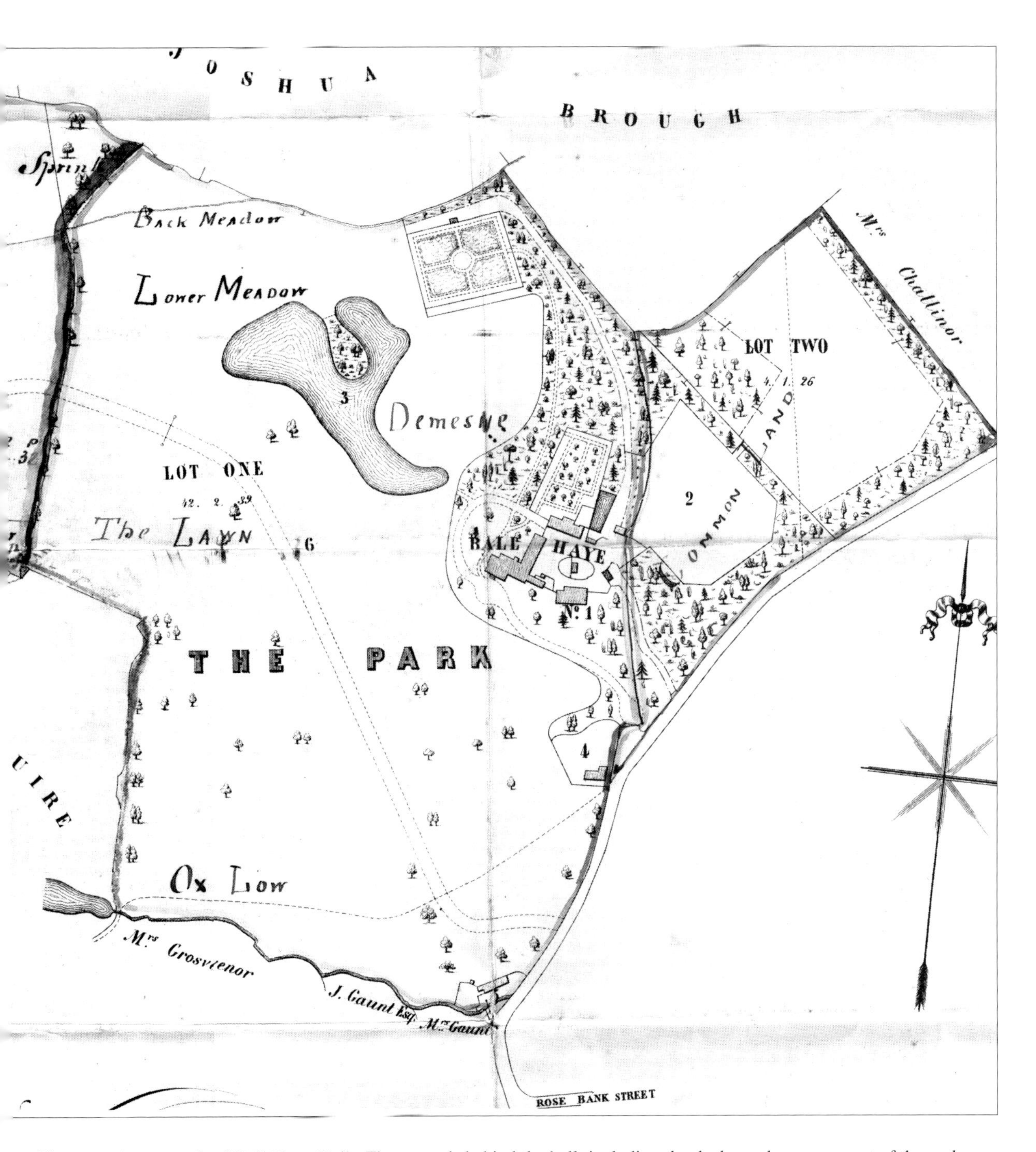

The extensive grounds of Ball Haye Hall. The grounds behind the hall, including the duck pond, are now part of the park (known by local people as "John Hall's gardens" - John Hall being a former resident and a prominent person in the town). The route that later became Park Road can be seen through the parkland.

Highfield Hall, home of Sir Arthur and Lady Nicholson.

Woodcroft Hall showing the elaborate extensions designed by Sugden and Son, but probably never fully executed.

Westwood Hall. Main entrance

Pickwood Hall, showing main entrance and terraced garden.

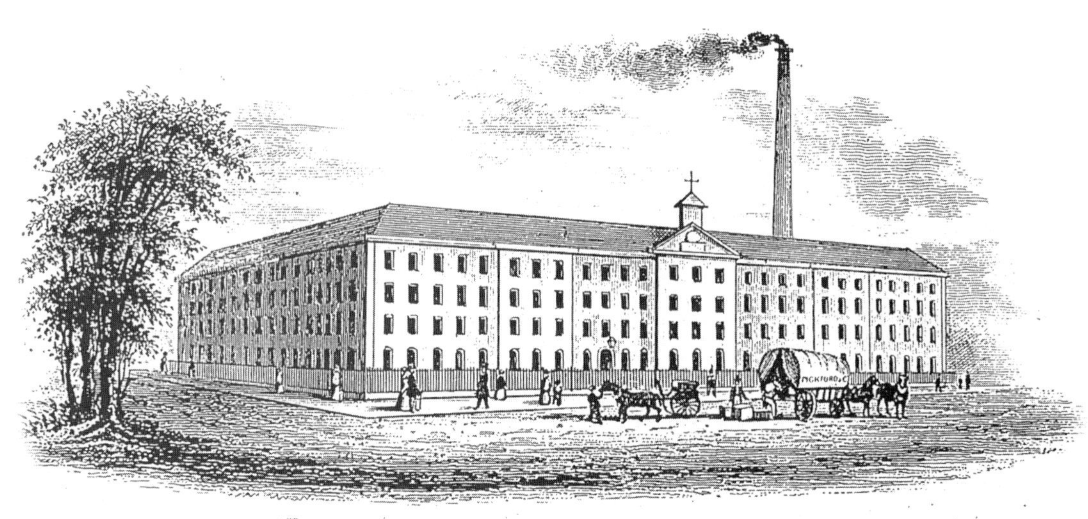

BRITANNIA SILK MILL

Russell and Clowes,

Silk Manufacturers,

LEEK. *Staffordshire.*

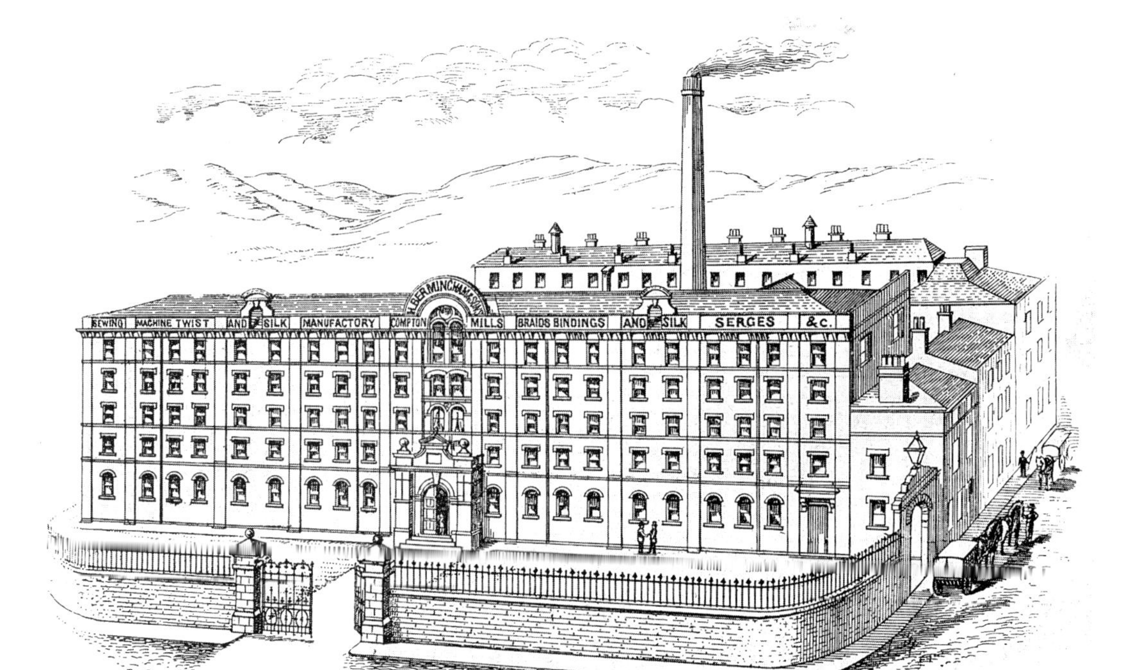

COMPTON MILLS.

CHAPTER ONE
On Silk

THE SILK WEAVING INDUSTRY was established in Coventry in the early seventeenth century, and by the later years of that century, silk had, quietly but firmly, and perhaps on a small scale, begun to make an impact on the Leek area as a new 'cottage industry'.

There was silk working in the Leek area long before the Huguenots came. The inventory of the goods of a certain John Wood, a silk weaver of Leek, is dated 1672, and shows a considerable investment in stock: undyed silk £179 1s, buttons and galloons £100, more silk at London £18, more silk for woofing £6, more silk to be charged at £110, and his total debts, good and bad, were £256 4s 2d. Even by seventeenth century standards, this represents a substantial business. It is interesting to note that Wood has stock in London, nearly 200 years before the 'London office' became the norm for local firms.

This significant inventory, which is held by Lichfield Joint Record Office, proves that, by this comparatively early date, the silk industry was well established locally, and pre-dates the revocation of the Edict of Nantes by 13 years, thus showing that escaping French Protestants did not introduce the industry to the Leek area, although the influx of thousands of Huguenot refugees obviously contributed to the introduction of revolutionary new ideas and methods in silk manufacture.

Clearly, as the industry became established locally, employment was found for a growing number of people, and the population increased accordingly. Richard Wilkes, writing in about 1750 states:

> *Leek is now become a considerable town; the buildings and lands are greatly improved; and a great trade for making buttons for men's cloaths of hair, mohair, silk thread etc. is here carried on with success. Many hundreds of poor people are employed in this manufacture.*

Also writing about the same time, Dr T. Pocock described Leek as *'a town of little trade except the making of thread, buttons and ribbon'*. It was a time when fashionable clothing worn by the gentry was enhanced by the silk covered buttons produced on a small scale but in great quantities in the cottage homes around the Moorlands.

Leek was strategically placed on the system of turnpike roads, and there was ample water in the area of a quality that was suitable for dyeing, so geographically conditions were ripe for development. The growing strength of the industry is demonstrated by the fact that, when John Lombe patented his water-powered twisting process in Derby, a mere thirty-odd miles distant, the silkmen of Leek became aware of this as a threat to their livelihood, and in 1734 united with other manufacturers from Macclesfield and the Lancashire towns in successfully campaigning against the renewal of Lombe's patent.

William Pitt (General View of the Agriculture of the County of Stafford, 1796) gives a good insight into the labour situation at that time. He states:

> *Leek has a considerable manufacture in the silk and mohair way; the manufactured goods from which are, sewing silks, twist, buttons, ribbons, silk-ferrets, shawls and silk handkerchiefs. In these manufactures, as by information from Messrs. Sleigh and Alsop, and Phillips and Ford, manufacturers, and others, are employed about two thousand inhabitants of the town, and one*

thousand of the adjacent country. In this trade some good fortunes have been made, and it has been very flourishing.

Trade directories from the late 18th and early 19th centuries reflect the continuing growth of the industry. Bailey's directory (1784) and Holden's directory (1809) list nine button, twist and sewing silk or ribbon manufacturers and two dyers. Parsons and Bradshaw's directory of 1818 lists 15 manufacturers and two dyers and, 16 years later, when White's directory was published in 1834, some 31 manufacturers were listed.

In the early nineteenth century, a contemporary writer, Samuel Bamford, who visited Leek in 1820, says:

In passing through the streets of Leek we noticed a number of weavers at their looms, and obtained permission to go into the weaving places and see them. The rooms where they worked were in general very clean; the work was all in the silk smallware line, and many of the weavers were young girls, some of them good looking, most of them very neatly attired, and many with costly combs, earrings, and other ornaments of value, showing that they earned a sufficiency of wages and had imbibed a taste for the refinements of dress. The sight of these young females, sitting at their elegant employment, producing rich borderings and trimmings, in good, well-aired, and well-finished apartments some of them approached by stairs with carpets and oil cloths on them, the girls also being dressed in a style which two hundred years before would have been deemed rich for a squire's daughter, was to me very gratifying.

Bamford was describing the typical weaving shades of Leek, some of which were at ground level, whilst others were located in the attics of workers' houses. Here the upper rooms are distinguished by the elongated windows, giving maximum light for maximum time, thus gaining the maximum production of goods in the working day. But was Bamford's view somewhat rose-tinted? Just why the young ladies of Leek made such an impression on him is not clear, and his views should be compared with later reports on working conditions at the time.

Working conditions and hours in the Leek silk mills were regulated by the terms of the 1833 Factory Act, which stipulated that children under 13 were allowed to work 10 hours a day. Reports indicated that most of them finished their day's work tired, for their work as helpers necessitated running backwards and forwards the 30 yards length of the loom all day, covering a distance of about 24 miles, usually barefooted.

The principle of half-time education was brought in by the 1844 regulations and, following the 1867 Factory Act, more powers of inspection and the enforcement of the law were given to the local authorities. The Leek Improvement Commissioners vested this responsibility in Robert Farrow (Sanitary Inspector). He was both diligent and efficient in the task, and exercised his authority responsibly, being particularly keen on the principle of half-time education. As a result, many more children began to receive education, and schools developed as a direct consequence.

Dyeing became a natural extension of the silk industry. The local water supply was of an ideal quality for dyeing processes, and Leek became famous for raven black dyed silk, pioneered by Joshua Wardle of Leekbrook. It was on this basis that Sir Thomas Wardle (1830-1909), son of Joshua, built his considerable reputation as a silk dyer, which led to his fruitful association with William Morris to produce silk and cretonne prints, where the skill of the dyer blended with the talents of the artist to create fabrics of great beauty. The association was somewhat stormy at times, for Morris laid down strict guidelines for the shades he was seeking, and insisted that they be followed exactly. Nevertheless, the two men became very firm friends.

The latter half of the nineteenth century was the period of great growth and prosperity in the Leek textile industry. It was during these later Victorian years that the various family firms of silk and textile manufacturers enjoyed their most significant progress. These factories varied in the numbers they employed, from a mere handful of workers to several hundred. These, too, were the years during which the architects, William and Larner Sugden, were most active in their work, giving Leek a splendid number of fine public buildings, Victorian architecture at its finest and most imaginative, built on the wealth generated in Leek at the time.

M.H. Miller's *Olde Leeke* included the following article on hand loom weaving. It is reprinted here in full as it gives a first hand account of the state of the industry at the time.

HAND LOOM WEAVING

ON January 1st, 1839, Mr. Joseph Fletcher, secretary to the Hand-loom Inquiry Commission, held an inquiry into the condition of the hand-loom weavers of Leek, and from a blue-book (kindly placed at our disposal by Mr. William Allen) we are able to give extracts from the interesting report and evidence:

Leek, which contains about 5,000 inhabitants, has long been the seat of the manufacture of broad silks of the best quality, and of plain ribbons by hand; upon the latter of which the manufacture by power has gradually encroached. There are yet about 150 broad-looms and 180 engine-looms in the town; but only half of the former and a third of the latter are now fully employed. About thirty of the broad looms have the jacquard machinery attached; but the small figures are produced by the alternate pressure of a number of treadles. The ribbon looms are employed chiefly in making plain black sarcenets, and scarcely any satins. Steam-power, however, has taken both the work and the workmen from this department, and now makes all the galloons.

The number ot steam engine looms is about l00

Those of Messrs. Carr	*20*
Glendinning and Gaunt	*10*
Worthington	*50*
Wreford	*50*
Ward	*50*

There are no power-looms making broad silks, though some are being erected. The power-weaving of ribbons, ferrets, and galloons, in those looms, is part of the whole system of silk. manufacture in the Leek factories, which embraces also the throwing and spinning of silk, and the twisting of it into sewing-silk, braids, etc. The principal occupation of the hand-loom weavers is in the production of black, checked, or figured silk neck-handkerchiefs, and a few gros-de-naples and figured gown-pieces of the first quality; the best plain black ribbons, and silk serges of superior qualities. They manufacture chiefly for the best home market, and all the principal employers conduct their business on the same principles; each firm throwing their own silk, weaving or twisting it, and disposing of their goods by their own agents to the retailer, or occasionally to the warehouse-man.

All have their own style of business and their own country connection. The beautiful raven black, which the dyers of Leek alone can give (perhaps on account of the qualities of the Churnet water, which runs by the town), forms some bond upon the black ribbon trade; although these dyers work also for Manchester, London, etc. The sewing-silks, twists, and buttons, are alone designed for exportation, either by the manufacturers or through merchants.

The hand-loom work is given out to "undertakers" warped and round. They are owners of a varying number of looms, and employ journeymen and apprentices, to the former of whom they pay the warehouse price, after deducting for loom rent, etc. The hand ribbon looms yet employed are chiefly worked by the female members of the undertakers' families, the power-factories having taken all the journeymen away from them; and there are no apprentices being brought up to this branch of the trade. Apprentices are taken into the broad trade, generally for seven years, commencing between the ages of eleven and fourteen.

The prices are all by the piece; handkerchiefs being paid for by the dozen, other broad silks by the yard, and ribbons by the piece of 36 yards. The following arc the lists of Messrs. Ellis, Russell, and Co., from which those of other employers do not materially differ:

Black sarcenet ribbons widths: 2, $7\frac{1}{2}$d.; 4, $9\frac{1}{2}$d.; 6, $11\frac{1}{2}$; 8, $1/1\frac{1}{2}$; 11, 1/4; 12, 1/7; 14. 1/11; 6, 2/3; 8, 2/7; 20, 2/10; 24 and 30, 3/6 and 4/6 per piece of 36 yards.

Plain black bandanas 32in., 5/-; 34in., 5/6; 36in., 6/6 per dozen.

Black Barcelonia, 3 threads 26in., 4/6; 28in, 4/6; 34in, 5/6; 36in, 6/6; 38in, 7/6 per dozen.

Black Brussels, 4 threads 32in, 6/; 34in, 7/-; 36in, 8/-; 38in, 9/- per dozen.

Fancy handkerchiefs from 6/- per dozen to 16/- per dozen, varying according to quality and pattern.

The broad-silk weavers, in 1834, endeavoured to get a formal agreement among the roasters to a list of prices, and several abortive strikes took place. The prices in the hand-engine loom have necessarily declined before the power competition, to the injury of the undertakers or first hands, but not of the journeyhand class, who are now working the power-looms themselves.

One of the principal masters supposes the nett weekly earnings of the power engine loom weavers to average 16/- per week, but the relieving officer of the union estimates it at much less. The hand engine loom trade is so disorganized by the withdrawal of all regular journeymen, that there are only the loom owner's own earnings and those of his family to be estimated. On 12 dys. of black sarcenets, the manufacturer above alluded to thinks about 11/- might be earned; or 10/6 if fire and light be deducted.

The earnings of the broad looms weekly, at the warehouse prices, are estimated by the same gentleman at about 25/- per week on handkerchiefs, and from 16/- to 18/- on figured goods; from which filling and fire and light have to be deducted. But the weavers whom I examined represent the average as much less.

There are about 40 undertakers in the broad trade; a considerable number of journeyhands; a few women, the wives of journeyhands; and a few apprentices. The undertakers appear to be a class superior in habits and condition to those of almost any other place; but those of the journeyhands are low; their wives are commonly piecers and doublers in the factories, wind for the sewing silk manufacturers, or are mill overlookers. They work commonly by the piece, but a woman's weekly wages are reckoned at 5/- to 5/6, except for doubling, which is because children early get employment in the factories, even at six or seven years of age; the silk mills being exempt from any limitation as to their age. Their wages increase from 1/- per week, when first admitted, up to 2/6 when about 13 years of age. Some are employed at quill-winding for the weavers.

The houses of the undertakers are many of them convenient and substantial buildings, consisting of four apartments on the ground and first floors, with workshop above. One of my witnesses pays £10 rent, 4/- street gas tax, 2/6 for highways, 12/- poor's rate, 3d. Easter dues, and 1d. church rate per annum, besides 6/8 water money. It is the journeyman class who are obviously more expressly the object of inquiry, on account of their poverty; and of these the most important body is the steam factory weavers. The relieving officer testifies that, during the fifteen months that the union has been formed, he has had no weavers on his books except through sickness, and these were among the poor journeymen, who live perhaps in £5 cottages. They have generally had families and though their homes betokened great poverty, they were clean, as also were their persons and dress, and those of their children. The town is notable for its cleanliness.

Embezzlement of silk at the factories prevails to an enormous extent, and has lately much increased. Receivers are readily found. There are, however, few dissolute people. The greater number not only send their children to Sunday schools, but go to places of worship themselves. Of the young men, many subscribe to the Mechanics Institute, especially for the winter, while in summer they are generally busy at cricket.

Except a small endowed school there is no public day-school, and nearly all the instruction which the children receive is at the Sunday schools. In the Wesleyan Sunday schools there are upwards of 1,000 children.

The hand engine loom undertakers recommend a tax on machinery, and the broad loom weavers desire a repeal of the corn-laws.

A more contemporary review of Leek's industries appeared in the annual journal 'Leek News' published each Christmas during the 1930s. This usually contained articles contributed by local persons having a particular insight into matters of local interest. This article, written by Mr. J B Cope, a leading member of a firm of knitwear manufacturers in Leek, is reproduced here in full.

FIFTY YEARS of LEEK INDUSTRIES.

A RETROSPECT by Mr. JB COPE.

LEEK'S industries have passed through many changes during the last half-century, to recall which, may interest many, particularly of this generation.

Suppose we take the year l880 as our starting point. Real silk sewing threads were without doubt the backbone of local employment, there being at that period about fifty manufacturers, large and small.

Spun silk and mercerised cotton as sewing mediums were in their infancy. The first spun silk made in Leek emanated from the factory of Messrs W S Watson and Co. in 1880. This branch was afterwards taken over by a number of local manufacturers, who formed The Leek Spun Silk Co., for that purpose. Later, about 1900, Messrs T and V Myatt laid down machinery for the same purpose but only carried it on for a few years, again in 1907 Messrs Brough, Nicholson and Hall installed machinery in the Fountain Mill, which had been taken over from Messrs G Bermingham and Co.

By this time mercerised cottons had become a big competitor with both net and spun silks for sewing purposes. The growing use of sewing machines in factories played a great part in the modifications required in all classes of sewing threads. Raven sewings, together with Yellow Barbers (as used by the boot and shoe trades) being all but extinguished and the make-up of others altered. Even embroidery silks, of which there were several notable brands turned out - probably the most used being Peri Lustre made by Messrs Wardle and Davenport - all suffered somewhat, from the advancement of mercerising which provided lustrous cotton to replace the silk.

Later on, the advent of artificial silk as an embroidery medium, led to more firms taking an interest in embroidery, crochet and hand knitting threads, an expansion which for some years created work for many busy hands, in the mills and at home. The craze for hand knit and crocheted jumpers showed what could be done with the new yarn.

BRAIDS.

During the early years under review, a very big trade was being done in braids, both for men's and women's wear. Tailors' braids by the millions of yards were turned out. These braids were made chiefly from mohair yarn, though many were mixed mohair and silk, and some of pure silk. Practically every man had a suit, of which, coat and vest were edge-bound with braid. Women's clothes were also ornamented with braids, but in heavier and coarser makes, mostly produced from worsted yarns, while men's were chiefly of the flat make and rarely more than one inch wide. Women's were of all types - so-called Russia braid, tubular braid, cords and flat braids, the latter in varying widths up to eight inches wide. A woman's outfit might carry something of all varieties with anything up to fifty or sixty yards in all.

In addition to these plain or self-coloured braids a very large amount was made mixed with tinsel threads in imitation of gold, silver, copper and steel, in addition to braids made entirely from these threads. To all these must be added corset cords - a silk covered cord with cotton centre, made in a wide range of brilliant colours and in large quantities. Eyeglass cord, surgical cord and fishing lines all from pure silk, also a lot of thick cord covered with worsted made into girdles with tassels and net-worked top.

Boot and shoe laces required immense quantities of mercerised cotton, which later largely superseded the polished thread especially for the better qualities for men's wear, and almost entirely for women's.

BRAID TRIMMINGS.

Braid trimmings were a big feature for several years, from about 1887, these were principally made from tubular braids, the patterns, being formed and sewn by hand, found employment for a number of women in the mills, and more at home. These braid trimmings besides being made and sold by the yard, were made in sets composed of collar piece, two cuff pieces, two panels for bodice front, and in many instances, a larger and wider panel for the skirt front.

Another feature was the making of so-called frogs, from flat braids, and Austrian knots from heavier tubular braids, both were graduated in sizes and finished with braided buttons, the making of which found employment for many wood-turners to supply the moulds over which the braiding was plaited.

In addition to these hand sewn trimmings, a large quantity was also being made on small hand looms and by other means, but these machine-made goods were largely made from real silk, with tinsel threads worked together, the variety of materials used being considerable. These machine-made articles carried on for several years, being lighter, more fanciful, and cheaper. No mention has been made so far of a cheap make of worsted braid, so-called llama braid, a quality which was much used for binding purposes, and for several years, in combination with a chenille pile which was worked down the centre, made a very popular skirt hem protector. This being while skirts were worn long, and often dragging on the ground. Many ingenious contrivances, in the way of dress suspenders, were being made. Changes in fashion gradually shortened the length of skirts, causing changes in braids for lighter sorts.

Other types of machines, with Jacquard effects, paved the way for artificial silk, which was coming, the earliest sample being received in 1893, with a request for a report on its utility. This sample was very small, but was made up as a fine braid and returned with the intimation that the sample was too small to form an opinion upon.in 1895 a large consignment of Chardonnet yarn was received in a variety of colours and sizes, this was made up in various ways including twisted cords, braids, etc., but mainly in wide braid which found a market as Ladies' ties. During the next few years other makes came to hand which were all difficult to manipulate, being troublesome to wind, and make up. It was often neccessary to have lamps burning under the machines, particinlairly in damp weather which influenced the yarn detrimentally. Large quantities of this early yarn were made up into multi-coloured braids for ladies' and gentlemens' ties.

WEAVING.

Weaving was chiefly centred in making Prussian bindings, ferretts, galloons and, similar smallwares, until a few years later, about 1900, when there was a big call for tubular casings. These were used for covering strips of steel in varying lengths from about six to ten inches long. These steel strips were for holding the seams of women's bodices straight and shapely. They were inserted in the tubular casing, the ends of the case turned over and sewn down; this found much employment for home-workers. The old hand-loom weavers had gradually become fewer, there being probably only three or four firms who still employed such - Messrs. Alsop, Downes and Spilsbury had several engaged making dress fabrics, tailors' serges - in black, white and colours, also furniture fabrics all in pure silk, in addition to silk handkerchiefs. They, also Messrs. G. Bermingham and Son were honoured by Royalty to provide special dress lengths.

Perhaps the chief development in the weaving trade took place about 1889. When the Jacquard smallware loom was introduced by Brough, Nicholson and Hall, these looms were early in use making Petersham ribbons, grograms, silk hat bands for the navy and also for schools with badges or names woven in colours, named skirt bands with the makers' name or brand mark, boot top bands, coat tabs and shirt labels, together with fancy galons which fashion favoured for a while, these were in conventional designs chiefly, in silk and tinsel on cotton warp. Later in 1893 came a demand for Beaded galloons, these were produced on the Jacquard loom, after slight modification, and by the aid of a special reed which could be adjusted to permit one or more beads to pass at a time. The beads came in packets of one hundred thousand ready threaded on short strings and had to be transferred on to continuous thread, wound on small bobbins for weaving, made in various designs and sometimes further embellished with sequins. This vogue lasted but a few years.

In this branch many single hand looms were also in use. With this type of loom one girl made one piece of galon varying in width from half to two inches. These hand looms had been in use since 1889, making many varieties of articles from furniture gimps, laces for academic gowns, to real gold military braid for officers' uniforms, together with a wide variety of braid trimmings, fringes and ruchings.

These ruchings were made from real silk braids from half to one inch wide, cut into short pieces about two inches long, some plain and others goffered or crimped and then woven in on a cotton warp ground up to four inches wide forming a deep feathery plush effect which was rich though heavy. The Jacquard loom was used for a similar article but in this the braid was very narrow and first put through a curling process. before weaving, the result was a good imitation of a feather ruche; they sold very extensively. This ruche vogue was utilised by procuring from Yorkshire, a fabric woven in strips of plush or astrachan effect materials, between each strip was a space of plain woven fabric, these were cut apart and a length of cotton wadding laid in. the edges turned over and sewn together thus creating a further variety and incidentally finding employment for home workers.

KNITTING.

1899 saw the introduction to Leek of the first knitting machine using a latch needle. It was a French machine for making gimp trimmings from small braids, cords, chenille, beads or anything which could be introduced for trimming purposes. Later it was used for making striped ties, but it was superseded by a German machine which was more versatile, I refer to the Sander and Graft machine.

1901-2 flat knitting machines were being used, - they were introduced for making pyjama girdles *primarily. On these machines was made a small range of knitted ties, from pure silk, spun silk, mohair, and art silk. The success of these which was immediate, led to other machinery being sought, amid the introduction of Standard machines, Berridge machines and Harrison machines. The Brinton machine introduced in 1905, by Wildt and Co. was the forerunner and type on which most of the tie and scarf machines have since been modelled.*

In 1904 came a loom type of machine with a Jacquard cylinder under the needles, the cylinder turning with each stitch and the needles being operated from cards which revolved with the cylinder. This machine was introduced for making pyjama girdles, but it proved unusuitable because the mechanism was not firm enough for thick soft cotton. But, on this machine, was produced the first motor scarf in 1905. This scarf was exactly as the later elastic stitch scarves, only of coarser make, made in spun silk in coloured stripes, with knitted tails for fringe. This machine was later superseded for more adaptable and easier worked machines, which followed in quick succession to keep pace with the expanding requirements.

Probably the next most important development came when Messrs. Wardle and Davenport introduced art silk hosiery which became so famous and widely imitated during and since the later war years.

More recent developments have included all kinds of under and outer wear, requiring the finest machines and the most versatile from a designer's point. Many of the more recent additions are within the knowledge of this generation, therefore need not be further enlarged upon. So seeing the space allotted has already been exceeded, I must now leave this review with the hope it has been interesting.

J. B. C.

Haregate Hall (from a Mackaness print)

An artist's impression, looking over Fountain Street, of the main factory on the Brough, Nicholson and Hall site. Note the two large water tanks.

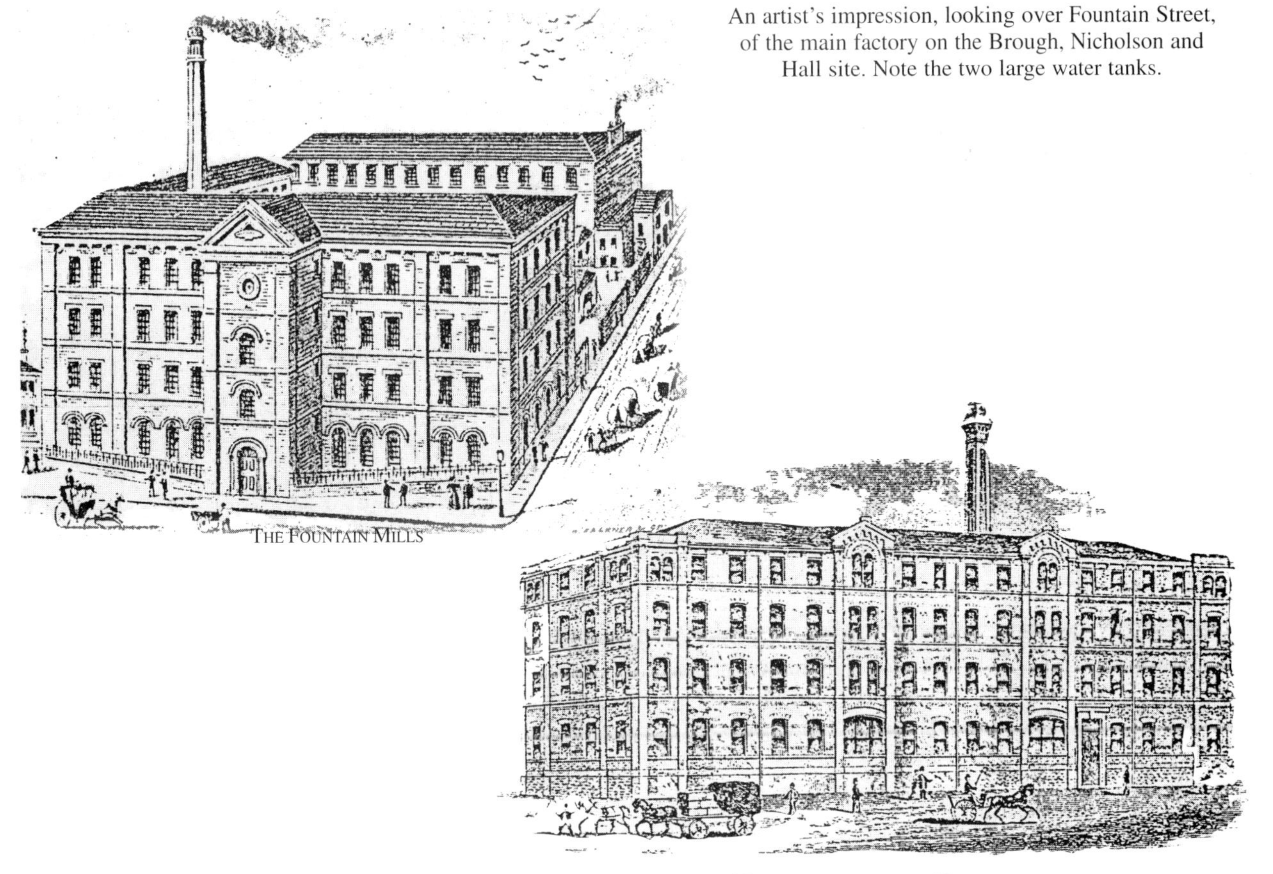

THE FOUNTAIN MILLS

THE ALEXANDRA MILLS

The very noisy braid plaiting shed.

Mohair winding room.

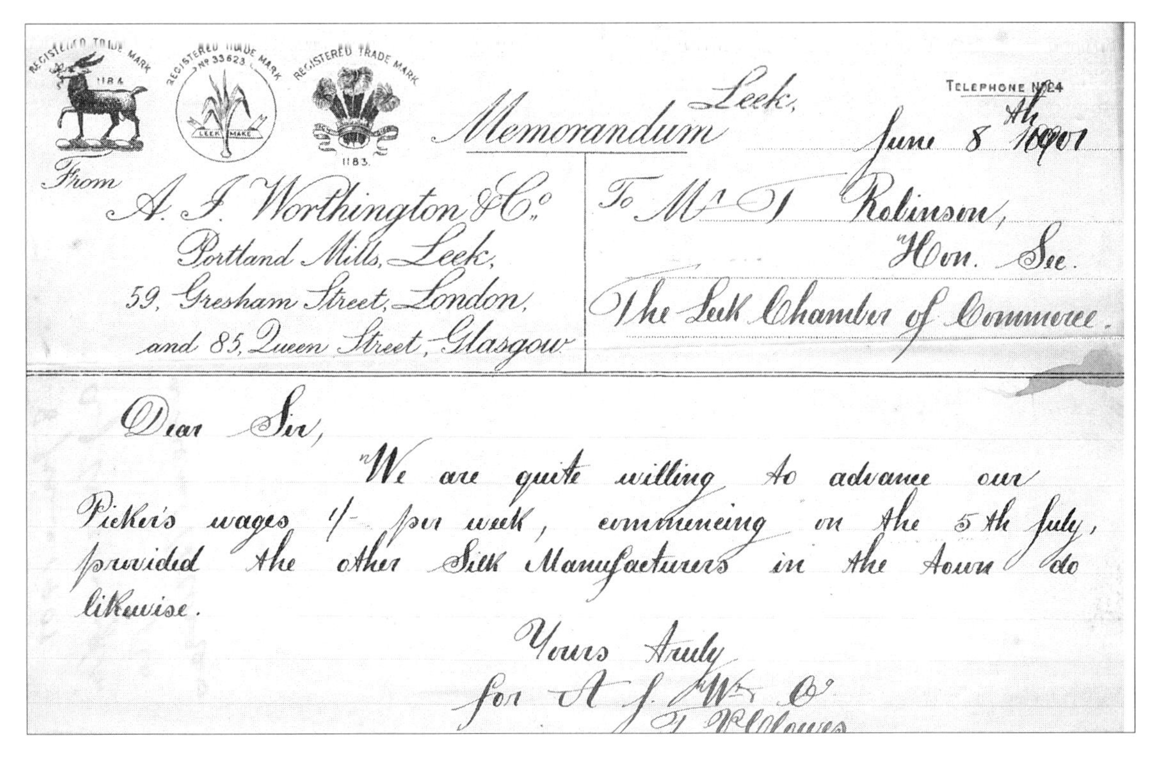
REGISTERED TRADE MARK 1184 — REGISTERED TRADE MARK No 33623 LEEK MAKE — REGISTERED TRADE MARK 1183

TELEPHONE No 24

Memorandum — Leek, June 8th 1901

From A. J. Worthington & Co.
Portland Mills, Leek,
59, Gresham Street, London,
and 85, Queen Street, Glasgow

To Mr J Robinson,
Hon. Sec.
The Leek Chamber of Commerce.

Dear Sir,

We are quite willing to advance our Picker's wages 1/- per week, commencing on the 5th July, provided the other Silk Manufacturers in the Town do likewise.

Yours truly
for A J Wr & Co

This stylish letter heading of A.J. Worthington and Co, illustrates the formal way in which labour negotiations were conducted.

Residents of upper Queen Street have put on their Sunday best for the photographer in 1912. The factory of A.J. Worthington and Co stands just beyond the junction, the photograph taken before the enclosed wooden bridge, with its public clock, was built over the road to connect the two parts of the factory.

The Leek Silk Twist manufacturing Society Ltd.

Silk twister with his young helper.

W.H. Nithsdale was the photographer of these mill interiors.

Silk manufacturers usually had elaborate printed letterheads to create a good impression with their customers.

Silk twisting shade, the Leek Silk Twist Manufacturing Society Ltd.

Manufacture of silk braids, Messrs Wardle and Davenport Ltd.

Lace tagging room, Brough, Nicholson and Hall Ltd, c 1897.

24th Dec, 1901

A. Nicholson Esq.

L E E K .

Dear Sir :-

With reference to the 12 o'clock Saturday closing : not havi[ng] had any further notice of a meeting in connection with this matter - and as I shall be away from home until Monday or Tuesday next, I write to you to let you know the result of a discussion we have had here on the subject.

We are of opinion that the discontinuing of the 5 minutes grace as discussed at the last meeting, is not a sufficiently serious and commercial scheme for us to work upon. The enclosed form of notice will give you an idea of the system we think it would be best to employ, and I should be glad if you would not mind letting me know your opinion of it, or, as I shall be away, would youm mind writing to W. & D. Ltd.?

Yours sincerely,

[signature]

N O T I C E . Jan.1st, 1902.

The law now requiring textile factories to close at 12-0(noon) on Saturdays - the hours of work will, (in order to obtain the 54 hours as before) in future, be as follows :-

Monday	Tuesday	Wednesday	Thursday	Friday	Saturday.
6 - 30	6 - 30	6 - 30	6 - 30	6 - 30	6 - 15
8 - 30	8 - 30	8 - 30	8 - 30	8 - 30	8 - 0
B'fast	B'fast	B'fast	B'fast	B'fast	B'fast
9 - 0	9 - 0	9 - 0	9 - 0	9 - 0	8 - 30
12 - 30	12 - 30	12 - 30	12 - 30	12 - 30	12 - 0
Dinner	Dinner	Dinner	Dinner	Dinner	
1 - 30	1 - 30	1 - 30	1 - 30	1 - 30	
5 - 45	5 - 45	5 - 45	5 - 45	5 - 45	

The pattern of the working week is defined in this correspondence from Wardle and Davenport Ltd.

The box making room at Brough, Nicholson and Hall Ltd, c 1897.
There was a high level of female employees in every department.

A typical dyehouse.

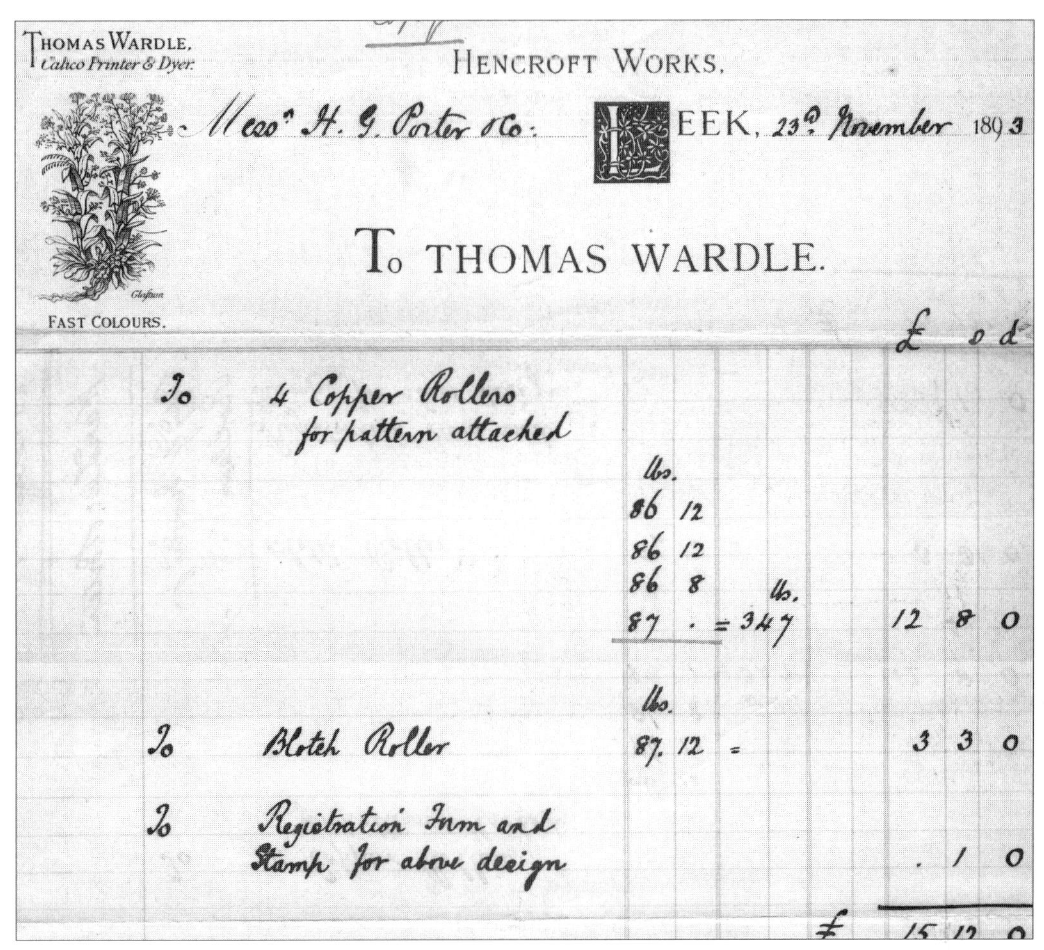

THOMAS WARDLE,
Calico Printer & Dyer.

HENCROFT WORKS,

Messrs H. G. Porter & Co: LEEK, 23rd November 1893

To THOMAS WARDLE.

FAST COLOURS.

				£	s	d
To	4 Copper Rollers for pattern attached	lbs. 86 12 / 86 12 / 86 8 / 87 .	= 347 lbs.	12	8	0
To	Blotch Roller	lbs. 87. 12	=	3	3	0
To	Registration Form and Stamp for above design			.	1	0
			£	15	12	0

Thomas Wardle, son of Joshua Wardle, of Cheddleton Heath, was born at Leek on 26th January 1831. He was educated at the old Leek Grammar School and Macclesfield. His skills and expertise as a silk dyer were sought out by William Morris, who, in his search for perfection in the colours for his fabric design, worked with Wardle at the Hencroft Works near the River Churnet on Abbey Green Road on visits to Leek between 1875 and 1877. Thomas Wardle travelled widely, and his visits to India and Kashmir led to his discovery of the excellent properties of Tussur silk. His knowledge of silk working proved to be a great asset to the industry in India. He was much in demand as a lecturer and advisor on all matters relating to silk and wrote a number of books and pamphlets on the subject. He was president of the Silk Association of Great Britain and Ireland, and was knighted for his services to the silk industry in 1897. He was also an expert on geology, contributing articles to the publications of the North Staffordshire Field Club and Sleigh's History of Leek. Arthur Wardle, son of Sir Thomas, joined the firm in 1881, and following the death of his father in 1909 the dyeworks moved to the other side of the river, a much larger site stretching along the Macclesfield Road where expansion led to the formation of Sir Thomas and Arthur Wardle Ltd. Churnet Works, Leek.

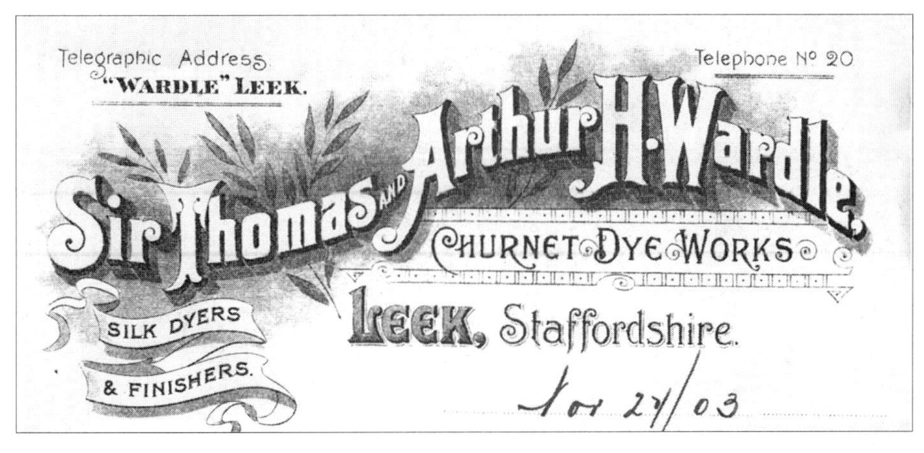

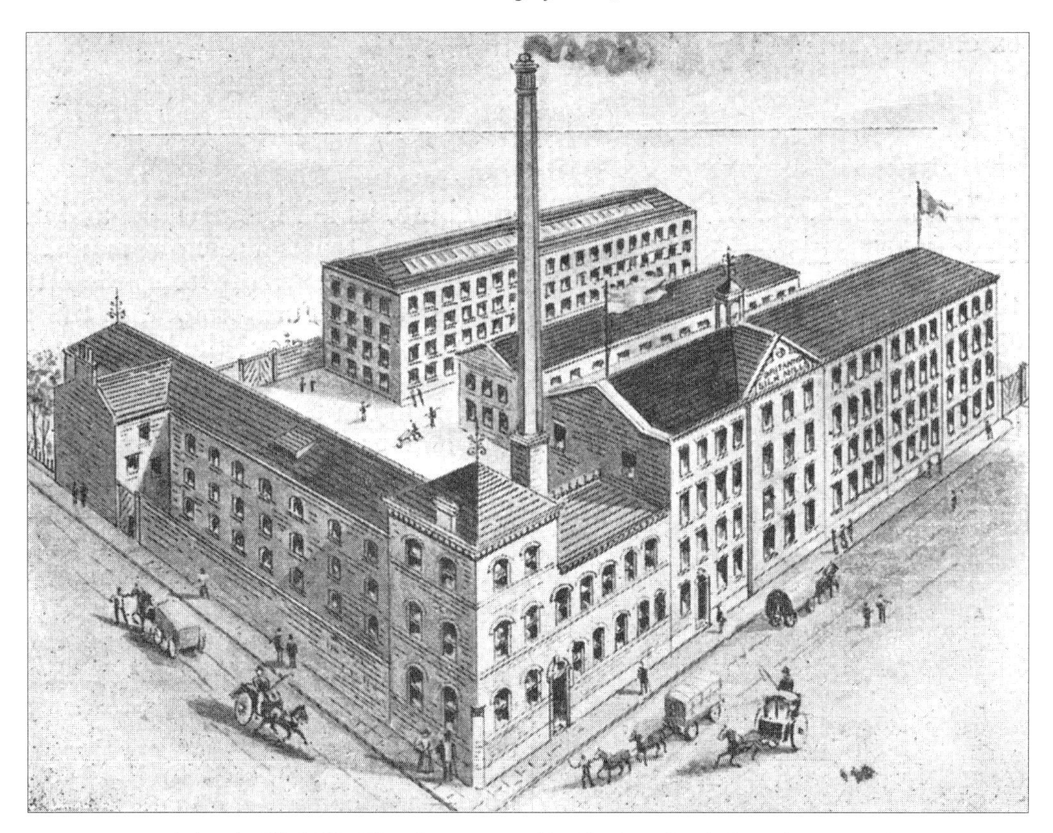

Brittania Silk Mills, West Street, owned by Stephen Goodwin and Tatton Ltd.

This fine example of Leek's Victorian factory architecture is Waterloo Mill. Built in 1895 for William Broster, it is seen at its best here, devoid of the buildings and streets which now surround it. The architect was James Gosling Smith.

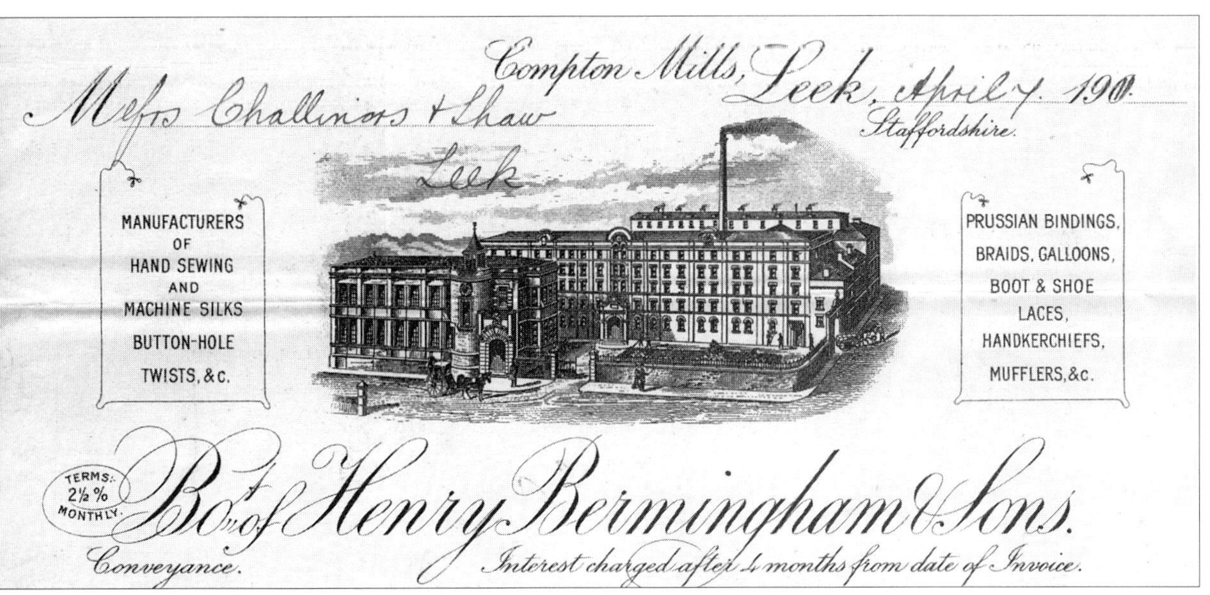

Compton Mills, Leek, April 7. 190
Staffordshire.

Mefs Challinors & Shaw
Leek

MANUFACTURERS OF HAND SEWING AND MACHINE SILKS BUTTON-HOLE TWISTS, &c.

PRUSSIAN BINDINGS, BRAIDS, GALLOONS, BOOT & SHOE LACES, HANDKERCHIEFS, MUFFLERS, &c.

TERMS:- 2½ % MONTHLY.

Bo^t of Henry Bermingham & Sons.

Conveyance.

Interest charged after 4 months from date of Invoice.

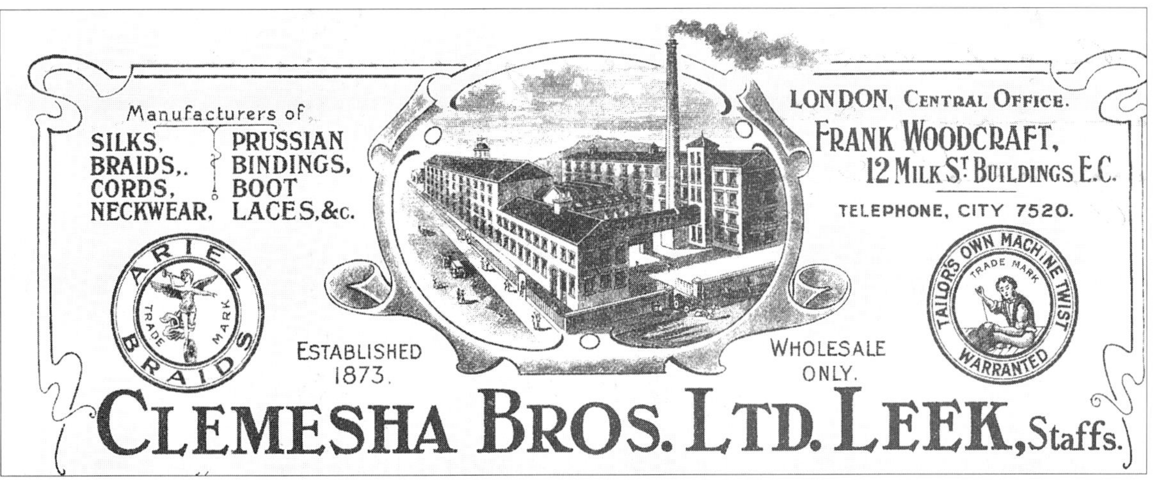

Manufacturers of
SILKS, BRAIDS, CORDS, NECKWEAR,
PRUSSIAN BINDINGS, BOOT LACES, &c.

LONDON, CENTRAL OFFICE.
FRANK WOODCRAFT,
12 MILK S^T BUILDINGS E.C.
TELEPHONE, CITY 7520.

ARIEL BRAIDS TRADE MARK

TAILOR'S OWN MACHINE TWIST TRADE MARK WARRANTED

ESTABLISHED 1873.

WHOLESALE ONLY.

CLEMESHA BROS. LTD. LEEK, Staffs.

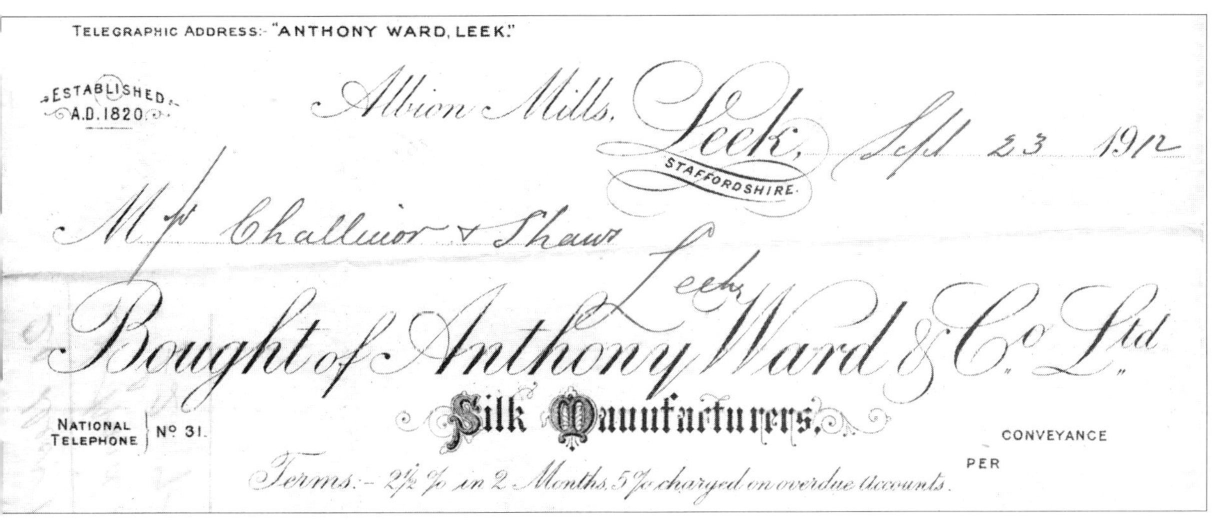

TELEGRAPHIC ADDRESS:- "ANTHONY WARD, LEEK."

ESTABLISHED A.D. 1820

Albion Mills, Leek, Sept 23 1912
STAFFORDSHIRE.

M^ss Challinor & Shaw
Leek

Bought of Anthony Ward & Co. L^td

Silk Manufacturers.

NATIONAL TELEPHONE No. 31.

CONVEYANCE PER

Terms:- 2½ % in 2 Months, 5 % charged on overdue Accounts.

These stylish letterheads are typical of the prestgious stationery used by most silk manufacturers at this period.

The shop of Thomas Mark, Printer and Stationer, Derby Street. The firm produced an almanac each year which contained much local information and a directory of traders.

CHAPTER TWO
On Print and Printers

THE EARLIEST RECORDED BOOKSELLER in Leek appears to be Joseph Needham, who had premises on the south-east corner of the Market Place. It was with Needham in the late 17th century (c.1668-70) that a young man named Michael Johnson served his apprenticeship. Johnson later moved to Lichfield, where he set up his own business as bookseller and stationer, and married Sarah Ford, a Warwickshire woman. A son was born on 18 September 1709 who was destined to become the great English lexicographer and man of letters, Dr Samuel Johnson. He became the intimate friend of the Scottish author James Boswell, whose Life of Dr Johnson portrays graphically Johnson's standing in the literary life of his day.

Boswell states: "*At that time booksellers' shops in the provincial towns of England were very rare, so that there was not even one in Birmingham*". It is therefore significant that Leek was able to support such a shop at the time, and an indication of the comparative prosperity of the town in the early 18th century. Inventories from that period which mention books are usually a sign that the person had considerable wealth. Perhaps even more significant is the fact that the seeds of Samuel Johnson's ultimate genius were sowed by his father's experience and learning with Leek bookseller, Joseph Needham.

Bailey's British Directory of 1784 is one of the few 18th century directories to include Leek. This early directory lists 35 tradesmen and professional people, and these too reflect the comparative prosperity of the town. Sixteen were engaged in some aspect of the silk industry, and the remainder include three surgeons, four lawyers, five grocers, two drapers, one druggist, one ironmonger, one fellmonger, one innkeeper, and one bookseller and printer - Joseph Needham, possibly the son of the previous Joseph Needham, since his young wife Anna died on 21 May 1778, aged 26, and is buried in Leek churchyard.

A later directory, The Universal British Directory of Trade and Commerce and Manufacture of 1793, shows, as might be expected, a much larger and wider representation of trades and professions, with the silk industry continuing its rise, and two booksellers are now listed: Thomas Bromwell and M. and C. Maddock. George Moore is listed as a bookbinder, and Francis Hilliard, a Bristol man, is a printer and bookseller occupying the premises formerly belonging to Joseph Needham.

By 1818 (Parsons and Bradshaw's Directory) William Hope is a bookseller, stationer and bookbinder in Custard Street, Charles Lowe a bookseller and stationer in Sheepmarket, and John Smith, also a druggist, in the Market Place, with charge of the post office in Spout Street. Francis Hilliard, still in business as a printer, has now moved to Scolding Bank, the area which is now Overton Bank. At the time he was the Parish Clerk, and in 1821 printed *A Selection of Psalms and Hymns* designed for the use of the Congregation of Cheddleton Church.

George Nall, from Bakewell, a versatile and comprehensive trader stocking most things from pencils, pens, account books and stationery items, to smallwares, patent medicines and musical instruments, was also a printer. His advertisement followed four closely-printed pages of items stocked:

LETTER-PRESS AND COPPER PLATE PRINTING
BOOKBINDING ACCORDING TO ALL THE VARIETIES OF MODERN TASTE

This Leek Directory of 1832 indicates that George Nall was distributor at the Stamp Office in Sheepmarket and, with W. Alcock, a Market Looker, a versatile and busy man indeed! These 19th Century tradesmen seemed to have boundless time and energy! Nall was an experienced printer, having been in partnership with Bemrose in Derby. Arriving in Leek around 1828 he first set up business in Spout Street, but was in Sheepmarket by the time White's comprehensive Directory of Staffordshire appeared in 1834.

William M. Hilliard, who joined his father's business in 1822, was trading in his own right in Church Street, leaving Francis to carry on with his public services as Parish Clerk on Overton Bank.

In 1834 George Nall was still in business in Sheepmarket, and his son Robert joined the firm as a partner, to form George Nall and Son, still in business in Sheepmarket in 1835 (Pigot's Directory) but moving to Custard Street by 1846 (William's Directory) where the firm was also agent for the Nottinghamshire Assurance Company. At the time the Post Office was in Custard Street with George Nall as postmaster. By then W. M. Hilliard had moved to the Market Place, and was agent for the Royal Exchange and Tradesman's Assurance Company. John Pilgrim is listed as a bookseller in Derby Street.

The business of George Nall and Son was sold to William Clemesha, listed in Kelly's Post Office Directory of 1868 as printer, stationer and bookbinder, 11 Stanley Street (formerly Custard Street, but now renamed). Clemesha pioneered the hand-powered flatbed machine in Leek, capable of producing 500 copies per hour.

In J. G. Harrod's Directory of 1870 William Clemesha is listed prominently as printer, stationer, bookbinder and account book manufacturer and lithographer, still at 11 Stanley Street. Also listed in this directory are: Edward Hallowes, bookseller, printer and stationer, Stockwell Street, (Hallowes had served his apprenticeship with Nall); C. R. Jones, bookseller, printer and stationer, Sheepmarket; Charles Kirkham, smallwares, hosiery and stationery, Derby Street; James Rider, printer, bookbinder, stationer, account book manufacturer and stamp distributor, registrar of births, deaths and marriages, and agent for Newton and Wilson's sewing machines, 6 Derby Street. (In 1864/5 James Rider was in Spout Street.)

No 6 Derby Street was destined to remain in the printing business for many years. James Rider was still there in 1872 (Post Office Directory), where he was also registrar of births, marriages and deaths for Leek district, and stamp distributor.

In Kelly's Directory of 1892 Thomas Mark, bookseller, printer and stationer was in business. Like many of his competitors, he was another versatile man, for he printed books, booklets and his own directory and almanac, as well as general jobbing work.

In 1896 W. H. Eaton occupied 6 Derby Street, and other printers listed are:

Clowes and Co, London Street;

J. Fogg, Stanley Street;

Thomas Grace, Market Place;

E. Hallowes, Stockwell Street;

Hill Brothers, Derby Street;

G. Hill, Stanley Street;

C. Kirkham, Derby Street;

M. H. Miller, Market Street.

Many printers from this period seemed to remain in business for only a short time, and their names are not well-known amongst old Leek traders. Perhaps competition was fierce, and prices were always keenly contested. The silk industry was always a great consumer of paperwork, and eventually several of the larger firms installed their own in-plant printing facilities.

Newspaper printing had, by the late 19th Century, become firmly established locally. Matthew Henry Miller is noted in the 1872 Directory as editor and proprietor of the Leek Times, Stanley Street. By 1892 (Kelly's Directory) the Leek Post was produced in Pickwood Road, with the North Stafford Newspaper Company as proprietors. Kelly's 1912 Directory shows the Leek Post published weekly by Hill Brothers (Leek) Ltd at 79 Haywood Street, and the Leek Times in Market Street by M.H. Miller, editor and proprietor.

The story of the dual publications of the weekly newspapers cannot be fully told without introducing the name of one of Leek's famous sons, Enoch Hill.

Enoch Hill was born in one of the small houses in Milk Street, Ball Haye Green. As a young man he had a great desire for knowledge and was diligent in his studies. In his early years he took an active part in the religious, social and municipal life of Leek, being closely attached to St Luke's Church and the Ball Haye Green Mission Church, and for many years a Sunday School teacher and lay reader. Virtually self-taught, he built up an extraordinary personal efficiency by self-improvement, and his perseverance was exemplary. He became acquainted with Mr John Sykes, headmaster of the Leek Grammar School, under whose influence and guidance he undertook a further course of private tuition.

He began printing in a shed behind his Milk Street home, and later went to work for Edward Hallowes, printer and stationer, in Stockwell Street; printing then became his first commercial enterprise.

He moved into a shop in Cawdry Buildings (Kelly's Directory 1892) where he established a stationery and printing business. But his main work was still to come. In 1895 he was appointed Secretary to the Leek United Building Society, a position which he held for seven years.

During that time he was elected to the Leek Urban District Council, on which he served for the remainder of his time in Leek. He played a major part as secretary of the Catering and Entertainment Committee for the local celebrations of the Coronation of King Edward VII.

In 1902 he was appointed secretary of the Halifax Permanent Building Society, and his career went from strength to strength. He became prominent in the Building Society movement nationally, holding a number of national offices and presiding at the Annual Building Societies Conference for several years. He also earned considerable distinction in banking circles, and was rewarded in 1928 with a knighthood.

Naturally, when he entered the Building Society profession, his printing business had to be offloaded, so he transferred his interest in it to his brothers thus forming the firm of Hill Brothers (Leek) Ltd. The firm took new premises in Haywood Street in 1900 and it was here that the Leek Post was printed for many years.

The Leek Post and the Leek Times ran concurrently for a number of years. At first the Leek Post was less successful, while the Leek Times enjoyed a much larger circulation. Because of this, it charged a higher rate for advertisements, and this ultimately led to a reversal, for the Leek Post, in spite of its poorer financial position, installed new and more efficient machinery, while the Leek Times became less efficient and more unreliable. This situation ultimately led to the Times being incorporated into the Post to form the Leek Post and Times in 1934.

Other jobbing printers during the early 20th century have included H. Sanders, who had premises in Gaunt Passage in 1909, and the Moorlands Press (proprietor W. T. Cook) in Pickwood Road. In 1901 Mr Fred Hill commenced business as a stationer and bookseller, and established a printing shop in a section of Haywood Mill, Haywood Street. John Maycock, a life-long friend of Mr Hill, was a printer.

After the end of the First World War Mr Hill purchased three cottages in Getliffes Yard, just off Derby Street, and almost opposite his shop premises at 58 Derby Street. The cottages were three storeys high, and Mr Hill made the three into one long building, removing an upper floor to make a more lofty building with a goods entrance opening on to York Street. The printing was done on the ground floor, and the upper floor was the paper store, cutting room and finishing department. The machinery was letterpress, and the staff were two journeymen, with assistance from newsboys from the shop, as their time allowed. Some of these boys became apprentices, and transferred to the print works, where they were able to learn the trade from composing type and printing, to folding, numbering and finishing.

The firm undertook a wide variety of jobbing work, much of this being provided by the local textile industry and other commercial enterprises in the town, as well as social printing and funeral work.

It was the combination of his experience in the printing trade, his strong connections with the public life of the town and his involvement with the Leek Chamber of Trade which put Fred Hill in a unique position to be able to produce Leek News.

He was for many years a member of the Leek Urban District Council, and Chairman in 1934/5. He became involved with the annual Leek carnivals which were held in the 1930s. Later he became a director of the Leek United and Midlands Building Society, and was a keen Rotarian.

Leek News was an advertising journal and as such was ahead of its time, being 50 years before the so-called free sheets of today. But the News was so much more than a mere free advertising medium it was a well-produced and well-illustrated journal containing numerous articles of interest.

The cost of production was completely covered by revenue from the advertisements, enabling it to be distributed free each Christmas.

Printed in his own workshop in Getliffes Yard, every word was set by hand composition. This involved much overtime for the men, and work would have to start in late October to ensure it would be out by Christmas. Much of the material in Leek News was the direct work of Fred Berrisford, who was employed by Mr Hill in the office. He did most of the proof-reading and wrote many of the unsigned articles, both long and short. On completion it was delivered free to every household in Leek, involving an army of delivery men and boys.

Each year a small de luxe edition of about 500 copies would be produced with a better quality cover, printed on art paper and sold for 3d each, mainly for people who perhaps wanted a gift copy to send to friends away.

About 5,000 copies of Leek News were printed each year for the 14 years between 1925 and 1938. During the 1930s Mr Hill experimented with the idea of a monthly edition of about 2,000 copies, but this was not as successful, and was abandoned because it took up too much time.

A major contribution for several years was the article by 'The Small Boy in the Market Place' - a nom-de-plume hiding the identity of Mr W. Warrington. His articles (see Ch 9) reflecting life in a small town, have something of the quality of Arnold Bennett about them. He played a leading role in the public life of the town, as a member of the Leek Urban District Council, and chairman of the committee responsible for Procession and Music for the celebration of the Coronation of the King and Queen in 1937, the year in which he was chairman of LUDC. He was a governor of Leek Westwood High School for Girls, and Leek High School. A talented musician, he was also deeply involved in local amateur dramatic and operatic societies.

His contribution, and the efforts of so many others, made Leek News a mirror, reflecting so much of the life of bygone Leek.

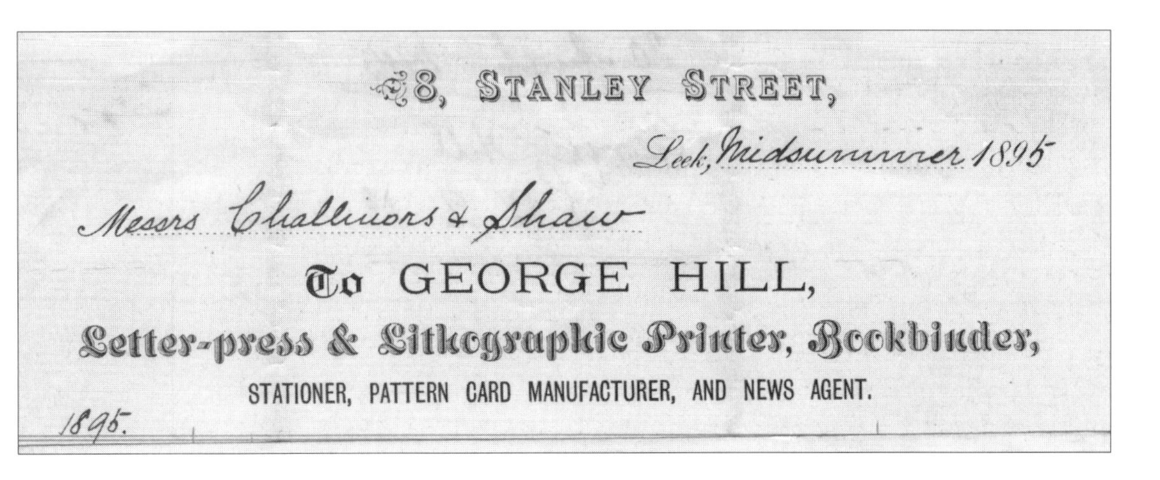

8, STANLEY STREET,

Leek, Midsummer 1895

Messrs Challinors & Shaw

To GEORGE HILL,

Letter-press & Lithographic Printer, Bookbinder,

STATIONER, PATTERN CARD MANUFACTURER, AND NEWS AGENT.

1895.

George Hill was a printer and stationer who also produced a wide range of local view picture postcards.

David Morris and Co, Printers.

Sir Enoch Hill, who became a leader in the building society movement. He became Secretary to the Halifax Permanent Building Society in 1902, and under his management the business grew to become one of the largest in the Country. In 1921 he became Chairman of the Executive of the National Association of Building Societies. He was knighted for his services to the building society movement.

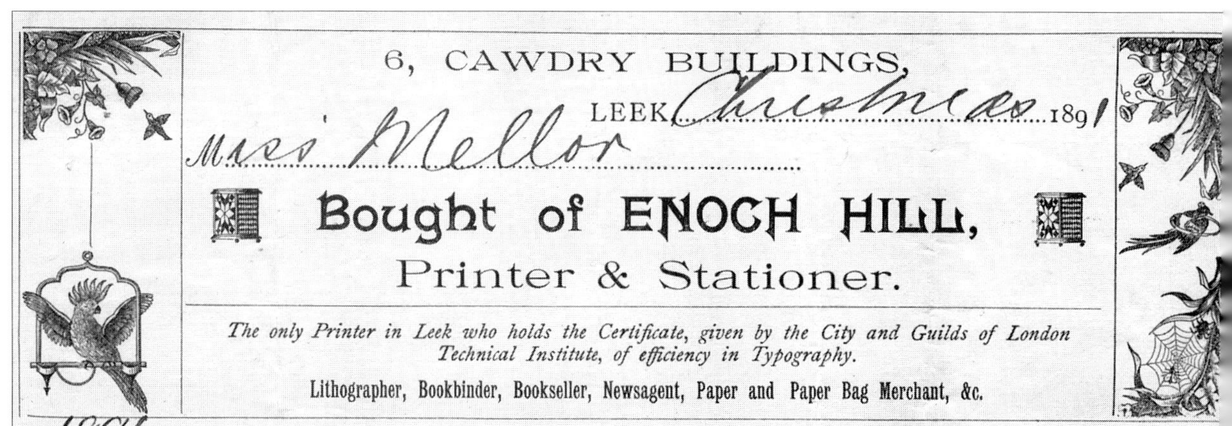

6, CAWDRY BUILDINGS,

LEEK, Christmas 1891

Miss Mellor

Bought of ENOCH HILL,

Printer & Stationer.

The only Printer in Leek who holds the Certificate, given by the City and Guilds of London Technical Institute, of efficiency in Typography.

Lithographer, Bookbinder, Bookseller, Newsagent, Paper and Paper Bag Merchant, &c.

11, STANLEY STREET,

LEEK, December 7 1870

Bought of WILLIAM CLEMESHA,

STATIONER, ENGRAVER,

LETTERPRESS & LITHOGRAPHIC PRINTER, BOOKBINDER, &C.

*** The London and Manchester Daily Papers and all Magazines received by early trains, and delivered as speedily as possible.

Eaton's - The Moorland Press, Derby Street.

WHOLESALE & RETAIL STATIONERY AND MUSIC WAREHOUSE

Royal Exchange Office, Sheep Market, Leek 18

J. Alsop Esq

To W. & M. Hilliard

Letter-Press & Copper-Plate Printer.

BOOKSELLER, STATIONER, BOOKBINDER

AGENT TO THE STAFFORD, MACCLESFIELD, & EVERY OTHER COUNTRY & LONDON NEWSPAPER

AUCTIONEER & APPRAISER.

BOOKS, MAGAZINES & OTHER PERIODICALS REGULARLY SUPPLIED FROM LONDON ON THE SHORTEST NOTICE

SOLE AGENT FOR MILNER'S PATENT FIRE PROOF SAFES.

W. and M. Hilliard, who also acted as auctioneers.

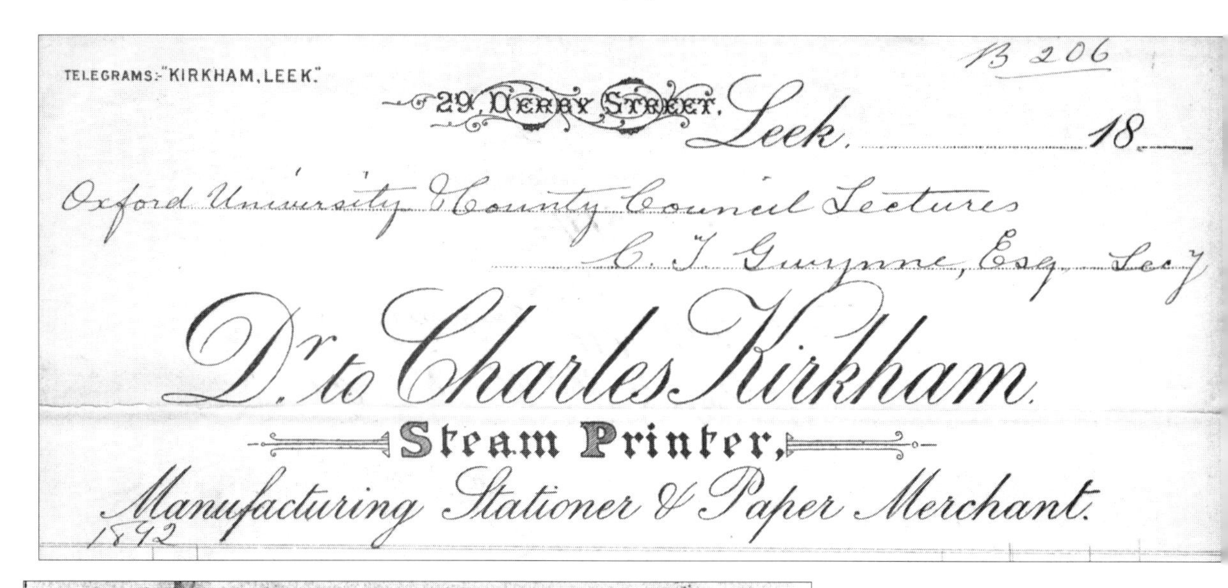

TELEGRAMS:-"KIRKHAM, LEEK."

B 206

29, Derby Street, Leek. 18

Oxford University & County Council Lectures

C. T. Gwynne, Esq. Secy

Dr. to Charles Kirkham.

Steam Printer,

Manufacturing Stationer & Paper Merchant.

1892

Charles Kirkham, printer, Derby Street.

Fred Hill, Printer, Stationer and Bookseller, Derby Street.

WANTED
A
BOY
JUST
LEAVING SCHOOL
with a view to later becoming
AN APPRENTICE
TO THE
LETTERPRESS PRINTING TRADE.

APPLY TO :—
FRED HILL,
PRINTER AND STATIONER,
DERBY STREET, LEEK.

DERBY STREET,
LEEK, Dec

Messrs Challinor & Shaw

Dr. to FRED HILL,
Printer, Stationer, and Newsagent.

PRINTING ACCOUNTS MONTHLY.
NEWSPAPER .. QUARTERLY.

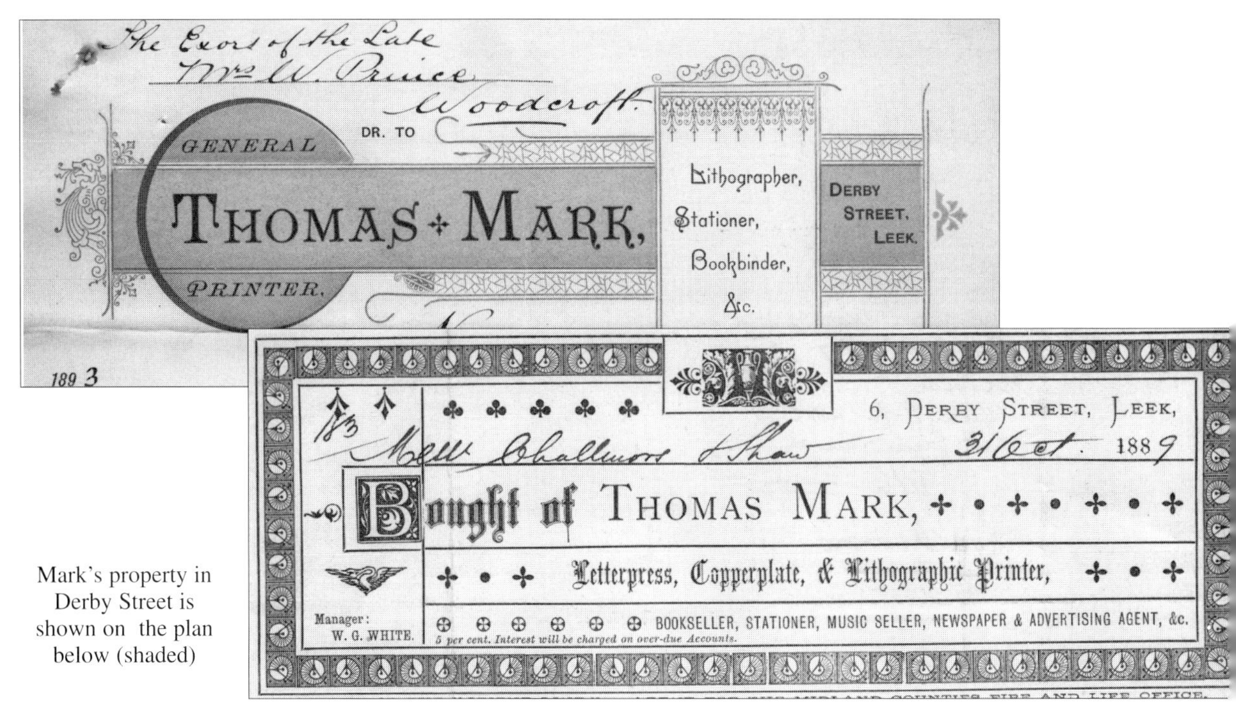

The Exors of the Late
Mrs W. Price
Woodcroft.

DR. TO

GENERAL
THOMAS + MARK,
PRINTER.

Lithographer,
Stationer,
Bookbinder,
&c.

DERBY STREET, LEEK.

1893

6, DERBY STREET, LEEK,
183
Messrs Challinor & Shaw 31 Oct. 1889

Bought of THOMAS MARK,

Letterpress, Copperplate, & Lithographic Printer,

Manager: W. G. WHITE.

BOOKSELLER, STATIONER, MUSIC SELLER, NEWSPAPER & ADVERTISING AGENT, &c.

5 per cent. Interest will be charged on over-due Accounts.

Mark's property in Derby Street is shown on the plan below (shaded)

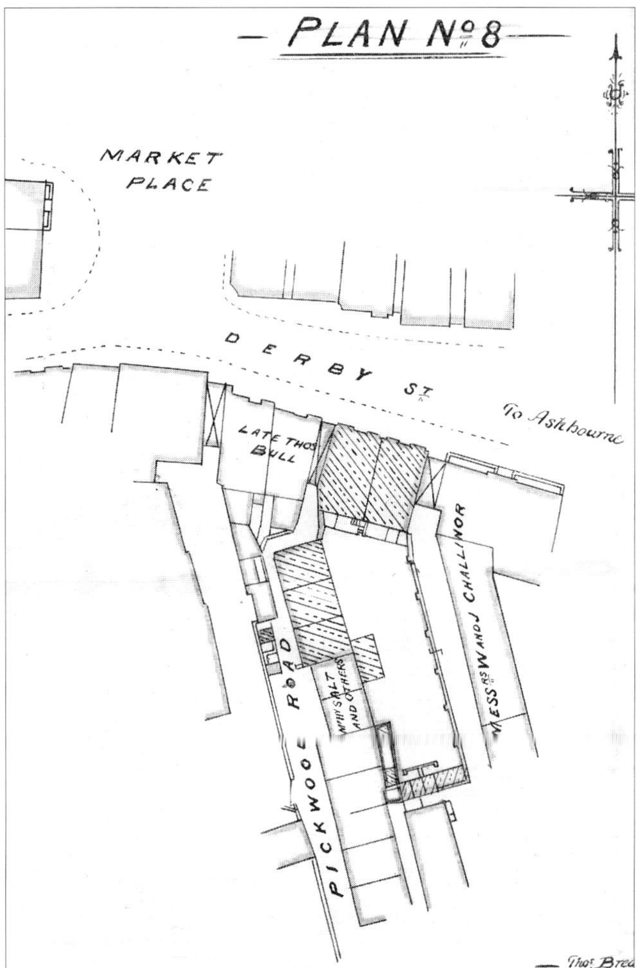

A typical advert for a local printer. The printing of memorial cards in the Victorian age, and after, was much in demand. They were widely circulated to friends and family

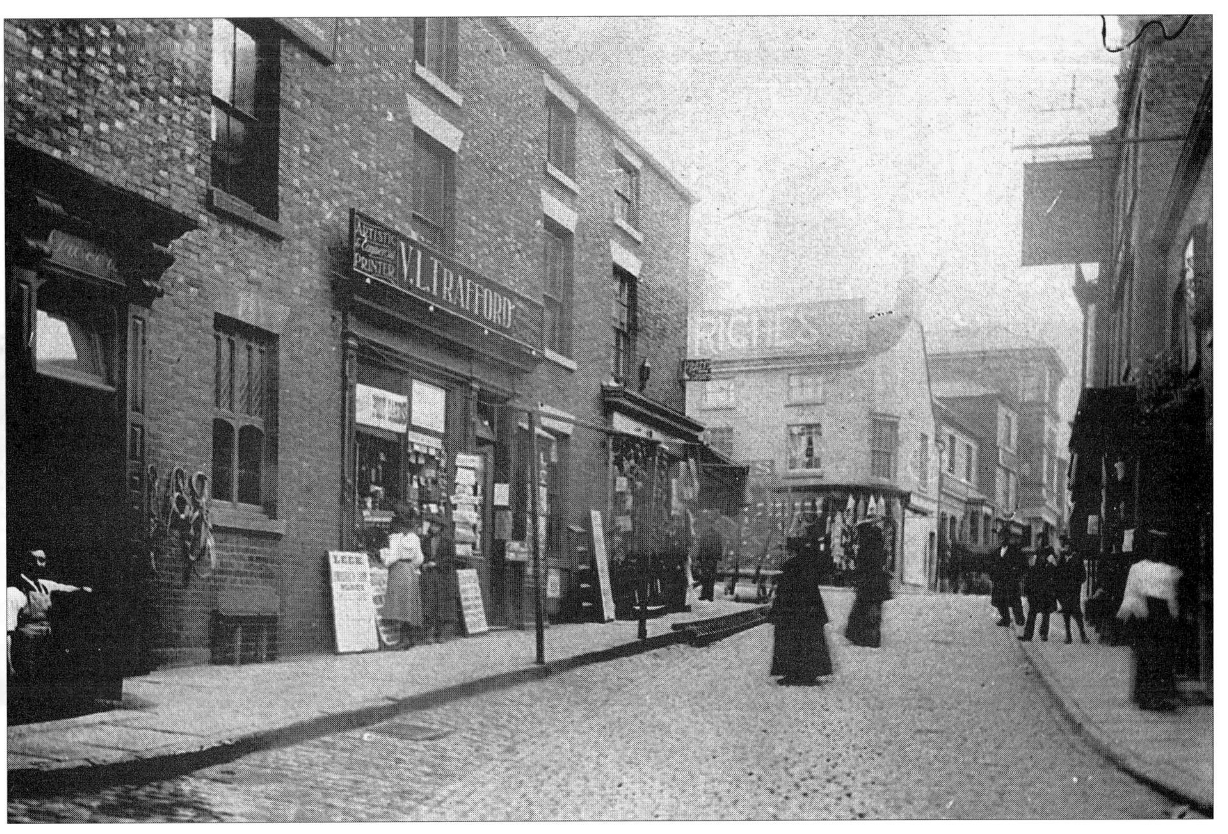

Mr. V.L. Trafford's Print Shop, Stanley Street.

J. Finney Vo's

Stockwell Street, Leek,

Messrs Challinor & Co.

TO EDWARD HALLOWES,

Letter-Press, Lithographic, and Copperplate Printer,

BOOKSELLER, STATIONER & BOOKBINDER.

LEDGERS, JOURNALS, DAY AND CASH BOOKS, RULED AND BOUND TO ORDER ON THE SHORTEST NOTICE.

New Books, New Music, Periodicals, &c., procured twice a week.

		£	s	d
1864, July 27	Printing 150 Crown Bills:–Sale of House Garden, &c. at Ladderedge	"	14	"
Aug. 5	Advertising Sale of the above House, &c. in the Staffordshire Sentinel (twice)	"	11	"
" "	Advertising Ditto Ditto Ditto in the Staffordshire Advertiser	"	6	"
J. & F. 5/9	Settled Mar. 23/65	£1	11	"

Edward Hallowes

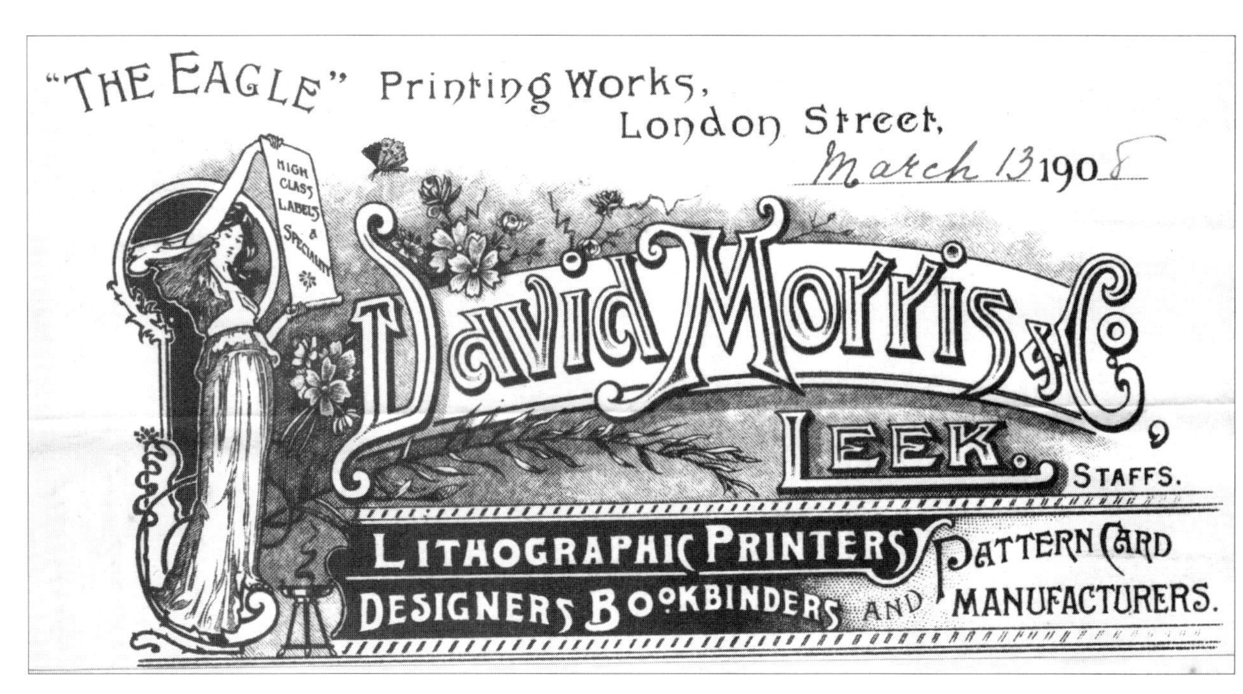
"THE EAGLE" Printing Works,
London Street,
March 13 1908
HIGH CLASS LABELS A SPECIALITY
David Morris & Co
LEEK, STAFFS.
LITHOGRAPHIC PRINTERS, PATTERN CARD
DESIGNERS, BOOKBINDERS AND MANUFACTURERS.

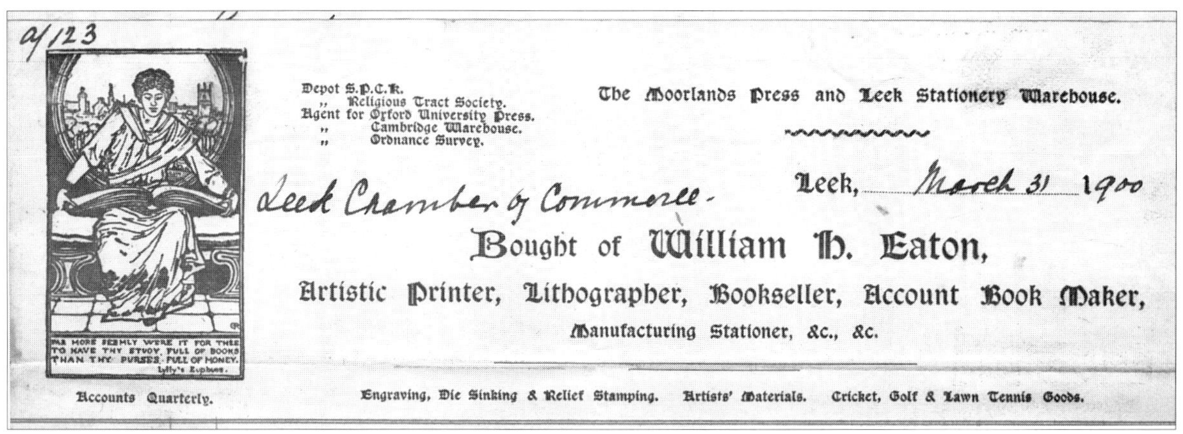
a/123
Depot S.P.C.K.
„ Religious Tract Society.
Agent for Oxford University Press.
„ Cambridge Warehouse.
„ Ordnance Survey.
The Moorlands Press and Leek Stationery Warehouse.
Leek Chamber of Commerce
Leek, March 31 1900
Bought of William H. Eaton,
Artistic Printer, Lithographer, Bookseller, Account Book Maker,
Manufacturing Stationer, &c., &c.
FAR MORE SEEMLY WERE IT FOR THEE TO HAVE THY STUDY FULL OF BOOKS THAN THY PURSES FULL OF MONEY.
Lylly's Euphues.
Accounts Quarterly.
Engraving, Die Sinking & Relief Stamping. Artists' Materials. Cricket, Golf & Lawn Tennis Goods.

63.
Leek Times Office, Market Street,
Mess Ceballivors & Shaw, Derby St.
LEEK, July 1 1895
Dr. to M. H. MILLER,
Legal, Commercial, and General Printer.
TELEGRAMS, TIMES, LEEK.
TELEPHONE, NO. 14.
TRADE MOTTO: QUALITY AND QUICKNESS.

The billheads of local printers naturally demonstrated the scope of the art of the typographer.

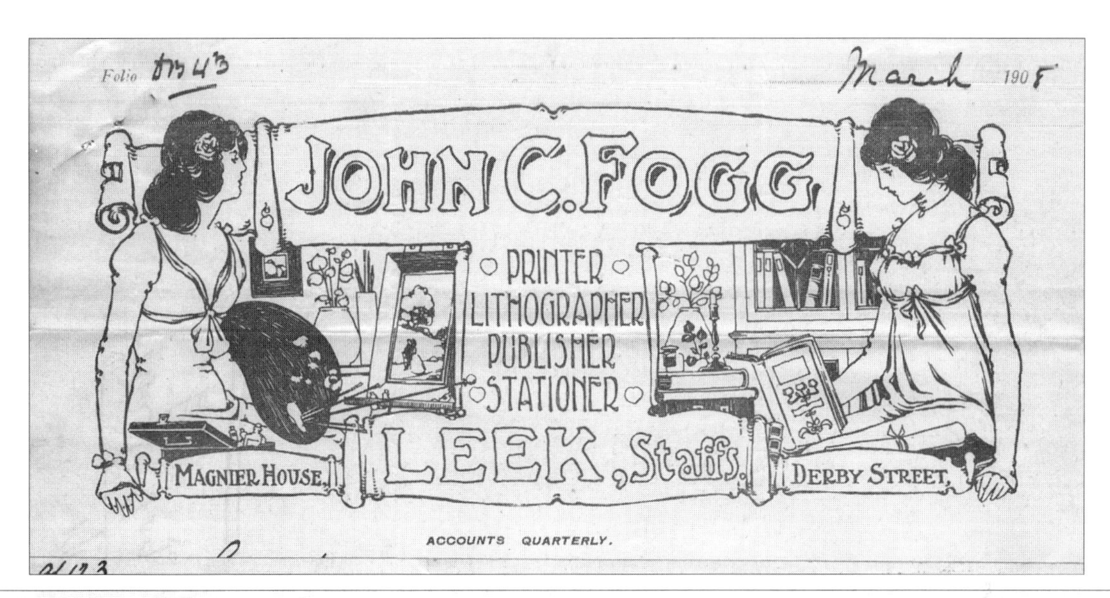

Folio

March 190

JOHN C. FOGG

PRINTER
LITHOGRAPHER
PUBLISHER
STATIONER

MAGNIER HOUSE, LEEK, Staffs, DERBY STREET,

ACCOUNTS QUARTERLY.

PHONE 420

W.R.

PICKWOOD ROAD,

At the rear of 6, Derby Street,

LEEK Sept. 22 1933

Messrs Thos. Brealey & Sons

Dr. to THE MOORLANDS PRESS,

W. T. COOK LATE W. H. EATON

PRINTERS, STATIONERS, BOOKBINDERS, Etc.

TERMS—Monthly Accounts. 2½ per cent discount if paid within 7 days. Under £1 Net.

The Firm's printed receipt form only recognised.

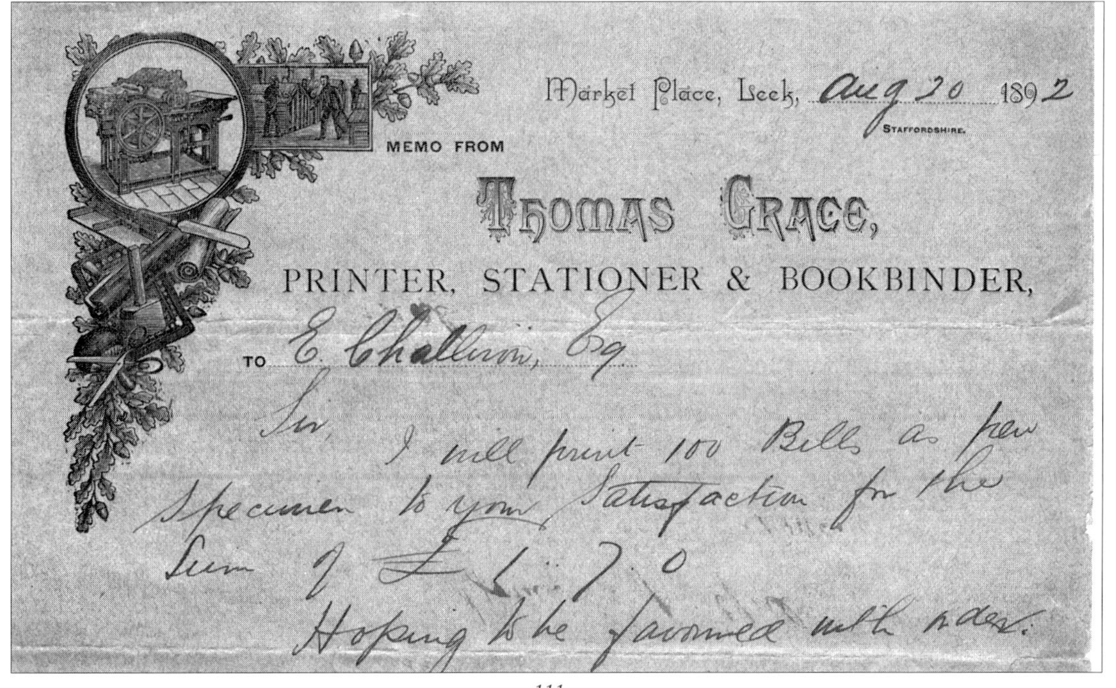

Market Place, Leek, Aug 20 1892

Staffordshire.

MEMO FROM

THOMAS GRACE,

PRINTER, STATIONER & BOOKBINDER,

TO E Challinor, Esq

Sir,

I will print 100 Bills as per Specimen to your Satisfaction for the Sum of £1.7.0

Hoping to be favoured with order.

Queen Victoria's Jubilee, 21st June 1887.

A religious procession in Derby Street. The preponderance of adults suggests Band of Hope, not Club Day.

CHAPTER THREE
On Parade

IN THE DAYS BEFORE the more sophisticated and spectacular outdoor entertainments of today, the traditional street parade was always a great crowd-puller. It was involving for spectators and participants alike, and Leek was no exception to the rule.

Leek people have always loved a procession, and have usually turned out in great numbers to witness any parade through the streets of the town. Civic and royal events and religious traditions have all been celebrated by a parade through the streets of the town, and war and peace have been commemorated in the same way.

Leek has always been fortunate to have a number of good brass bands, which would enhance any procession, and give it some style and spectacle. The Volunteer Band, the Temperance Band, the British Legion Band and numerous Scout bands have given their services, and, in more recent times, the Salvation Army Band has always been favoured with competent musicians. These, together with jazz bands, pipe and drum bands, military bands and marching bands have always ensured that local parades will go with a swing. One of the most spectacular and auspicious parades ever to be assembled in Leek was that which marked the opening of the Nicholson Institute on Thursday, 16 October 1884. The event was fully described in a graphic and detailed article in Leek News.

The Institute celebrated its 50th anniversary in 1934, the year in which Mr Fred Hill, the publisher of Leek News, was the chairman of Leek Urban District Council. What better reason for giving the Nicholson Institute extended coverage in his annual publication?

The annual Chairman's Sunday parade, following a church service, officially marked the start of the year of office of the particular town councillor who was Chairman that year. The parades usually involved all the civic heads, councillors and council officials, magistrates and the many and various organisations, clubs and societies in Leek, as well as scouts and guides. It was, in effect, the whole life of the town out on parade. The parades are still held today, by Leek Town Council, when a new Town Mayor is appointed each year. The Staffordshire Moorlands District Council Chairman's Sunday takes place in the Moorlands town which the chairman for that year represents, and not necessarily in Leek.

A similar gathering assembles by tradition on Armistice Sunday in November each year for the parade to the Nicholson War Memorial, where poppy wreaths are laid by civic heads and representatives of other organisations, with the British Legion playing a leading role.

Coronations, jubilees and Royal weddings have usually been celebrated in Leek by parades and street parties, as have also the victory celebrations following the two world wars.

One of the earliest Royal weddings to be celebrated with a splendid parade was that of the marriage of Princess May to the Duke of York on 6 July 1893. The streets were bedecked with flags and banners, and exceptionally fine weather made the day memorable. Every society, school, institution and religious denomination was represented in the parade, headed by the Improvement Commissioners, and there was a fine assembly in the Market Place, where the local volunteers, under the command of Captain Smith, fired a Royal Salute in front of Foxlowe.

Royal proclamations have also been marked by civic parades and due ceremonial. The proclamation of King Edward VII took place on Wednesday 6 February 1901, of King George V on Wednesday 11 May, 1910 and that of King Edward VIII on Saturday 25 January 1936, each a distinctly civic occasion, supported by a parade, as the accounts printed in Leek News reveal.

Originally known as Cap Sunday, Club Day continues as an annual event. This Sunday School Festival has its roots back in the early 1800s. It was the custom on the first Sunday in September for the children to parade through the town and assemble in the Market Place, where several hymns were sung. The girls wore white caps trimmed with a frill, hence the name of the day. The conductor for many years was Mr Richard Cutting, a silk manufacturer, sergeant in the Leek Loyal Volunteers, one of the Leek Improvement Commissioners and a prominent and devout Methodist, being Superintendent of the Leek Methodist Sunday School at Mount Pleasant from 1808 until his death in 1856. During most of those years he conducted the hymn singing in the Market Place, where the hymns would be introduced by his loyal friend and colleague, Mr James Wardle, also a Commissioner, a member of the old Leek Savings Bank and one of the first teachers of the Leek Methodist Sunday School, being treasurer from 1808, surviving his contemporary, Richard Cutting, to die in 1862. Mr P. A. Rayner later became the regular conductor.

W H Nithsdale captured the crowds on the edge of the Market Place in this animated 1906 Club Day scene

This Cap Sunday festival drew so many people into Leek that the inns became crowded and, fearing that this might lead to some desecration of the sabbath, the festival was moved to the first Friday in August, when it became known as Club Day, a name which it carries to the present time. Now it is traditionally held on the third Saturday in July. This Annual Sunday School Festival involves churches of all denominations, including Roman Catholics - a truly ecumenical affair.

A similar procession was held annually during Edwardian years. This was the Band of Hope Demonstration, and it was a largely Free Church affair, the Band of Hope movement being closely allied to the Temperance movement. The much photographed demonstration held on June 29 1907 was typical of many. It was led by the Congregationalists, with their minister, Rev John Hoatson (1900-1910), and lay leaders Messrs Isaac Heath, George Brookes and J. Giles.

It will be clear that most local parades have been of a celebratory nature. Only occasionally has there been any form of 'protest' procession. One exception was the Trades Demonstration on 22 June 1907, one week before the band of Hope demonstration. It was a very large procession, with hundreds of workers taking part, and even more onlookers lining the streets. The event was widely photographed by W.H. Nithsdale, the Inland Revenue agent in Leek, whose camera often recorded local scenes and events at that time.

A parade of a different kind took place on 22nd June 1907, the great Trades Demonstration, when several hundred people took part and even more lined the streets. The event is captured here by the camera of W H Nithsdale as the parade rounds the corner of St Edward Street.

Officers and sergeants of the Leek Volunteers 1904
Front: J Poultney, W Peach, Lieut E H Brunt, Capt B Wardle, Lieut W F Challinor, W Lowe, J J Biggar
2nd: W Read, P Copeland, G Bostock, W Doxey, F Bode
3rd: W Berresford, W Hammersley, C W Robinson, W Stubbs Back: T Swadling, L Tatton, T Bestwick, G Gilman

Probably the earliest photo of the Leek Volunteer Band, taken by P A Rayner outside Ball Haye Hall c.1882. The band, considered one of the best in Staffordshire, gave open air concerts to large audiences in the Market Place on Monday evenings in summer. Front: J McCall, J Birch, W Hall, G Perkin, W Brooks, W Goodwin, A Fisher, S Shenton, G Wood
Back: C Goodwin, J Goldstraw, Sgt Mee, Samuel Gee (conductor). E Vigrass, E Piercy, J Woodings, T Ball, J Goodwin

Officers and sergeants of the 1st Volunteer Battalion North Staffs Regiment (1 Co) Leek.
Front: Lieut B R Hall, Capt W F Challinor, Major B Wardle, Lt Col T J Smith, Lt Col G D Goodman, Surg. Lt Hardwicke
Middle: J Boughey, W Peach, W Read, G Gilman, J Poultney, R Trafford, W Berresford, E Hassall, T Currie, W Doxey, W Woodings
Back: W Stubbs, C W Robinson, F Bode, G Bostock, L Tatton, W Hammersley, A Wood, W Lowe

Band of the 1st Volunteer Battalion, North Staffs. Regiment (1. Co) Leek. The group was taken shortly after Sgt W Doxey had taken over as bandmaster from J Woodings (appointed 1891).
Front: F Tipper, W Berresford, W Doxey, Major B Wardle, G Edwards, J Woodings, R Armitt, N S Fergyson
Second: F E Fox, W R Walwyn, F Sherratt, T Moran, G Towers, W Ratcliffe, E Hambleton, W Ball, T Hanson, G Johnson
Third: W Dresser, W Wood, L Dale, C Hollinshead, J Prince, S Howard, W Woodings, A Wood, T Hambleton
Back: T Swadling, A Mellor, T Biddulph, E Bennett, W Hammersley

The Leek Volunteer Band in procession at the bottom of Ashbourne Road.

The Leek Temperance Prize Band 1907 - one of several local bands that enjoyed success in the Edwardian years.

An early Club Day scene - the banner party of Brunswick Methodist Sunday School assembled in Regent Street schoolyard.

An old Club Day procession at the bottom of Compton.

A typical Edwardian Club Day scene in Stockwell Street illustrates the great support that this festival always enjoyed. It was a time when participants and spectators alike dressed in their Sunday best for the occasion.

A Club Day procession in St Edward Street c.1902

An extremely wet Chairman's Sunday parade, 1907.

The Band of Hope procession in Stockwell Street, 29th June 1907.

Another annual procession, often difficult to distinguish from Club Day, was that of the Band of Hope. This church-based temperance movement usually had more support from adults than children. This suggest that this is the Band of Hope in Compton. The background, c 1900, shows the row of terraced cottages, including two shops, which lined the western side of Compton making the road only 12 feet wide at this point. The cottages have now been demolished and the road now follows the line of the retaining wall.

The crowded Market Place at the Band of Hope demonstration.

The rallying point for the Band of Hope demonstration was always the Market Place, where a short service was held. Decorated hats were the order of the day for the ladies taking part.

The General Election 1910. Successful candidate Heath.

The Coronation in 1911 was the occasion for a procession, seen here entering Church Street.

The band of the 1st Volunteer Battalion, North Staffs. Regiment (1 Co) Leek is seen here leading a military funeral to Leek Cemetery on 18th July 1907. Privates Henry Bennett and John Bode had been accidentally drowned whilst fishing in Rudyard Lake.

The scene at the graveside in Leek Cemetery where full military honours were observed.

The 1910 Coronation Parade in Derby Street.

The old Leek Battery (3rd battery, 231st Brigade RFA, 46 th North Midland Division) is seen here at Leek Drill hall. The band is the 3rd Battery Band which had a good reputation. The officers were Lieut Faulkner Nicholson, Major Challinor and Lieut. Basil Nicholson.

Friday 14th August 1914 was the day the old Leek Battery marched off to war. In this picture the battery has just left the Drill Hall in Alma street and is entering Belle Vue from Frith Street. Major Challinor is in the lead on his horse 'Trumpeter'.

The Battery has now reached Derby Street and many Leek people have turned out to give them a send-off.

Wagons are seen here piled high with equipment as the column enters Ashbourne Road. This photograph was taken by W H Horne, a local photographer who recorded the event at different points along the route.

Limbered wagons passing from Derby Street to Ashbourne Road.

Major Challinor heads the column as the battery leaves Leek passing through Lowe Hill bridge.

Ball Haye Green carnival - a float to celebrate the end of the First World War.

Ball Haye Green Carnival just after the First World War.

The victory parade following the end of the First World War.

Royal Visit to Leek and the Roches, 1872.

Duchess of Teck. Countess of Shrewsbury. Duke of Teck. Mr. P. L. Brocklehurst. Earl of Shrewsbury.
Viscount Ingestre can be seen seated on the wall above the Countess of Shrewsbury

Crowds of guests assemble on the Roches for the visit of the Princess Mary of Cambridge and the Duke of Teck, 23rd August 1872

CHAPTER FOUR
On Kings and Princes

OVER THE YEARS Leek has had comparatively little direct contact with Royalty. Visits by members of the Royal Family have usually been strongly supported by the local silk industry, which is an indication of its standing and importance, and, indeed, of the personalities connected with it.

The following paragraph from the Leek Times of Saturday, 26 January 1901, with its amusing footnote, is a summary of the position up to that time.

LEEK AND ROYALTY

In 1085, the town was a royal possession, and in 1208 King John signed its charter. Edward II came to Leek in 1318, and in 1559 Queen Elizabeth gave the town's tithes to Sir Raufe Bagenalle. Nearly 200 years elapsed before royalty again set foot in Leek, and then it was in the person of Charles Edward, the Young Pretender, who invaded the moorlands in 1745. Twenty nine years ago the Duke and Duchess of Teck passed through Leek on a visit to the Squire of Swythamley, and in 1895 the Duchess came specially to acquaint herself with the silk industry, in which she took a deep interest. Last year, as will be remembered, the Duke and Duchess of York paid a visit to Leek and opened the Technical School.

An old-time correspondent to the Leek Times said: "My recollections of the ox which was roasted when William IV was crowned are not very bright. I remember more of the barrels of beer than meat. After the barrels had ceased rolling when empty, the people who were full commenced rolling and some of them carried on above a bit."

The reference to the visit of Edward II in 1318 suggests that it was to the alleged assembly of the King, two Roman Catholic cardinals, nine English bishops and many magnates of the land which, it is said, took place on 7 August 1318, between Leek and Horton, for the purpose of the reconciliation, and exchange of the kiss of peace, between the King and his kinsman Thomas, Earl of Lancaster, who had long been in dispute with each other.

Early Royal visits are often clouded by legends, traditional stories and even myths. Of the later Victorian and Edwardian Royal visits there are much more reliable records and accurate contemporary press reports. There is, however, no record that Queen Victoria ever visited Leek during her long reign. The following paragraph from the Memorial Edition of the Leek Times of Saturday, 26 January 1901 is nevertheless interesting:

THE QUEEN AT LEEK

It is not generally known that when the late Queen was about six years old and known as Princess Victoria, she paid the only visit of her long life and reign to the Metropolis of the Moorlands. The incident is described by Mr. Daniel Rogers, aged 86, who 76 years ago lived at the cottage on the right-hand side of the road near the bridge at the bottom of the bank leading to Upperhulme. He clearly remembers the Duchess of Kent, accompanied by the Princess Victoria, driving through the village from Buxton to Trentham. At the bottom of the bank he took off the slipper, and the Duchess of Kent gave him a half sovereign in gold. Mr. Rogers, however, is not able to say where the horses were baited at Leek, but he thinks it was at the Roebuck or Red Lion. He very much regrets having parted with the coin.

On Friday, 22 August 1872 the Duchess of Teck (Princess Mary of Cambridge, cousin of Queen Victoria) and the Duke of Teck visited the area as guests of P. L. Brocklehurst Esq, of Swythamley Park.

They had been staying at Alton Towers during the week, and were brought to Leek by special train, accompanied by the Earl and Countess of Shrewsbury, Lord Ingestre and other gentry.

The Earl and Countess of Macclesfield, with Mrs Cruso and Mr W. Challinor welcomed the distinguished visitors. Huge crowds had assembled round the station, and the route from the station to the Market Place was one mass of decorations, triumphal arches, and flags of all nations.

The crowds were dense around Foxlowe, Mrs Cruso's home, where the party alighted for refreshments, and the Princess appeared at one of the upper windows to acknowledge the applause of the crowd. The party then proceeded via Buxton Road to the Roches, where they were received by Mr Brocklehurst and escorted to Rock Hall. From here they ascended the Roches, where a seat had been carved out of the rock for the Princess to rest. This so-called 'Queen's Chair', with its engraving commemorating the event, is still to be seen. The party then descended, to go on to Swythamley Hall for lunch, with a distinguished guest list, returning to Leek after 6 o'clock, where the great crowds still waited to give them an enthusiastic send-off.

Although they were not accompanied by a royal visit, the 50th and 60th anniversaries of Queen Victoria's reign were celebrated in great style in Leek, in an upsurge of patriotic fervour so typical of the times, as ordinary citizens seized the opportunity to bring a little excitement into their lives.

It was one of the hottest days of the summer of 1887 when over 5,000 schoolchildren and adults gathered in the Cattle Market to celebrate Queen Victoria's Jubilee on 21 June in spectacular style.

In a great display of fervour and patriotism the Blue Ribbon Army Band played Rule Britannia and the Earl of Shrewsbury's Band God Bless the Prince of Wales, while Mr P. A. Rayner conducted the hymn-singing. The third and fourth verses of the National Anthem had been specially adapted for the occasion by a Leek man, Mr W. Johnson.

The great procession which followed was headed by the band of the 1st Volunteer Battalion, North Staffordshire Regiment, followed by the town's Magistrates, Commissioners, Ministers and Clergy, with the hundreds of children and the Friendly Societies of the town.

After parading through the streets around the town centre the procession made its way to the Pickwood Recreation Ground, where Mr William Challinor formally handed over to the Chairman of the Commissioners the Deed of Conveyance of the land his gift to the town. The children were then presented with a commemorative mug, and were entertained to tea.

To mark the Jubilee, an ox, the gift of Mr Edwin Trafford, a Leek butcher, was roasted and served to about 800 elderly and poor of the town, in the Market Place.The great day ended with various sports and amusements, including dancing, tug-of-war, races and jumping competitions and, as darkness fell, a grand display of fireworks, with bonfires and beacons on the hills around Leek.

The town was en fete again ten years later, to celebrate 60 years of Queen Victoria's reign - the Diamond Jubilee. The celebrations started on Sunday 20 June when all the churches held special services. Tuesday dawned, a hot sunny day, the factories were closed, and the people turned out in thousands. Public buildings, shops and houses had all entered into the spirit of the occasion, decorated in splendid fashion. The house and gardens of Mr B. B. Nixon, Ballington House, proved to be a great attraction, illuminated by Chinese lanterns and fairy lights hung in the trees. The grounds were open to the public from 9 am and attracted many visitors. Collections were taken in aid of the Cruso Nursing Fund. The Leek Temperance Band played popular selections on the terrace.

The Market Place had Venetian masts erected around the perimeter, from which stretched festoons of flags, Chinese lanterns and some 2,000 fairy lights.

Both the Volunteer and Temperance Bands performed in the Market Place during the day, and in the afternoon some 5,000 Sunday School children, together with town councillors, magistrates, civic leaders and representatives of the services and other local organisations all assembled in the Market Place, for singing conducted by Mr W. H. Eaton. The Chairman of the Leek Urban District Council called for three cheers for Her Majesty, before a huge procession, led by the Volunteer Band, paraded round the streets of the town. At dinner time hot-pot was served out at the various bakehouses to poor people. It consisted of beef steaks, potatoes, onions and gravy, and about 1,000 people were fed. Mr John Fallon gave eight loads of potatoes and Mr W. Walker of the Leek Brewery gave four 36 gallon barrels of beer, which were consumed with gusto!

Jubilee day ended with a fireworks display at the Pickwood Recreation Ground, and bonfires on high points at Lask Edge, Horton, Gun, Morridge, Ferny Hill, Crown Point, Cheddleton and Stanlow.

Towards the end of Queen Victoria s reign two more Royal visits took place, both connected with the Leek Technical Schools. On 24 July 1899 the ceremony of laying the foundation stone was performed by Millicent, Duchess of Sutherland. The chairman of the Leek Urban District Council was Mr Andrew Morton JP. and Mr John Hall was chairman of the Technical Instruction Committee.

Twelve months later, on Saturday, 28 July 1900 the actual opening of the Leek Technical Schools was performed by HRH the Duchess of York (later Queen Mary). On the same occasion HRH the Duke of York laid the foundation stone of the Carr Gymnasium, on the same site.

The Royal Party arrived at Leek station at 3.00pm, where Sir Thomas Wardle presented Mr Wright, chairman of Leek Urban District Council, Major General Phillips, Mr J. Hall, Mr A. Nicholson and Mr J. Challinor to the Royal visitors, before the party entered waiting carriages to drive via Broad Street, St Edward Street, Church Street, Market Place and Stockwell Street to the new Technical Schools. The Royal party visited the Brough, Nicholson and Hall factory before leaving by train at 6.30pm.

Thirteen years later, on 23 April 1913 the Royal couple renewed their acquaintance with the town, and their obvious interest in the silk industry, as King George V and Queen Mary. The King and Queen first visited Wardle's Churnet Dye Works. They then followed the route via Belle Vue, Garden Street, Westwood Road, Barngate Street, Cruso Street, Broad Street, St Edward Street, Sheepmarket, Market Place (where, it being a Wednesday, the traditional open-air market attracted their attention), Derby Street, Ashbourne Road to the factory of Brough Nicholson and Hall Ltd, in Cross Street.

Here they were met by Sir Arthur and Lady Nicholson, Mr J. Hall JP, Mr H. Salt, and Mr A. H. Moore JP, who had completed 50 years with the firm. The spooling and winding departments were visited, then Mr J. Howe Hall and Mr J. Tatton escorted their Majesties round the knitting department.

At the spun silk department Mr A. Falkner Nicholson and Mr Bernard Hall escorted the King and Queen through the mill. At the close of the visit to the factory Sir Arthur Nicholson presented their Majesties with silk scarves of their choice.

The Royal party then proceeded to Market Street, where they were received at the Town Hall by Mr T. Mason JP (chairman), Mr C. Watson (vice-chairman), and members of Leek Urban District Council, together with Mr W. Allen (law clerk), and Mr H. Henshaw (clerk).

From the Town Hall the Royal party travelled by way of Stockwell Street, Church Street and Belle Vue to Highfield hall, where they were the guests of Sir Arthur and Lady Nicholson. At Highfield the King, who obviously shared an interest, saw several of Sir Arthur's prize shire horses, including the champion mare.

Throughout the visit the streets of the town were highly decorated, and local people turned out in crowds. Several arches had been erected, and banners and pennants were in abundance.

The scene in St Edward's Street shows the parade to celebrate the wedding of Princess May to the Duke of York 6th July 1893.

TO

VICTORIA BY THE GRACE OF GOD OF THE United Kingdom of Great Britain and Ireland Queen, defender of the faith.

May it please your Majesty

We the Improvement Commissioners of the Town of Leek, in the County of Stafford, in General Meeting assembled, most humbly offer to Your Most Gracious Majesty our Hearty Congratulations on the Attainment of the Fiftieth Year of Your Majesty's Glorious Reign, thankfully acknowledging the Goodness of Almighty God in sparing Your Majesty to Witness the inauguration and completion of the many Valuable Works of Public Usefulness and Benefit which have so distinguished Your Majesty's Beneficent Reign.

We gratefully recognise the remarkable progress which has been made during the Victorian Era in Education, Art, Science, Commerce, the Improvement of the Law, and in Social and Religious Life, thereby contributing to the happiness and material Welfare of your people, to an extent never before known in the History of this or any other Country.

When periods of Distress and Calamity have occurred, Your Majesty's Sympathy has shone forth, and assistance has been rendered, giving a high example to others and solace and hope to the sorrowful; and now, in this Year of Jubilee of Your Majesty's Reign, we beg to record our Sincere and Loyal Admiration of the Royal and Womanly Conduct which has, on all occasions, so well characterised Your Majesty; and we earnestly pray that Your Majesty may long be spared to Reign over a Peaceable, United, Happy, and Increasingly-Prosperous People.

As Witness our Common Seal, the Thirty-first day of May 1887.

Richd. Shaw, Chairman.

The loyal address prepared by the Leek Improvement Commissioners for Queen Victoria's Golden Jubilee 1887.

To Their Royal Highnesses
The Duke and Duchess of York.

May it please Your Royal Highnesses,

We the Leek Urban District Council offer to Your Royal Highnesses, on behalf of the Inhabitants, a Loyal and Hearty Welcome on your visit to Leek.

We are duly conscious of the exceptional honour conferred upon the Town by your presence here to-day, showing as it does the deep interest which is taken by Your Royal Highnesses in the development of the Silk Industry which provides occupation for so large a proportion of the inhabitants of this locality, and also in the Educational and other Agencies having for their object the Intellectual, Social and Physical improvement of the people generally.

We sincerely hope that Your Royal Highnesses will meet with much that will please you here and will increase the interest in the Town and its inhabitants which is evidenced by your presence to-day for the purpose of Opening the New Technical and Silk Schools and Laying the Foundation Stone of the "William [illegible]" Public Gymnasium.

It is a cause of sincere satisfaction to the Council that Your Royal Highnesses have so honoured our Town, mindful as we are of the visits on two occasions of Her Late Royal Highness Princess Mary Adelaide Duchess of Teck, who took great interest in Leek and its Industries and whose Memory will long be honoured and revered by the people.

We earnestly hope Your Royal Highnesses will retain pleasant recollections of your visit to the Metropolis of the Moorlands, and we heartily assure you of the attachment and loyalty of its inhabitants to Her Most Gracious Majesty the Queen and all the Members of the Royal Family.

Given under the Seal of the Council, this 28th day of July in the Year 1900.

Robert Wright Chairman
[illegible] Clerk
William Allen Law Clerk

The illuminated address prepared by Leek Urban District Council for the visit of the Duke and Duchess of York, 28th July 1900, when they opened the Leek Technical Schools.

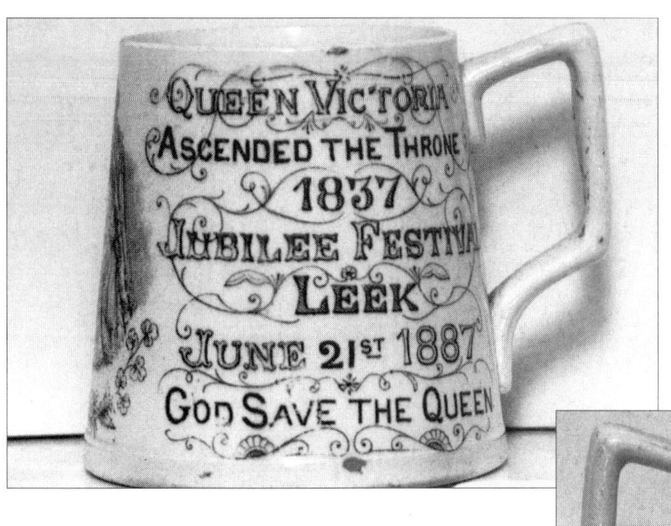

Queen Victoria's Golden Jubilee 1887 commemorative mug presented to 5000 school children on June 21st 1887 at Pickwood recreation ground by William Challinor, solicitor of Pickwood Hall.

Proclamation of King George V on Wednesday 11th May 1910.

The gathering at Highfield Hall, home of Sir Arthur and Lady Nicholson, on 23rd April 1913, on the occasion of the visit of King George V and Queen Mary.

The Royal party and guests at Highfield Hall, 23rd April 1913.

King George V with Mr Falkner Nicholson, inspecting Sir Arthur's famous shire horses at Highfield Hall. The mares paraded before the King included 'Pailton Sorais' and 'Mollington Manners' - winners of many prizes at shire horse shows. Sir Arthur purchased the stallion 'Hoe Forest' from George V.

Royal occasions always attracted great crowds in Leek. On 28th July 1900 the Duke and Duchess of York visited the town to open the new Technical Schools, lay the foundation stone of the Carr Gymanasium and visit Brough, Nicholson and Hall. Here the Royal party is seen arriving at Leek station (site of the present day Safeway).

The visit of King George V and Queen Mary April 23rd 1913. The royal visitors are seen here at the factory of Brough, Nicholson and Hall Ltd.

CHAPTER FIVE
On the Fields

THERE IS AMPLE EVIDENCE that the Victorians and Edwardians of yesterday's town took their sport seriously. The economic growth and prosperity of Leek during the later years of the 19th century is reflected in the fact that Leek was able to support horse-racing of a high standard, involving the gentry, and even the nobility.

Furthermore, a number of the men who were drawn to Leek by its growing textile industry became deeply involved with cricket, rugby, football and other sports.

In many ways Leek was ahead of the times in the establishment of organised sporting clubs. As early as 1876, Leek supported a cycling club. Known then as the Leek and Moorlands Bicycle Club, it is probably the oldest cycling club in the country still operating today.

Another local cycling club was the Ball Haye Green Wheelers, the weekend run being the highlight of the week for many working-class folk, an escape to the fresh air of the hills and moors. In those days before the motor car, cycling was not only a healthy exercise, but the means of opening up the countryside to a broad cross-section of the townspeople.

Cricket in the summer and football in the winter were, of course, the main sporting activities. Both sports were played to a high standard locally, and many star players took the field. The level of competition was fierce as, alongside the development of Leek industrially, works teams emerged, enabling several league and cup competitions to be held. Right into the 1950s a keenly contested knock-out cricket competition was held, with evening matches of limited overs involving works and club teams. Many were the exciting close finishes as the evening shadows lengthened across the lovely little Beggars Lane ground! There were cries of *"Give 'im a flashlamp"* as umpires gave dubious decisions in the gathering gloom.

Between 1833 and 1867 horse racing was held regularly in Leek, usually in October each year. In 1868 Leek Races became North Staffordshire Races, the autumn meeting being held at Leek.

The races were always well-organised, and supported by prominent citizens of the town, whose generous annual subscriptions made the venture financially viable. On the other side of the coin, of course, there was money to be made, for much organised sport had, for many years, involved finance, either in the form of betting and wagers, or in games and matches being played for a cash stake on the result. This often led to bitter rivalry, even in the most traditionally gentlemanly of sports.

The first record regarding Leek Races states:

LEEK RACES 1833
will take place on
Monday and Tuesday the 21st and 22nd October
over Birchall Dale Course.

The stewards were Francis Cruso and John Heathcote, William Alcock was Clerk of the Course, and George Keates secretary and treasurer.

The rules were strict, and stated, for example:

No person will be allowed to erect a Booth, Shed or Stall until he has agreed with the Clerk and paid his subscription. Also dogs found on the Course will be destroyed and every person crossing the adjoining fences or in any way wilfully trespassing will be prosecuted.

The Subscription List for 1833 produced a total of £90, the list reading like a directory of the gentry of the day, headed by two MPs, John Davenport and Edward Buller.

The 1833 treasurer's statement showed a balance of cash in hand of £3 7s 6d. In 1835 the treasurer at the time, Dr Daniel Colquhoun, produced a balance sheet showing £15 10s 6d in hand. The stewards were Samuel Milward and John Acton. In those early years entries were usually small, the maximum normally being six horses, and often less. Nevertheless the races were clearly popular, enjoying regular support. Balance sheets during the early years never showed a large profit, the income being largely paid out in prize money to the winners. Each year there was a payment to Mr. Hockenhull, for the use of the Course and to the Leek Band, in addition to the regular expenses of printing, postage, advertising, beer for the band and casual labour to maintain the course.

An odd entry in the subscription list for 1844 is a gift of 10 shillings from someone listed as 'An enemy to races'. That year James Bloore was the Treasurer, and John Heathcote Hacker (solicitor) and A. J. Worthington (silk manufacturer) were the stewards. (There were no races in 1843.)

At a meeting at the George Inn, Leek on 17 September 1849 a committee of five was appointed to organise and promote the Leek Races, to take place in Wakes Week each year. The first five members were Messrs John Wain, Abraham Howes, John Whittles, B. Smith Walters and James Robinson. Later Mr James Bloore was appointed treasurer.

The Racing Committee met at the King William IV Inn, Church Street on 6 October 1851 to inspect the proposed new ground at Leek Edge as to its condition and suitability on which to hold the proposed Races. However, in 1863 the Leek Races were still being held on the Birchall Dale Old Course. Thomas Maskery was Clerk of the Course, a position which he held for a number of years, and the treasurer was Mr William Allen. The accounts showed a healthy balance in hand of £50 3s 6d.

In 1867 the Leek Races were held at the Highfield Park Course, and the entries were higher, with up to nine horses in some races. Next year, 1868, the event assumed the title of the North Staffordshire Races, Autumn Meeting, Leek. The prestigious list of stewards was Lord Alexander Paget, Lord Berkeley Paget, Captain Hyde Smith and W. F. M. Copeland Esq, with Thomas Maskery still holding the office of Clerk of the Course.

The races held were the Churnet Valley Stakes (a field of nine); the Hunter and Yeomanry Stakes (a field of four); the Ladies Purse (a field of six); the North Staffordshire Handicap (a field of eleven); the Highfield Stakes (a field of ten) and the Horton Stakes (a field of five).

In 1870 the races were held at Highfield on 8 and 9 August. Mr T. Maskery continued his service as Clerk of the Course, and the distinguished team of stewards was Lord Waterpark, Lord Henry Paget, Lord Alexander Paget, Lord Berkeley Paget, Capt Hyde Smith, P. L. Brocklehurst Esq, Robert Bentley Esq and W. M. Copeland Esq. These names indicate the involvement of the Jockey Club in Leek Races.

This distinguished gathering is a clear reflection of the growth, importance and prosperity of Leek during these later Victorian years.

The first record of a cricket club in Leek is in the formation of the Leek and Moorlands Cricket Club in 1844. The relevant extract from the original Minute Book reads:

At a meeting held at the Leek Town Hall on the 20th May, 1844:
Resolved that the club be called the Leek and Moorlands Cricket Club. Mr. Sawkins was appointed treasurer, and Mr. J. G. Whittles, secretary. That the rules as read be adopted, and 30 copies printed by Mr. Nall for the use of members. That a meeting be called by circular to be held at the Town Hall at 7 o clock on Wednesday, the 22nd instant, for the purpose of confirming the rules and receiving their subscriptions.

WILLIAM CHALLINOR, Chairman

At the subsequent meeting it was resolved *"that the field occupied by Mr. Leech at Barnfields, be taken at the rent of £5 per.year."* The first list of members ran as follows: Wm. Badnall, W. P. Morley, G. Sawkins, William Milner, E. S. Walters, John Ward, T. Redfern, jun, H. Sleigh, L. Hunt, A. J. Worthington (H.M.), The Rev J. Barnes, William Challinor, J. Challinor, J. G. Whittles, G. A. Smith, J. Nall, J. Robins, jun, A. Wedgwood, Joshua Smith, T. Carr, jun, and E. Heaton.

The first organised match was against Norton CC on Monday 30 June 1845, but there is no record of the result.

During its first year, the club's matches tended to be somewhat spasmodic, mainly internal games between teams of club members. A number of new members joined: Samuel Phillips, J. H. Hacker, G. Samkind, Mr Jennings, Mr Maskery, Mr Cartwright, Mr Davidson, Mr Bagnall, Mr Henry Johnson, Mr Kingswood, Mr A. Homes, Mr Souter, Mr Ellis, Mr J. Andrew, Mr W. H. Gaunt, Mr T. Wardle, and William Arckoll.

As with the Leek Races, the main body of support came from the town's more prominent citizens - the silk manufacturers and the professional classes.

The early recorded matches tended to be low-scoring affairs, pitches being more favourable to bowlers than batsmen. Round-arm bowling was first introduced on 27 July 1848 in a match with Cheadle, when J. Redfern, home from Rugby School, first practised the art, taking seven Cheadle wickets for 35 runs. The match, played over two innings, saw Leek the winners by the narrow margin of two runs.

The statement of expenses in 1848 is both interesting and amusing:

Laying the ground £3-3-9
Paid for cart and horses and ale for men 19-0
Players and umpires dinners £3-5-6
New cricket ball 7-6
Expenses for band £1-4-0 (A band appears to have been an essential feature of these early sporting occasions!)
During 1848, several players joined the club who were working on the Churnet Valley Railway, which was under construction at that time.

On 8 April 1851 Mr A. J. Worthington became the Club's chairman, Mr W. B. Badnall vice-chairman and Mr William Allen secretary and treasurer. The committee was Messrs G. Bloore, W. Arckoll, E. S. Walters, J. Gaunt and L. Ellis.

For a match against Congleton, expenditure included sending a bellman round the town crying the match, umpires and scorers expenses, dinners and refreshments for match, toll-gate expenses, mowing and watering the ground with a barrel of water and horse and man, a pair of leg guards and pair of wicket-keeping gloves, plus six shillings for impounding Mr. Davenport's sheep through the gate of the field being left open.

An important date was 1852, when John Davenport Esq gratuitously gave the use of the Beggars Lane ground for the club.

Mr J. Heathcote Hacker was elected president and Mr E. S. Walters vice-chairman. The first professional player appears to have been J. Copson who in 1855 was paid one shilling per match, with a free dinner and £1 per year for carrying the club's baggage.

In those early years, matches began in the early morning, so that an innings could be completed before luncheon.

By 1851 a new club, Leek Albion, had been formed, and a match was arranged in which Leek fielded 11 players and Albion 15. Nevertheless, Leek won, scoring 115 to Albion's 73. The return match was played at Pool End during the Leek Wakes (20 and 21 October) over two innings, the combined score of the Leek Eleven 163 to the Albion's 15 score of 94.

Another local club was formed in 1861 by the local Volunteers Company but, in their early matches with the Leek club, they always appeared to be the losers.

An important name in Leek cricket is that of Robert S. Milner. He played his first match against Ashbourne, and recollected the occasion to Mr Tom Tipper:

> *I remember very clearly, playing this match. I was about 16 years old, and just home from school for my holidays. Mr. William Allen invited me to play at Ashbourne, so I went home to ask my mother's permission to go. This she at once granted, and she also provided me with the wherewithall for my expenses. When my turn came to bat, Mr. Allen was in, and he said to me when I was about to receive my first ball, "Keep your bat straight, Robert". At the second ball he said," Well played, Robert"; but when the third ball bowled me for a duck he exclaimed," Oh, d... it"!*

R. S. Milner, however, was destined to play a much more significant role in the later history of the club. Many players, at all levels, have made an inauspicious beginning to their careers, and gone on to greater things.

Between 1862 and 1865 several more junior clubs were formed, notably the Recreation Club, connected with the Congregational Church, and the Gladstone Club, mainly drapers and their assistants. These clubs had the use of the Beggars Lane ground, while Leek played on Slater's Field (site of Langford Street today), before moving to Highfield in 1867.

Such was the dominance of the Leek Club in those years that a number of matches were played against teams with larger numbers of players. On 18 August 1866 a Leek XI played a match against a combined team of 22 players, over two innings. The 22 scored 48 and 45 and Leek's score was 75 in their first innings, going on to win by eight wickets. The 1867 season opened with a match at Highfield, the Leek XI against the Recreation Club's 18, Leek again the victors. A second eleven was now formed by the Leek Club.

In 1871 the officers of the Club were: H. L. Johnson Esq, President; Thomas Wardle FGS, and Joseph Flowers Esq, Vice Presidents; Mr P. Dalgliesh, Treasurer; Mr J. Black, Secretary; Mr R. S. Milner, Captain; Committee: Messrs J.W. Critchlow, R. S. Milner, John Plant, F. J. Milner, Henry Lightfoot, J. G. Smith, John Gould, George Hill, D. Dunwell.

In that season, the Captain, R. S. Milner. headed the batting averages, and George Peacock the bowling. R. S. Milner, who died on 4 February 1925, captained the Club from 1867 to 1882, and was President from 1887 to 1889. A professional coach, Amos Hind, was engaged in 1872.

On 5, 6 and 7 August 1875 a Yorkshire County XI visited Highfield to play a Leek 22. The match was marred by rain, and Yorkshire scored 100 and 63, Leek replying with 74 and 41 for 6 wickets. A Nottingham County XI played 18 of Leek next year, 1876, Leek scoring 39 and 49 and Notts 61 and 28 for 3, winning by 7 wickets.

W.W. Farrands, a Notts bowler, was engaged by Leek for the 1877 season, when the County XI returned to play Leek again. The scores were 71 and 77, Farrands taking a hat-trick for Leek, who replied with 88 and 16 for when time was called, play having been delayed by rain.

On 15 May 1880, after an early morning start, Leek, playing Burton-on-Trent, made their record score of 368, a score which has never been surpassed. Burton had scored 17 for 2 wickets at the close.

In 1886 Mr B. C. Glover, owner of Highfield Hall, died. He was a Vice-President of the club, and had always allowed free use of the Highfield Ground. In the Jubilee year, Mr A. Nicholson took over Highfield Hall, and continued the free use of the ground.

Mr R. S. Milner became Club President in place of Mr H. L. Johnson, who had left the town, having served 16 years as President.

The 5-ball over was introduced in 1889 and on 5 May that year Mr F. J. Milner died, aged 37. From 1872 to 1885 he was the Hon Secretary, Treasurer and Second XI Captain. 1890 saw the foundation of the North Staffs Cricket League, and Leek CC went through the season without defeat.

The 1892 season started tragically, when C. Rothera, the Leek professional, 28-years-old and a native of Bradford, stopped a smart return of caught-and-bowled with his left hand. He became unwell and left the field. He later recovered, and prepared to return to the field. On being told that the innings was almost over, he passed a joke with those present, then collapsed and died. Williams Bates, an ex-Yorkshire and England player, was engaged in his place. He had toured Australia with the M.C.C.

In 1893 Leek joined the North Staffs League and, after a poor start, finished in fifth position. 1894 was the 50th anniversary of the Club, marked by the visit of an MCC XI on 3 and 4 August. The weather, unfortunately, was poor, and MCC batted first on the Friday, scoring 178 for 3 wickets, when play was abandoned for the day. The game resumed at 11.00 am on Saturday, and MCC took their score to 201 for 4 declared. Leek scored 87 all out, when torrential rain put an end to the match.

1895 was another significant year for Leek cricket, when Leek Highfield was formed as a separate club, Leek CC continuing to play at the new ground at Beggars Lane. The split occurred as a result of a dispute concerning the payment of match fees which the Cricket Club wanted to levy on the working-men players. There was a good deal of acrimony, and Arthur Nicholson intervened taking the view that such fees were unreasonable, and a man of ability should be allowed to play, irrespective of his social class. The dispute turned out to be very bitter - almost a class war, in fact - and Nicholson threatened to withdraw the free use of the ground at Highfield if the club persisted with its policy. The club was split on the issue, some members broke away and continued to play as Leek Cricket Club, on the Beggars Lane ground. The remainder stayed at Highfield, Playing as Leek Highfield Cricket Club.

Leek Highfield's first professional was Walter James Bagshaw, a medium-fast left-arm bowler from Attercliffe, Sheffield.

Next season, 1896, Leek Highfield were admitted to the North Staffs League, and the first meeting of the two clubs, on a hot day at the Beggars Lane ground on 11 July, resulted in a draw. Leek declared at 162 for 8 wickets, and Highfield replied with 85 for 7. The return match was played at Highfield on 1 August, and again a large crowd attended. Highfield batted first, and scored only 14 for 8 wickets, but rallied to achieve a total of 40. In failing light, Leek passed this total for the loss of 5 wickets, but as soon as the winning hit was made, with Dr J. McClew and W. Vickerstaff at the wicket, the rain began to fall heavily.

In 1898 Leek won the championship of the North Staffs League, Highfield finishing in eighth position. That same year the Leek and District League was formed. An outstanding player for Leek Highfield during those years was Jerry Pace, a talented bowler who once took all 10 wickets for 32 runs against Bignall End, and regularly headed the bowling averages for his club.

At the turn of the century, in 1900, Leek Highfield 2nd XI were champions of the Churnet Valley League, and into the twentieth century Leek cricket continued successfully to attract a good level of support and interest.

In 1908 the generosity of the Nicholsons was demonstrated when Mrs Nicholson wiped off the Club's debt and gave two silver cups for batting and bowling; in 1911 Sir Arthur Nicholson presented a new pavilion to Leek Highfield. The 1911 season also saw Jerry Pace taking 102 wickets at an average of 11 runs per wicket, but unfortunately Leek Highfield were relegated from the League.

Several prominent players from both clubs lost their lives in the First World War:

Leek: Capt R. F. Johnson, Pte H. A. Tudor, Pte J. Doxey, Pte E. Chapples, Lt C. C. Watson, Major F. Davenport, Abel Arnott;

Leek Highfield: Lt B. L. Nicholson, Pte W. Baskerville, Pte Harvey Hunt, Pte H. Hulme, Pte J. Mycock, Pte E. Thornton.

The devasting number of casualties in the war decimated many local cricket clubs, and consequently, after the war, teams were weakened. However, in 1919 Leek and Leek Highfield settled their differences and amalgamated, making one strong club out of two weakened ones. In this strength, the new Leek Cricket Club enjoyed considerable success in the 1920s.

In 1920 the Beggars Lane ground was purchased. In 1922 a loving cup was presented by the Club to Sir Arthur Nicholson on his 80th birthday, the Club continuing to use the Highfield ground as its main base.

In 1924 Jerry Pace completed a total of 1,000 wickets in the North Staffs League, and was presented with the ball with which he took the 1,000th wicket.

Also prominent among the bowlers during those successful years was C. J. Taylor, while A. Rider was a prolific batsman.

In 1939, Mr H. Ball was made a Life Member and Vice-President of the N. S. League in recognition of his 50 years membership with Leek Cricket, serving as Chairman for several years. Mr John Tatton, who purchased Highfield Hall, and following the Nicholson tradition, continued to allow free use of the ground.

Facilities for playing football in Leek in the 1870s were scant, for there was virtually no established recreation ground at the time. Cricket and football would be played on waste ground, wherever there was room for a pitch. Such open spaces were to be found where Bath Street and Ford Street now stand, the Cattle Market site, Leonard Street and Shoobridge Street, Macclesfield Road, Spring Gardens, Beggars Lane or Nab Hill. Often, if the games were unauthorised, the jackets of the lads would be impounded by the police, their owners having later to collect them from the Police Station, then at the top of Mill Street, where a stern caution was usually issued.

Britannia Street Recreation ground, then called Maddox and Phoenix Croft, and owned by Mr and Mrs Argles, was brought by the Leek Improvement Commissioners in 1870, and a few years later Gladstone Street and Chorley Street were built upon it. Westwood Recreation Ground was opened in 1879, and in Jubilee Year Mr William Challinor presented the Pickwood Recreation Ground to the town on 21 June.

The first recorded football match took place on 15 October 1870. Organised by the Recreation Club, two Leek teams opposed each other, and the game was played under the Rugby Rules. Although the Leek Times stated that regular games would be played, weather permitting, there is no record of any such games until late 1873.

On 11 October 1873 an announcement appeared that a meeting would be held at the Swan Hotel on the following Thursday evening for the purpose of establishing a football club in connection with the Leek Cricket Club, which was then flourishing. The Club was formed, training commenced, and the Rugby Rules were learned with a view to starting competitive matches. On 17 January 1874 a practice match was played on the White Lion ground at Bridge End. Matches, however, were sporadic, one being played against Stoke, and one against Langley, near Macclesfield, Leek the winners on both occasions.

The first match between Leek and Macclesfield was played on the White Lion ground on 4 March

1876, and ended in dispute. Leek players alleged that their opponents displayed a total lack of knowledge of the rules, apparently a case of anything goes!

Another unusual match took place the following week, on 11 March 1876, when the first fifteen opposed the next thirty - and the fifteen easily defeated the thirty by two goals and three tries to nothing.

In December 1876 the local Volunteer Corps formed a football club, and played a match with Leek Football Club, under the Rugby Rules.

It was during the 1876-7 season that Leek adopted the Association Rules, the first recorded match played on 20 January 1877, against Uttoxeter. The result was a win for Uttoxeter by one disputed goal to nil. There was no referee, and the two umpires were both Uttoxeter men, so the Leek players claimed a draw on the grounds that the umpires had erred in favour of their own side! (Note: Endon, however, were the pioneers of Association Football in the Moorlands, for they formed their club on 16 November 1876 and played their first match against Normacot on 23 December 1876.)

Following the establishment of Association Football towards the end of 1876, many clubs were formed in the Potteries and North Staffordshire, and the game became popular, with good crowds turning up to watch matches.

Rugby Union Football continued to be played during the winter on a ground to the north of Highfield Hall. A number of players played cricket there in the summer and football in the winter.

Early in 1877 the Leek Club left the Bridge End ground, moving to the Britannia Street Recreation Ground for a spell. The first match between the two local sides, Leek and the Volunteers, was played on 10 February 1877. The result was Leek 1, Volunteers 0.

On 10 March 1877 two matches were played at Leek on the same day, one under the Association Rules and the other under the Rugby Rules, the Association game drawing the larger crowd. The first season, 1876-77, was successful for the Leek club, twenty games being played and only six lost.

The Staffordshire Cup was established the following season, Leek playing their first cup-tie on 13 October 1877, beating Cobridge College by one goal to nil. In this match the cross bar was used instead of the tape, and each side provided an umpire. The second round of the cup saw the first meeting between Leek and Stoke, with Stoke the winners by one goal to nil.

By this time, the ground at Westwood Lane was in use, and Leek was enjoying a successful season; the 1st team played 13 matches, won 12 and lost only one (against Stoke in the Cup 2nd round), the 2nd team played 11 matches, won 5 lost 4 and drew 2. The list of officials shows the close involvement with cricket in summer and football in winter in the case of a number of men: President: H. L. Johnson, Vice-Presidents: R. S. Milner (who also played as a goal-keeper) H. Brunt, E. Fynney, T. Wardle, W. H. Hammersley, Dr Gailey, J. Robinson, A. Nicholson, W. Allen and F. J. Milner (a versatile, all-round sportsman). The secretary was Mr S. Henshaw, Mr Bruce was treasurer, and Roland Sleigh and James Gwynne Captains of the 1st and 2nd teams respectively.

The winter of the season 1878/79 was severe, with heavy snow in January. Nevertheless, the game continued to attract a good measure of public support, with large crowds at most matches. It was a practice at this time for clubs to borrow players from other clubs, and on 5 October R. Sleigh of Leek played for Stoke against Notts County. There appears to have been a certain amount of needle between Leek and Ashbourne. In a match played on 23 November 1878 the Ashbourne team refused to accept the offside rule, and played the game according to their own interpretation of the rules. Again on Thursday evening, 13 February 1879, another match was played at Ashbourne, under floodlights. Ashbourne won 4-1, but the lighting was said to be unsatisfactory, usually going out when the Leek men got near the Ashbourne goal!

A record gate of over 1,000 attended the match at Leek on 1 March 1879, when Leek played a strong Stoke team. The score at half-time was 1-1, and Stoke scored what was alleged to be an offside goal just before time, when the game was brought to an abrupt conclusion!

The biggest victory ever scored by Leek in a Staffordshire Cup Tie was 11 goals to nil, against Hanley Providence, at Leek on 14 October 1882. On 24 February 1883 Leek reached the semi-final of the Staffordshire Cup when they were beaten by Stoke, at Stoke, by 4 goals to 3.

Such was the level of interest in, and measure of success of, the Leek Club that they entered the English Cup in 1884, but unfortunately their first venture into this higher competition was not successful, for they were beaten by Northwich Victoria by 4 goals to 3. Next season, however, they fared much better, defeating Macclesfield away from home by the convincing margin 5 goals to one. Leek reached the 3rd round of the English Cup, and on Saturday 3 January 1885 the historic match with Queen's Park, Glasgow took place on the Westwood Lane ground, before a crowd of about 3,000. The match was exciting, and Leek lost by the narrow margin of 3-2.

Leek, however, enjoyed more success in a local cup in the season 1887/88 when, on 28 April, they played Stoke in the final of the Charity Cup. Leek won by 2 goals to one, in spite of being a goal down at half-time and, when they arrived back at Leek Station, a large crowd had assembled to greet the victors.

The growth of interest in local football during the late 19th and early 20th centuries is demonstrated by the emergence of a number of junior and works teams. Among the more successful were: Leek Scriveners formed in 1878; Leek Wasps, who enjoyed some success in the 1880s and 90s; The Volunteer Club formed in connection with the local Volunteer Corps; The White Star, playing in 1890, and mainly organised by Mr J. Bermingham; Pickwood Vale who came into prominence in 1890/91, when they won the Baskerville Cup; Pickwood Rovers who became defunct during the season 1892-93; Leek Alexandra FC formed in 1913, and recognised as one of the best junior clubs in the district, enjoying much success in league and cup competitions; Ball Haye Green FC, a popular and successful team, who tied for the championship of the Leek and District League with Brough's works team in the season of 1901/02; Leek YMCA, winners of the Leek Combination Cup, season 1906/07, and Leek St Mary's, the losers to Leek YMCA after a replay. Leek Fire Brigade held what must be a unique record in the annals of football: they never lost a match! The reason was that they only ever played one match, against a Leek Police XI in 1898.

Sport in Leek has therefore occupied a prominent place in relation to the national perspective. The early horse races were recognised by the Jockey Club. Its cricket teams have employed First Class County players, and, in turn, contributed players to that level of the game, even to the international level. A number of the football teams who played against Leek teams are still in existence, and playing in the English leagues. Rugby and hockey have also supplied players who have gone on to international status. Boxing, athletics, swimming and golf have all produced local champions who have gone on to greater achievements. And even the more cerebral sport of chess has had its high performers on the national scene! High status, indeed, for a small market town.

OVER BIRCHALL DALE COURSE.

LEEK RACES.

CONDITIONS.—Entries for the North Staffordshire, Birchall, and Free Handicaps, to close and name to Mr THOMAS MASKERY, Clerk of the Course, on or before the 19th September, and the Weights to appear in BELL'S LIFE on the 30th September, 1865.

Every Rider to appear in Jockey costume. - No Gambling allowed on the Ground.

The Winner of the Hunter's Stake will not be allowed to start on the second day without the consent of the Committee, and then to carry such additional weight as they think proper. All disputes to be settled by the Committee, or whom they may appoint, and their decision to be final, and not subject to appeal to any Court of Law. Four Horses to start for each Race, or the public money will not be given without the consent of the Committee. The owner of a Horse running in the Hunter's or Tally Ho! Stakes must prove the pedigree of his Horse if, and when required by the Committee. Each Horse to pay 2s. 6d. for scales and weights. The Colours of the Riders must be declared at the time of entry, and any Jockey changing his Colours will be fined 10s. 6d., the same to be paid at the time of weighing, or he will not be allowed to ride. Any objection against a Horse running in the Hunter's or Tally Ho Stakes must be made in writing, on or before Tuesday, the 17th of October, 1865. The objector will be required to deposit 10s., and in the event of the objection not being sustained, such deposit will be forfeited, and paid over to the Race Fund.

No person residing out of the Parish of Leek will be allowed to sell upon the Course, either Wines, Spirits, Ale, or other fermented Liquor.

No person will be allowed to erect any Booth, Stall, or Standing, on the Course, without having first agreed and paid for the same, with the Clerk of the Course. The Entrances for both days Races (except the Handicaps) must be made in writing, and delivered to Mr. THOMAS MASKERY, Spout Street, Leek, between the hours of 7 and 9 o'clock, on Saturday Evening, October 14th, 1865. To start at 1.30 p.m., prompt.

R. JOHNSON, of York, Handicapper.
THOMAS MASKERY, Clerk of the Course.

JAMES RIDER, PRINTER, SPOUT STREET, LEEK.

The Birchall Dale Course was the original venue for the Annual Leek Races, usually held in October.

NORTH STAFFORDSHIRE RACES.

AUTUMN MEETING, LEEK,

OCTOBER 19th AND 20th, 1868.

STEWARDS.

LORD HENRY PAGET,

CAPT. HYDE SMITH, & W. F. M. COPELAND, Esq.

CONDITIONS.—Entries for each day's Race must be made in writing and delivered to the Clerk of the Course on or before SATURDAY, the 17th October, 1868. Any objection against a Horse must be made in writing before going to Scale; the objector will be required to deposit 10s.; and in the event of the objections not being sustained such to be forfeited and paid over to the Race Fund. Four Horses to start for each Race or the Public Money will not be given, without the consent of the Stewards.

All disputes to be settled by the Stewards, or whom they may appoint, and their decision to be final, and not subject to any further appeal whatsoever. Each Horse to pay 2s. 6d. for Weights and Scales. Every Rider to appear in correct jockey costume. To start at ONE o'clock promptly. No Gambling or Mock Auction Carts allowed on the Ground.

Special Trains will run from the Pottery Towns at a return Fare of One Shilling. For time see Company's Bills.

T. MASKERY, Clerk of the Course.

C. R. JONES, PRINTER AND BOOKSELLER, LEEK.

LEEK RACES.

OVER THE BIRCHALL DALE OLD COURSE.

A Winner of the first day will not be allowed to start on the second day without the consent of the Committee, and then to carry such additional weight as they think proper. All disputes to be settled by the Committee, or whom they may appoint, and their decision to be final. Four Horses to start for each Race, or the public money will not be given without the consent of the Committee. The owner of a Horse running in the Hack Stakes must prove the pedigree of his horse, if required by the Committee. Each Horse to pay 2s. 6d. for scales and weights. Entrance money must be paid at the time of entry, or the horse will not be entitled to the Stake, though a winner. The Colours of the Riders must be declared at the time of entry, and any Jockey changing his colours will be fined 10s. 6d., the same to be paid at time of weighing, or he will not be allowed to ride. Any objection against a Horse running in the Hack Stakes must be made in writing, and handed to the Clerk of Scales at, or before, the weighing of the Jockey riding the Horse objected to. No person residing out of the parish of Leek will be allowed to sell upon the Course, either Wines, Spirits, Ale, or other fermented Liquor. No person will be allowed to erect any Booth, Stall, or Standing on the Course without having first agreed, and paid for the same, with the Clerk of the Course. The Entrances for both days' Races must be made in writing, and delivered to Mr. THOMAS MASKERY, Spout Street, Leek, between the hours of [illegible] and [illegible] o'clock, on Saturday Evening, Oct. 17th, 1863.

JAMES RIDER, PRINTER, LEEK.

THOMAS MASKERY, Clerk of the Course.

The well organised Leek races were a strong feature of Victorian Leek.

Ball Haye Green Football Club played on Isaac Bailey's field in Novi Lane, when this picture was taken in 1901. They were well supported and often attracted crowds of 2000. Front: F Dale, A Brown, R Green, S Pickford, E Sherratt. Players behind: E Tatton, F Whitter, S Ratcliffe, E Shenton, J Burnett, C Ball, A Naden. Officials: H Wilson, J Cottam, J Perry, J Smith, H Biddulph, TS Myatt, D Porter, C Rhead, A Green, G Rider, G Burnett, J Day (Sec)

Brough, Nicholson and Hall Ltd ran several teams and this large group of players was photographed c.1936. Colonel A Falkner Nicholson (in raincoat) is seated left on front row.

Two photos of Leek YMCA who were winners of the Leek Combination Cup 1906-7.
Photo above: Front: V Finney, A Bowyer, J Smith, R Carr, E Ratcliffe
Middle: A Knight, H Nichols, W Bowyer, G E Plant. Back: G Towers, A Goodwin, H Ellerton, G Bagshaw
Officials: T Clarke, M Newsome, M Cope, A Ford, H R Sleigh, E R Campling, R Johnson, H J Cope.

Leek Cyclists Club outside the Duke of York Inn, Derby Street, which served as their headquarters for a while.
The members are seen here in carnival mood.

The Leek Cyclists' Club formed in 1876 is one of the oldest in the country and has never lacked support.
This photo is in 1910 at the home of T Smith Myatt, Daisy Bank.

One of Captain Byrom's shooting parties at Abbey farm in the 1930s. Front: Mr Hine, - - , Mr Nash, Mrs Byrom, Capt Byrom, Miss Watson, Gen. Phillips (Ashenhurst), Mrs Standring, Dr Hammersley, Sgt Major Allen (Swan Hotel), D Cumberlidge. Middle: Mr Eardley, E Cumberlidge, W Cumberlidge, Capt Colville, Charles Watson, T Hampson (Woodlands), J Meakin (Westwood Manor), E Challinor, A Standring (Dunwood), T Hudson, S Cade, H Stonehewer, Mr Deakin, Mr Broadhurst, Mr Pimlott, J Osborne. Back: Mr Beresford, B Preston, M Conway, J Prime, Mr Lockett, E Chapman, Mr Harrison, Mr Deacon, A Armitt, Mr Phillips, M Stonehwer, Mr Marshall, 'Mick', G Viggers.

In the early 1900s local cricket was thriving in the Leek area. One of the most successful teams was Westwood Rovers, who played in the strong Leek and District League and were champions 1900-2
Front: J Goodwin, G plant, J Hazelhurst, G E Plant (captain), J Sheldon, W Birch,
Rear: S Poyser, E Bowyer, A Birch, C Goodwin, G Earls, C Green, E Vigrass, H E Rendall, W Dresser, W Poyser, G Bagshaw, C F Bowyer (Sec).

The Leek Hornets in 1897, a junior team connected with Leek Football Club.
Front: H Shufflebotham, C Lovatt, W Bromfield (later MP for Leek), J Barnett, J Heath
Middle J Birch, A Brindley, C Trafford. Back: A Rogers (sec), F Johnson, A Brunt, J Hill.

Pickwood Vale FC were the first winners of the Baskerville Cup in 1890-91. The team, founded 1887, enjoyed much success in local competitions. Front: M A Cope, J Lovatt, H Mellor, E Putnam, R Baker. Middle: H Quinn, F Nixon, T Goddard. Back: E Chapman, E Nixon, G E Bagshaw.

Another successful local team in season 1906-7 was Leek St Mary's. The final of the Combination Cup was contested on 30th March 1907 by the YMCA and Saint Mary's which the YMCA won 2-0.
Front: C E Goodwin, J Grahame, J Alsop, H Hill, M Conway Second: H Cope, Trafford, H Fitch, A L Kidd, Jim Moss
Rear (officials): J Moss, W Cope, J Morgan, C Gell, S Mitchell, S W Bailey, J Furby, J Drury, A Moss, P Birch, G Fisher.

The Duke of York Inn, Derby Street was the headquarters of the Leek Harriers Athletic Club. Seen here in 1895.
Front: S Goldstraw, R Hardy, H Peach, G Moores, W Trafford Middle: F Hilton, E Hambleton, G Mayers, G McKinsey, E Bull,
Back: J Taylor, E Goldstraw, J Fisher, J Lowe, J Wardle, W Peach, G Gyte, A Rex, F Pearson, S Taylor, W Hilton, H Walters

In late Victorian times the only bowling green in Leek was at the Abbey Inn (which at some time was known as the Bowling Green Inn) on Abbey Green Road and reputed to be centuries old.
Front: W Goldstraw, W Garner, B Flanagan, J Matthews. Back: S Cartwright, J Williams, J Smith, H W Nixon

This football team holds a unique record - they never lost a match. Not only that, they only once came near defeat. On 3rd December 1898 a challenge match took place between the Leek Fire Brigade Eleven and a Leek Police Eleven, the Fire Brigade winning by a single goal - and this was the only match they ever played!
Front: C Malkin, J Carding, J Day, A Carding, W Davenport. Middle: H Henshaw, W Tatton, J Amson, H Alcock, H Buxton, T Alcock, C Mycock, W Carding. Back: S Perkin, R Carding, S Billing, J Creighton, J Beckett, A J Halton, J Pace

LEEK PHILOTHESPIAN CLUB.

"The Play's the thing.."
HAMLET, II, 4.

PROGRAMME.
OF THE
Amateur Theatricals,
IN THE TOWN HALL,
On Thursday and Friday Evenings,
12th and 13th November, 1891.

"Call forth your actors by the scroll."
Midsummer Night's Dream, I, 2.

"My heart speaks you are welcome."
Macbeth, III, 4.

Manager .. .. Mr. J. Wardle.
Stage Manager .. .. Mr. J. Newall.
Musical Director .. .. Mr. S. H. Mee.
Scenic Artist .. .. .. Mr. H. W. Campling.

DOORS OPEN AT 7. COMMENCE AT 7-30. CARRIAGES AT 10-30.

"SOLD FOR A PENNY."
II Henry VI. IV. 2.

THOMAS MARK, PRINTER, LEEK.

The Leek Philothespian Club was an early amateur dramatic society formed during the 1880s. It gave many performances for charity.

VICTORIA THEATRE
Cattle Market, Leek.
Proprietress & General Manageress .. Mrs. M. C. SINCLAIR.
Patron .. .. .. SIR HENRY IRVING.

MONDAY, March 25th,
Special Production of the Famous HISTORICAL DRAMA, entitled—
A WOMAN'S AMBITION
Or, ENGLAND in A.D. 670.

Wulfere (King of Mercia) ... ... Mr. David Sinclair
Rollo } (his Sons) } ... ... Master Harry Miller
Ulfred ... ... Miss Nellie Warner
Edgar (the Hleot of the Hough ... Mr. Hector Audreys
Egbert ... ... Mr. W. Curtiss
Bishop Chad (of Lichfield) ... ... Mr. Alf. Miller
Ptolemy ... ... Mr. Harry C. Sinclair
Robert ... ... Mr. H. Chad
Oswy ... ... Mr. E
Werebode ... ...Miss Alice Sinc
Queen Erminilda ... ... Miss F. C
Gurtha ... ... Mrs. Chad
Rosa ... ... Miss Ada C

NOTE.—This Drama was played with great success last year and th year before under the title of "A Daughter of Babylon."

TUESDAY, March 26th,
A Beautiful EMOTIONAL DRAMA, entitled—
A MOTHER'S SIN
Or, THE FRENCH EAST LYNNE.
To be followed by SINGING and a FARCE.

WEDNESDAY, March 27th,
The ever-popular IRISH DRAMA, entitled—
THE COLLEEN BAWN
Or, THE BRIDES OF GARRYOWEN.
To be followed by SINGING and a FARCE.

A travelling theatre (often called 'rag and stick' theatres) frequently visited Leek. They performed in a portable auditorium, pitched on the old cattle market site.

CHAPTER SIX
On the Stage

LEEK AMATEUR MUSICAL SOCIETY was established in 1866 and gave its first concert in the Temperance Hall, Union Street on Tuesday, 8 May 1866. The first officers of the society were: President, Rev B. Pidcock; Secretary, Miss A. Milner; Treasurer, Mrs Alsop; Librarian, Mr W. Dishley; and Conductor, Mr J. W. Powell. The vocal members met for regular practices on Saturday evenings, and the Society gave two or three concerts each year, with additional performances of oratorios such as Handel's Messiah at Christmas and Mendelssohn's Elijah, usually during Lent.

Often guest vocalists were engaged, and the orchestra was reinforced by members of 'Mr. Halle's Band, Manchester', as it was described in the programme for the performance of Elijah on 24 March 1879. The Society's 50th concert was given on Monday, 18 December 1882, when Mrs Holt of Sheffield and Mr Macdonald of York Minister were the guest soloists.

Although the concerts were usually musically successful, the annual financial statements often showed a deficit, and it was sometimes necessary, as in 1893, to hold a Sale of Work to make up the balance. For many years Dr J. J. Ritchie was the President, and the regular Conductor was Mr J. Gwynne, with Victor Prince as Honorary Secretary. Concerts were later held in the Town Hall and, by the time the Society gave its 90th concert on 18 December 1899, the orchestra was considerably larger. In 1902 the Society regretfully announced the resignation of Mr and Mrs James Gwynne, the conductor and accompanist for over 20 years. Victor Prince was the conductor when the Society gave its 100th concert at the Town Hall on Monday, 11 April 1904. Later conductors were John Cope (1909) and Carl Oliver (1913).

Leek Orchestral Society was formed in the 1890s; the stated aim of this society being *'the cultivation and practice of orchestral music, as it is the only one of its kind in the district which enables young people to practice together. For this object it claims the support of all'.* Its President was Sir Thomas Wardle, Treasurer Mr H. Moorhouse and Secretary Mr W. Stubbs.

Many of the musicians associated with the Leek Amateur Musical Society (where the emphasis was on choral works) were also members of the Leek Orchestral Society, and James Gwynne was the conductor, followed in 1921 by Fred Wood. The concerts were usually held in the Town Hall, and saw the emergence, in the second violins, of a man who was destined to play a dominant role in future amateur musical and dramatic performances in Leek and in the public life of the town - William Warrington. The society ceased in 1926 for lack of support.

Leek Amateur Operatic Company was formed in 1895, and quickly established a sound reputation with its productions of the well-known Gilbert and Sullivan operas. Its first productions were Trial by Jury and HMS Pinafore, the latter repeated in 1897 by popular demand. The profits from the first production were given to the Nicholson Institute Picture Purchase and Exhibition Fund.

The Society had a distinguished patron, the Duchess of Sutherland, and in the company's 1901 production of 'The Yeomen of the Guard' Victor Prince was the conductor, and William Warrington appeared in the orchestra. By 1910 he had become Chairman of the Committee, the society being re-formed as the Leek Amateur Opera Society in 1909. Among the leading players in those early years were Kineton Parkes (the town's librarian and curator), W. E. Brindley, Marcus Prince, Edward Challinor, W. J. Hudson, Mrs Kineton Parkes, Florence Parkes, Florrie Wright, Phyllis Bilton and Alice Wood. The early productions were held at the Town Hall but, for the 1910 production of Patience, the company moved to the Grand Theatre. The orchestra was formed by the Leek Amateur Orchestral Society and the Grand Theatre Band.

The company's years of greatest success and popularity followed the First World War and continued into the 1920s. The venue was always the Grand Theatre, and these annual Gilbert and Sullivan productions received good support from the people of Leek. Mr W. Warrington became the producer, and the mantle of the leading comic roles fell on Mr A. D. Price, a science teacher at Leek High School, who played these famous characters with great skill.

The Leek Amateur Opera Society occasionally made a departure from Gilbert and Sullivan to stage variety entertainments for various charities. In 1925 Mr Warrington produced an entertainment in aid of the National Society for the Prevention of Cruelty to Children. The performers were: Mrs Jim Chell (Gertrude), Miss Dorothy Jackman, Mrs Lionel Sneyd (Irene) and Messrs Jim Chell, Charles Gell, Harold Grace, Harry Owen, Leonard Salt and Bert Sharpe. The programme amusingly records:

> *'The London Co-optimists commence their programme by announcing that the various performances appear by kind permission of their different managers and others. We can only state our performers appear, in the case of married men, by permission of their respective spouses, and in the case of the unmarried ones, by permission of the various young men and maidens who have a lien on them.'*

The programme consisted of sketches, comedy and musical items, and an old fashioned farce called Bobby Settles Down.

Leek Philothespian Club was formed in the 1880s, this dramatic society adopted as its motto 'The Play's the Thing'. One of its leading members was Mr John Wardle who, as actor and manager, was largely responsible for the Club's popularity. He played many leading roles, including those from Shakespeare, and on one memorable occasion obtained special permission from Sir Henry Irving to perform 'The Dead Heart', a drama of the French Revolution; his performance in 'The Bells' was also noteworthy. A. E. Quinn was a leading player of comedy roles with the company and, when he retired, Jimmy Crombie followed in his footsteps. Nellie Robinson and the Vigrass sisters were the leading female performers.

The Philothespian Club gave many performances for charity, on one occasion playing at the old Longton Theatre in aid of the North Staffs Royal Infirmary. Performances in Leek were often supported by the Leek Orchestral Society, conducted by Mr James Gwynne, who played during the intervals. The company, however, had its own musical director, Mr S. H. Mee, the stage manager was Mr J. Newall and the scenic artist Mr H. W. Campling. The company ceased productions of plays about 1910.

The Moorland Players operated in the 1930s, again involving William Warrington as producer. They performed plays in the Churnet Hall, Cheddleton and the Grand Theatre at Leek, where films would be shown on the first three nights of the week, with the Moorland Players on the last three nights.

The Grand Theatre and Hippodrome theatre and cinema was formally opened on Monday, 13 December 1909 by Mr John Ernest Ingham, Chairman of the Leek Urban District Council. There was a lavish music hall performance, with several professional artistes at the opening performance and during the week concluding with 'Special animated pictures on the Grand Bioscope'.

The Foxlow Follies: during the First World War, Foxlow, formerly the home of Mr and Mrs Cruso, was used as a Red Cross Hospital, and in December 1918 a programme of entertainment was presented by the soldiers to mark the fourth anniversary of the opening of Foxlow, at the Town Hall. The programme notes are amusing, and the whole affair appears to have been hilarious, reflecting no doubt the joyful mood of the times, when the war, which had been so devastating, was over.

The Old Temperance Hall, which stood in Union Street, was originally a chapel, erected by a small breakaway movement in the Leek Congregational Church. A group left the main Derby Street church in the 1830s, and set up their own church. They were reunited with the Derby Street Church in the 1850s, following the retirement of their minister, Rev Robert Goshawk. This made a much stronger church, as numbers increased, which led to the planning of the new Congregational Church in Derby Street, which opened in 1863. The Union Street building was sold to the Temperance Society, and became known as the Temperance Hall. The building was frequently used to stage various entertainments by the Musical Society and the Orchestral Society and for the production of plays, sometimes by travelling companies, but more frequently by local amateurs.

For many years an outstanding feature was the Penny Readings given every Saturday night to packed houses. Mr E. Mountford, the teacher of music, was chiefly responsible for providing the entertainment, and the concerts he staged gave endless delight to hundreds of Leek people.

Many well-known local people took part, including Mr William Challinor, Mr M.H. Miller, Mr J.G. Beckett, Mr Ralph de Tunstall Sneyd, Dr Ritchie, Mr J. Lovatt, Mrs Hobson (readings of Lancashire sketches), Mr W. Doxey (popular songs) and Mr Sam Godwin (a nigger-minstrel performance). The programmes usually included instrumental, vocal, humorous and dramatic items. Oscar Wilde lectured at the Temperance Hall in February 1884 but the audience was reported to be small. The Temperance Hall later became a skating rink, and was used for a time by the Salvation Army, before their own headquarters were built in Salisbury Street, ending its days as the Majestic Cinema, burned down in 1961.

The Philharmonic Society: there is a record that this newly-formed society held its subscription concert in the Swan Hotel Assembly Room on 24 October 1839 - an early contribution to the cultural life of Leek.

During the summer of 1884, the Volunteer Band and Theatricals gave regular concerts in the Market Place on Monday evenings (weather permitting); the conductor was Samuel Gee.

In his article in the Leek News of 1935 *The Small Boy in the Market Place,* Mr W. Warrington recalls memories of the old Volunteer Theatricals in the 1880s in which Sergt. Bolstridge took part:

> *"I recollect how his movements so reminded us of him as our Drill Instructor teaching us to 'Right turn, smartly come to attention', etc. And his dialogue was about as intelligible as his words or command. 'As unt' (eyes front) and so on. I remember his entrance (in She Stoops to Conquer) when he came to say farewell to Julia seemed like "Left, right, left, alas Julia! Left, right, left, right, right turn, attention, feet at an angle of 45 degrees. I-come-to-bid-you-a-long-farewell".*

The writer recollects that at their earlier performances professional actresses were engaged for the female roles, one such being Miss Rose Seton, the eminent Shakespearean actress , but later local young ladies took part - Miss Alice Sherratt, Miss Alice Birtles, Miss Tillie Slater, a step-daughter of Mr Travis who lived in the Market Place and whose clocks are now collected by connoisseurs. "Of later performances, I remember Mr Willie Young, Mr Marcus Prince, Mr Edward Challinor, Segt. W. P. Govier and others."

The article goes on to recall that "during the 1890s there were several performances of Old English

THE GRAND THEATRE AND HIPPODROME LEEK.

Proprietors - - - - Messrs. The Leek Theatre Co., Ltd.
Managing Director - - - MR. JAMES BIBBY.

EFFICIENT ORCHESTRA.

General Manager - - - - - MR. JAMES BIBBY.
Stage Manager - - - - MR. H. ROBINSON.
Musical Director - - - MR. H. W. GOLDSTRAW.

Monday, December 13th, 1909,

Formal OPENING at 6-45 p.m. by

JOHN ERNEST INGHAM, Esq.

F.C.I.S., J.P. Chairman of the Leek Urban District Council.
When the Band of the 3rd North Staffordshire Artillery Battalion will be present, by kind permission of Major Challinor.

To be followed by the Opening Performance.

and during the Week.

7 p.m. TWICE NIGHTLY. 9 p.m.

EXPENSIVE ENGAGEMENT OF

THE DUNVILLES

Speciality Comedy Musical Performers. In their latest achievement "Little bits of this and that."

The SISTERS DELMORE

Vocalists, Sand, and Step Dancers.

The TWO LYRICOS Tenor & Soprano Vocalists.

ELLIOTT & ELLIOTT

DUETTISTS AND DANCERS.

Comedies in which the lead was taken by Miss Trissie Allen, and I remember how utterly charming she was as Lady Teazle , in which performance, I think, A. E. Quinn took Sir Peter. In 1894 I saw her as Miss Hardcastle in 'She Stoops to Conquer', and Lieutenant Gimson from the Potteries, a very clever actor, who also used to play with the Old Volunteers, took Tony Lumpkin. If I were asked what was the very best amateur stage setting shown in Leek, I should unhesitatingly say it was in this play. It was designed and carried out by Mr Tom Wardle (another son of Sir Thomas Wardle) and Mr W.R. Kean, the assistant art master at that time. At this performance Mr Langfield Ward (uncle of Mr John Ward) wrote and recited a prologue which impressed me beyond measure".

During the early 1900s a local pantomime was presented each year at the Town Hall, in which the principal parts were taken by Mr Harry Ind, as the dame, and his sister Amy as the principal boy. Later, after the First World War, and into the 1930s, professional companies performed pantomimes at the Grand Theatre.

Live theatre was brought to Leek in Victorian and Edwardian times by a number of travelling shows, known colloquially as the' rag and stick' theatre. Their method was to travel in large waggons which would be assembled together to form an auditorium and stage, with a canvas roof - hence the name. One such company which visited Leek regularly around the turn of the century was Mrs M. C. Sinclair's Victoria Theatre, which claimed as its patron the eminent thespian, Sir Henry Irving. The company usually performed a different play each evening, ranging from traditional Victorian melodramas, which would no doubt stir the emotions of the Leek play-goers, to screaming farces, designed to send the audience home happy. The theatre boasted boxes, stalls, pit and gallery, and must have given a full evening's entertainment, for it commenced at 7.30 pm, and offered half-price seats after 9 o'clock!

Another travelling theatre company was the Bijou Theatre, manageresses Misses Mitford and Bond. This company presented musicals with songs and dances, as well as straight plays.

In 1864 Middleton's Marionettes had a small tent theatre in the Cattle Market. Every night at the conclusion of the performance the manager would address the audience: "Ladies and gentlemen, on behalf of the proprietor, Mr. Middleton, I return you his sincere thanks for the mark of your patronage and approval". He would then go on to announce the following night's production - sometimes a heavy Victorian drama, sometimes a traditional story such as Babes in the Wood, sometimes a song and dance show.

The Leek Literary and Mechanics Institute or the 'Mechanics', to give it its popular name, played a large role in the cultural and educational life of yesterday's town. Founded in 1837, rising, as it were, from the ashes of an older one dating from 1781, it had its home in a substantial building in Russell Street. Educational facilities were almost unknown at the time, and the work done by the 'Mechanics' was of the utmost importance.

The names of some of the men who founded and managed the institution reads like a roll-call of most of the town's prominent citizens at the time. Among those early pioneers were James Alsop JP, Joshua Brough JP, John Brough JP, Dr Ritchie, Sir Thomas Wardle, William Challinor, John Cruso, Rev John Sneyd JP, Joseph Challinor, Richard Place, Rev J. Hankinson, William Sugden, Rev R. Goshawk, W. S. Brough JP, Rev W. P. Bourne, Edwin Brough JP, C.T. Gwynne MA, Rev Carr Smith; M. H. Miller, R. S. Milner, J. G. Beckett, Thomas Shaw, John Robinson JP, Thomas Carr, A. J. Worthington, W. D. Badnall, H. Bermingham, John Ward JP, Robert Farrow, John Sleigh and many others.

Originally lit by candles (there is a bill in 1842 for 'new snuffers'), it later changed to gas. In the early days newspapers were provided only occasionally, and fiction was never in the library. All this changed after 1860, when an Art School was formed.

The study of science and technology was introduced. A Debating Society was established, as well as a Chess Club and musical classes. Regular lectures, concerts and dramatic entertainments were frequently given, and the names of the artistes and lecturers is proof that the highest standards were always set.

The Russell Street building opened in 1862, cost £869, and was designed by William Sugden. The money was raised by donations, life memberships, bazaars and fetes, one such being held at Alton Towers, when local manufacturers closed their mills to allow support. By 1867 the Institute was free from debt, and there was a balance of £40 in the Building Society. There was a warm and well-lit Reading Room with papers and magazines to suit all tastes, a well-stocked library and the Billiards and Games Room was much used and appreciated. The Institute was on a sound basis, and would continue as such until the Nicholson Institute was opened in 1884.

Although it was not designed with stage facilities, the Nicholson Institute has played an important role in the cultural life of Leek since 1884. It was given to the town by Joshua Nicholson, silk manufacturer, and was designed by William and Larner Sugden. It was to house a library, reading room, museum and art gallery, school of art and a meeting room where lectures and musical recitals could be held - a function which it still performs to this day. And it was at the Nicholson Institute that the man who contributed so much to the amateur stage in Leek - Kineton Parkes - worked as curator, librarian and head of the School of Art.

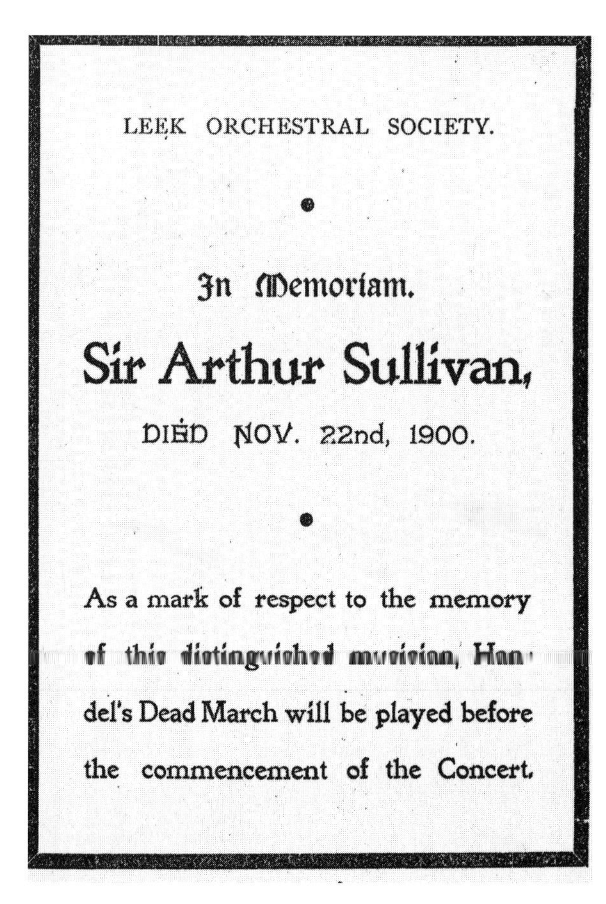

LEEK ORCHESTRAL SOCIETY.

In Memoriam.

Sir Arthur Sullivan,

DIED NOV. 22nd, 1900.

As a mark of respect to the memory of this distinguished musician, Handel's Dead March will be played before the commencement of the Concert.

BON MARCHE, For Ladies' & Children's MILLINERY, Etc.

Established 1843. Stanley Street, Leek.
KINSEY (Late HARROD,) DEALER IN PLAIN & FANCY BASKETS,
Glass, China, Earthenware, Bohemian Glass Vases, and Fancy Goods.
TEA SETS A SPECIALITY.

14, Talbot Street,
JOHN HAMBLETON,
BOOT & SHOE MAKER.
Repairs neatly and promptly executed.
Good Workmanship Guaranteed.
All kinds of Ladies' and Gents' Boots and Shoes in stock.

9, SHEEP MARKET, LEEK.
T. NEWELL,
Family Grocer & Provision Merchant.
A choice selection of First-class Provisions.

Alliance Buildings, Derby St., Leek.
J. S. BURTON,
Pork & General BUTCHER,
Only Best Quality English Meat kept.
Pickled Tongues. Home-rendered Lard.
Corned or Spiced Beef to order.

ST. EDWARD STREET, LEEK.
Branch :—RUDYARD. (Market Place on Saturday).
MATTHEW KNOWLES, High-class Pork & General Butcher.
Home-made Sausage and Black Puddings.

Try **A. E. Duddington,** For Good Value in
CROCERIES, FRUITS & CONFECTIONERY.
GLADSTONE STREET CORNER, near Theatre.

29, St. Edward Street, (opposite Post Office.)
R. & A. Thomas, MILLINERS AND FANCY DRAPERS.
Gloves, Hosiery, Fancy Neckwear, Laces, Haberdashery, &c.

LEEK UNITED
PERMANENT BENEFIT
BUILDING SOCIETY.
Established 1863.

INVESTORS.—A safe Three and a half per cent. Investment free from deduction of Income Tax.

WITHDRAWALS PAID ON SHORT NOTICE.

BORROWERS.—Advances promptly made on approved securities at low rates of Interest.

Reserve Fund £16,400. Annual Income £50,000.

Prospectuses and full Particulars (Free) from Messrs. HACKER & ALLEN, Solicitors, Leek; or the

Offices :—43, St. EDWARD STREET, LEEK.
William Walley, Secretary.

BON MARCHE for all the Latest Styles in BLOUSES.

The Grand Theatre and Hippodrome presented many traditional music hall shows.
This elaborate programme was printed by the local firm of David Morris and Co.
It illustrates the lavish style which was the hallmark of this printer,
reminiscent of the Pre-Raphaelite designs associated with William Morris.
The splendid selection of advertisements include many well-known Leek traders.

Blue Ball Inn. Wines and Spirits.

H. ELLIS, 5, BALL HAYE STREET.
HIGH-CLASS BOOT REPAIRS.
Gents.' from 2/9; Ladies' from 1/9; Hand-sewn a Speciality.

NAG'S HEAD, Mill Street,
Proprietor: H. J. Jacobs.
MARSTON'S BEERS ONLY.
Wines & spirits of the best quality. ... Cigars.
Good stabling. FREE & EASY EVERY SATURDAY.

J. PHILLIPS.
Don't forget our address when requiring IRONMONGERY
'Phone 6Y.
12 & 14, Stockwell St., Leek

Established 1883.
KNIGHT BROS.
Clothiers, Outfitters & Ladies' Tailors,
West Street, LEEK

After visiting the Theatre, call and inspect
J. BRINDLEY BAILEY'S
Choice selection of
MANTLES, COSTUMES, COATS, BLOUSES, ETC.,
35, Derby St. & Market St., LEEK

There's no trouble with CYCLES bought at **BODE'S,** Agent for
RUDGE WHITWORTH, SINGER'S, ROBIN HOOD & CHASE CYCLES.
REPAIRS. ACCESSORIES. GRAMAPHONES AND RECORDS.
39-49, ASHBOURNE ROAD.

For High-class MEAT at Reasonable Prices try
RIGBY & Co., Butcher
HIGH STREET,
Next to Theatre. LEEK.

17, Market St., next to the Town Hall, Leek.
A. F. PORTER,
Ladies' Costumier & Gents' Tailor.
Costumes, Habits, suits.
Morning Orders Executed Promptly.

BLACK'S HEAD HOTEL
Now under New Management. AND STABLE YARD, EVERYTHING of the BEST QUALITY.
Teas and Refreshments provided at reasonable prices. PRO., HENRY NICHOLLS.

33, Broad Street, LEEK.
G. HAMBLETON, Wholesale and Retail
TOBACCO & CIGAR MERCHANT.
British, Havana, Mexican & Manilla Cigars.

THOS. GRACE,
Telephone 56. BUILDER, CONTRACTOR, JOINER, and BUILDER'S MERCHANT,
Broad Street, LEEK

DOES IT EVER OCCUR TO YOU
to wonder why you wear an ordinary looking shirt, Cap, or Tie, when something distinctive in style and Quality costs you no more at
WARRINGTON'S, DERBY ST.

COG & PARTRIDGE, DERBY STREET
Proprietor: T. BATEMAN.
SALT'S celebrated ALES & STOUTS.
Wines and spirits of the Finest Quality.
ACCOMMODATION FOR CYCLISTS.

Cash & Co., LEEK
Specialists in all kinds of FOOTWEAR
PERCY CASH, Manager.

J. Miller & Sons, LADIES' & GENTS' TAILORS
General Outfitters,
Telephone No. 1073. Piccadilly, HANLEY.

DAVID MORRIS & CO., LTD., FOR ALL CLASSES OF
PRINTING & ACCOUNT BOOKS,
"EAGLE" Printing Works, London Street. LEEK.

IN GALLON JARS 1/4.

S. HAMBLETON & SON,
Broad Street, LEEK.
THE NORTH STAFFORDSHIRE FURNISHING WAREHOUSE,
Reliable Furniture at competitive Prices

ASK FOR Ross Watson & Co's **OLD GAUL,**
THE FINEST BLEND OF SCOTCH WHISKEY.
Agents G. & J. MUNRO & Co. Limited, Leek.

The Grand Theatre & Hippodrome,
LEEK.

Proprietors	Messrs. The Leek Theatre Co., Ltd.
Managing Director	James Bibby.
Stage Manager	H. Robinson.
Musical Conductor	H. W. Goldstraw.

PROGRAMME.

1.—OVERTURE ... ... Orchestra

2.—PHIL HERMAN, Vocal Comedian, In Song and Story.

3.—M'DLLE ROSELTHA, International Skipping Rope Dancer and Quick Change Artiste.

4.—MISS MARIE D'ALCOURT, Illustrated Songs.

5.—BILLY HURST & GEORGE FREDERICKS, In their Speciality Comedy Act, entitled:— "THE MAN IN CHARGE."

6.—The SISTERS DELMORE, Vocalists, Sand and Step Dancers.

7.—The TWO LYRICOS, In Musical Comedy Act, "THE HIGHWAYMAN."

8.—The SPRING ELLERS, Trick Barrel Jumpers.

9.—Mr. JOHN WHEELAN, Tenor Vocalist.

10.—The DUNVILLES, Speciality, Comedy, Musical Performers.

11.—GRAND BIOSCOPE PICTURES.

MATINEE, SATURDAY AFTERNOON, Doors Open 2, Commence 2-30,
SPECIAL PRICES FOR SCHOOL CHILDREN.

Children in arms not admitted.
The Management reserve the right to refuse admission to any person.
No seats guaranteed unless booked. No Money returned.

Hall & Co., Caterers, Victoria Cafe & Commercial Hotel
St. Edward Street, LEEK.

WESTWOOD MANOR COAL & IRON CO., LTD.,
Depot: STRANGEMAN STREET (back of Post Office),
BEST HOUSE COAL, COBBLES, SLACK AT THE DEPOT OR DELIVERED.
Telephone:—83. Leek.

REUNINGER, PORK BUTCHER and CONFECTIONER, 26 & 27, MARKET PLACE, LEEK.

The ELECTRIC LIGHTING THROUGHOUT
this Theatre was carried out by
JOHN RICHARDS,
ELECTRICAL ENGINEER,
60, St. EDWARD STREET,
LEEK, Staffs.

THE
Leek & Moorlands Building Society,
IS THE LARGEST BUILDING SOCIETY IN STAFFORDSHIRE.
Having an Annual income of about £150,000, and a Reserve Fund of over £50,000.
Total Receipts to the end of 1908 £3,516,000.
To same date Advanced on Mortgage £1,700,000.
Bonuses allotted to its Members exceed £51,000.
To Investors.—Good Security and Interest. Sums from 1/- upwards received at any time.
Apply for Prospectus and further information to
Mr. FRANCIS BILLING, Secretary.
Offices:—15, Stockwell Street, Leek.

THE WHITE LION, ASHBOURNE ROAD, LEEK.
Proprietor: JOHN OWEN.
Marston's, Thompson, & Evershed's celebrated Burton Ales and Stout in fine condition.
Wines, Spirits and Cigars of the finest quality.
OLD AND NEW FRIENDS WELCOME.

38, St. EDWARD STREET, LEEK
DEPOT FOR HIGH-CLASS GROCERIES AND ITALIAN AND FRENCH WAREHOUSE GOODS.
A large assortment of Rowntree's and Cadbury's CHOCOLATES, FANCY BOXES, etc.
E. Riley (Late Bastin)

WADDINGTONS'
FOR HIGH CLASS PIANOS AT LOWEST PRICES
HIGH-CLASS ENGLISH PIANOS.
LOW PRICES. EASY PAYMENTS. 25 YEARS' WARRANTY.
From Factory to Public direct.
S. TAYLOR,
37, DERBY STREET, LEEK.

H. EDDOWES has always a choice selection of FASHIONABLE DRESS GOODS, LADIES' COATS, COSTUMES, DRESS SKIRTS, &c.
The old established shop for Horrockses Calicoes, Flannelettes, and all reliable Drapery Goods.
5 & 7, Sheep Market, Leek.

JOHN C. FOGG, PRINTER,
LITHOGRAPHER, PUBLISHER, STATIONER.
MACHIER HOUSE, DERBY STREET, LEEK, Staffs.

EDWIN PHILLIPS,
16 & 18, Stockwell Street, Leek.
Plumber's Work carefully carried out on sanitary Principles.
HOUSE DECORATION.

Salter & Salter, (1900) Ltd.,
Makers of RELIABLE FOOTWEAR,
32, St. EDWARD STREET.

ALES, WINES AND SPIRITS OF THE BEST QUALITY.
Catering in all its Branches.
STATION HOTEL RUDYARD, Proprietor: C. W. CLAYTON.
L. WHITTLES & SON.

The programme of live acts is followed by "grand bioscope pictures" - a hint of the coming age of cinema.

Leek gets its own purpose-built theatre for live performances, the Grand Theatre and Hippodrome in High Street in 1909.

Leek Amateur Operatic Society's production of 'HMS Pinafore', November 1895:
Back: J G Beckett, M Prince, E Challinor, V Prince, S Prince
Second: Mrs Kineton Parkes, Miss Ada Allday, Kineton Parkes, W E Brindley
Front: Miss Florence Parkes, Miss Lexy Munro.

17 F. S. FELTHOUSE 17

The increasing popularity of moving pictures led to the theatre becoming a cinema with only occasional live shows. The New Grand is seen here with its typical 1930s facade, in this fine view, looking down High Street from Sheepmarket.

The following selection of programmes of the Leek Amateur Musical Society illustrates the wide range of musical and choral items tackled

LEEK AMATEUR MUSICAL SOCIETY.

FIRST CONCERT,

IN THE TEMPERANCE HALL, UNION STREET, MAY 8, 1866.

Solo Flute, Rev. Dr. Armstrong. Solo Pianoforte, Rev. C. A. Barker. Solo Violin, Mr. J. F. Cadman.

Vocalists, The Leek Amateur Musical Society. Accompanist, Miss Andrew. Conductor, Mr. Powell.

PROGRAMME AND BOOK OF WORDS.

See the Chariot.

CHORAL GLEE .... *W. Horsley.*

SEE the chariot at hand, here, of love,
Wherein my lady rideth!
Each that draws is a swan or a dove,
And well the car love guideth.
As she goes all hearts do duty
Unto her beauty,
And, enamour'd, do wish, so they might
But enjoy such a sight,
That they still were to run by her side,
Thro' swords, thro' seas, whither she would ride.

Have you seen but the bright lily grow,
Before rude hands have touch'd it?
Ha' you mark'd but the fall o' the snow,
Before the soil had smutch'd it?
Ha' you felt the wool o' the beaver?
Or swan's-down ever?
Or have smelt o' the bud o' the briar!
Or the nard in the fire?
Or have tasted the bag o' the bee?
O, so white, so soft is she!

Ben Jonson.

Violin Solo.

AIR No. 7, with variations..... *De Beriot.*
MR. CADMAN.

Since first I saw your face.

MADRIGAL.................. *Ford*, 1620.

SINCE first I saw your face, I resolved
To honour and renown you;
If now I be disdain'd
I wish my heart had never known you:
What I that lov'd,
And you that liked,
Shall we begin to wrangle?
No, no, no! my heart is fast,
And cannot disentangle.

The sun, whose beams most glorious are,
Rejecteth no beholder,
And your sweet beauty, past compare,
Made my poor eyes the bolder:
Where beauty moves,
And wit delights,
And signs of kindness bind me,
There, O there! where'er I go,
I leave my heart behind me.

Martin, the Man at Arms.

SONG .... *Loder.*

MARTIN, the man at arms, stalwart and strong,
Keeps watch on the turret high,
Now humming the snatch of a rude bower song,
Gazing now on the star-lit sky;
He looks to windward; he looks o'er the lea;
All around is calm and still,
Save the kine in the fold, lowing lazily,—
And the tinkle of the rill,
While full and low floats down below
The sentinel's deep "Good night!"

He halts and he harkens! a quick, light step
Is heard on the turret stair;
What flutters so white in the clear star-light?
'Tis the veil of a damsel fair:
"Who goes there? Lady fair—so please you, declare,
Why here at this lonely hour?"
Oh! its only Nannette, the pretty coquette
That waits in my lady's bow'r.
Speak low, speak low, if you'd not have her go
Before you can say "Good night."

He has shorten'd his stride, and she trips by his side,
With the starry sky above,
And Martin once more tells o'er and o'er
The tale of his long tried love:
Grave, sly, and demure, she listens be sure,
And then looks him through with a glance,
But all he can get from the cruel coquette
Is, "Man at Arms, shoulder your lance!"
Then its ah! and its oh! there now, do let me go,
For my mistress is calling—"Good night."

W. H. Bellamy.

The first concert was held on May 8th 1866.
The comprehensive programme printed the words in full of all the works performed.

Rules of the Leek Amateur Musical Society.

OFFICERS FOR THE YEAR 1866.

THE REV. B. PIDCOCK, PRESIDENT.

MRS. ALSOP, TREASURER. | MISS A. MILNER, SECRETARY.

MR. Wm. DISHLEY, LIBRARIAN.

CONDUCTOR, - - - - - MR. J. W. POWELL.

COMMITTEE.

Miss Bamford.	Miss A. Nixon.	Miss Smith.
Mr. Beckett.	Mr. Jos. Johnson.	Mr. Ritchie.

VOCAL MEMBERS.

Mr. Alcock.	Mr. Bowers.	The Rev. J. Hankinson.	Miss A. Nixon.
Mrs. Alsop.	Miss Bowers.	Miss Johnson.	Mr. Richmond.
Miss Andrew.	Miss Chesterton.	Miss E. Johnson.	Mr. Ritchie.
Miss Bamford.	Mr. E. L. Cooper.	Mr. Jos. Johnson	Mr. H. Simpson.
Miss S. Bamford	Miss Critchlow.	Mr. S. Johnson	Miss Smith
Miss E. Bamford.	Mr. Wm. Dishley.	Miss Lightfoot.	Miss A. Smith.
Miss F. Bamford.	Mrs. Jno. Hall.	Miss A. Milner.	Mr. C. Vigrass.
Mr. Beckett.	Miss S. Hammersley.	Miss K. Nall.	Miss Woolliscroft.
	Miss A. Hammersley.	Miss Nixon.	

HONORARY MEMBERS.

Mr. Alsop.	Miss Clowes.	Dr. Goodman.	Miss Van Tuyl.
Mrs. Challinor	Mrs. Cruso.	Mrs. Henry Johnson.	Mr. T. Wardle.
Mrs. Wm. Challinor.	Mrs. Ellis.	Mrs. Milner.	Mr. G. Wardle.
Mrs. J. Challinor.	Mrs. Fynney.	Mrs. Ritchie.	

1. That this Society be called "THE LEEK AMATEUR MUSICAL SOCIETY," and consist of Vocal and Honorary Members.

2. That the annual subscription of Vocal Members be from 5s. to 20s., each 5s. entitling the member to one Ticket for the Concerts. The subscription of Honorary Members to be 20s. per annum, for which four Tickets for the Concerts will be given. All subscriptions to be paid in advance.

3. That the business of the Society be managed by a Committee, to be elected at the Annual Meeting from both classes of members, and to consist of President, Treasurer, Secretary, Librarian, and six others—five to be a quorum.

4. That the Annual Meeting be held as near to the first of October as convenient.

5. That candidates for membership be proposed and seconded by members in their respective handwriting, such proposition to be sent to the Secretary two days previous to the weekly meeting. The election to be by ballot and three black balls to exclude.

6. Private Concerts to be given—not less than two in each year. The Committee to select the music for weekly practice or public performance, and the sole direction to rest with the Conductor. No member to take part in any general performance without having attended a sufficient number of weekly practices.

7. Any alteration of, or addition to general rules, to be made at an annual or special general meeting.

8. That only Visitors, non-residents in the town be allowed to come to the practices.

MEETINGS FOR WEEKLY PRACTICE ARE HELD ON SATURDAY EVENINGS AT 6.30.

The officers and members of the choir in 1866 are listed here.
The society was supported by many of Leek's prominent citizens and the rules suggest that the Society was run on sound principles.

LEEK AMATEUR MUSICAL SOCIETY.

IN THE

TEMPERANCE HALL, LEEK,

ON

TUESDAY, THE 16TH DAY OF DECEMBER, 1873.

ORCHESTRA:

1st Violin: Mr. F. Vetter, of Manchester.
2nd Violin: Mr. F. P. Walwyn. Viola: Mr. G. A. Smith.
Violoncello: Mr. Tomlinson. Double Bass: Mr. Cundiff.
Flute: Mr. Mee. Cornet: Sergt. Kelly, of Macclesfield.
Drums: Mr. Mc'All. Harmonium: Mr. Mountford, of Silverdale.
Conductor: Mr. Powell.

THE MESSIAH is a great Christian *Epos*, or descriptive poem—for music is poetry—having for its subject Man's Redemption; and it belongs to the same class of art as the *Paradise Lost* of Milton. But while Milton's epic only comprehended a part of that vast theme which required the *Paradise Regained* to complete his design, Handel has here placed before us, in the words of the inspired writers themselves, and in music which adds depth, solemnity, and power, even to the language of inspiration, the whole of that ineffable scheme of goodness and mercy to which mankind must ever look for consolation and hope. The poem is divided into three parts. The first part contains the promise of the Saviour, as given in the words of Isaiah and the other Prophets of the Old Testament; the announcement of His advent to the "Shepherds in the fields, keeping watch over their flocks by night;" and a picture of the blessings attending His mission. The second part paints His passion, death, and glorious resurrection; then describes the spread of His holy word into all lands, notwithstanding the rage of the heathen; and closes with the divine strain of rejoicing, the matchless "Hallelujah!" The third part relates to the second coming of Christ, the resurrection of the dead, and the final accomplishment of the Redeemer's mission. It is an ascertained fact, incredible as it may seem, that this greatest of all existing Oratorios was begun and completed, by one gigantic effort, within the space of two-and-twenty days. It was composed in 1741.

W. CLEMESHA, STEAM PRINTER, STANLEY STREET, LEEK.

Oratorios such as Handel's Messiah were often performed with great enthusiasm before large audiences.

LEEK

AMATEUR MUSICAL SOCIETY.

PRESIDENT—REV. B. PIDCOCK, B.A. TREASURER—MRS. CRUSO.
SECRETARY—MR. E. GUBBINS.
COMMITTEE—
MRS. HOWARD, MISS E. BAMFORD, MR. BECKETT, MR. LOCKETT,
MISS A. H. MILNER, MISS SMITH, MR. DISHLEY, MR. RITCHIE,
CONDUCTOR—MR. POWELL.

THE

FOURTEENTH CONCERT

WILL BE GIVEN ON

TUESDAY EVENING, DEC. 5th, 1871,

IN THE

TEMPERANCE HALL, LEEK,

WHEN THE PROGRAMME WILL COMPRISE—

The Market Chorus from "Masaniello," the Anvil Chorus from "Il Trobatore," Jackson's Glee, "The Sisters of the Sea," The Prayer from "Mose in Egitto," by Rossini, Pinsuti's Serenade "In this Hour of Softened Splendour," Bishop's Glee "Spirits Advance," and

SOLOS AND DUETS,

BY MRS. ALSOP, MISS SMITH, REV. F. W. PIERCY, AND MR. BECKETT.

DOORS OPEN AT HALF-PAST SEVEN, CONCERT TO COMMENCE AT EIGHT.
A Cloak Room and attendance provided.

BOOKS OF WORDS CAN BE OBTAINED IN THE HALL.

CARRIAGES MAY BE ORDERED FOR TEN O'CLOCK.

ADMISSION TO THE GALLERY: Three Front Rows, One Shilling; Back Seats, Sixpence.
Tickets sold by Mr. Clemesha, Mr. Rayner, and the Vocal Members.
The Body of the Hall is reserved for the holders of Subscribers' Tickets.

W. CLEMESHA, PRINTER, LEEK.

Some challenging works were included in the 1871 concert. The concerts were originally performed in the old Temperance Hall, Union Street.

Leek
Amateur Musical Society's
EIGHTY SEVENTH CONCERT
GIVEN IN THE
TOWN HALL ON MONDAY DECEMBER 13th, 1897.

HAYDN'S
"CREATION"
(PARTS I & II)

STANFORD'S
"REVENGE"

PRINCIPALS.

Mrs. GLOVER-EATON,
Gloucester and Worcester Festivals.

Mr. ALBERT MONAGHAN,
Principal Tenor, York Minster.

Mr. JOHN RIDDING,
Turner's Opera Co. and Carl Rosa Opera Co.

ORCHESTRA.

First Violins.
Mr. V. V. Akeroyd (Liverpool)
Miss Mabel Smith
Mr. T. Knight
Mr. W. Hill
Mr. V. Prince
Mr. G. Sheldon
Mr. J. Rider
Mr. F. Wood

Second Violins.
Mr. H. Sedgwick (Manchester)
Mrs. J. Gwynne
Mr. J. Dishley
Mr. J. Garner
Mr. J. Goldstraw
Miss Ward
Mr. W. Warrington

Violas.
Mr. J. Holme (Manchester)
Mr. F. Walwyn
Mr. E. Pickford

Violoncellos.
Mr. F. G. Collinson (Liverpool)
Dr. Johnson
Mr. F. Johnson

Contra Bass.
Mr. G. Yates (Manchester)
Mr. W. Hall

Flutes.
Mr. J. Hambleton
Mr. J. Hill

Oboe.
Mr. S. Gwynne
Mr. G. Brooks

Clarinets.
Mr. F. Norton (Manchester)
Mr. G. Rider

Bassoons.
Mr. F. Foulds (Manchester)
Mr. A. Haslam (Southport)

Horns.
Mr. W. M. Riley Manchester
Mr. A. Gaggs (Manchester)

Trumpets.
Mr. B. Holtham
Mr. G. Goodwin

Trombone.
Mr. A. Bill

Tympani.
Mr. H. Moorhouse.

Side Drum.
Mr. Bennett

Bass Drum.
Mr. Locksley

Piano.
Mr. W. H. Eaton.

Librarian.
Mr. F. Billing.

CONDUCTOR: MR. JAMES GWYNNE.

TOWN HALL, LEEK.

The Amateur Musical Society
WILL GIVE THEIR 107th CONCERT
On THURSDAY, DECEMBER 19th, 1907.

Mendelssohn's Oratorio.
"ELIJAH."

PRINCIPALS:
MISS GERTRUDE BLOOMFIELD,
SOPRANO.
MISS GRAINGER KERR,
CONTRALTO.
MR. WEBSTER MILLAR,
TENOR.
MR. HERBERT PARKER,
BASS.

THE LEEK ORCHESTRAL SOCIETY,
ASSISTED BY MEMBERS OF THE NORTH STAFFS. ORCHESTRA.

Conductor - - - - - - Mr. JOHN COPE.

DOORS OPEN 7. CONCERT 7-30. CARRIAGES 10-15.

CLOAK ROOM AND ATTENDANCE PROVIDED.

All communications, etc., to be addressed to the Hon. Sec.
MR. J. B. COPE, 20, SHOOBRIDGE STREET.

Leek Amateur Musical Society.

Programme & Book of Words

OF THE

FIFTIETH CONCERT

ON

Monday, Dec. 18th, 1882.

On this occasion the Society will be assisted by

Mrs. HOLT, OF SHEFFIELD, SOPRANO

Mr. MACDONALD, OF YORK MINSTER, TENOR

And by the following Orchestra,

First Violins ... MR. F. BROWN, Manchester.
" S. BENN, "
" MACDONALD, Congleton.
Second Violins... MR. G. SOURBUTTS, Manchester.
" P. A. RAYNER, JUNR., Leek.
Violas ....MR. H. MILLER, Manchester.
" F. P. WALWYN, Leek.
Violoncellos ... ..MR. J. WALTON, Manchester.
" HARVEY, Leek.
Double Bass......MR. J. CROXALL, Manchester.
Flute ....DR. MOSS, Congleton.
Clarionette.........MR. WADSWORTH, Manchester.
Oboe ....MR. W. COULTON, Manchester.

CONDUCTOR :—MR. SAMUEL GEE, R. A. MUS.

SAM RIDER, PRINTER, DERBY STREET, LEEK.

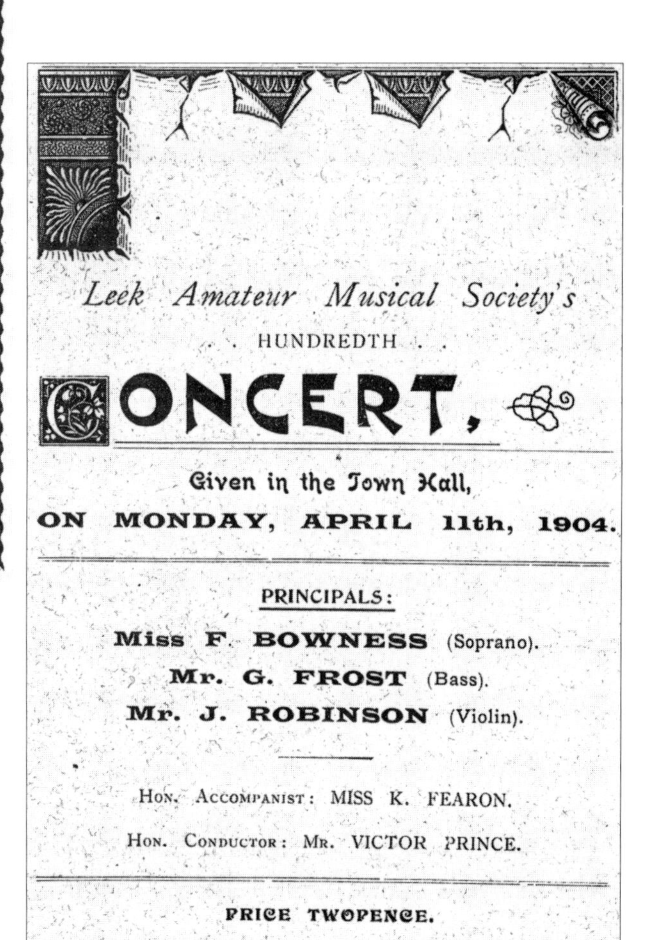

Leek Amateur Musical Society's

HUNDREDTH

CONCERT,

Given in the Town Hall,

ON MONDAY, APRIL 11th, 1904.

PRINCIPALS:

Miss F. BOWNESS (Soprano).
Mr. G. FROST (Bass).
Mr. J. ROBINSON (Violin).

HON. ACCOMPANIST: MISS K. FEARON.

HON. CONDUCTOR: MR. VICTOR PRINCE.

PRICE TWOPENCE.

JOHN C. FOGG, PRINTER, DERBY STREET, LEEK.

THE GRAND THEATRE, LEEK.
Repertoire—
Trial by Jury.
H.M.S. Pinafore.
Pirates of Penzance.
Iolanthe.
Yeomen of the Guard.
THREE NIGHTS ONLY.
Thursday, Mar. 31, Friday and
Saturday, April 1st & 2nd, 1910.
THE
Leek Amateur Opera Society
PERFORMANCES OF
Gilbert & Sullivan's Original Æsthetic Opera,
PATIENCE;
Or, Bunthorne's Bride,
by permission of Mrs. D'Oyly Carte, of the Savoy Theatre, London.
UNDER THE PATRONAGE OF
HER GRACE THE DUCHESS OF SUTHERLAND.
SPECIAL SCENERY AND COSTUMES.
PRINCIPALS, CHORUS, & BAND OF SIXTY PERFORMERS.
Orchestra:—
The LEEK AMATEUR ORCHESTRAL SOCIETY:
and The GRAND THEATRE BAND.
Doors open at 7-30. Performance at 8. Carriages at 10-30.
THE MOORLANDS PRESS, LEEK.

Special costumes were hired from London for this 1910 production of 'Patience'. When the society performed the opera in 1921 the costumes were dyed locally by Mr R Clowes. Appropiately the designs were inspired by the Pre-Raphaelite tradition and the stage decorations were from designs by the Leek Embroidery Society, echoing Leek's William Morris connection.

LEEK AMATEUR OPERA SOCIETY.

CAST.

Colonel Calverley, the 35th Dragoon Guards	Mr. George White
Major Murgatroyd, " " "	Mr. W. E. Brindley
Lieutenant, the Duke of Dunstable "	Mr. Hy. Farrington
Reginald Bunthorne, a Fleshy Poet	Mr. Kineton Parkes
Archibald Grosvenor, an Idyllic Poet	Mr. Charles Till
Mr. Bunthorne's Solicitor	Mr. J. E. Lillie-Mitchell
The Lady Angela (Rapturous Maidens)	Miss Florrie Wright
The Lady Saphir (Rapturous Maidens)	Miss Phyllis Bilton
The Lady Ella (Rapturous Maidens)	Miss Alice Wood
The Lady Jane (Rapturous Maidens)	Miss Lewin MacWhirter
Patience, a Dairy Maid	Mrs. Parkes Darby

CHORUS OF RAPTUROUS MAIDENS.

Mesdames and Mdlles.: Nan. Audley, Nellie Bamford, Mary Bilton, Annie Bowyer, Doris Cartlidge, Edith Eaton, Kate Eaton, Alice Goodwin, Dorothy Gwynne, Ethelwyn Gwynne, Rosie Heath, Dorothy Jackman, Tina Powner, Ada Reynolds, Emily Rowley and Dolly White.

CHORUS OF OFFICERS OF DRAGOON GUARDS.

Messieurs: W. E. Beacham, Geo. Cartlidge, Wm. Creighton, Shirley Dix, Percy Eaton, Wm. E. Gwynne, R. Hunter, Fred Keates, H. R. King, Max Parkes, Geo. Pickford, Henry Robinson, Wm. Slater, Herbert Sumerling, Dudley Willmer.

ACT 1. SCENE—Exterior of Castle Bunthorne.

ACT 2. SCENE—A Glade.

* * *

LIST OF SUBSCRIBERS.

Mr. Wm. Allen
Mr. R. Audley
Mr. Harold Blades
Mrs. Bockett
Mr. G. Bowyer
Mr. Harry Carding
Mr. Geo. Cartlidge
Mr. John Cartwright
Mrs. Ed. Challinor
Mr. W. E. Challinor
Mrs. Evershed
Mr. Harold Goodwin
Mr. Harold Henshaw
Dr. J. M. Johnson
Mr. H. J. Johnson
Mr. A. Meakin
Mr. A. H. Moore
Mr. A. F. Nicholson
General Phillips
Mr. Marcus Prince
Mrs. Ronald Rider
Mr. Thos. Robinson
Mr. Thos. Shaw
Mr. John Shorter
Mr. Sidney Stannard
Mr. Jas. Swindells
Mr. Joseph Tatton
Mr. Anthony Ward
Mrs. A. H. Wardle
Mr. G. C. Wardle
Mr. Charles Watson
Mr. W. S. Watson
Mrs. Whittles

Leek Amateur Opera Society.

PATRONESS:

HER GRACE THE DUCHESS OF SUTHERLAND.

PRESIDENT:

Dr J. M. JOHNSON.

TREASURER:

Mr. C. S. Anderson, Parr's Bank.

CHAIRMAN OF COMMITTEE:

Mr. W. Warrington.

COMMITTEE:

Mr. F. J. Bermingham
Mr. W. E. Brindley
Mr. F. Carding
Mr. N. Carr
Mr. W. Creighton
Mr. P. J. Eaton
Mr. F. Goldstraw
Mr. H. Henshaw
Mr. D. Willmer
Mr. R. Hunter
Mr. H. R. King
Mr. G. Pickford
Mr. M. Prince

Conductor: Mr. Wm. H. Eaton.

Accompanist: Mr. Tom Forrester

Stage Managers: Mr. George White, Mr. Kineton Parkes.

Honorary Secretaries: Mr. Harold Goodwin, Mr. Kineton Parkes.

Wardrobe Keepers: Mr. W. Norman Carr, Miss Marion Carr.

Prompters: Mr. Ernest Darby, Mus. Bac., Mr. W. A. Furmston.

In charge of Seating:

Mr. Wilfred H. H. Eaton, assisted by Messrs. C. S. Anderson, F. J. Bermingham, Fred Carding, Frank Goodwin, Harold Goodwin, Harold Henshaw, Norman Lewis, Dr. MacKinnon, Jack Tatton, Horace Thompson, Sidney Stannard, and G. T. Stevenson.

Orchestra:

Violins: Messrs. W. Goldstraw, F. Wood, F. Knight, H. Knight, J. Newall, — Powner, V. Prince, J. Robinson. *Violas:* J. Dishley and H. Brough. *Violoncellos:* Dr. Johnson and F. Mountford. *Contra Bass:* A. Knight. *Flute:* G. Goldstraw, *Oboe:* S. Gwynne. *Clarinets:* A. Rider, J. Rider. *Bassoon:* E. G. H. Childe. *Cornet:* C. Goodwin *Trombone:* A. Bill. *Tympani, etc.:* H. Moorhouse.

* * *

Special Costumes by Messrs. B. J. Simmons, Covent Garden, London.
The Ladies' Sporting Jerseys in Act II. by Mr. W. Warrington, of Derby St., Leek.
The Hats by Mesdames Stubbs & Hardy, of St. Edward Street, Leek.

William Warrington, an outfitter by trade, was a great influence on the amateur entertainments of the day.

Rudyard Reservoir, from an old print.

The construction of Rudyard Lake was authorised in 1797 to provide the Trent and Mersey Canal Company with extra water needed for the Leek branch of the Caldon Canal. It took three years to build. It soon established itself for recreation and a century later the dam head promenade featured a skating rink, dancing and other amusements.

CHAPTER SEVEN
An Edwardian Playground

JOHN LOCKWOOD KIPLING was born in 1837, the son of a Methodist minister in Yorkshire. As a youth he travelled to London in 1851 to visit the Great Exhibition. This clearly influenced his artistic talents and ambitions; eight years later he was in Burslem, working as a pottery-designer for Pinder, Bourne and Co.

For such an educated and artistic young man the industrial Potteries in the mid-nineteenth century might well have been barren ground, were it not for the influence of the Methodist minister in Burslem, Rev Frederick Macdonald, who put young John Lockwood Kipling in touch with a group of others with similar artistic and intellectual tastes and qualities. It was through his association with this Burslem Pre-Raphaelite group that John Kipling was invited by his employer's daughters, the Misses Pinder, to a picnic party at Rudyard Lake in the early summer of 1863. Also in the party were Rev Frederick Macdonald and his sister Alice.

Two years later John Lockwood Kipling married Alice Macdonald in London, on 18 March 1865. Immediately after the wedding ceremony, the Kiplings sailed for India, where John was to take up an appointment as head of a new Art School in Bombay. Their first child was born at Bombay on 30 December 1865 and was christened Joseph (after his grandfather) and Rudyard (in recognition of the place where his parents first met each other).

Thus, the name of this little North Staffordshire village was perpetuated for all time in the annals of English literature, for Rudyard Kipling was destined to become one of the foremost writers and poets of the later Victorian years, eventually to be awarded the Nobel Prize for Literature.

Guests at the Pinders' picnic party could well have travelled from the Potteries to Rudyard by train, for this is what many people did in those days, with Rudyard Lake providing a fashionable venue for a day out. The site of the lake, Rudyard Gorge, was formed in the Ice Age, providing an ideal natural location for the lake, which is, of course, man-made.

It was authorised by Act of Parliament in 1797 as a reservoir to feed the Caldon Canal when the Leek branch was being cut, an additional supply of water being urgently required to relieve problems on the main line, particularly in times of drought. The lake was thus created in a splendid scenic setting, with wooded banks on either side.

The coming of the railway in 1849 opened up Rudyard to the visitor, and in due course visitors flocked in by the train-load. In its heyday Rudyard was a busy station, reflecting the great popularity of the village as a tourist attraction in those bygone days. It employed a large staff, considering its rural setting, and had extended platforms to cope with the long excursion trains bringing hundreds of visitors at weekends and holidays. Rail traffic through Rudyard doubled between 1904 and 1906, as tourists and day trippers came from far afield. The North Staffordshire Railway Company did much to promote the attractions to the potential visitor. The company's printed guides waxed lyrical about the advantages of the area, one such stating:

'RUDYARD LAKE - The Windermere of the Midlands. Fishing, Boating, Bathing, Golf. Arrangements can be made for camping-out in delightfully wooded, sheltered nooks on the borders of the Lake.'

Another, referring to the lake, stated:

'It is a splendid sheet of water and the number of pleasure boats which visitors can obtain at

moderate charges has been increased of late; there are also two motor launches. The Lake has also been stocked with over 30,000 fish.'

A golf course was operated by the railway company, situated at the head of the lake, in a splendid setting with fine open views. Originally with nine holes, it was doubled to 18 holes in 1910, during the peak years of Rudyard's prosperity as a tourist centre. In 1908 tickets at two shillings per day could be obtained from the stationmaster or the professional in charge of the course. Visitors wishing to use the golf course could travel by one of the lake steamers, or by train, alighting at Rudyard Lake Station (at the head of the Lake) opened in 1905 and renamed Cliffe Park Halt in 1936. Cliffe Park Hall, a splendid, solidly-built, castellated house built about 1830, served as the golf house for the railway company's golf course. It later became a youth hostel.

The 1908 guide, referring to the golf course, goes on to state:

'The Links have been favourably reported on by professionals, and a comfortable pavilion for the use of members of the Club is in full working order. The terms of membership of the Rudyard Lake Golf Club are: Gentlemen: Entrance fee One Guinea; Annual subscription One Guinea. Ladies: Entrance fee 10/6; Annual subscription 10/6.'

The lake itself, of course, has always been the central attraction at Rudyard, and there is a long tradition of water-based activities such as boating, sailing and fishing. The lake is over two miles in length and up to a quarter of a mile wide.

Captain Webb, famous as the first person to swim the English Channel, visited Rudyard on Monday, 25 June 1877 to take part in what was advertised as a 'Grand Aquatic Entertainment.' Webb's share in the proceedings was, however, somewhat disappointing. The crowd of spectators, said to be over 20,000, expected him to do something spectacular, like swimming the length of the lake and possibly back again, but he only swam underwater for a short distance.

A contemporary report of the event states that a large grandstand and refreshment tent had been erected at the southern end of the lake. The weather was perfect, and there were a number of swimming races, including the All England Contest, won by Beckwith of London in a close finish. The Beckwith family played a prominent part in the proceedings, Miss Agnes Beckwith being, at the time, a world champion swimmer. There was a race between a man and a dog trained by Professor Beckwith, the dog being the easy winner! The last event was an amusing contest: walking along a greasy pole for a live pig. The pig, however, managed to escape, and fell into the water. Further entertainments on the day included dancing on the lawns, skittles, shooting competitions at the rifle galleries, and the skating rink.

The advertisement of the event particularly emphasised that:

'The bathing costumes being full and complete, the most fastidious of either sex, may, with propriety, be present at this Entertainment'.

The broad promenade formed by the dam at the southern end of the lake was the scene of a number of entertainments and amusements in the past, and crowds massed to watch. Circus-type entertainments were sometimes held, and it is recorded that an African 'Blondin' once performed there.

A skating rink was opened on Thursday, 1 June, 1876, using Plimpton's Patent Roller Skates for which the proprietor, Mr Joseph Thornley, had the sole concession for the district. The rink was open every day (except Sunday), mornings 11am to 1pm, afternoons 2.30 to 5.00pm, and evenings from 6.00 to 8.30pm. Admission was one shilling for adults, children under 12 sixpence, hire of skates sixpence.

In the notoriously bleak North Staffordshire winters, Rudyard Lake was often frozen, providing an additional free entertainment - ice skating. In the big Freeze of 1895 there were 16 weeks of frost, with the lowest temperature of 30 degrees below zero on 9 February.

During February 1895 a fire broke out in Mr Chester Thompson's boathouse on the lakeside, and the Leek fire engine, a horse-drawn Firefly Manual struggled through the deep snow in the woods. The ice was 18 inches thick, and the firemen had to hack a hole to obtain water. After the fire, instead of returning by the difficult roads through the woods, the fire engine was pulled across the frozen lake by firemen and skaters. The week following the fire, the Leek Volunteers held a route march in the Longsdon area, and afterwards paraded on the frozen lake. People came from far and wide to skate, and races were held at weekends.

The western edge of the lake is lined with a number of substantially built boathouses. One such, of outstanding appearance, a splendid brick and stone structure overlooking the water, was built for the Davenports by the Leek architects, Sugden and Son. This is known as the Lady of the Lake.

In the woods on the western bank two houses are built in close proximity to each other - the lower one blocking the view of the other. Local tradition has it that the lower one - Spite Hall - was built out of spite, to spoil the view of the other, Rudyard Villa, in some dispute between the two owners - hence its name. An early North Staffordshire Railway Guide also points out that originally, to add to the spite as it were, the owner placed on the roof ridge a number of griffins' heads, their grinning faces turned towards the villa, but these have been removed.

Rudyard village itself has many good, solid well-built houses, many having the appearance of good-class Victorian town houses, perhaps a little out of place in this rural situation, but again reflecting the growth and prosperity of Rudyard at that time. The solid-looking Methodist Chapel, with its fine window facing the road, is another indication of Rudyard's status in the past, its series of foundation stones indicating the generosity of local residents. Rudyard also has two substantial hotels, one of which was built by the railway company to boost their interest in the tourist potential of the area, and a former miners' convalescent home, which was used largely by the collieries of North Staffordshire.

A prominent feature of the village is the Memorial Stone. This stands at the junction of Lake Road and Whorracks Bank, from where it was quarried in 1897, the Diamond Jubilee year of Queen Victoria. The rough-hewn stone has many dates engraved on its dressed faces - royal events, national events, war and peace - in effect, a potted history in stone of the past century, and as such a symbol of much of the time encompassed by this personal selection of Leek's history.

Winter on the frozen lake, with Lowry-like figures muffled against the cold.

Rudyard Vale, showing Spite Hall and Rudyard Villa.

W.H. Nithsdale's photograph (c 1905) has captured much of the spirit of Rudyard - the train by the lakeside and the boat trips on the Lake.

This peaceful scene is typical of the countryside surrounding Rudyard Lake.
Looking from the western side with the railway following the opposite bank.

An evening scene with reflections in the calm water capturing the spirit of Rudyard Lake.

Boating has always been a great attraction at Rudyard. Here the boats and landing stage are crowded with visitors.

This winter scene shows the overspill weir at the dam head.

The North Staffordshire Railway Company were quick to exploit the potential of Rudyard to attract visitors, and from 1850 many developments took place. This picture of the village overlooks the railway and shows the long platform required to cope with the long excursion trains which brought many thousands of visitors to Rudyard.

One of the sound investments by the railway company was the establishment of the Hotel Rudyard. Opened in the 1860s, it has seen many changes over the years and various proprietors initiated a whole range of entertainments. This picture c. 1912

The railway line alongside the Eastern side of the lake.

The first tee at the golf links developed by the railway company at the northern end of the lake.

A woodland path at Rudyard.

The railway company's tea pavilion at Rudyard was another of their enterprises.

The neat interior of the Pavilion Tearoom, overlooking the lake, captures the spirit of the age

Rudyard Lake from the Chalét, North Stafford Railway.

The North Staffordshire Railway Company developed its own Tea Chalet, overlooking the Lake

An essential feature of a summer outing to Rudyard - Granelli's ice cream. The ice cream cart of Agostino Granelli was a familiar sight in the village. The Granelli family were based in Macclesfield and Leek.

The railway track ran very close to the edge of the Lake, on the eastern side.

The end of a busy day for the operators of boat trips on the Lake.

Amongst the features of the Lake are the boathouses on the western bank, the most impressive of which is 'The Lady of the Lake'. It was designed by the Leek architects Sugden and Son in 1893. The figure of the lady is built into the chimney.

Rules and Regulations of Rudyard Skating Rink.

1. No one should stand upon the floor within skating limits, or so as to obstruct the entrance to the place or the view of others.
2. Never cross the floor in passing to or from a seat; always follow the direction of the skaters around to place.
3. Throwing any substance or spitting on the floor is dangerous, and will not be permitted.
4. No cane, stick, string, or other similar article, should be taken upon the floor by skaters.
5. In skating round the circuit, all will observe a uniform direction, taking great care never to interfere with the movements of others.
6. No skater should stop in the circuit, except to assist a lady.
7. Pushing, tripping, racing, "tagging," or taking hold of each other's garments, or any rude and dangerous actions, are strictly forbidden.
8. Skating should only be practised upon the floor assigned for that purpose.
9. Gentlemen without Ladies should take great care never to trespass upon the time or space set apart for Ladies or Gentlemen with Ladies.
10. Ladies and Gentlemen are respectfully requested to avoid skating against the seats or walls, or subjecting the skates to any other rough usage that will damage them.
11. No smoking allowed.

A cheerful compliance with the above, and a careful regard for the comfort and enjoyment of others, is respectfully requested.

Beginners should first walk slowly around the Room a few times before attempting any rapid movements.

Skaters should learn to put on and take off their Skates.

On taking off the Skates, please buckle together and return them to the Skate Room.

The skating rink at Rudyard lake was opened 1st June 187 The rules and regulations wer very strict and precise.

Below:
Lake Road with the Memorial Stone on the left.

Harper's Gate
Wesleyan Sunday School.

A
MAGIC LANTERN
AND
SERVICE OF SONG
ENTERTAINMENT,
WILL BE GIVEN ON
TUESDAY, MARCH 12th, 1889,
ILLUSTRATIVE OF
"CHRISTIE'S OLD ORGAN

PICTURES:

1 Introduction.
2 Treffy at Home.
3 Christie Listening.
4 Treffy's Fall.
5 Christie and Treffy Alone.
6 Treffy's Last Out.
7 Treffy Low Spirited.
8 Christie's First Out.
9 First Visit to Mabel's
10 Christie Calls the Doctor.
11 Christie Tells Treffy "Only a Month"
12 Mabel Learns to Play.
13 Mabel Points to Heaven.
14 Christie Outside Mission Hal
15 Interior of Mission Hall.
16 The Minister and Christie.
17 Mabel Sends Flowers to Tre
18 Minister Visits Old Treffy.
19 Treffy's Death.
20 The Vision.
21 Christie Alone.
22 Christie Overcome.
23 Christie Ill.
24 Minister Visits Christie.

To Conclude with a Series of Amusing Pictures.

DOORS OPEN AT 6.45, TO COMMENCE AT

Admission 1d. each, a few Reserved Seats 3d. each.

A typical Victorian Methodist entertainment at Rudyard

WESLEYAN CHAPEL,
HARPER'S GATE, RUDYARD.

THE
ANNUAL TEA MEETING
AND A
SERVICE OF SONG
Will be held in the above Chapel,
ON THURSDAY, OCTOBER 17, 1878,
TEA ON THE TABLES AT 4 O'CLOCK.
SERVICE OF SONG AT SIX O'CLOCK.

PROGRAMME.

BEFORE JEHOVAH'S AWFUL THRONE. ...		THE CHOIR.
SONG.	... Arise and Shine.	MISSES EDE AND WHITE.
SONG.	... ...	MR. MEAKIN.
SONG.	The Children's Heavenly Home.	MISS AUSTIN.
RECITATION. ...	... Only a Tear.	MISS EDE.
SONG.	Welcome to Glory ...	THE CHOIR.
ANTHEM.	"Praise the Lord, O Jerusalem."	MESSRS. MEAKIN, WALKER, AND OTHERS.
SONG.	The Christian Martyr. ...	MISS TRYTHALL.
RECITATION.	"The lips that touch liquors shall never touch mine."	MISS WHITE.
SONG.	... White Robes. ...	MISS EDE.
SONG.	Waiting and Watching.	MRS. WOOD & MISS HILL.
SONG.	... Only Waiting. ...	MISS WHITE.
SONG.	... ...	MR. AND MISS E. WALKER.
SONG.	The Dying Child. ...	MISS HODGKISS.
SONG.	... The Life Boat. ...	MISS TRYTHALL.
SONG.	In the silent Midnight Watches.	MISSES CORBISHLEY & HODGKISS.
ANTHEM.	"Cry out and Shout."	MESSRS. MEAKIN, WALKER, AND OTHERS.
SONG. ...	... Shall we meet beyond the River.	THE CHOIR.

The Train leaves Leek at 3-28, Returning from Rudyard at 8-50.

Tickets for Tea and Service of Song, One Shilling each, may be had of Mr. E. Hallowes, Printer, or from any of the friends.

THE PROCEEDS TO BE GIVEN TO THE HARMONIUM FUND.

This great Methodist event at Rudyard must have taken a full four hours. It was possible to travel from Leek to Rudyard by train at very convenient times. The words of the second recitation would no doubt be inspired by the Temperance movement.

GRAND AQUATIC ENTERTAINMENT
AT
RUDYARD LAKE,
MONDAY, JUNE 25th, 1877.

CAPTAIN WEBB
HAS THE HONOUR TO ANNOUNCE THAT HIS FIRST GRAND
AQUATIC FETE
WILL TAKE PLACE ON THE ABOVE DATE.

The Programme will embrace the following:—

ALL ENGLAND SWIMMING CONTEST,
First Prize, £5. Second Prize, £3, Third Prize, £1. Distance, Half-a-Mile.

ALSO, AMATEUR COMPETITION!
First Prize, Silver Cup, value £5. Second Prize, Gold Medal. Third Prize, Silver Medal. Distance, Quarter of a Mile.

YOUTHS' SWIMMING RACE
Open to all under 16 years of age. First Prize, a Gold Medal. Second Prize, Silver Medal. Third Prize, Badge.

The Talented Beckwith Family, viz:—

PROFESSOR BECKWITH,
MISS AGNES BECKWITH,
(The Champion Lady Swimmer of the World.)
MASTER WILLIE BECKWITH
Will Perform their Unique Feats of Natation.

MAN AND DOG SWIMMING RACE.

Rescue from Drowning exemplified, by Two Talented Swimmers!
COMIC PART.—The Greasy Pole and Live Pig, also Duck Hunt.
For which Prizes are given.

CAPTAIN WEBB
Will give a Representation in miniature of the Channel Feat, &c., &c.

A GRAND STAND will be erected to accommodate Several Hundred Spectators.

Some idea of the event can be obtained from the following condensed report of the proceedings :—

"The weather was everything that could be desired," and over 20,000 people were present, the great bulk of which assembled at the South end of the lake where a large grand stand and refreshment tent had been erected on the lawn.

The events that were most generally appreciated, however, were the natation performances by the Beckwith family. This included undressing in the water, an imitation of the actions of a drowning man, and swimming with hands and feet tied. And an exhibition by Miss Agnes Beckwith, the champion lady swimmer of the world

The report of this part of the proceedure reads as follows :-"As slight feature of his famous channel feat, he took some refreshment from the boat which accompanied him and swam a short distance under water to show his powers of endurance. He was followed by Professor Marquis Bibbino, and Mr. Collins, who delineated what is known as the raft scene. The last event was a very amusing and even exciting contest, namely walking along a greasy pole for a live pig. The pig, however managed by some means to escape from the trammals in which he was confined at the end of the pole and fell flop into the water amid shouts of laughter by the spectators."

"This brought the outdoor proceedings to a close," the report proceeds, "but before the departure of the trains there was ample time for further enjoyment, such as dancing on the lawn, skittles, shooting competitions at the rifle galleries, and on the skating rink which was crowded."

From Leek News

Rudyard Lake.

GREAT

SKATING CONTEST

WILL TAKE PLACE ON

SATURDAY NEXT, JANUARY 17th, 1891.

To Commence at 2 p.m.

Mr. Gili, at the Rudyard Hotel, will offer a number of

Suitable Priz

TO BE COMPETED FOR

By Ladies, Gentlemen, Yo

and Girls.

ALL ENTRIES F

NO CHARGE FOR A

THOMAS GRACE, PRINTER, MARKE

NORTH STAFFORDSHIRE RAILWAY.

Cheap Half Holiday Excursion to

RUDYARD LAKE,

ON SATURDAY, JUNE 29.

Engagement at an Enormous Expense of the Origina

AFRICAN BLONDIN,

THE PRINCE OF THE AIR!

This is his last performance in England, previous to his departure to Melbourne, Australia, and America, having arranged to re-cross Niagara.

LAST FOUR DAYS.

Will cross the Lake at Four o'clock in the Afternoon, and Seven o'clock in the Evening.
THURSDAY, JULY 4, at Four o'clock in the Afternoon, and Seven o'clock in the Evening.
SATURDAY, JULY 6, at Four o'clock in the Afternoon, and Seven o'clock in the Evening.

This wonderful performer has astonished thousands by his daring and marvellous exploits on the high rope. On this occasion he will CROSS RUDYARD LAKE.

By the kind permission of Mayor M. A. Bass, M.P., and the Officers, the Splendid PRIZE BAND of the BURTON RIFLE CORPS, under the Leadership of Mr. Twells, will accompany the Trip, and play a choice selection of Music.
The LEEK BRASS BAND & STRING BAND will Play for Dancing.

WALKING!!

MR. F. ALLNUTT

WILL WALK

50 MILES IN 10 HOURS!!

On the Green adjoining the Lake at Rudyard, on SATURDAY, 14TH JULY,
To Start at 10-30 a.m., prompt.

AN EFFICIENT BAND will be in attendance.

Admission: Sixpence and One Shilling each.

A variety of events advertised in an 1878 newspaper cutting.

Drapery and Boot Department, St. Edward Street.

CHAPTER EIGHT
The Co-operative Movement in Leek

IT WILL BE CLEAR from the foregoing chapters that the social structure of the town of Leek in the mid-19th century was ripe for the development of the Co-operative Movement. Industry and commerce were prospering, the population was increasing and more and more people were getting their own houses. On the wages paid in the factories, working-class folk had to be thrifty, and money management was not a natural skill with the majority. The principles of investment and savings had yet to be learned. The building societies were in their infancy, and there was a need for a more broadly based organisation to cater for the wider needs of the people.

This would involve not only facilities for savings and investment, but also the provision of shops, where goods of all kinds would be available at reasonable prices, with loyalty benefits for those who shopped in them. It was a commercial venture outside the bounds of normal commerce, where individual tradesmen would only have an eye to their own profits, and one which would take a good deal of faith and courage to set up. Under this revolutionary new scheme, the people would have an actual share in the businesses they traded with.

The date for the foundation of the Co-operative Movement in Leek is usually stated to be March 1859. According to the souvenir booklet published to celebrate the Jubilee Year of the Society in 1909, a manufacturer named Miles Simpson had moved to Leek from Middleton in Lancashire, bringing with him a group of his workers who had been involve with the Co-operative Society in Middleton. George Eastwood, who had the experience of working on a Co-operative Society committee, took the initiative, and launched the idea that if twelve men could be found to take up a one pound share each, a society could be formed.

George Eastwood and Thomas Woodcock undertook the responsibility of collecting one shilling a week from such potential members as preferred to spread their payments over a period. Seven of the intending members took advantage of this arrangement. Early in 1859 it became clear that the required number of shareholders would be forthcoming, and a small cottage on Clerk Bank, owned by a tailor named Armitt, was taken, and the members, now twelve in number, proceeded to furnish their little shop. The spirit of co-operation and determination within the group was evidenced by the fact that the shop was completely fitted up by their own labour.

The first seven members were George Eastwood, Thomas Woodcock, Nathan Taylor, Jonathan Grindrod, William Hyde, John Howarth and George Tomlinson. Others who joined very early were:

JOHN ABRAHAMS
GEORGE ARMITT
WILLIAM BAILEY
JOHN BARNETT
WILLIAM BOWCOCK
HENRY BRADLEY
CHRISTOPHER CHADOCK
WILLIAM DISHLEY
THOMAS GALLIMORE
NATHAN GAYES
EDWARD GRAHAM
JOHN GREEN
CHARLES GRINDROD
WILLIAM HEYWOOD
WILLIAM HORNE
JAMES HORNE
GEORGE MASON
SAMUEL HENRY MEE
SAMUEL MELLOR
WILLIAM MERRITT
SAMUEL MORLEY
JOHN MORRIS
SAMUEL MORRIS
JOSIAH MOTTERSHEAD-HIBBERT NEWALL
WILLIAM OWEN
THOMAS PALMER
GEORGE PLANT
JAMES PLANT
JOHN PLANT
VERNON POOLE
GEORGE RANDELL
JAMES SHAW
THOMAS SHAW
JAMES SCHOFIELD
WILLIAM STEEPLE
GEORGE TURNER
JOSHUA TRAFFORD
FIELDING WHISTON
LUPENE RIDER
ELIZABETH ROGERS
ALICE CRAIG

It is interesting to note that there are just three ladies - the last three named - on the list.

The Society, first known as the Leek and Moorlands Industrial Provident Society, gradually grew, and the little converted cottage soon became inadequate for the needs of the growing society. In the early sixties the Society moved to a larger shop just over the road, on Overton Bank, which had formerly been a grocery and provision shop.

As the Society continued to grow its rules were prepared for submission to the Registrar of Friendly Societies, and on April 24th 1860 the Society was duly enrolled. This meant that the Society had to have formally appointed officials, and Jonathan Grindrod became its first President. The Secretary was Thomas Gallimore, and William Horne was Treasurer and Manager. Thomas Booth and Samuel Henry Mee were appointed Auditors. Most of the work done was unpaid, and the shop was only open in the evenings and on Saturday afternoons. It would be many years before the shop was open all day.

In 1868 the first Annual Party was held in the Temperance Hall. The membership was then approaching 300, and increasing sales and profits meant that the dividend to members had risen from 3d to 1s 3d in the pound. At that time there was a slight downturn in the Society's affairs. There was differences of opinion amongst the membership and a number of members withdrew not only their capital but their trade. However, the Society weathered the storm, and gradually stability was attained. In 1875 it became possible to open during the daytime, and this signified a period of firm progress.

Thomas Gallimore died in 1876, and James Ratcliffe became Secretary. In 1879 the Committee acquired much larger premises in Ashbourne Road, where a bakery department was set up, together with grocery and provisions. This enabled the Society to bake its own bread, and signified a period of great growth. The Society invested in the newly-formed Co-operative Wholesale Society, which ensured the supply of quality goods at reasonable prices. A Penny Bank was established at Ashbourne Road in 1880 to encourage the children of members to save their own small sums of money.

The Overton Bank shop became the Boot and Shoe Department in 1881, and in 1882 the first branch grocery shop was opened at Ball Haye Green for the convenience of members residing in that district. The bakehouse was extended in 1890, and a coal department established in 1894. Other branch shops were opened - Picton Street (1895), Buxton Road (1904), Mill Street (1907) and at Compton. A Drapery Department was established at 39, St. Edward Street in 1897, to which the Boot and Shoe Department was later transferred, and continued there until 1907.

1896 was memorable in the history of the Society, for it marked a forward step in the movement towards the emancipation of women. The Leek Women's Co-operative Guild was founded, and its first meeting was held at the Coffee Tavern on October 14th, when 16 members were enrolled. Meetings were later held in the William Morris Labour Church on Overton Bank, recently leased from the Quakers. The Guild members met regularly to discuss subjects relating to the Co-operative Movement and social reform. Two of its members, Miss A. Provost and Miss Kidd, took up positions with the Central Committee.

Another big forward step was the rebuilding of the Central Premises on Ashbourne Road in 1899. Larner Sugden was the architect and Thomas Grace the contractor, and the new building housed offices and boardroom, grocery, provisions and bakery. The upper floor comprised a large hall - usually known as the 'Co-op Hall' - where public meetings, functions and social events were held.

In 1911 the Leek and Moorlands Co-operative Society embarked on a new venture in High Street. Here an imposing, large emporium was built, designed by the Burslem and Leek architect, Reginald T. Londen. This fine building housed a variety of departments, including furnishing, boots and shoes, tailoring, drapery and pharmacy. From the upper floor windows of this shop you could look over High Street to the little shop on Clerk Bank, where the Society was founded in 1859.

The Committee in the Society's Jubilee Year, 1909
Seated: John Ernest Ingham (Secretary and Manager), William Provost (President), Samuel Poyser.
Middle row: Joseph Henry Mather, William Henry Palmer, Charles William Green
Back row: William Merritt, James Lilley, Alfred Walthall, Henry Horne.

Women's Guild Committee
Seated: Mrs Hazelhurst, Miss Leah Provost (Secretary), Mrs Fernyhough (President), Mrs Hassall
Middle: Mrs Ball, Mrs Eaton, Mrs Lee, Miss B. Provost. Back: Mrs Grindrod, Mrs Barlow, Mrs Birchenhough, Mrs Rowley

The Co-operative movement has a long history in Leek. The Leek and Moorlands Industrial Provident Society Ltd, as the society was first called, established its first shop in 1859 in a small cottage - second from the left - on Clerk Bank.

In 1904 the Leek and Moorlands Co-operative Society purchased these cottages on the corner of Buxton Rd and Osborne St and opened this branch to relieve the pressure on the nearby Ashbourne Road shop. The branch was extended in 1906.

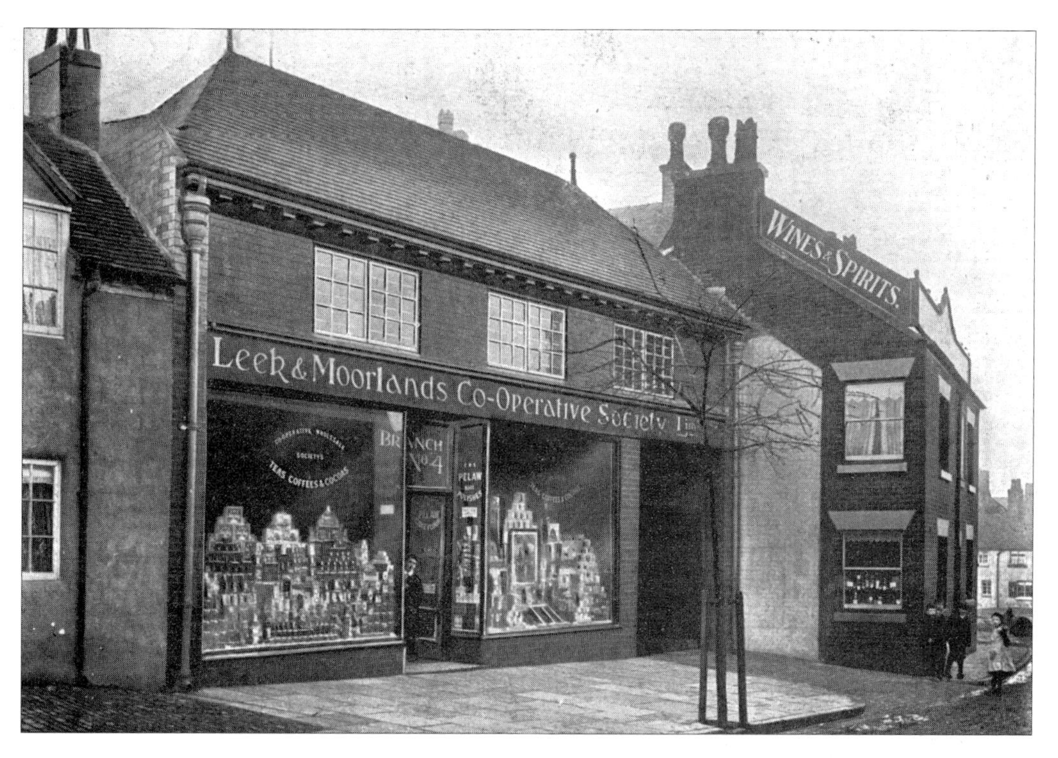

Mill Street Branch, opened 1907.

Ball Haye Green Branch, opened 1882. Note the Co-op delivery cart. A larger, purpose-built shop was later opened on the opposite corner of Milk Street. By the end of 1882, sales, which in 1879 were £5768, had more than doubled to £11,886.

A group of carly members still living in 1909.
Seated: Joseph Trafford (82), John Morris (87), Nathan Taylor (84), Charles Merritt (82)
Standing: George Hambleton (74), William Steeple (74), Samuel Mellor (76)

Heads of Department, 1909
Seated: Henry Farrall (Ball Haye Green), Mrs Robinson (Boot and Shoe), George E. Newsome (Central), George Rider (Drapery
Middle: Arthur Pickford (Mill Street), Harry Howard (Buxton Road), George Hy. Sheldon (Picton St), William Morris (Bakery
Back: John Barnett (Cobbling), William Lovatt (Stables), Arthur Meakin (Office), George Wm. Eckersall (Coal).

The Stables, Field Street, erected 1905.
The Co-op made deliveries of coal, bread and milk by horse-drawn carts.

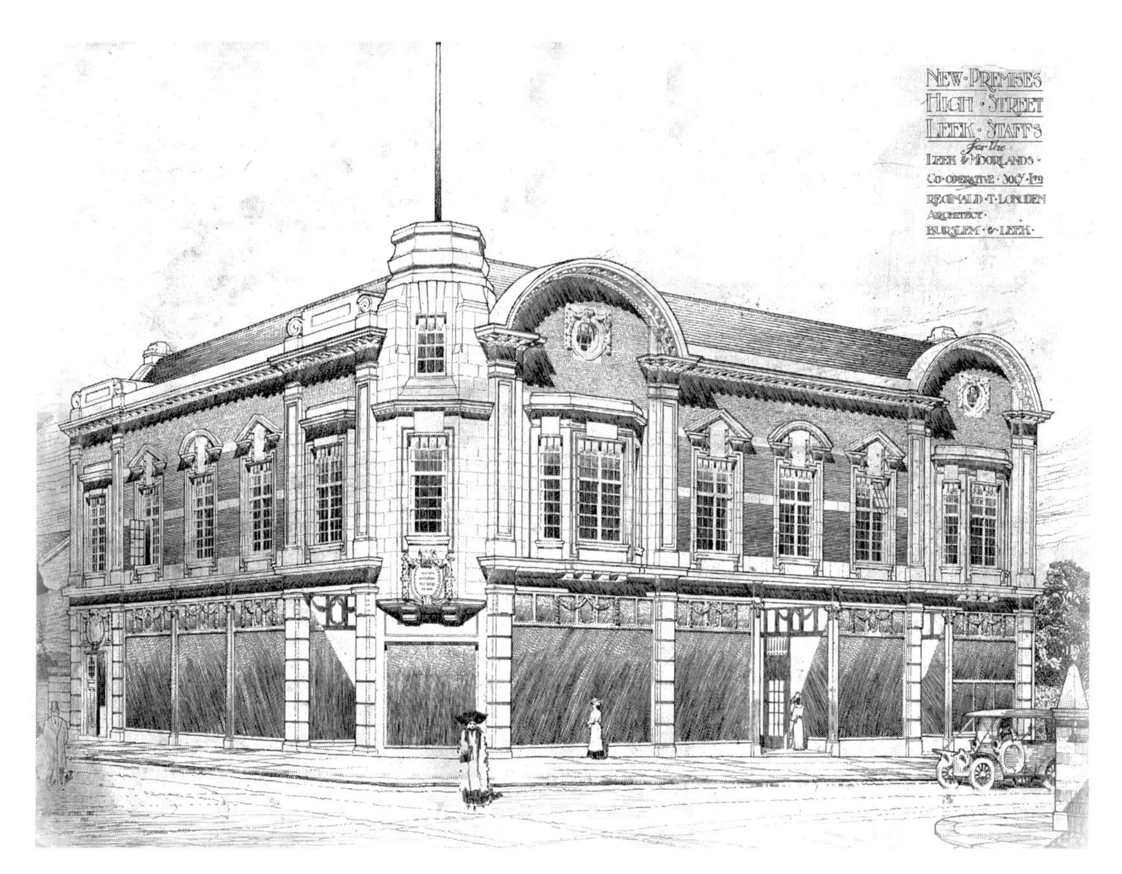

Reginald T. Longden was the architect of the Society's new premises in High Street (1911).

LEEK NEWS.

CHRISTMAS SHOPPING NUMBER.

No 0006. DECEMBER, 1930. Threepence.

CONTENTS.

Group of Workmen and others engaged on the erection of the Leek Technical Schools, 1900.

Top Row
1 J. Eliner
2 Tom Oliver
3 G. Sales
4 J. Haywood
5
6 H. Birkenhead
7 E. Sherrat
8 H. Atkinson
9 J. O'Hara
10 H. Biddulph
11 H. Grace
12 A. Woodings
13 J. Jones
14 A. James
15

Second Row
1
2 W. Salt
3 H. Ball
4 F. Bradley
5 T. Goldstraw
6 T. Salt
7 J. Goldstraw
8 C. Mason
9 A. Wright
10 P. Wright
11 W. Merritt
12 R. Cowell
13 T. Lindop
14 R. Sorrell
15
16
17

Third Row
1 A. Grace, stand'g
2
3 H. Slater
4 W. Wood
5
6 J. Nixon
7 J. W. Ward
8
9 J. Horne
10 H. Brown
11 J. Brooks
12 J. Billing
13 R. Horne
14 J. Simpson
15 E. Evans
16 H. Smith
17 J. Bowcock

Fourth Row
1 — Scholes
2
3 P. Plant
4 J. Lowe
5 J. Turner
6
7 Ernest Birch
8 J. Curtis
9 Edward Birch
10 M. Minton
11 H. Hobson
12 Walter Lay
13 Vinct. Robinson
14 T. Vickerstaff
15 E. Bendall
16 E. Sheldon
17 J. Fallows
18 J. Deakin
19 E. Bullen
20 H. Birchenough

Fifth Row
1
2 J. Condlyffe
3 H. Porter
4 T. Carpenter
5 Edgar Wilmer
6 A. Vass
7 E. Spare
8 D. Wilmer
9
10 David Hibbert
11 C. Stretch
12 H. Hammond
13 G. Mollatt
14 Will Carding
15 R. J. Wragg
16 Geo. Hocknell
17 Geo. Trafford
18 A. Pegg
19 T. White

Sixth Row
1 H. Grace
2 J. Carding
3 M. Carding
4 K. Parkes
5 T. Grace
6 Larner Sugden
7 G. Wood
8 — Broadbent
9 A. Carding
10 W. A. Overfield
11 H. Sugden
12
13 F. D. Galt
14 W. H. Gal
15 R. Walwy
16 — Porter
J. Grace (s
in front)

CHAPTER NINE
Victorian and Edwardian Images from Leek News

Queen Victoria's Jubilee, 1887.

OX ROASTED IN MARKET PLACE.

The gentlemen included in the group are—left to right—Mr. W. H. NIXON, Mr. EDWIN TRAFFORD, (who gave the ox), Mr. E. TRAFFORD, Mr. M. H. Miller, Mr. W. PILKINGTON, Mr. M. CARDING, Mr. H. BRUNT, Mr. J. C. CLEMESHA, Mr. J. STAFFORD.

MENTION is made on another page of this issue, of the great events that took place in Leek on the occasion of the celebration of Queen Victoria's Jubilee.

One outstanding event in connection with those celebrations was the roasting of a whole ox in the Market Place—an event which will still be vividly remembered by many who at that time took a young and eager interest in the proceedings.

The photograph reproduced above shows the ox that had the honour of playing the principal part in this event. It was a fine animal— generously given by Mr. Edwin Trafford, the well-known Leek butcher, then of Stanley Street, but later of the Market Place.

The ox, which had been roasted at an earlier hour, was cut up at 10 o'clock in the morning and distributed amongst 700 to 800 old people— bread and tea being added to complete this sumptuous repast.

Dr. J. Mountfort Johnson.

Medical Officer of Health.

IT will, I am sure, come as a surprise to many of our readers to learn that the Town of Leek had only had two Medical Officers of Health over a period of 78 years. The first appointment was made by the Local Commissioners on the 11th November, 1867, when the late Dr. John James Ritchie was appointed. The late Doctor, who is still remembered by many of the older inhabitants, continued in this position to 1901, having carried out his duties 42 years.

Dr. J. M. Johnson, whose photograph we have reproduced above, was appointed to the position on the 5th of March, 1901, and is to-day ably filling this position after 36 years. Dr. Johnson is now in his 77th year and we offer to him our sincere congratulations on his excellent service to his native Town.

The report of the Medical Officer for the month of June, 1884, shows the average age at death to be **34½** years, whilst in 1937 for the month of September the Medical Officer's report shows the average age at death to be **67** years, almost double what it was 53 years ago. A splendid testimony, surely, to the progress made in recent years by the Medical Profession, together with the improvements that have been provided in better sanitation, pure and wholesome food and water.

Leek 100 years ago.

IN the light of a town's development, a hundred years comparatively speaking is not a long time—a mere couple of generations—and yet when we try to imagine what Leek was like a century ago we realise what tremendous strides the town has made in the intervening period.

Towards the end of the reign of George IV the little moorland town comprised 1,250 houses inhabited by about 7,000 people, who then, as now, were chiefly employed in the silk trade.

It is interesting to read over the list of streets, namely, Spout street, Derby street, Stockwell street, Custard street, Market place, Sheep market, Church street, Church lane, Mill street, Compton, Buxton road, Ashbourne road, Ball Haye street, Union street, King street, Schooling bank (Overton bank), Schoolhouse bank (Clerk bank), New street, Albion street, Fountain street, Leek Moor, White's Bridge, and Spooner's lane. These were the only thoroughfares and were lit by gas, a hundred lamps costing two pounds per year for lighting.

There was only one Church of England establishment and that of course was the Old Church, of which the Rev. T. H. Heathcote was the Vicar, and the Rev. James Turnock, Curate. The Wesleyans had two places of worship, at Bank Field (Mount Pleasant), and Ball Haye Street, a school chapel. The ministers were the Revs. Richard Wintle and James Dunning, but it was in this year that a third minister was deemed necessary, and three years later, in 1832, the Rev. Joseph Hargreaves was appointed, Mr. James Wardle giving £50 a year and house rent free towards his support. There were nearly a thousand members of the Wesleyan Church and the Sunday School had as many scholars.

The Independents had a Chapel in Derby street on the site of the present chapel, the Rev. J. Morrow being pastor.

The Quakers met occasionally on Overton Bank, and the Primitive Methodists had their services in Back Sides.

The government of the town was partly vested with Messrs. Thomas Smith, Samuel Millward, Anthony Ward and Richard Cutting, the overseers, William Alcock, the solitary constable, Charles Booth, the town crier, Messrs. J. Griffin and Josiah Brunt, highway surveyors, Benjamin Rice, governor of the House of Industry, or the Workhouse, and the Revs. T. H. Heathcote and John Sneyd, and Mr. Edward Trafford Trafford, the justices of the peace.

Railway travel was only being thought of in those days. The Mail Coach rattled out of Leek daily for London at one o'clock, and arrived at a quarter before one. At the same times the Mail arrived from and left for Manchester. A horse post went out to Warslow, Longnor, Hartington, and other places at two o'clock on Mondays, Wednesdays and Fridays. Passenger coaches also went out for London, Manchester, and Birmingham. On certain days carriers' carts journeyed to Ashbourne, Burslem, Butterton, Buxton, Congleton, Cheadle, Chester, Hanley Longport, Lane End, Longnor, Bakewell, Sheffield, Macclesfield, the Potteries, Stone and Stafford, Stockport, Manchester, and Uttoxeter. Canal boats plied between Leek London, Liverpool and M[illegible].

Three of the seven schools in town were in Derby street. There the Misses Babbington had a ladies' boarding school, and Miss Morrow and the Rev. J. Morrow had charge of the other two. In addition to these there was the Free Grammar School conducted by the Rev. James Turner, one at Compton, taught by Miss Ridout, one in Church street taught by the Rev. Cornelius Bromby, and another in Mill street taught by Mr. William Shufflebotham.

MR. W. S. BROUGH,

Distinguished Staffordshire Public Man.

Staffordshire Sentinel, 6th Nov., 1917.

BY the death of Mr. William Spooner Brough which took place at his home in Buxton Road, Leek, on Monday, 5th Nov., 1917, the county has lost one who, until infirmity limited his activities, was among the best known men in Staffordshire. At Leek, in the county town, and in the Potteries, he was a familiar figure. His genial and hearty manner, his inexhaustible fund of good spirits, his large-hearted generosity, and his catholic culture made many proud to claim his friendship. His public work alone deserves fullest recognition, but beyond that he was an art collector of rare insight and knowledge, an artist of considerable ability, a bibliophile and an omniverous reader, a botanist and an archæologist. His passing, though in the fullness of years, will be widely regretted.

Within a fortnight of his 77th birthday, he had been very infirm for several years, and his attendance at county meetings and public functions had been very limited for a long time. His last act was characteristic of his profound kindliness and deep sentiment. On Monday morning he was wheeled to the cemetery at Leek, where a servant of his was laid to rest a year ago. He placed some flowers on her grave and returned to his home. Later, he had a seizure and passed away. During his illness he had been visited by the Earl of Dartmouth, Lord Hatherton, and Sir Reginald Hardy, who, with many others prominent in the county, were among his personal friends.

Born in 1840, an only son, he came of an old Staffordshire family. As far back as the 16th century, a Thomas Burgh, otherwise Brough, was established at the Frith under the Roches. At the farm there—Frithbottom Farm as it is called—his father Mr. Joshua Brough, was born. Mr. Brough was educated at the Leek Grammar School and the Mill Hill Public School, but to an only sister, who married the late Mr. John Beavis Brindley, first Recorder of Hanley, he confessed his indebtedness for his early love of literature. Leaving school at the age of sixteen, he was bound apprentice to the firm of Messrs. T. & T. Brough & Co., silk manufacturers, of Leek. In 1868 he became a partner in the business, and continued there until 1880, when he ceased his connections with the firm.

Subsequently, he went to London and became intimately associated with art and artists. The late Sir Thomas Wardle and he were for a time partners in an art collector's shop in Bond street, London, and it was at this period that he made the acquaintance of William Morris, Burne-Jones, Whistler, and other leaders of the art movements of the time, with some of whom he became very intimate, particularly with William Morris, who in books issued from the Kelmscott Press speaks of "My friend Will Brough."

[illegible] who had the pleasure of Mr. Brough's personal acquaintance, and a knowledge of the treasures contained in his modest home—beautifully situated on the Buxton road and near the Ball Haye Park which he laid out for the recreation of the people of Leek—know how wide and discriminating was his taste as an art collector. His rooms were filled with art treasures—representative examples of etchings, mezzotints, and other prints, oil paintings and water-colours by the famous artists of the past. His prints covered representatively Rembrandt to Whistler, and included also examples earlier and later. He loved to delve into his cabinets and to enlarge, to the understanding visitor, on the merits and beauties of a famous etching. His pictures were many. He prided himself on the possession of a Velasquez and a Cuyp, and his collection includes also Rossetti's beautiful "Santa Lilias," and paintings by Ford Madox Brown, Burne-Jones, Turner, Whistler the French impressionists of the Barbizon School, the later Dutch painters, besides David Cox, Copley Fielding, Peter de Wint, and many others. His collection was one for the artist to revel in with sheer delight. The writer recalls an exhibition of the North Staffordshire Arts Society held at Trentham Hall, not long before its demolition, to which Mr. Brough lent a wonderful collection of Whistlers, Corots and other workers of the Barbizon painters, as well as a few remarkable pieces by the Brothers Maris, the modern Dutch masters.

Of his public work he would prefer to be remembered chiefly for his care of discharged prisoners. He was a Justice of the Peace whose interest in prisoners did not end with the sentences he imposed. Many owed their reclamation to him; some of his efforts, of course, ended in failure. He laughingly, but not without a note of sadness, told the story of a discharged prisoner to whom he gave a new start in London. At Euston one day he met his protege who "kindly" offered to carry his bag. Mr. Brough never saw again the protege or the bag. In 1883 he was appointed a county justice, and became a visiting justice at Stafford Gaol. For years he had been hon. sec. of the North and South Staffs. Discharged Prisoners' Aid Societies.

Mr. Brough had been a member of the County Council since its formation and was an alderman at the time of his death. His principal work in that connection was concerned with the erection of Cheddleton Asylum, being at the time Chairman of the County Lunacy Committee. He took a wide and practical interest in county and local government, and was for years also a member of the Leek Board of Guardians.

In 1879 he was elected a fellow of the Royal Historical Society. For twelve years he was hon. sec. to the Leek Mechanics' Institute. For many years he had been a member of the North Staffordshire Field Club, occupying the presidency in 1878. His addresses to the members of this club were on "The Flora of Rudyard," "The Literature of Botany," "The Arthurian Circle" and "My Old Wall," the last-named being delivered in 1878 when he occupied the the position of president. In the same year he read a paper on "Wootton and its Associations," pointing out that [illegible] there endeavoured to naturalise foreign plants and wrote part of his "Elements of Botany." On behalf of the Club Mr. Brough welcomed the members of the British Archæological Association to North Staffordshire in 1895, his inaugural address delivered at Stoke containing much valuable matter relating to the antiquities of this part of the county. Another address of his was that delivered at the North Staffordshire Technical Museum in May, 1891, on "Book Illustration," a subject on which he was justly regarded as an authority.

A Group of Congregational Sunday School Teachers & Workers taken about 1885.

Back Row—Wm. Hall, (Librarian), Arthur Lockett, Spencer Warren with his Son and Daughter, Thos. Booth, Henry Salt, Mr. Phillips Arthur Nicholson, A. Sumerling, Dr. J. J. Ritchie, John Jackman, Joseph Lovatt, John Rudkin, Geo. H. Bailey, Geo. Brookes, Charles Hancock, W. J. Moorhouse, Joseph Shaw, Gus Carr.

Middle Row—W. H. Johnson, Miss Ritchie, Miss Ives, Miss Hankinson, Miss Marsland, Rev. J. Hankinson, Miss Ball, Miss Pollie Ratcliffe, Isaac Heath, Miss L. Carr.

Front Row—Miss Overfield, Miss Sugden, Miss Dishley, Miss Singer, Mrs. Jackman, Miss Booth, Miss Lizzie Heath.

IN naming the ladies and gentlemen in the above group, which was taken some forty-five years ago, we have taken the liberty of using the names they were known by at that time.

There are thirty-seven people in the group. and as every one was an earnest worker in the Congregational Sunday School, it gives some idea of the strength and usefulness of the Congregational Church of that day, and also of the valuable and very wide influence it has had upon the life of the town.

GROUP OF LEEK LIBERALS, 1895.

Back Row—R. Thompson, T. W. Billing, W. Whetstone, R. Bott, S. Hammond, C. Ward.
Second Row—R. Naden, J. Carter, J. Fogg, E. Carter, W. Stannard, A. Nixon, G. Hall, A. Tatton.
First Row—H. J. Cope, T. Porter, G. Cope, W. Eaton, T. Heywood, H. Moorhouse, W. S. Mears, F. Bode.

THE group reproduced above reflects something of the enthusiasm and interest that were taken in politics locally some thirty-five years ago. In those days Liberalism in Leek was very much alive, and the late Mr. Robert Pearce (afterwards Sir Robert) whom almost everyone in Leek affectionately knew as "Bobby" Pearce had no lack of supporters.

The late Mr. M. H. Miller writing in the *Leek Times* of the 1895 election said: "A parade of some score bicyclists with their machines bedecked with Liberal colours, and carrying cards bearing the instruction Vote for Pearce, was a source of considerable interest and was altogether a most effective spectacle"

This election of 1895 was the first Mr. Pearce fought in Leek—He was then opposed by the late Mr. Charles Bill. The poll at this, and Mr. Pearce's subsequent elections, were as follows :—

Opening of the Leek Branch of the North Staffordshire Railway.

From the Staffordshire Sentinel, 2nd November, 1867.

YESTERDAY, the new line of railway from Stoke to Leek, or more exactly, from a point beyond Bucknall on the Biddulph Valley line, to a point on the Churnet Valley line near Leek, was opened for passenger traffic. There were goodly numbers of passengers by the trains yesterday, and considerable jubilation by the good people of Leek, the day being observed as a semi-holiday by them. Mr. W. Challinor liberally devised a good luncheon, to which he invited the directors, and officials of the railway, besides a number of the inhabitants of Leek and the Potteries. At Leek Station a band was playing, an evidently gratified crowd had assembled, and, on alighting at the Leek Station, the visitors were welcomed by Mr. Challinor, and then entered vehicles which had been provided for their conveyance, the band meanwhile playing loyal tunes. A vehicular procession was then formed, and was preceded by the band, and followed by a large crowd. In this order the Compton schoolroom was reached, and here a *recherche* luncheon was provided by Mr. Duessen, of the Red Lion Hotel.

The chair was occupied by Mr. W. Challinor, who was supported by Lieutenant-Colonel Pearson, Chairman of the North Staffordshire Railway Company; R. H. Haywood, Esq., W. Brownfield, Esq., directors of the company; and the Rev. G. E. [illegible] of Leek, Mr. P. Brocklehurst, of Swythamley, and many other gentlemen of the town and neighbourhood. The schoolroom was neatly decorated, and over the Chairman's seat was the inscription, "Success to the North Staffordshire Railway."—After the excellent meal had been discussed, the Chairman gave the loyal toasts, and followed them up with, "The Clergy of the Diocese," "The Army, Navy, and Volunteers," "The Lord Lieutenant and the Magistrates," all which toasts were duly acknowledged. The Chairman said it now devolved upon him to propose the toast of the day, "The health of the Chairman and Directors of the North Staffordshire Railway Company, and success to their new undertaking, the branch line of railway between Stoke and Leek." (Loud applause). It had happened as an accident, that he was the humble representative of his fellow townsmen in welcoming the directors and officials of the railway, not only in their official capacity, but also on account of their personal qualities. (Applause). They had completed a branch which, though short, would materially conduce to the convenience, comfort, and prosperity of the town of Leek. (Applause). The state of things in Leek, and the considerable district round it, with respect to communication with the Pottery towns, had been most difficult and inconvenient. Either the people of Leek had had to go round by North Rode or by Uttoxeter, the result being that on reaching either of those places, they found themselves ten miles further off than they were when they started. Like the schoolboy in going to school, they could say that for every step forward they had taken two steps backwards—laughter—and had therefore to turn their backs upon their destination to reach it. (Laughter). Now, however, they would not have to turn their backs on Stoke in order to reach it, for they had a straightforward line, and instead of having to travel forty miles, they would only have to traverse a distance of eleven miles; and he was sure that the company, in forming that branch, had established a link which would be of advantage to both districts, as well as to the company providing the accommodation. (Applause). He would hear mention that he had received letters from Lord Shrewsbury, Mr. Kynnersley, Mr. Smith Child, and other directors of the company, expressive of their regret that they could not be present at that meeting, and wishing God speed to the branch that day opened. The Ashbourne and Hanley branches had paid well, and he trusted that the Leek branch would pay as well or better. (Applause). They saw above him what had been adopted by the railway company, the Staffordshire knot. They had all read of a certain classical knot which had to be cut, and most of them knew something of another knot, the matrimonial, which could rarely be untied nor cut—(laughter)—but which nevertheless had been, he trusted, productive of the greatest benefits to them. But the Staffordshire knot was a fastening the origin of which was involved in considerable mystery; he had never heard what it meant, yet he would venture to hope that, as represented on that occasion, it would prove a bond of union between Leek and the Potteries, tying together in friendly unity the trades and manufactures of North Staffordshire. (Loud applause). While the people of Leek were willing to assist the company as customers, on the one hand, he trusted the company, on the other hand, would assist the people of Leek in little matters of arrangement which were of importance to the trades of the town, and that both would work harmoniously together for their mutual interest. (Applause). He was very happy that he was the medium of conveying the thanks of his fellow townsmen to the directors for their attendance that day, as well personally as in respect of the great undertaking they had carried out. He begged to propose the "health of the Directors, coupling with them the names of Colonel Pearson, Mr. Haywood, and Mr. Brownfield, trusting that the company would long have the benefit of their direction, and that they might long enjoy health and prosperity." (Loud applause). Colonel Pearson said it fell to his lot to thank them for their hearty reception of the toast so kindly proposed. He was unaccustomed to occupy such a position before the general public, but it did not require much eloquence to say that he and his co-directors really valued the kindness which had that day been exhibited to them, and that he hoped the directors would long hold the good opinion they had been kind enough to express. Too often, railway directors were at variance with the public, because it was forgotten that the directors had the shareholders to think of first, and that they could not, without injury to the shareholders, bring the rails to every one's door. He trusted the good people of Leek would see, when the arrangements of the new branch should be completed, that the directors had done the best they could, as quickly as they could, consistently with their duty as trustees of the shareholders; and that the Staffordshire knot would really prove a knot of unity. (Applause). He was induced to believe it would be so, by the heartiness of the reception which had been that day accorded to the directors. (Applause). He could only say that he wished the branch had been made years before, and now it was opened, he was sure the general manager would give to Leek every accommodation that could be given with justice to the shareholders. (Loud applause). The Chairman and others then proposed the health of Mr. Forsyth, engineer to the company; Mr. Morris, General Manager; Mr. Samuda, Secretary; Mr. Challinor and others, which were [illegible] and responded to.

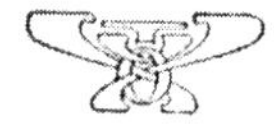

The Old Leek Grammar School, taken at the time of the Royal Jubilee Celebrations, 1887.

Back Row.—Peter Bluett, W. Breton, R. Rushton, C. Hammersley, E. Hammersley, J. J. T. Sykes, J. Sykes (Headmaster), H. Massey, H. Knight, S. Stannard, S. Trafford, E. W. Bridgewood, C. Bluett, T. Cantrell, G. Timmis.
MiddleRow.—Percy Bluett, W. Lea, H. Walker, W. Lovatt, T. Maskery, D. Fergyson, W. Clowes, H. Bluett, T. Bamford, E. Blades, E. Hill.
Front Row.—R. Brealey, A. W. Ellerton, R. Scarratt, F. Taylor, G. Govier, W. Jones, R. Govier, A. Walker, V. Jones.

AMONG the scholars included in the above group of Leek Grammar School boys, which was taken in Jubilee Year, are many that have since attained and are at present occupying prominent and responsible positions in the professional, commercial, and public life not only in Leek but also in important centres throughout the Empire. Most of these boys are now fathers, some of them are grandfathers, and it will afford not a little interest to their off-spring and younger acquaintances to see them as they appeared in their boyhood days.

A group of Leek Men in New Zealand, Xmas, 1906.

Back Row—E. Bullen, G. Bailey, H. Meakin, R. Bailey, T. Wood, T. Hambleton, G. Stanyer, A. Simpson
Middle Row—W. Heath, T. Plant, J. Baxter, J. Heath, A. Dale, H, Porter, F. Hassall, E. Amson.
Front Row—C. Bonsall, E. Brough, J. Rod, J. Rod, jun., W. Newall, F. Brooks, E. Goodwin, G. Ball.

THE photograph reproduced above is of unusual interest, and inasmuch as it was taken twenty-six years ago this Christmas at a spot some 12,000 miles away from home, it is a remarkable group—a gathering of twenty-two Leek men in New Zealand !

Mr. Rod, the host, who can be seen with his son in the front row, was for many years a very good friend to Leek men arriving in New Zealand, and was instrumental in finding situations for many of them.

To mark their appreciation of Mr. Rod's many kindnesses, these "strangers in a strange land" decided to club together and present him with a gold watch. This they did, and the above photograph was taken on the occasion of the presentation.

Mr. W. Newall, whom many will remember seeing on his recent visit to this country, is in the centre of the group. It is interesting to note that when Mr. Newall built his house, which is near Wellington, he christened it "Rudyard House."

THE FIRST ANNUAL REPORT, OF THE

Leek Benevolent Burial Society,

Established December 13th, 1840.

ADDRESS.

WE, the Officers of the above Institution, beg leave to lay before an enlightened Public, a statement of the pecuniary affairs of this Society. Its prospects during the first stage of its infancy have been of an animating and cheering nature. When we take a retrospective view of its rise and progress, under the blessing of Almighty God, we stand astonished to witness such great effects produced from such little causes.

It is gratifying to the thinking mind to consider that our united efforts have been the means of affording relief to the wants of our suffering fellow creatures. Since the commencement of this Institution, various have been the vicissitudes to which some of its members have been called to endure; some have been arrested by he cold hand of Death, and have been called out of time into a never ending Eternity.

Thus the surviving relatives have through the medium of this Institution, been enabled to inter their deceased friends decently and respectably, and thus the cordial balm of consolation has been timely administered to alleviate their distress, so that the hearts of the Fatherless, the Orphan, and the Widow have been made to rejoice.

We further beg to return our grateful acknowledgements to the Humane and Benevolen who have so kindly come forward and subscribed their names as Honorary Members; likewise to those who have given their Donations in aid of its funds. We hope many may see the utility of the Institution, and follow so praiseworthy an example, and we trust that the Nobility and Gentry of LEEK and its Vicinity, may be led to appreciate its merits, and give it their patronage and support, as the establishment of this Society has been the means of removing many incumbrances, which in some cases would have devolved on the Rate Payers.

We humbly hope by a steady adherence to the strict rules of economy and justice, which principles are the basis on which this Society is founded, we trust the succeeding year may surpass the preceding. We beg to return our sincere thanks to the Collectors of each division, for their unwearied exertions in the discharge of their respective duties, as nothing has been wanting on their part to promote the interest of the Society. We presume this Institution has the pre-eminence over that of others, hence its ob ect is to embrace from the cradled infant of six weeks old, to the hoary head of fifty years, (providing they be in health,) and in case of death ample provision is made for their decent interment.

"Therefore in the morning sow thy seed, and in the evening withhold not thine hand, for thou knowest not which shall prosper, whether it shall be this or that, or whether they shall both be alike good."

The subjoined is a statement of our affairs during the past year—Funerals 26. Amount paid for Funerals £93 12s. 0. Members 1155. The extra money paid £41 2s. 9d. Amount of Cash in the Treasurer's hands (Thomas Carr, Jun., Esq.) £50. In Sub-Treasurer's hands (Mr. John Mien) £21 9s. 7½d.

OFFICERS.	COMMITTEE.		HONORARY MEMBERS.
GEORGE PARKER, *President.*	MATTHEW COPE,	JESSE RUSHTON,	MR. W. M. HILLIARD, STATIONER.
RICHARD SCHOFIELD, } *Inspectors.*	WILLIAM AINSWORTH,	SAMUEL HOWARD,	MR. G. NALL, DITTO.
JOSEPH BIRCH, JUN., } *Inspectors.*	JAMES ASH,	WILLIAM KEATES,	MR. G. RIDER, CLERK of LEEK CHURCH.
JOHN MIEN, *Sub-Treasurer.*	SAMUEL TURNOCK,	JOSEPH BRADLEY,	MR. U. WAMSLEY, PUBLICAN.
JOHN TAGELL, *Secretary.*	WILLIAM BIRCH,	RICHARD GOODWIN.	MRS. LASSETTER, DITTO.
THOMAS CARR, JUN., ESQ., *Treasurer.*	JOSHUA MOSS.		MRS. HAWKINS, DITTO.

FIRST QUARTER,

Dr.

Date		£.	s.	d.
1840.				
Dec. 13,	By [illegible] 1..	0	3	8
20,	Ditto	0	6	8
27,	Ditto	0	13	0
31,	By Messrs. T. Carr & Co. Donation	1	0	0
..	By Mr. France, ditto	0	5	0
..	By J. Davenport, Esq., ditto	0	10	0
..	By a Friend	0	2	6
1841.				
Jan. 3,	By Cash received	0	14	8
10,	Ditto	1	6	9
17,	Ditto	1	14	1
24,	Ditto	1	19	5
31,	Ditto	2	7	0
Feb. 8,	Ditto	2	14	11
15,	By Mr. Hammersley, donation	0	10	0
..	Ditto	3	1	7
22,	Ditto	3	3	1
Mar. 1,	Ditto	3	13	6
..	By a Friend	0	10	0
8,	By Cash	4	0	6
15,	Ditto	4	1	10
21,	Ditto	3	15	3
28,	Ditto	4	3	5
Apr. 5,	Ditto	4	1	5
..	By Articles sold	3	2	10
..	By Mr. Hilliard's ditto	0	1	5
..	By Mr. Nall's Donation	0	1	1
		£48	3	7

Cr.

Date		£.	s.	d.
1840.				
Dec. 15,	To Paper, Books, &c.	0	3	11½
18,	To 2 Men's expenses memorializing	0	5	0
..	To expenses attending the *establishment of the Institution*	2	0	0
27,	To 4 Money Bags	0	1	7
..	To Mr. Nall's Account	3	9	10½
..	To Coals and Candles	0	0	11
1841.				
Jan. 10,	To Enroling Articles	1	1	0
..	To Post Office Order	0	0	5
..	To William Johnson	0	0	5
17,	To a Man memorializing	0	2	0
..	To Paper, Ink and Candles	0	1	1
..	To Postage, Candles & Coals	0	1	10
..	To James Mayers	0	2	0
..	To Committee Meeting	0	3	4
.	To William Johnson	0	1	3½
..	To Stamps and Committee	0	3	8
..	To Gas		1	3½
..	To Collectors' and Officers' Salaries	6	17	4
16,	To Committee	0	3	4
..	To Mr. Hilliard's Account for Printing	4	0	0
..	To Committee	0	4	0
		19	4	4
..	To Cash in Sub-Treasurer's hands	28	19	3
		£48	3	7

SECOND QUARTER,

Dr.

Date		£.	s.	d.
1841.				
	By Balance last Quarter	28	19	3
Apr. 12,	By Cash received	3	19	4
19,	Ditto	4	3	8
..	By Mr. Sawkins' donation	0	5	0
..	*By Mr. Wm. Challinor*	0	5	0
..	By Mr. R. Sterling	0	5	0
..	By Mr. J. Gaunt	0	5	0
..	By Mr. J. Howes	0	2	6
..	By Mr. Charles Lockett	0	2	0
..	By Mr. Rigby	0	2	0
..	By Mr. Winfield	0	5	0
..	By Mr. Thurstan	0	2	0
..	By Mr. G. Bull	0	2	6
..	By Mr. Thomas Johnson	0	2	0
..	By Mr. W. Hine	0	2	0
26,	By Cash	4	4	10
May 3,	Ditto	4	1	1
10,	Ditto	4	2	4
17,	Ditto	4	1	9
23,	Ditto	4	2	7
30,	Ditto	4	7	4
June 7,	Ditto	4	1	11
14,	Ditto	4	13	6
21,	Ditto	4	7	9
..	By Entrance Money	0	2	6
28,	By Cash	4	4	5
..	By Entrance Money	0	5	0
July 4,	By Cash	4	4	6
..	By Mr. Nall	0	1	1
..	By Articles Sold	0	5	2
..	By Mr. Alsop	0	5	0
		£86	13	0

Cr.

Date		£.	s.	d.
1841.				
Apr. 12,	To Giving Quarterly Meeting	0	1	0
..	To Candles, Nails, & Postage	0	0	9
..	To 2 Men's expenses memorializing	0	5	0
..	To preparing Room	0	1	3
26,	To Blot Paper	0	0	2
..	To Box	0	14	0
..	To Paper, Candles, Pens, and Holders	0	2	6
..	To William Johnson	0	0	9
..	To Committee Meeting	0	6	0
..	To Mary Mellor, London Road, 42	3	12	0
..	To Henry Smith, Gettliffe's Yard, 1	3	12	0
..	To William Wood, Buxton Road, 18	3	12	0
..	To Mary Simpson, Albion street, 41	3	12	0
..	To Ebenezer Worthington, Prospect, 1	3	12	0
..	To Ann Gratton, London Street, 37	3	12	0
..	To Mary Plant, London st. 19	3	12	0
..	To Elizabeth Allison, Preston, 35	3	12	0
..	To Officers' Wages	6	16	0
		37	3	11
	To Cash in Treasurer's hands	49	9	1
		£86	13	0

THIRD QUARTER,

Dr.

Date		£.	s.	d.
1841				
	By Balance last Quarter	49	9	1
July 12,	By Cash received	4	13	4
19,	Ditto	4	3	1
26,	Ditto	4	10	4
Aug. 2,	Ditto	4	4	6
9,	Ditto	4	7	3
16,	Ditto	4	10	8
23,	Ditto	4	10	8
30,	Ditto	4	4	9½
Sep. 6,	Ditto	4	10	6½
13,	Ditto	4	9	9½
20,	Ditto	4	15	8½
27,	Ditto	4	7	1½
Oct. 3,	Ditto	4	11	7½
[illegible]	[illegible]	[illegible]	[illegible]	[illegible]
		£112	10	8½

Cr.

Date		£.	s.	d.
1841.				
Oct. 10,	To Officers' and Collectors' Salary	7	7	0
18,	,, Preparing Room	0	1	3
..	,, Allowance attending ditto	0	0	6
Aug. 2,	,, Writing Paper	0	1	2
9,	,, Candlesticks	0	3	0
19,	,, Candles	0	0	7
..	,, Pens and Pen Holders	0	1	6
Sep. 13,	,, Governing Committee,	0	7	6
27,	,, Sub-Treasurer's Salary	0	5	0
..	,, Candles	0	0	7
Oct. 20,	,, Ditto	0	0	7
July 12,	,, John Hargreaves, Mill-street, 80.	3	12	0
14,	,, Sarah Cope, Clerk's-bank	3	12	0
16,	,, Mary Thompson, London-road, 47	3	12	0
Aug. 11,	,, Hannah Rigby, West-street, 77.	3	12	0
22,	,, Mary Cope, Kiln-lane	3	12	0
Sep. 2,	,, Mary Smith, Buxton-road, 70	3	12	0
20,	,, Elizabeth Hill, Mill-street	3	12	0
26,	,, Jane Lovatt, Belle-vue, 19	3	12	0
27,	,, Jane Stonehewer, Mill-street, 69	3	12	0
Oct. 7,	,, William Moss, Spout-street, 80	3	12	0
..	,, A. E. Keates, London-road, 10	3	12	0
		£51	12	6
	By Cash in Treasurer's hands, (T. Carr, Jun. Esq.)	50	0	0
	By Ditto in Sub-Treasurer's hands, (Mr. J. Mien)	10	18	2½
		£112	10	8½

FOURTH QUARTER.

Dr.

Date		£.	s.	d.
1841.				
	By Balance last Qnarter	60	18	2½
Oct. 17,	By Cash	4	4	0½
25,	Ditto	4	4	0
..	By Mr. Rider's Subscription	0	5	0
Nov. 1,	By Cash	4	17	3½
8.	Ditto	4	10	16
15,	Ditto	4	12	3
22,	Ditto	4	8	11
29,	Ditto	4	12	9
Dec. 5,	Ditto	4	4	11½
12,	Ditto	4	13	5½
		£101	11	8½

Cr.

Date		£.	s.	d.
1841.				
Oct. 17,	To Officers and Collectors	4	14	6
..	,, Candles and Coals	0	1	
Nov. 1,	,, Blot Paper	0	0	7
21,	,, Candles	0	1	2
..	,, Ink	0	0	3
..	,, Paper	0	0	5
Nov. 8,	,, Edith Hill, Mill-street	3	12	0
9,	,, Mary Beards, Stockwell-street, 70	3	12	0
13,	,, William Ingham, Market-place, 60	3	12	0
18,	,, Elizabeth Abraham, Mill-street, 25	3	12	0
..	,, Ann Ball, Kiln-lane, 47	3	12	0
Dec. 5,	,, Mary Abbott, Spout-street, 43	3	12	0
11,	,, Mary Brook, [illegible]	[illegible]	[illegible]	[illegible]
		30	2	1
	By Cash in T. Carr's, Jun., Esq. Hands	50	0	0
	By Cash in Sub-Treasurer's Hands	21	9	7½
		£101	11	8½

W. M. HILLIARD, PRINTER, &c., MARKET-PLACE, LEEK.

LEEK · IMPROVEMENT · ACT.
1855.
First Commissioners elected under the Leek Improvement Act, 1855, at Election held on 25th September 1855
JAMES ALSOP
JOSEPH BENTLEY
JAMES BERMINGHAM
THOMAS BIRCH
JOHN BROUGH
JOSHUA BROUGH
JOSIAH BRUNT
THOMAS CARR
JOHNCRUSO
NATIAN DAVENPORT
MOUITFORT FYNNEY
MAT'HEW GAUNT
SIMON GETTLIFFE
ROBERT HAMMERSLEY
JOHN LOVATT
GEORGE MASSEY
JAMES RIDOUT
JOHN RUSSELL
SAMUEL TATTON
JOHN WARD
THOMAS WEST
JOHN WESTON, Senr.
JOHN GIBSON WHITTLES
GEORGE YOUNG
Members of the Leek Urban District Council 1905
THOMAS HENRY BOOTH
ROBERT WRIGHT, J.P.
ANDREW MORTON
THOMAS SHAW
ALFRED HOWARD MOORE, J.P.
HENRY ALLEN
JOHN ERNEST INGHAM, F.I.C.S.
CHARLES WATSON, J.P.
THOMAS MASON
THOMAS HENRY MORTON
GEORGE TAYLOR STEVENSON
HENRY DAVENPORT
GEORGE NEEDHAM HAMMERSLEY
HENRY WEST BRASSINGTON
WILLIAM HALL
ALFRED FLOWER
SAMUEL MILLWARD PRINCE
ROBERT SCHOLEFIELD MILNER
JAMES CORNES
WILLIAM BARNFATHER
HUGH RICHARD SLEIGH, J.P.
THOMAS WHITTLES
JOSEPH RATCLIFFE
ARTHUR HASSALL
HENRY ALLEN (VICE CHAIRMAN)
WILLIAM ALLEN (LAW CLERK)
Given under the Common Seal of the Council this 24th day of October 1905.
Chairman
Clerk
Law Clerk

Leek reaches 3rd Round of the English Cup.

IN the 80's of last century, Leek football was probably at its zenith. Something of the proud record of those days has been mentioned elsewhere in this issue.

But probably the greatest match in which the Leek team ever took part was that played against Queen's Park (Glasgow) in the 3rd round of the English Cup, fifty years ago this season.

Below we give the teams and the description of the match as it appeared in the Press of that day.

QUEEN'S PARK.		LEEK.	
P. McCallum, Goal.		E. Hassall, Goal.	
J. Harvie,	Backs.	F. Byrne	Backs
W. Arnot,		G. C. Wardle	
C. Campbell,	Half-Backs.	G. Tudor,	Half-Backs.
J. McDonald,		J. Smethurst,	
W. Anderson,	Forwards.	H. E. Whittles,	
W. Harrower,		W. Vickerstaff,	Forwards
R. Christie		M. Rider,	
A. Hamilton,		H. Stonehewer	
J. Lambie,		J. Brentnall,	
D. S. Allan,		W. E. Allen,	

The photograph recently taken at Mr. G. C. Wardle's home includes the only five Leek players still living who played in the Queen's Park Match.

G. C. WARDLE W. VICKERSTAFF
J. SMETHURST H. STONEHEWER J. BRENTNALL

The great Queen's Park Match.

On Saturday, January 3rd, 1885, the great historic struggle between Queen's Park, Glasgow, and Leek, took place at Leek. From the moment it was known that Leek had been drawn against the famous Glasgow organization, the greatest interest was manifested in the match, and as the time drew near for the contest the excitement became intense. Of course it scarcely entered the mind of anyone before the match that the comparatively unknown Moorland team would wrest the victory from their powerful antagonists, but all who knew the true form of the Leek men felt fairly confident that the match would not prove the walk-over it looked upon paper. Under all the circumstances it was naturally expected that a great crowd of spectators would be seen on the Westwood Lane ground when the event was ripe for decision, and the Saturday afternoon proved that these hopes were entirely realised, upwards of three thousand persons being present, including a number of ladies.

Mr. R. Browne umpired for Queen's Park, and Mr. T. Armitt for Leek. Mr. J. Pope, of Wednesbury, officiating as referee.

It will be seen that the visitors played two halves and six forwards.

The home team won the toss, and at 2-50 the ball was kicked off by the visiting centre forwards. After a short period of pressure by the visitors, McCullum was called upon to save his charge. This roused the visitors effectually and they gained several corners, but were unable to pierce the strong defence of Leek, until a slow shot travelled over the goal-line before Hassall, who was looking after the man, could get at it. Other corners fell to the visitors, but were unproductive, no score resulting from a corner during the game. Once about this period of the game a gleam of hope was seen for Leek when the ball got past the Glasgow backs, but the goalkeeper kicked down the field and a pretty scrimmage in the Leek goal ended in the visitors scoring No. 2, Anderson for the second time giving the final touch. Hassall saved finely from the kick-off, and then Rider was hurt, and was scarcely able to play his usual game afterwards. The play became more even, and Leek made a determined rush, and were rewarded with a fine goal off Vickerstaff, the feat being greeted with enthusiastic cheers. The visitors' custodian was again called upon to save from a shot from Allen, and until half-time was whistled the game was of a very even and interesting character, the score being two goals to one in favour of Glasgow when the whistle blew. The second half of the game was even more keenly contested than the first. For a short time the ball was kept in the Glasgow territory, and encouraged by the frantic cheers of the home supporters, the Leek forwards missed a goal by a few inches only. Leek secured two corners, and then Anderson had hard lines at the other end, the ball hitting the post and going out. Soon afterwards, however, he had better luck and with a swift shot he registered the third goal for the visitors. Queen's Park now reduced their forwards to four, and presented a magnificent defence, in which Campbell and McAra played an important part, and this was the more necessary as Bryden, having strained his ankle, was of very little use. Leek made many furious onslaughts one of which was rewarded by Allen scoring just beneath the bar. The Glasgow umpire objected, stating that the ball had gone over, but Mr. Jope decided for Leek; amidst terrific cheers. Towards the close, Vickerstaff had a grand chance of equalising, but at the supreme moment, and within a few yards of the goal, he slipped on the frozen ground, and Queens' Park kicking out, and thus wasting valuable time, were left the winners of one of the finest and best contested games ever seen on the Leek ground, by three goals to two. Christie, McCullum, Campbell, Anderson and Hamilton were the best of the visitors on the day's play, whilst Byrne, Wardle, Hassall, Vickerstaff, Allen and Smethurst did wonders for Leek, all the rest of the team playing up well. After the match, the visitors were entertained at dinner by the Leek club, at the Swan Hotel, Mr. R. S. Milner occupying the chair and Mr. G. C. Wardle the vice-chair. Mr. Campbell, in responding to the toast of the Glasgow team, complimented Leek upon their play, stating that the game was very even, and that they had nothing to boast of in their three goals to two victory. It was one of the best, pleasantest and hardest games the Queen's Park had ever fought, and they should return to Glasgow with the most pleasant recollections of Leek. There was nothing, in his opinion, to prevent Leek taking a leading position amongst the best of Association players, and he hoped at some future time to have the pleasure of playing against them again. The *Manchester Guardian* of the Monday following said, "Leek gave Queen's Park a surprisingly hard nut to crack, but notwithstanding this the famous Scotch organization seem bent on lifting the cup."

Men's Bible Class, West Street Wesleyan Sunday School

CORONATION DAY, 22nd JUNE, 1911.

BACK ROW—W. Osborne, J. Erisley, C. Sherratt, G. Pickering, W. H. Pickering, T. Hunt, J. A. Vigrass, H. H. Goodwin, H. Rhead, T. Vigrass, H. Rushton, H. Brentnall, T. Higginbotham, G. Crombie, W. Vaughan, T. Burgess, H. Morton, A. Nixon.

3rd ROW (Standing)—W. Clowes, S. Bayley, A. Hunt, A. Bayley, H. Bayley, F. Goodwin, J. Bonsall, T. Bloor, S. Bayley, F. Kelsall, A. J. Kent, D. Ingham, A. Prime, J. Loxley, J. Hall (Supt.), J. Wood, H. Morriss, J. Morriss, W. Morriss, A. Leadbeater, J. Bayley, J. Swindlehurst, H. Ralphs, A. J. Hine, G. Hulme, H. Brockhurst, H. Bayley, E. Fernyhough, W. Marren, B. Farrall.

2nd ROW (Sitting)—H. Bal., J. Bayley, W. Ward, J. Morrow, H. Lomas, A. Gibson, D. Lovatt, T. Goodwin (Teacher), L. Ball, L. Ball, J. Gaunt, S. Murray, G. Stonier, S. Goodwin, A. Leadbeater, W. Ainsworth.

FRONT ROW—F. Gosling, F. Owen, W. Turner, W. Ball, W. Brentnall, S. Owen, T. Wardle, A. Worthington, W. Rhead, E. Matthews, W. Hudson.

EVERYONE connected with Sunday School work knows how the numbers and the interest ebb and flow, and how difficult it is to retain the interest of people in this work after they have passed the age when they are transferred from the junior and intermediate section and take their places among the seniors. So many competing interests claim the time and attention of adults that a really efficient and well attended senior school can only be obtained by patient and thorough preparation and a close personal interest in those whose names are on the books.

West Street School has had a long list of devoted teachers and officials who have carried on a tradition which has been handed down from men whose ambition was to serve their fellow men and who used the medium of the school to inculcate the principles in which they believed and which had served to carry them through the difficult and often baffling periods of life.

Like all institutions of its kind the School has had periods when the attendance has been large and the interest well sustained. The accompanying photograph shows a very remarkable group of men taken in 1911. This group is the Men's Bible Class, which at that period was led by the late Mr. Thos. Goodwin, who, during the later years of his life, gave much time and thought to his weekly meeting with these men, and looked upon the position he held as a signal honour crowning many years of active service in various spheres of the Methodist Church with which he had been associated from childhood.

Born of sturdy Methodist stock, in the parish of Quarnford, where his father laboured on a farm and his mother made silk buttons for the factory at Leek, he was put to work in the coal pit at the tender age of five years, when one of his duties was to pull the small wagons of coal to and from the coal face to the loading positions. There was no compulsory elementary education in those days, but as he grew older his family gravitated to Leek where the night school met his thirst for knowledge and he began to gain that love of literature and general education which he pursued right to the end of life. In order the more efficiently to teach and preach the truths of the Bible, after attaining the age of fifty years he began to learn the Greek language so that he might read the books of the New Testament in the original, and many were the happy hours he spent in elucidating problems which arose during the weekly discussion.

A glance at the photograph will bring to mind memories of men who have become eminent in the life of the town and others who have migrated to various countries in the Empire, there to influence the life of the community, and doubtlessly a sight of this group will serve to remind many of those pre-war days and possibly act as an incentive to others to continue the work which has been a source of benefit to the moral and spiritual interests of this town.

THE BEST AMATEUR PERFORMANCE IN LEEK

THE SMALL BOY OF THE MARKET PLACE.

SOME months ago I read a criticism in a local paper of an amateur performance which stated that it was the best amateur performance ever held in Leek.

While not questioning that statement I wondered how the critic, who had been so short a time in Leek, could know, and my mind went back and back until it became the small boy's (of the Market Place, if you like) even then interested in amateur performances and all pertaining thereto. Back from the local Amateur Acting Societies at present existing, through the Leek Amateur Opera Society's twenty years, the Moorlands Amateur Operatic Society, and the Wounded Soldiers' performances at the Town Hall during the four years of war, then to the local pantomimes in the early years of the 1900's; the first, Leek Amateur Operatic Society of the 90's and the frequent Amateur Theatricals in which Miss "Trissie" Allen (Mrs. W. G. Challinor's brilliant sister) was the bright particular star; on through the Philothespian Club which was formed in the 80's, to the old Volunteer Theatricals which was my earliest personal recollection of Amateur Acting.

Continuing, I recalled the accounts which Mr. A. H. Moore gave me of performances in the 70's, and Mr. J. G. Beckett's even earlier amateur activities. Looking over his criticism of the Leek Amateur Opera Society's performance of "The Mikado" I see that he wrote: "My memory went back for more than sixty years" incidently of this performance he said "'The Mikado' is the greatest success yet achieved by any local Society. . . . It would hardly be possible to suggest any improvement)." If in 1922, Mr. Beckett's recollections covered a period of more than sixty years, we are carried back to about 1860; then I remembered seeing in the William Salt Library at Stafford, a programme of an amateur performance held in Leek in 1840 or thereabouts, in which Miss Challinor's name appeared; therefore we have now about a century of amateur acting to investigate before we can really know which *was* the best amateur performance ever given in Leek.

So let us return from this point. Touching the 40's I have only to say that the Challinors as a family have now been amateur actors for almost a century—maybe earlier but I am only dealing with my own knowledge. There was the Miss Challinor whose name was in the programme mentioned above, and I have distinct recollections of Mr. W. G. Challinor in theatricals, and still more distinct recollections of his son, Colonel Challinor (who I believe also acted with the Cambridge U.D.C.) and now his niece, Mrs. Peter Johnson, is carrying on the family tradition, and in her last part in "Mr. Pim Passes By" was particularly delghtful—in fact the production of this play has distinct claims to be one of the best amateur performances in Leek.

Progressing to the 60's of which Mr. Beckett talked so much (I remember how he generally prefaced his criticisms in the "Leek Times"—of which he seemed to act as Art Critic—with reflections of what he and his contemporaries did in the 60's and 70's so that a parody of the famous Gladstonian query was frequently quoted and became a standard joke in the Leek Amateur Opera Society:—"What did Beckett do in '63 ?)." I think some good work must have been done then for he was a thorough artist and interested in all artistic pursuits. I remember seeing him perform "Shylock," perhaps thirty years later (than the 60's referred to) but I was then flippant enough to be more interested in how he sharpened his knife in the trial scene, on the wooden boards of the Town Hall stage, than his histrionic efforts. I also saw him perform "Samuel" in the "Pirates of Penzance" with the Old Leek Amateur Operatic Society, but then he was old—at least in my arrogant youth I thought so—and I was not much impressed by his performance. Nevertheless, I think in his day he must have been an asset to the amateur movement of his time. There was also a young lady I knew in my youth, who I believe was a contemporary of Mr. Beckett's and who, according to her own telling, had been a leading local amateur actress—Miss Woodhead. I say a "young" lady for although she must have been about seventy, she was still very young, not only in her outlook but in her spritely figure, due it was rumoured to her daily habit of leaping on and off the sofa—thus anticipating, if somewhat primitively, modern rejuvenating treatment.

Naturally, of the 70's I have no personal recollections, but Mr. A. H. Moore used to give great accounts of performances in this period, in which his wife played and another leading lady of whose name I am uncertain. I think it was Miss Lightfoot. I suppose it would be during this period that Mr. M. H. Miller, editor of the "Leek Times" appeared as an amateur actor, and, if he was as entertaining as he was in private life, I should think he was very good.

Next we come to the 80's and with the later years my own personal recollections begin. Certainly my criticism of this period would not be of much value. I clearly recollect being highly critical of the extraordinary length of the men's Georgian waistcoats, which were new to me, in—would it be "She Stoops to Conquer" or "The Rivals"? I think the former, because I have very definite recollections of the latter play by the old Volunteer Theatricals in which Sergt. Bolstridge took part. I think it might be taken as genuine criticism if I said he was not a good actor, for I recollect how his movements so reminded us of him as our Drill Instructor teaching us to "Right turn," "Smartly come to attention," etc. And his dialogue was about as intelligible as his words of command "As unt" (eyes front) and so on. I remember his entrance when he came to say farewell to "Julia" seemed like "Left,-right,-left-alas-Julia! Left,-right,-left,-right,-right-turn,-attention,-feet-at-an-angle-of-45 degrees. — "I-come-to-bid-you-a-long-farewell." My recollection of individual performers at this time is very hazy. At their earlier performances I think professional actresses were engaged, as it was considered "fast" for local ladies to take part. I remember great excitement when Miss Rose Seton, "the eminent Shakespearian actress," came to perform, and I quite felt we were seeing Ellen Terry's or Mrs. Kendal's equal and was much impressed with her snakelike movements.

I do, however, remember at the performance of "The Rivals" previously mentioned falling violently in love with Miss Alice Sherratt, a young lady who was then much in the public eye, and whom I thought supremely beautiful with her bright corn coloured hair and china complexion. I also remember Miss Alice Birtles (who was reputed to be very accomplished), and Miss Tillie Slater, acting "Lydia Languish," a step-daughter of Mr. Travis, who lived in the Market Place and whose clocks are now collected by connoisseurs. Of later performers, I remember Mr. Willie Young, Mr Marcus Prince, Mr. Edward Challinor, Sergt. W. P. Govier and others.

It was in the 80's also that the Philothespian Club was formed, and it s surprising that a Dramatic Society of fifty years ago should have been "formed on modern lines" (as the fashion papers have it) like the many modern Amateur Dramatic Societies of to-day. Their motto, "The Play's the Thing," headed their programmes, not "Charity's the Thing" as many are now. There always seems to me something rather dishonest and self-convicting in this. By all means give your profits to charity if you have any, and if you can afford it, and perform when you can to help a charity, but that is not the reason for the existence of an Amateur Acting Society—"The Play's the Thing" as the Philothespian Club advised fifty years ago. On looking over an old programme of theirs I also saw the quotation "Our true intent is all for your delight"—and they did delight Leek people for many years.

The principal performer in this Club was Mr John Wardle and for years people talked of "Johnnie" Wardle. It is true he had his failures, as for youthful parts such as "Romeo" and other juvenile leads he was ill-suited. Nature had not given him the romantic appearance, or the "golden voice" one hears so much about to-day, but his performance in "The Bells" set the whole town talking the day after, and it was said that Mrs. Cruso, the "Queen of Leek" (which term then had a different meaning from the modern Town Carnival Queen) and who acted as such, had personally congratulated him on his performance.

retain a very clear recollection of the thrill his performance gave me as "Cardinal Richlieu" (1894) in the scene where he draws the circle of sanctuary round his ward

A. E. Quinn, I should say without hesitation, was the best amateur comedian ever seen in Leek. In "Paul Pry" and "The Librarian"—an adaptation of "The Private Secretary"—translated from the original German by Mr. Fred Wardle (a son of Sir Thomas Wardle) and even as the "First Grave Digger" in "Romeo and Juliet" his performance was perfect. After he gave up, Jimmy Crombie followed in his footsteps with much cleverness. There were other men who were good but space forbids mention of them. Their women actors are more difficult to assess. The older plays seemed to have such difficult women's parts but Nellie Robinson was a born comic actress and I think two actresses like the Vigrass sisters would be acquisitions to any Dramatic Society of to-day. In writing of the Philothespian Club I am referring to the time when Wardle and Quinn were leading spirits. The Club continued for a long time afterward but I did not see the later performances.

In the 90's the first Leek Amateur Operatic Society was formed—I think in 1893—and the "The Lord-High-Everything-Else" of the Society was Mr. Kineton Parkes, a most delightful man and a born showman, and my recollection of this Society was that it was run on showman's lines. Mr. Parkes seemed to be Business Manager, Secretary, and Producer and took all the principal parts. Not that he was not good—indeed he was excellent—but it is bad for a Society for one man to rule *and* take the principal parts. His sister, Florence, was perhaps the best soubrette Leek has given us, but the Society as a whole lacked talent. It was eminently a "fashionable" event—not a Society for producing amateurs in the best way. The first night was a sight Leek seldom sees with all the "upper teen" (as the then Town Hall caretaker's wife termed it) of North Staffordshire attending. In one respect they were very fortunate and that was in the delightful scenery painted by Mr. Craigmile, the then Art Master. I wonder what has become of it? His drop scene of Leek, from Ladderedge (when Ladderedge was entirely rural) and some of the other scenery would have made highly pleasing frescoes for the Town Hall walls.

During the 90's also there were several performances of Old English Comedies in which the lead was taken by Miss Trissie Allen, and I remember how utterly charming she was as "Lady Teazle," in which performance I think Quinn took "Sir Peter." In 1894 I saw her as "Miss Hardcastle" in "She Stoops to Conquer" and Lieutenant Gimson from the Potteries, a very clever actor, who also used to play with the Old Volunteers, took "Tony Lumpkin." If I were asked what was the very best amateur stage setting shown in Leek, I should unhesitatingly say it was in this play. It was designed and carried out by Mr. Tom Wardle (another son of Sir Thomas Wardle) and Mr. W. R. Kean, the assistant Art Master at that time. At this performance Mr. Langfield Ward (uncle of Mr. John Ward) wrote and recited a prologue which impressed me beyond measure—that a local person could do this, *and* in rhyme too, was beyond my comprehension and I immediately classed him as a Goldsmith, or Browning. How one's ideas change! When, thirty years afterwards, in the same Hall, I wrote a prologue and most of the entertainment, I thought so little of it that nobody beyond the players knew I had written anything.

During this period I remember a wonderful performance of "He, She, and It," a most difficult short play, acted with consummate skill by Miss Blagden, a connection of Mrs. Cruso's. I think Mr. Fred Wardle took the part of "He."

Early in the new century for several years a local pantomime was given at the Town Hall, in which the principal parts were taken by Mr. Harry Ind and his sister Amy. I should say the former as a pantomime "Dame" and the latter as "Principal Boy" have yet had no local rivals, for their performances were excellent.

In the next decade the Leek Amateur Opera Society was formed. It is not for me to dilate on the activities of a Society with which I was connected for twenty years, but I think no record of local amateur acting would be complete without mention of Miss Phyllis Bilton, Mr. A. D. Price, and Mr. Charles Gell. Miss Bilton might then have been fittingly described in Sir James Barrie's happy phrase "A rogue in porcelain." Has there ever been an amateur actress that Leek took to its heart as it did Miss Bilton, and deservedly so, I think? And was there ever such a delightful stage-lover in Leek, as Mr. Charles Gell? If so I haven't seen him and as regards Mr. A. D. Price, I have never disguised the fact that I think he was one of the cleverest amateur actors I have ever seen. In the earlier years I should also mention Mr. George Cartlidge and the meteoric appearances of Miss Mary Bilton and Miss Biddy Swift, both of whose amateur careers were cut short—the former by marriage and the latter by adopting the stage as a profession. Everyone who saw him will remember Mr. Wilfred H. H. Eaton, whose connection with the Society was cut short, as he left to join Miss Horniman's Company at the Gaiety Theatre, Manchester and later was producer for Vedrenne and Eadie.

And so we are now back from where we started with the four acting Societies in the Town, with whose work you are acquainted and one of which, according to the criticism I mentioned at the commencement of this article, has given the best amateur performance ever given in Leek.

My own private opinion is that according to most criticisms in most local papers, the best performance will not be given until the last one reported before the Great Trump, after which there will be no one to dispute the statement.

LOCAL GOVERNMENT IN LEEK.

1825 —— 1855 —— 1935

As the first local Improvement Act was passed in 1825—one hundred and ten years ago, and the second in 1855—just eighty years ago, it seems fitting that in this 1935 edition of "Leek News," we should take a backwood glance over the history of Local Government in Leek and try to form some idea of the progress that has been made during that time.

Prior to the passing of the first Act in 1825, the streets, highways and roads in the town were managed by Highway Surveyors and Parish officers appointed at vestry meetings, and the expense levied by rates in the same manner as was done in other small towns and in country parishes.

There were very few streets in Leek at that time. Footpaths were numerous, however, but these were narrow, unpaved, and always in a bad and dirty condition. The site of Deansgate, Market, York, Ford and Bath streets was pasture land. South and East of Derby street there was Pickwood road, then known as Backsides; Brook st., which was much narrower than it is to-day and which was then known as Workhouse street; Broad street, formerly known as Canal street and Spooner's lane, which was much steeper than it is to-day and dropped down to the level of the present Railway Station; then there was Compton; Ashbourne rd., then known as Leek Moor; Ball Haye street; Fountain st.; part of Portland street; Brunswick street; and Buxton road; all the rest was grassland, intersected by various footpaths, with an odd building or two dotted here and there. And with the exception of West street, Mill street, and the property in the neighbourhood of the Church, the same may be said of the site of all the present streets to the West of St. Edward street. On the North side of Derby street there were Union street, New street, and Stockwell street which was narrow and ran down into quite a valley—the "road" from there to Ball Haye Green was very narrow, and was known as "The Hole."

Very little provision was made for the supply of water. There was a tap in Fountain street which was used by the residents of that street and also by the people living on Ashbourne road, but in times of scarcity it ran so slowly people had to wait for hours or fetch their water from the Buxton road springs. The greater part of the town, however, depended upon wells or the water of the Churnet, and that "was often impregnated with noxious matter," we are told.

Sanitary arrangements, drainage and sewerage were equally primitive. An open sewer ran down the Cattle Market side of Fountain street and emptied itself into a cesspool close to where the Public Baths now stand, and similar conditions prevailed in other parts of the town. No arrangements were made for the emptying of the privies—each individual householder having to make his own arrangements for that and for the disposal of his household refuse. Streets were unswept and filth was allowed to accumulate almost everywhere.

There were no lights or lamps in the streets or footpaths and on dark nights the inhabitants had to carry a lanthorn or grope their way about as best they could. The streets were not named and the houses were not numbered. The maintenance of law and order depended upon one solitary constable in the day time, and on three or four old watchmen (or "Charleys" as they were called) at night. On their rounds these gentlemen used to call out the hour of the night and the state of the weather. One of them, Phillip Mulvaney (an old naval man) was once censured for not calling out the hours of the night. The next time he was on duty he stopped outside the house of the gentleman who had taken him to task, and in a thunderous voice loud enough to waken the whole neighbourhood called out. "Past twelve o'clock and a star-light morning." Then he added "How d'yer like dat?" The reply he is reputed to have received is unprintable.

At the time the 1825 Act came into force, and for more than a decade afterwards, there were four watchmen in the town, viz. Dan and Joseph Osborne, John Walters, and George Bowcock, who was universally known as "Nosey" Bowcock, "in just recognition," we are told, "of his very prominent nasal organ." "Nosey," according to history, was a lover of "the cup that cheers," and was very frequently the victim of many practical jokes played on him, not only by the children of that day, but also by such a responsible and respectable a fraternity as the doctors of the town. He died in 1846 and is buried in the Old Church Yard.

There was no proper Cattle Market. The cattle fairs were held in the streets; chiefly St. Edward street, Church street, Sheep Market, Stockwell street, and on the old Cattle Market where the Monument now stands, and the filth, inconvenience, and confusion that [illegible] to be occasioned by the scores of cattle, sheep and pigs that were allowed to wander about these narrow streets on fair days can better be imagined than described.

The Act contained a recital to the following effect:—

"Whereas the Streets, Highways and other public places are not lighted, watched, or properly cleansed, it would tend greatly to prevent thefts, robberies, disturbances, and other unlawful proceedings, which in the night time are frequently committed in the said Town, and would add to the personal safety, comfort, convenience, and advantage of the inhabitants . . . . . if the Streets, Highways, Market Place, and other Public places in the said Town were properly and effectually lighted, watched, and cleansed, and the present nuisances abated."

Thirty-four gentlemen were appointed Commissioners for executing the powers of the Act. Their qualification was the possession of property of the annual value of £50, or personal property to the amount of £1,000. They were empowered to erect Gas Works or to enter into contracts for the lighting and cleansing of the town, to prevent future projections into the roadways, to employ watchmen and erect watch boxes, but were not empowered to repair the highways.

The work the commissioners were called upon to perform was not of an exhilarating nature. Ideas in the provision and development of public services were in their infancy. They had neither the money nor power to indulge in spectacular developments, and progress was therefore necessarily slow. But the introduction of street lighting, and such improvements in the water service as the meagre supply would allow, plus other small improvements which were gradually introduced, were of immense benefit to the inhabitants. The two outstanding acts of this first Board of Commissioners were the building of the Public Baths which were opened on the 21st June, 1854, and the purchase of the Gas Works in the same year for £6,124—a step for which they were much censured by the inhabitants of that time.

After thirty years of slow but steady progress the Commissioners began to feel the need of wider powers to enable them to carry out a number of badly needed improvements which, under the first Act, they had no power to undertake. Since the date of the first Act the population of the town had practically doubled and many of the wants that were only mildly felt fifteen or twenty years earlier were now urgently needed. A considerably increased supply of water and an efficient system of sewerage were both very badly needed, and as the death rate, which was very high in Leek at that time, was felt by many enlightened people to be directly attributable to the lack of these two services something had to be done. Certain street improvements, which the Commissi[illegible] were without power to effect, were also long overdue, and as the only burial places in the town (viz: St. Edward's, St. Luke's and the Mount Churchyards) were practically full, a Cemetery, also, was badly needed.

Consequently, in January, 1855, the Commissioners determined to promote a new Act.

This second Act, commonly known as the Leek Improvement Act, 1855, came into operation on the 31st July of that year, and is usually spoken of as being the beginning of municipal government in Leek. It gave the Commissioners powers enabling them

LOCAL GOVERNMENT—continued.

to purchase, compulsorily, lands for the following purposes, viz :—a Cemetery, Cattle Market, General Market, Town Hall, and for the widening and improving of streets as well as for the purchase of Market Rights and Tolls, and the Waterworks. The Act of 1825, which was limited to an area of 1,200 yards from the bottom of the Market Place, was repealed, and the limits of the town were extended to a circle the radius of which was 1,500 yards measured from the centre of the Market Place, and the number of Commissioners was reduced from thirty-four to twenty-four.

The first election under this new Act of 1855 took place on the 25th September of that year. There were sixty-four candidates for the twenty-four seats, and it is interesting to note that despite the importance of the occasion and the extraordinary interest which the election must have aroused, only 240, out of an electorate of 608, troubled to record their votes.

This apparent apathy on the part of the electorate, however, had no adverse effect on the enthusiasm and high-mindedness of the Commissioners who secured election. They realised the importance and the responsibility of the powers that had been entrusted to them, and with far-seeing judgment they and their successors carried out many important reforms to which the people of to-day are indebted for many of the amenities and advantages it is their privilege to enjoy in this eightieth year after the passing of the Act.

One of the first Acts of the new Board was to purchase the Waterworks. At that time the reservoirs, springs, pipe lines, and many rights and privileges appertaining thereto were owned by the Earl of Macclesfield, and it was a fortunate move for Leek when, in 1856, the Commissioners decided to buy them ; the price being £11,000. Although the supply had been considerably improved and extended during the previous thirty years, it was still totally inadequate for the needs of the day. Out of 2,117 houses that then comprised the township only 1,260 were connected to the supply : the remainder being still dependent upon wells or the Churnet. The new Commissioners, now having bought the works, immediately commenced to extend the services and within two years the number of houses supplied rose from 1260 to 1732. In 1861 the Potteries Water Board went to Parliament to obtain control of the Watershed comprising the Springs at Upperhulme, but fortunately for Leek the Commissioners, owing largely to the initiative and ability of Mr. William Challinor, successfully opposed the application, and secured the award of a protecting clause that enabled them to develope the springs at Upperhulme, which have since provided such an abundant supply for the people of Leek.

The position as regards sanitation and sewerage was very serious and the Commissioners were immediately faced with a tremendous responsibility. The death rate in Leek had risen from 22 in the 1,000 in the year 1851 to 30 in the 1,000 in the year 1856, and was still increasing. At this time the town was destitute of proper and efficient drainage ; cesspools were universal, being studded about in all parts of the town, and the scavenging department consisted of two old men and a donkey cart. Medical opinion stated that if proper sanitary improvements were carried out the death rate should be reduced by a third and the average length of life, which was much shorter in Leek than the rest of the country, should be correspondingly increased. Improvements were necessarily slow at first, but soon experts were called in and on their recommendation it was decided to carry out a comprehensive scheme at a cost of £10,000. The provision of this scheme for the disposal of sewage, and the provision of a much improved water supply had so marked an effect on the health of the town that the mean age at death, which for the period 1851-60 was only 24 years, was, within the next ten years raised to 32 years, and within the next ten years Leek from being one of the worst towns in the County became one of the healthiest. Furthermore, so well has that progressive policy for the provision of essential health services been continued that to-day the mean age at death is 59 years—a standard that has few equals in the Kingdom. Moreover, the new Sewage Disposal Works at Leekbrook and the new Water Scheme at Poole End, both provided within the last two years, are expected to meet any need that is likely to be experienced in Leek for many years to come.

The Market Rights and Tolls which belonged to Mrs. Grosvenor, then of Stockwell House, and Mr. E. Rooke, of Leeds, were bought in 1859 for £4,140 plus £302 expenses, and thus the Ancient Market Rights passed into public ownership ; an acquisition for which all Leek people must thank the Commissioners of that day. In 1874 the site of the present Smithfield Market was purchased from Mrs. Shoobridge, part of it being laid out as a cattle market ; and the remainder was used as a Town Yard. The cattle fairs which up to that time had been held in the streets were then transferred to the new market. When the new Town Yard was opened in Cruso street in 1894 the whole of the Smithfield site was utilised.

Whole pages could of course be written on the benefits the town has derived from the work so faithfully and disinterestedly performed by the Commissioners and their successors, the Urban District Council, who superseded them in 1894. The work of the Lighting Committee alone would provide copy for columns of matter. Both the Gas and the Electricity Departments are providing services that are probably unsurpassed by any town in the country, and all of it has had to be built up from very small beginnings.

Much could also be said on the many extensive street improvements that have been carried out during the past fifty years, as for instance : the bottom of Buxton road ; the corner of Buxton road and Osborne street, where the old Pig and Whistle used to be ; the corner of Brook street and Russell street, the bottom of both Compton and St. Edward street, Belle Vue and Kingsway, Newcastle road, the clearing of the old Globe Yard and the making of High street, and many others.

Another outstanding feature is the work of the Housing Committee. No town of its size in the country has a finer housing scheme or a better record for housing, no less than 800 houses having been built in Leek since the war.

The Baths, the Fire Brigade, the Cemetery, the Butter and Poultry Markets, the Isolation Hospital, the Park, and other similar public properties all stand as evidence of the able and valuable work that has been performed on behalf of the town and its people by those public-spirited men, who have shouldered the work and responsibility of Local Government in Leek during the past eighty years, but space is limited, room must be found in this Journal for other matters, and these notes must come to an end with the mere mention of the foregoing features, each of which in itself would provide something of a romance.

Back Row—W. Davenport. W. Woodings. E. Gee. David Dick. W. Bould, and R. A. Crombie.
Middle Row J. Pegg. J. Gibson, Joe Yates. R. Pitt. J. Fowler, and H. Parr.
Front Row—W. Whetstone. G. Clowes, G. Swindlehurst. H. Prime, Mrs. Gould. C. Kirkham. H. Yates. and E. Yates.

The above group was taken on the occasion of an outing from the "Earl Grey," Ashbourne Road, some twenty-four years ago, and is published because of the number of well-known Leek gentlemen who comprise the group. Also equally well known to many Leek people of mature age, is Mrs. Gould, the very kindly and popular landlady of the "Crewe and Harpur," Longnor, where the photograph was taken and where the party were entertained to dinner.

THE LATE M. H. MILLER

MATTHEW HENRY MILLER was the founder of Leek's first newspaper and was born in Birmingham on 7th February, 1843, being the third son of James and Eliza Miller. He was educated at Severn Street School, was apprenticed to Josiah Allen, of Livery Street, and in 1864 came to Leek to conduct the printing business of Mr. Robert Nall, of Stanley Street.

His first connection with the Press was as correspondent for the "Birmingham Daily Post," a position he occupied for more than forty years. He was also on the outside staff of the "Sentinel," and for many years did local service for the "Staffordshire Advertiser." On 30th July, 1870, in which year he married Annie Lovatt, the daughter of John Lovatt, silk manufacturer, of Leek, on 26th September, 1870, who predeceased him, he commenced the publication of the "Leek Times," using a partly printed London sheet and printing two pages of Leek news. The task was one of considerable difficulty, the trouble being to persuade the tradesmen of the town to advertise every week instead of once a year in "Old Moore's Almanack."

However, the modest sheet was a success, and its size and price were adjusted to meet the altered circumstances

Its career was followed with great interest throughout North Staffordshire and Mr. Miller's fearless criticism of local, county, and national affairs soon resulted in the paper gaining a considerable circulation which increased as the years rolled on.

Although Mr. Miller was a keen Liberal, the "Leek Times" espoused neither cause—its columns were open to Liberal and Conservative parties. Its democratic sympathies were however well known, and in local trade disputes the workers were always sure of warm hearted support. Charitable objects too, found the paper of inestimable value, and the founding of the successful Cruso Nursing Fund which has done so much good in the town was largely due to Mr. Miller's enthusiastic support. Nonconformity, too, found in the paper a real friend and many were the tributes paid by local leaders to its unswerving help. The "Leek Comet" was another of Mr. Miller's ventures. This was a paper published each Wednesday and was designed to attract farmers and others attending the Leek Market. Owing to lack of support publication was discontinued after a few months. Early in the life of the "Leek Times" Leek's historian, the late John Sleigh sent fragments of local and county history and mainly through him the Editor was caused to take an interest in the past life of his adopted town. As a consequence, a modest little book of 168 pages was issued under the title of "Leek Fifty Years Ago." Then followed in 1891 "Olde Leeke," and so warm was the welcome it received that a second volume was published in 1900. A number of other publications bear his name.

Mr. Miller won considerable personal influence in North Staffordshire and was greatly respected. Although, outspoken in tone, he was scrupulously clean in aim and sentiment and the "Leek Times" was followed with keen interest. He was a founder of the Birmingham Press Club, one of the first of its kind in the kingdom, and was a member of the Council of the Institute of Journalists.

In other ways, too, he made himself useful. Soon after coming to Leek he took part in public entertainments and his effort as a humourist and elocutionist secured him not a little popularity. Indeed, he was always ready to do anything for the benefit of good causes. Many of our old readers will well remember him as being an active member of the old Volunteer Theatricals and also of the old Penny Readings, entertainments which used to be held at the Temperance Hall—now the "Majestic" Picture House in Union Street.

He died on 25th October, 1909.

NICHOLSON INSTITUTE.

DESCRIPTION OF OPENING—16TH OCTOBER, 1884.

A MAN who, fifty years ago when many employers and others of that class considered the education of the working classes to be a source of real danger, possessed the vision, the means, and the bigness of heart to erect and present to the town of his adoption so magnificent and beneficient a gift as the Nicholson Institute, must, by every consideration, have been a truly great man.

Today, after half-a-century of progress in every sphere of life, it still stands out as a contribution of inestimable value toward the enrichment of the minds and the uplifting of the lives of the people of Leek, and indeed amongst local benefactions, there is from that aspect, only the Milner Bequest that is comparable with it.

How great must have been his regard for the highest welfare of his less fortunate fellow-men! He was not only a man of remarkable business acumen, and an outstanding man in industry, he also possessed a fine taste and discernment that enabled him to grasp and appreciate the value and the true beauties of art, learning, and literature. It was in fact because of his knowledge of the inestimable and imperishable benefits that accrue to those who cultivate a taste for such things, and his regard for the people of Leek that he presented this magnificent gift to the town.

Such a man was Joshua Nicholson. To him and this splendid gift he gave to the town, we might well apply the spirit of Wren's well-known epitaph in S. Paul's—"If you seek his monument, look around you."

Born at Luddendenfoot, near Halifax, in 1812, he was given the usual schooling of his class of that day and was then apprenticed to a well-known draper and silk mercer of Bradford. Possessing rare abilities and the diligence to make the best use of them, he quickly won the complete confidence of his employer, and soon showed promise of carving out for himself a great career. Though diligent in business he made time for reading and for religious work, and early in life he also began to take a keen interest in political and social work.

On leaving Bradford he spent a few years in Huddersfield and then at the age of 24 he came to Leek to take up the position of representative to Messrs. J. & J. Brough and company. How arduous and trying those duties must have been in the old coaching days one can better imagine than describe; few trains, no motor cars, no taxis or tram cars, roads incredibly bad, and all kinds of weather to be faced often on long journeys on the unprotected box seat of a (comparitively) slow moving coach—his job was indeed some task!

But young Nicholson's heart was in his job. He counted not the hours nor the effort, and his unflagging diligence, determination, and ability, which soon made him one of the most successful men on the road, eventually placed him at the head of his firm, and later enabled him to make that firm one of the best known in the kingdom.

Business was never allowed to absorb all his energies or his interests, however, and throughout his life he was a keen and social worker, an ardent Liberal, and a devoted Congregationalist.

He took a particularly keen interest in the youth of the town, and was always an enthusiastic and generous supporter of all movements tending to assist in the improvement of the physical, mental, and moral condition of both young men and young women.

It was with this end in view that, ten years before the building of the Institute, he formed an idea of founding an institute which would provide the young people of Leek with facilities for study, and at the same time stand as a memorial to the life and work of Richard Cobden, of whom he was a great admirer. And it was from this idea of founding a Cobden Club that his determination to build the Nicholson Institute eventually evolved. A growing realisation and a deepening conviction of the need for a greater and broader means of self-improvement for the young people than could be provided by the club he first visualised, coupled with increasing business success, led him to drop his earlier proposal and to concentrate upon the foundation and building of the magnificent building presented and opened to the public just half a century ago.

THE OLD GLOBE YARD.

THE above photograph of the old Globe and the entrance to the Globe Yard, will revive many memories of former days in the minds of scores of Leek people who knew it before it was swept away some thirty years ago, and not a few will recollect with renewed pleasure the many occasions on which they sacrificed their weekly half-penny in purchasing the twisted sticks of Shallcross's toffee, which was then the favourite sweetmeat with the great majority of Leek people.

To the young people of this generation it will probably be "news" to learn that before the construction of High street, the Globe yard was the way most frequently taken by pedestrians when proceeding from St. Edward street to the West end of the town, and although only a narrow passage was one of the busiest by-ways in the town.

DURING the latter part of last century there were few people better known or more highly respected in Leek than was Peter Cannings.

For nearly half a century Mr. Cannings was the Headmaster of the National Schools, Clerk Bank, and later of the Parish Church Schools.

As a headmaster he had few, if any, superiors. He possessed exceptional gifts both for teaching and leadership, and none was ever more successful in getting the best out of the scholars under his care. Of his personal influence one cannot speak too highly. It was such that men who have passed the allotted span of three score years and ten, and whose school days lie well over half a century behind them, still remember and acknowledge with gratitude and affection the help and guidance they received under his care.

In the year 1873, as a token of their affection and regard, his pupils and past pupils, presented him with a gold watch and chain, the watch being inscribed as follows :

> "Presented to Mr. Peter Cannings, Master of the National Schools, Leek, for a period of 30 years, by his past and present pupils as a mark of their sincere respect and esteem, and in grateful acknowledgement of his services.
>
> Leek, 14th Nov. 1873.

It is interesting to note that this watch is now in the possession of Mr. Thomas Grace of Dampier Street, who, as one of Mr. Canning's pupils, was present at the presentation ceremony in 1873, and to whom the watch was left as a legacy.

Chartist Rioters invade Leek August, 1842.

MOST of us have heard varying accounts of the Chartist Riots of August, 1842, when a contingent of between four and five thousand men "armed with staves and bludgeons" marched into Leek from the direction of Congleton and Manchester on their way to the Potteries.

The approach of so large a body of men naturally aroused considerable consternation in the town, and to prevent looting, all the public houses, shops, and many private houses, were shut and strongly barricaded. One gentleman, Mr. Simon Getlyffe, Provision Dealer, of the Market Place, after securely barricading his premises, tried to make doubly sure by the simple expedient of writing the brief inscription TO LET in big bold letters right across the front of the shutters. A strategic move for which he afterwards had to suffer considerable chaff from his friends and neighbours.

The following account of the events of this exciting week-end, which we hope will be of interest to our readers, is reprinted from the *Staffordshire Mercury* of August 27th, 1842 :—

This town, like too many others, has been the scene of the greatest excitement during the week. It was currently reported on Saturday and Sunday, the 13th and 14th, that some thousands of rioters would come into the town from Congleton early on Monday morning. This report was first set afloat by about ten men who came into the town on Saturday evening and went from house to house very impudently demanding money and goods. On the following morning these fellows proceeded to Warslow Wakes and there commenced spending their booty in drunkenness and debauchery. That the town might not be unprepared, summonses were served upon 500 of the male inhabitants on Sunday, signed by the Rev. John Sneyd and Matthew Gaunt Esq., two magistrates of the County, to attend at eight o'clock on Monday morning at the Town Hall, to be sworn in as special constables. Expresses were sent off for soldiers, but could not obtain any, except the Newcastle and Pottery troop of Yeomanry Cavalry, who arrived in the town about eight o'clock, commanded by Captain Tomlinson, and were stationed in the Market Place nearly the whole of the day. Early on Monday morning groups of men kept arriving in the town, armed with large sticks, clubs and pistols, and between nine and ten o'clock it was supposed several thousands came in a body, headed by a band of music. They marched into the Market Place, where the Cavalry and special constables were stationed, and brandished their huge club sticks over their heads, at the same time hooting at the cavalry and constables, and causing the greatest alarm. Captain Powys went in front of the mob on horseback and read the Riot Act, but no attention was paid to it and the crowd proceeded to different parts of the town to ascertain if any of the factories were at work, and to stop them. After which they again congregated in the Cattle Market, where a cart was procured for their leaders to speak from. Several of them addressed the mob and at the close of their speeches strongly advised the workpeople of Leek to join them in the morning to go to Burslem to urge the inhabitants of that town and other parts of the Potteries to assist in gaining what they termed their rights. During the day groups of the mob perambulated the town and went from door to door demanding money, etc., and threatening with violent language those who would not give them what they demanded. All the public houses, shops, and many private houses were closed, their doors being strongly barricaded, window shutters closed, and curtains drawn down, which gave the town a very mournful appearance, as if all the houses, etc., were deserted. Early the following morning the Cavalry were called away to Burslem and marched out of the town on account of its being made known that the mob would proceed there. About five o'clock two parties went round the town beating up with drums, collecting the mob and many inhabitants of Leek to go, and even used forcible means to compel those who were not willing to go with them, and they marched out of the town about six o'clock headed by a band of music, shouting and brandishing their weapons as they went.

Happily no serious clash took place in Leek, and the damage done was neither very serious nor very expensive. But the news of their approach had created widespread alarm and their presence in the town kept everyone on tenter-hooks. Altogether it was a very uncomfortable time for the law-abiding citizens of this quiet little town and as can be well imagined it was a welcome relief when the mob took its departure for Burslem.

Not very many Leek men seem to have been persuaded to join the rioters. But a number were "captured" by the mob and compelled to accompany them to the Potteries. Amongst these few were four brothers of the name of Heapy—members of a family that lived in Mill Street—and in a clash between the troops and the rioters, which occurred in Smallthorne Road, Burslem, William Heapy was killed by a shot fired by one of the troops. At the inquest several witnesses desposed seeing the deceased in front of the mob cheering them on and expressed the opinion that he was one of the leaders. His cousin, a Leek young woman, who identified him, however, denied the evidence of the previous witnesses, declaring that the deceased and his brothers were stood in the Market Place, Leek, where the deceased was employed as a shoemaker, when the mob came along and he and his three brothers were seized by the rioters, who forced them to the front of the mob and to lead the way to the Potteries.

This witness was very voluble in her explanations and talked a great deal about the deceased having put twenty sovereigns in his watch pocket that morning to pay something connected with a teetotal club ; but on the deceased being searched by the direction of the coroner, it was found there was no watch pocket in his suit. This threw considerable doubt on the witness's testimony and it was remarked by one of the jury that even if the deceased had been compelled to march in front of the mob they could not have compelled him to throw a stone or excite the mob. The jury returned a verdict of "Justifiable Homicide."

Old Thoroughfares Re-Christened.

IT may be of some interest to readers of Leek's ancient history to place upon permanent record the following list of ancient places the names of which have been changed :—

Old name	New name
Custard Street ...	... Stanley Street
Spout Street ...	...St. Edward Street
Spooner's Lane ...	... Broad Street
Canal Street ...	... Broad Street
Workhouse Street	... Brook Street
Barn Gates ...	... West Street
Nix Hill	...Wellington Street
Back Sides ...	... Pickwood Road
Newtown... ...	... ...King Street
Cope's Yard ...	... Gettliffe's Yard

The Old Grammar School which we reproduce above, was built by the Earl of Macclesfield in 1723 and although badly handicapped by the lack of any endowment, it was the premier school of the town from that time till it closed in 1901.

The report of the Schools Enquiry Commission of 1868 contains a report on the Leek Grammar School and the following is an extract :—

" There is a building traditionally called a grammar school, and used as such, which was built by Lord Chancellor Macclesfield in 1723. The Earls of Macclesfield exercise the right of appointing a master to teach in this building, but there is no endowment attached and the master has to make repairs at his own cost. . . . . . .

Meanwhile, a bonâ fide Grammar school continues to be held in Lord Macclesfield's building under a really competent master, who probably would not have bestowed himself upon Leek but for rather exceptional circumstances.

The building, which, as might be expected is in rather bad repair, consists of an upper and a lower room. The lower one is unfurnished, and used as a romping place for the boys. The teaching goes on in the upper room which is low, badly ventilated and has desks along the wall.

The master being unable to keep an assistant finds his time very much scattered. The boys, though only twenty four in number, are of all degrees of age and attainment and want education for very different purposes. Some want the simple commercial education, others a little Latin and mathematics, for the preliminary legal examination, others the elements of classics, with a view to going on to some higher school. The town is one where a Grammar school of the middle order might certainly flourish. It has a population of about 9,000.

Its manufacture is prosperous, and it acts as a capital to the moorland district of Staffordshire. What is wanted is a school which should give the elementary education, that is now given at Leek in a cheap commercial school, and at the same time do what the commercial school cannot do—act as a feeder to some higher school."

Probably the most successful period the school ever enjoyed, was the last thirty years of its existence. Under the headmastership of Mr. Joseph Sykes and of Mr. John J. Sykes, it rose to a high position in public esteem. Many men who are now holding responsible positions in professional or business life, owe much of their success to the excellent training they received during that period.

When the present High School was opened in 1901 however, the old Grammar School, to the sincere regret of many, came to an end.

Below we reproduce a group of the pupils attending the Grammar School at that time.

G. Hill, C. Morton, P. Riches, F. Mountford, C. Bermingham, J. Brough, A. Anglebeck, Mr. Cutliffe. Mr. Sykes
C. Swift, G. Breton, W. Winter, R. Audley, R. Timmis, S. Riches, W. Sheldon. W. R. Eddowes.
P. Sheldon (kneeling), F. Ainsworth, Leo Bermingham, H. Middleton, G. Marshall, H. Newall,
H. Field, N. Eaton. T. Pebworth, Elaine Scarratt.
E. Bayley, H. Hill, V. Hill, R. Ford, J. Ford.

Group of Pupils, Leek High School, 1902.

BACK ROW—1, W. Hill, 2, C. Morton, 3, N. Eaton, 4, G. Hill, 5, G. Breton, 6, E. Bermingham, 7, W. Eddowes, 8, G. Bermingham, 9, F. Gatton, 10, L. Bermingham, 11, J. Tatton, 12, B. Brooks.

2nd Row—1, M. Hunt, 2, B. Rigby, 3, E. Steele, 4, M. Craze, 5, G. Shaw, 6, E. Birch, 7, M. Brookes, 8, J. Brealey, 9, C. Salt, 10, D. Brealey, 11, G. Trythall 12, M. Pebworth, 13, B. Salt, 14, C. Bermingham, 15, G. Marshall.

3rd Row—1, N. Sowter, 2, A. Goodwin, 3, R. Bailey, 4, J. Hoatson, 5, R. Carr, 6, F. Rushton, 7, E. Summerling, 8, W. Hulme, 9, H. Newall, 10, A. Bailey, 11, E. Poyser, 12, P. Riches.

FRONT ROW—1, J. Shaw, 2, H. Bailey, 3, W. Hall, 4, T. N. Hulme, 5, I. Hammersley 6, S. Cartwright, 7, L. Craze, 8, A. Baskerville, 9, H. Leek, 10, H. Middleton.

Opening of the Coffee Tavern, 1878.

THE opening of the Leek Coffee Tavern, which took place on Tuesday evening, November 12, 1878, was quite an auspicious event.

The idea had originated amongst the supporters of the Temperance Cause in Leek; the purpose being to provide the working-man with an alternative place to the public-house in which to meet his friends, and indulge in friendly social recreation.

The chief promoters were Messrs. J. Challinor, A. Nicholson, J. J. Ritchie, and Capt. Colvile; Mr. Nicholson, one is led to assume, doing the lion's share of the work.

The report of the opening says: "The building had been beautifully fitted up, and every attention had been paid to the requirements of comfort and expeditious trade. Before the opening of the institution, the quality of the refreshments was well tested by a large party of ladies and gentlemen, and a chorus of satisfaction was the verdict." On adjourning to the reading room, where a large crowd had assembled, Mr. Hugh Sleigh was called to the chair.

On rising, Mr. Sleigh, who was warmly received, expressed the pleasure it gave him to be present on that occasion, and said the Leek Coffee Tavern was intended principally for the working classes of Leek. They all knew the British workingman was quite as intelligent and well-inclined as other members of society. True, he was somewhat of a gregarious nature. He would have society somewhere—he wanted the exchange of thoughts and sympathies with his fellows. Frequently his home was not a place where he could take a friend, and unfortunately he was surrounded by places which were rather productive of evil than good. He (Mr. Sleigh) did not want to say all these places were of that character, but when they were abused, as they often were, they were productive of mischief to society. Fortunately for the workingman there had been introduced in many towns establishments under the names of Coffee Taverns, in which he could obtain refreshments that would be beneficial to him and at the same time meet his fellows and exchange thoughts and feelings, the effects of which could not fail to be of advantage to him.

He (Mr. Sleigh) regretted that he was not better acquainted with the working of these establishments. From his own experience, he could say that if such places as these had been in existence in his earlier years he should undoubtedly have taken advantage of them, and he advised the working classes of Leek to do so, and concluded by wishing the Leek Coffee Tavern every success.

Other speakers followed, including Mr. J. J. Ritchie, who said the reproach was frequently made against teetotallers that they were always urging people to keep from public-houses, without finding other places to which they could resort. The promoters of the Leek Coffee Tavern were anxious to meet that charge. He would tell them how they intended to conduct the institution. The building would be open from 6 a.m. to 10 p.m. Many persons would be glad to get a cup of coffee, cocoa, or tea as they went to work early in the morning, instead of going, as many did, to the dram shop, they could come here and obtain what would do them good. There would be soup ready every day at twelve o'clock, but they could not expect soup ready all the day over.

Another feature in connection with the institution was this—that the working people of Leek could bring their meals here, and eat them free of charge. Indeed the promoters would be glad to see them. He had often seen working men sit down on the curb-stones in the street and eat the meals they had brought with them in the morning. They could come here and eat them without being charged anything, and if they liked they could have a cup of coffee or tea. But if they did not purchase anything they would be perfectly welcome to come. The other portion of the building would be used every Wednesday as a Settling Room for people attending the markets. A place would also be provided where those who like tobacco could enjoy a smoke. He hoped that all classes—particularly the working classes would avail themselves of the institution, as the promoters were anxious to make it successful.

He wished it to be understood that it was the intention of the promoters to devote any profits which might accrue to establishing a similar institution in some other part of the town.

LEEK DAY SCHOOL FOR GIRLS.

PHOTOGRAPHED ABOUT 1897.

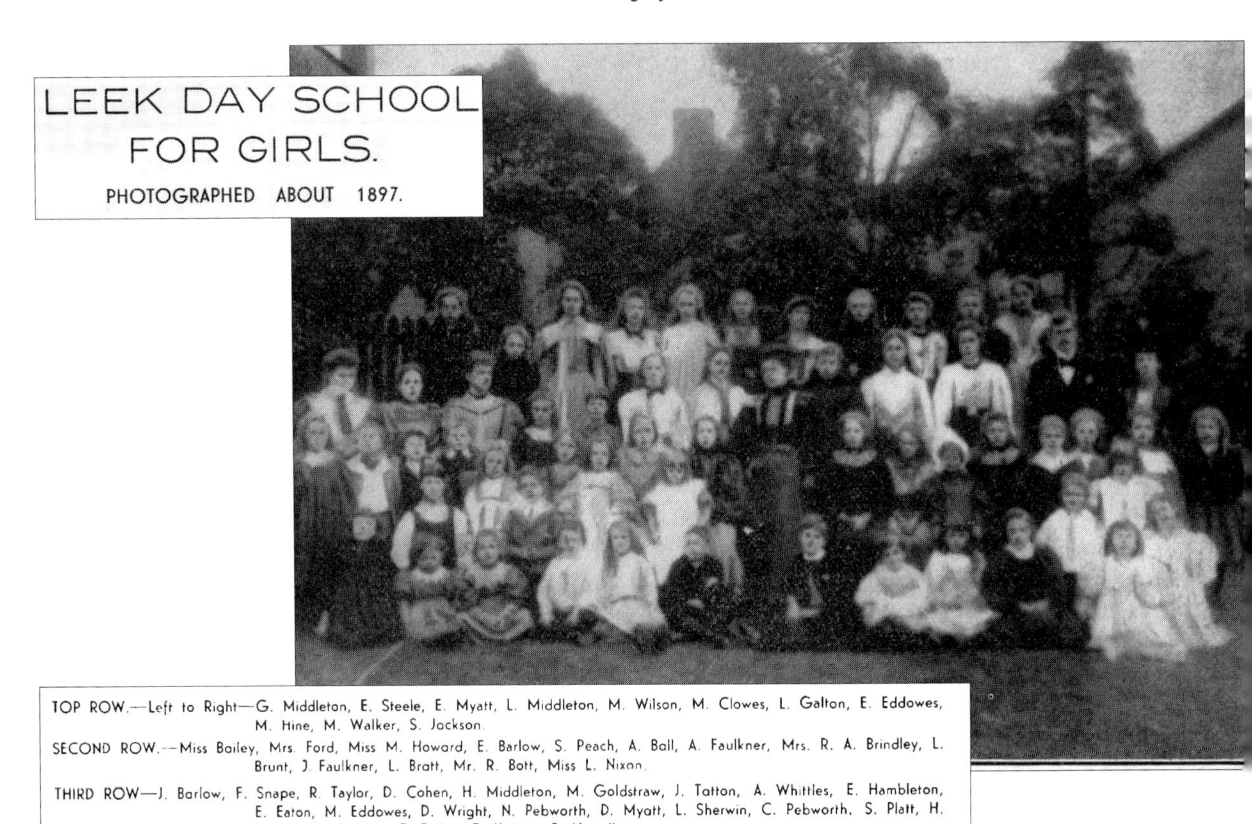

TOP ROW.—Left to Right—G. Middleton, E. Steele, E. Myatt, L. Middleton, M. Wilson, M. Clowes, L. Galton, E. Eddowes, M. Hine, M. Walker, S. Jackson.

SECOND ROW.—Miss Bailey, Mrs. Ford, Miss M. Howard, E. Barlow, S. Peach, A. Ball, A. Faulkner, Mrs. R. A. Brindley, L. Brunt, J. Faulkner, L. Bratt, Mr. R. Bott, Miss L. Nixon.

THIRD ROW—J. Barlow, F. Snape, R. Taylor, D. Cohen, H. Middleton, M. Goldstraw, J. Tatton, A. Whittles, E. Hambleton, E. Eaton, M. Eddowes, D. Wright, N. Pebworth, D. Myatt, L. Sherwin, C. Pebworth, S. Platt, H. Newall, M. Ellerton, E. Tudor, E. Keates, J. Newall.

BOTTOM ROW—M. Pebworth, E. Clowes, M. Clowes, E. Ford, E. Rider, T. Pebworth, G. Marshall, L. Wood, C. Eaton, M. Walker, M. Flint, C. Richmond.

West Street Sunday School Class, 1910, - Teacher, Miss Catherine Rayner.

Fourth Row—Nellie Ball, Maud Mitchell, Edith Birch, Nellie Taylor, Pattie Hunt, Annie Metcalfe, Betsy Trafford, Jennie Metcalfe, ———, Pattie Clayton.

Third Row—Maud Shatwell, Mary Clayton, Jennie Ball, May Mitchell, Emma Fitch, Eliza Birch, Miranda Hudson, Hannah Fitch, Ellen Perkin, Nellie Metcalfe, Annie Parr, ———, Ethel Poyser, Edith Bagshaw, Edith Robinson, Lizzie Millward.

Second Row—Lily Palin, Edith Sheldon, ———, ———, Florrie Merritt, Lizzie Moseley, Miss C Rayner, May Carding, Amy Billing, Lizzie Ainsworth, Maud Rowley.

First Row—Hannah Ainsworth, Lottie Dale, Edith Hollinshead, Annie Wardle, Lizzie Cureton.

Mrs Cruso

If I spoke of "THE HOUSE," to the present residents of the Market Place, I wonder how many would know what I meant? They would probably say, "what was The HOUSE?" like someone, who recently said to me, "Who WAS Mrs. Cruso?" But all of us who lived in the Market Place some fifty odd years ago, when I was "The Small Boy of the Market Place,"knew what THE HOUSE was because it was where Mrs. Cruso lived at the top of the Market Place—now the Trades and Labour Club.

It never had any name as far as I am aware, although some people inaccurately called it "The Manor House" which was one of the several names borne by the house now "The Red Lion." Mrs. Cruso had no need for a name for her house. "Mrs. Cruso, Leek," was sufficient and so it seems as strange to me to be asked "Who WAS Mrs. Cruso," as to be asked "Who was Queen Victoria," for I think Mrs. Cruso was known as Queen of Leek as much as Queen Victoria of England.

The first article I wrote for the "Leek News" was about Mrs. Cruso and the great position and influence she held in the Town practically until the end of her life at the age of eighty-one, and now it has been suggested that I should write the impressions of a small boy of over fifty years ago, of her house—THE HOUSE—as it was when she lived in it from the early 50's to the early 90's.

Since those days the exterior of THE HOUSE has not been altered with the exception an additional door on the Stockwell Street side and the interior is the same as regards the reception rooms and principal bedrooms, but the Kitchens and "Domestic Offices," as such parts of a house of this description were called, are altered beyond recognition and it is the vast size of this part which will be of interest, and perhaps amusement and wonder in comparing it with those of the houses now being built in the town.

But let us pull the brass front door bell (one of a long row in the back hall with curly spring tops to act on the clapper) and curb one's impatience while the butler takes off his green baize apron, lets down his deep linen cuffs, puts on his tailcoat and opens the door with a dignified sweep and a deferential bow. The Hall is much the same now as it was then excepting that there was no inner door and screen, and the walls were papered with hideous varnished marble paper.

The first door on the left was the Dining Room and the ultra modern young decorator will be surprised to learn that the walls were painted in "off white" shades. I remember the small sensation—small sensations were frequently caused in those pre-penny illustrated paper days—when Mrs. Cruso returned from London with the idea of having her Dining Room walls painted a "dark" white and stencilled all over in pure white. It took weeks to do and didn't seem to achieve anything to make the room any less dismal, with its huge family portraits, thick crimson curtains under heavy gilt pelments, and ponderous mahogany furniture, although the long dining table at night looked very bright and sparkling, with its amount of glass and silver—the latter including numerous silver branched candlesticks which were the only illumination, and also the many bowls of flowers although her head gardener was not great at floral decoration. At first glance they looked like coloured cauliflowers, an arrangement which he never varied, for I recall about a dozen years later when Mrs. Cruso sent my sister her wedding bouquet, it was a large, solid, close packed head of white camellias, &c., in a lace paper holder, instead of the graceful "shower" bouquet then the fashion.

The next room to this was the Drawing Room, its large bowed window from floor to ceiling took up the end wall and looked over the Park and Roaches. It had an elaborate gilt cornice from which hung green brocade curtains with heavy cords and tassels. I think the furnishings were mostly green but there were so many chairs, tables, chiffoniers, fauteuils, ottomans, what-nots, &c., that I have not a very clear recollection excepting a large round pedestal table near the centre of the room around which there was a set of Queen Anne dressing stools in cross stitch needlework and a table near the fireplace on which were displayed silver trowels, mallets, &c., souvenirs of foundation stone layings. There was much handsome china and tall glass shades with waxflowers, and a beautiful crystal candelabra, and silver scones round the walls for no gas was allowed beyond the red baize door, which divided this part of the house from the servants quarters.

There was only one room opening off the other side of the Hall as the vast Kitchen arrangements took up the remainder of the ground floor. This room faced the street and was called the Study although I should say it was little used except for smoking by gentleman visitors. *Continued*

THE HOUSE—CONTINUED.

I think originally it must have been Mr. Cruso's business room, (it is strange how little one heard of MR. CRUSO), for it was furnished much like a lawyer's office with double desk, arm chair and bookcases. There was also a large closet off it which one imagined full of deeds, &c., and it had an escape door opening into the back hall. This back hall was reached from the front hall through the silent swinging red baize door studded with brass nails, and on the right side was the back staircase—much more imposing than the iron and stone front staircase—in front of which was a huge wooden coal box as large as the coal house of a small modern house, and further on, the door to the Servant's Hall, about the most depressing room I have ever seen. The walls were panelled half way up with rush matting which was, with the remainder of the wall, painted drab. It was lighted in the daytime by a window looking on to a dull brick wall and at night by a solitary naked gasjet over the fireplace in the corner. There was a built-in cupboard in the wall in which, I remember a black Jack for supper beer was kept, and it was furnished by a long table with backless forms on either side and a rush seated arm-chair at the top for the coachman, who presided. The Housekeeper and Butler had their meals in the Housekeeper's room.

On the opposite side of the back hall was the kitchen door over which hung a long row of bells with curly springs and under them were the names of the various rooms to which they belonged. I recollect one had "The Brown Room" painted under it and I wondered what a Brown Room could be. It sounded so dismal and I pictured another drab Servant's Hall. But when you entered the kitchen that was anything but drab for it was a large lofty place and well-lighted from the roof by a turreted skylight. It had no windows in the walls as there were rooms all round it. Half of the left side, as you entered, was taken up by an enormous range with spits, hangers, pothooks and all the impedimenta of the complete old-fashioned range, and next to it was another complicated cooking contraption. It was rather like a hot counter in an hotel, but the bottom had two separate stoke-holes for fire and the top was hot enough to cook with the numerous spotless copper saucepans of all sizes, which decorated the wall over these two ranges. Next to these was a marbled topped pastry table with a fixed pestle and mortar incorporated in it and then an enormous wooden dresser, the top scrubbed to an incredible whiteness. Over this were narrow shelves on which the copper lids to the saucepans were kept, each lid having a long polished steel handle. On the opposite side was another companion dresser and high over it, store cupboards on the wall, between them was hung a great display of polished pewter dish-covers some large enough for a baby's bath.

Over this kitchen reigned Agnes Charlesworth, such a cheerful, bright, pink & white round faced cook with a frank all-square-and no-nonsense air about her. I believe she was just as frank with Mrs. Cruso. I remember hearing that she went into the kitchen one morning to order dinner and finished by saying "and I think, a small roly-poly." "Aye," replied Agnes, "I thought it would have to be a roly-poly." Mrs. Cruso laughed and said "Well, Agnes *mayn't* I have a roly-poly?" This kitchen provided not only food for Mrs. Cruso and her household, and few, except the invalids who received them knew of the delicacies prepared for them there and not many, except those in want, knew of the baskets of food that were given away.

The following amusing anecdote is recorded as having taken place in this kitchen when Mr. Mills, a well known attorney, lived there before the Crusos. A half-witted (?) boy was sent with a message for Mr. Mills to which an answer was required. It was a very cold morning and the lad was sent to the kitchen to warm himself. A large dog lay across the hearth and in a short time the boy was heard saying "Ger out, ger out wi' thee." The cook said "You needn't be feared, the dog won't hurt thee." "I know he wunner," said the lad, "but if yo gimme some bread and cheese he'll tak it on me, yo see if he doesna." !

In the middle of the kitchen on the right hand side was the entrance to Mrs. Heath,s (the housekeeper's) room, such a cosy little room with its bright fire, easy chair, rocking chair and warm snug curtains. There is always something cosy and "safe," to a small child, in a room off a room. I think I was a little in awe of Mrs. Heath. She looked so very dignified in her long black dress, black silk apron and black lace cap with lappets (I think that is what they were called). Mrs. Cruso and Ann herself wore the same kind of cap but the other maids wore a crocheted affair shaped like a small oval d'oyley. I don't think Mrs. Heath could have been as awesome as I imagined her because she frequently gave me one of her famous Queen Cakes which she kept in a tin box in her room, but I was awed by her sharp enquiring nose and the way she looked "inside" you through her old fashioned, narrow, spectacles.

Next to Mrs. Heath's room was the butler's pantry, and my recollections of this room are not as clear as of the remainder of "THE HOUSE" because although I may perhaps have been wrong about Mrs. Heath I definitely was awed and rather afraid of the butler. He was so super-dignified, so ultra-magnificent in his stiff white linen collar and cuffs—one up to his ears and the other down to his knuckles—and his grand aloof unapproachable manner. I recollect this room had a wall table all round with a lead sink at one end and under the table, a special cupboard for the forward stock of wine (which he fetched as required from the wine cellar below) and there were also plate cupboards above. I remember him once entering the kitchen and saying in reference to Mrs. Hugh Searight (Mrs. Cruso's niece who had just arrived on a visit and was renowned for her fashionable "hour glass" figure) that her waist was no wider than the Selzogene of soda water which he was carrying.

Opposite the entrance to the kitchen was a passage with larders on either side, the smaller being the game larder. I should think these two larders and the passage would occupy almost as much land as a small modern house. Beyond this, was the scullery—a large, high, dark stone-flagged place rather suggestive of the gloomy hall of an old country mansion. There seemed to be dismal black doors in all directions, one of which was the entrance to the staircase to the menservants' quarters which however at this time was not used as the men servants lived out. It was in this scullery that the under gardener used to bring the daily supply of vegetables, grapes, etc., from the greenhouses and also where the old man (I have forgotten his name although I remember his humorous Irish-looking face) brought the milk from "Cruso's Fields" that part of the Park which contains the lower pond—then two ponds with the path to the next field between them.

It was with the scullery that I chiefly associate the kitchen-maid, Lizzie Cumberledge, whom I looked upon as the heroine of this house as she had a "follower," for the others were all long past the age of young men (at least so it seemed to me) and they mothered her accordingly. Her father was the game-keeper and once had a terrible night affray with poachers somewhere near Packsaddle Hollow.

All the time I remember THE HOUSE, the only changes were kitchen-maids who left to get married. Lizzie's predecessor had quite a romance having fallen in love with Bateman, the footman, a tall well set-up young man—as footmen were supposed to be in those days—and looked very handsome in his livery. They wanted to get married, but unfortunately a more eligible "parti"—as such were described in the novels of that day—appeared, to whom much against her will she was married and Mrs. Cruso provided the trousseau and wedding breakfast at her house. I well recollect seeing the wedding party issue from the front door and walk past the Vicarage to the Church.

Next to the scullery was the laundry—the exact opposite to that gloomy place—for it was all so clean and bright with its large high windows. This place also had tables all round which were scrubbed as white as those in the kitchen and in front of them was a kind of raised platform, the purpose of which I never knew, but it was grand for playing "pretending" games, as it would accommodate itself to any purpose required. Next to the laundry was the wash-house—another large place—but I have little recollection of that as there was nothing much in it that appealed to a small child and we only used it to get through into Bowcock's yard, which opened up a fresh and unlimited field of adventure, for from there you could get down to Betty's Yard and on to the Stable Yard and through a door in the wall there, to Cavendish Square and Dicky's Gutter.

The Stable Yard, the stable, coachhouse and other buildings are still there, although their glory of "spit and polish" is departed. No wonder the coachman was irritable and ill-tempered when we attempted to play in this immaculately kept place, where everything was groomed and polished, carriages, horses, harness—even to the broad fringe (was it called a "plait"?) of plaited straw running the whole length of the stalls; and the harness room where everything harness, brasses, bits and so on were polished until they glittered in rivalry with the equally bright fire, and over all there was such a delicious smell of polish, vinegar, horses, dubbin and hay.

But however ill-tempered the coachman may have been, his wife made up for it. The living room of their cottage next to the stables would have sent an artist in raptures over its blue and white checked gingham curtains and frilled covers on settle and arm chairs near a blazing fire in the old fashioned grate, tricked out with brass embellishments and vying in polish with her husband's harness, and a high mantelshelf full of brasses and quaint chinese glass pictures from her son, who was in China. She also had a hospitable tin box like Mrs. Heath's only hers contained sponge cakes. Off the Stable Yard was the Drying Ground, now used as a nursery garden for the Park.

I find I have wandered, child-like, a great distance from THE HOUSE proper, so will take you back to explore the remainder of it. On the first floor was the morning room with a similar window to the drawing room over which it stood. From this window was (and is) a magnificent view of the surrounding country from the Cloud to Morridge. It was a comfortable room with many shelves of books and behind it was Mrs. Cruso's dressing room with a built-in wardrobe running along the whole of one wall and the usual furniture of that day, toilet table, washstand, screen, writing desk, comfortable chintz easy chairs, and a fine old bureau with a cupboard over it containing neat little drawers, inside which she kept much of her jewellery and trinkets. I think I was disappointed when Ann, her personal maid, once showed me this jewellery. Perhaps I was very young and expected a glistening array of coronets, tiaras, and diamond necklaces like one saw in Christmas almanacks of Queen Victoria, or like those the leading actress in the Rag and Stick Theatre wore ; but the strings of pearls, ear-rings, bracelets, pendants, etc. were not massive enough to impress me, except a very beautiful many pointed diamond Star, which seemed to run about in my hand like liquid fire when I held it. Ann told me that was her most valuable jewel.

It was no wonder Mrs. Cruso thought so much of Ann, such a perfect specimen of a confidential maid, if she were not the ideal children's nurse, so fond of children as she was and so understanding and always the same—even her dress was always the same. She might have stepped out of " Cranford " with her black lace and violet-ribboned cap tied under her chin and her dress like a crinoline, without a crinoline, if I may be so Irish, and of course the fancy black silk apron and list slippers. I don't know how long she was with Mrs. Cruso but certainly from the middle 60's until Mrs. Cruso's death in 1893.

Next to Mrs. Cruso's dressing room was " His Lordship's Bedroom." I think it was so called because it was where the Earl of Macclesfield slept when he visited THE HOUSE which he did from time to time to inspect his estates in the district or to shoot over his preserves. There was great activity at these times with dinner parties and visiting—Sir Philip Brocklehurst, Colonel Heath of Biddulph Grange, General Phillips of Ashenhurst, the Sneyds and others being among the guests. Most afternoons the carriage would drive up to the door with the coachman in his best livery, with silver buttons embossed with the crest and " Pro Cruse," striped waistcoat, top boots, white breeches, stock, etc., and Bateman, the footman, in his waisted box-coat down to his heels, silk hat with cockade, looking very handsome, and standing at the carriage door with his linen dust-rag (or fur, according to the season) which he carefully tucked round the Countess and Mrs. Cruso, then leapt nimbly on to the box beside the coachman, folded his arms and the carriage would drive off.

Returning to the bedrooms : The room next to " His Lordship's " was " The Master's." Both these rooms had enormous beds with glazed chintz curtains which stood out in stiff crackling folds and the same chintz was used for sofa and chair covers and window curtains. The beds were very high and I think there was an intriguing little set of steps covered with carpet to mount into them in one of the rooms. In addition to there being no gas, there were no bathrooms in THE HOUSE and of course " H. and C. " was not thought of in bedrooms. There were enormous wash-stands with double sets of toilet-ware on them, including two jugs and basins and one little one in the middle which I thought of in these childish days as father, mother and the baby, and as no babies ever seemed to visit the house, wondered what the little set was used for. In place of a bathroom, a large flat iron bath about a yard in diameter and a quarter of a yard deep and shaped something like a giant's patty pan was brought in and placed on a thick plaid rug like a horse cloth. What work it must have been for the footman, whose work it was to fill and empty them every day !

Between these two rooms was a dressing room over the front entrance and it was from the window in this room that the Conservative used to return thanks—if elected. This reminds me of a typical story of Mrs. Cruso's chivalrous spirit and broad outlook.

At one election when the Liberal Candidate was returned and was being chaired past her house she bowed to him and waved her hand and when some of her Conservative friends remarked on this she replied, with her great gift of fairness and dignity, " He is now my Member." The same gentleman who told this tale reflected on the anomoly of the Times when a woman of Mrs. Cruso's intelligence, position and wealth had no parliamentary vote but her undergardener had.

On the first floor, besides various house-maids closets, there was another bedroom and dressing room, which was much more modern than the others, for I remember it had not such an enormous bed and was not so heavily furnished. It was called the Blue Room and was furnished in plain blue and had long mirrors to the floor and other modern touches. I think it was regarded as the young ladies' room. I recall once going into this room with Ann when THE HOUSE was full of visitors for the Leek Invitation Ball—locally called the " Gentry " Ball,—and for the Yeomanry Ball the night after, and she opened the wardrobe doors and displayed with great importance two very grand white brocade dresses complete with bustles which she said were the dresses the two Misses Heath of Biddulph Grange were to wear and that they had worn them when they were presented the previous season at Queen Victoria's Drawing Room.

There were more bedrooms on the next floor—Mrs. Cruso herself slept there after her husband's death—but I don't remember much about them, as being mostly occupied, I don't suppose I went into them. There were also some rooms called the bachelors' wing and of these I only remember the baths and horserugs. Emma the other housemaid seemed to be in charge of these rooms and was quite different from the other maids. Somehow she amused me very much—I thought of her as a ventriloquist's doll. She had a mouth down at the corners much like these dolls and a rather " mezzled " face and plaintive croaking voice. She definitely was not born for joy.

The garden was rather dreadful according to modern ideas with its rows of scarlet geraniums, yellow calceolarias, and white marguerites, edged with blue lobelia. It had an " unloved " look about it and I don't think Mrs. Cruso's tastes ran in that direction although I may be wrong, but I recollect that when I was older and was allowed—under Ann's supervision—to take books from the morning room and read in the garden I never saw her there. There was, and of course still is, a magnificent view from the garden and it always fills me with surprise that you may walk from the Market Place right into the country in the depth of the house.

Looking back I think that THE HOUSE expressed Mrs. Cruso and her age. It was solid, open and dignified. It was comfortable, enduring and gracious. It was plain, homely and straightforward. There was nothing little or mean about it. All these characteristics expressed Mrs. Cruso who lived in an age when importance was attached to the graciousness and dignity of living, and now both Mrs. Cruso and THE HOUSE are gone—that is THE HOUSE as she and her generation knew it.

* * * * *

When I was old enough to stay up and go outside to hear the church bells tolling out the old year, Mrs. Cruso, wrapped in a fur cloak with the hood over her head and still a straight upright figure, although she must then have been nearer eighty than seventy, might have been seen walking smartly backward and forward across the front of the house. As the tolling bells ceased and the New Year was rung in, my sister and I would go across to her and wish her a Happy New Year, which seemed to please her, for she would shake hands with us and patting our shoulders return our good wishes, and we felt sure she *was* pleased as she turned and went in THE HOUSE—quite alone.

Top Row—D. Gwynne, E. Blades, N. Whittles, K. Watson,
Fifth Row—E. Tudor, M. Walker, J. Cartwright, M. Morton, K. Gearing, E. Blades, G. Blades, J. Challinor,
Fourth Row—L. Broster, A. Yates, N. Barlow, L. West, F. Birmingham, E. King, W. Breton,
E. Platt, Evelyn King, D. Barlow,
Third Row--Miss Harris, M. Flint, K. Platt, A. Platt, B. Swift, Miss Potts, A. Whittles, J. Shaw,
J. Platt, P. Gwynne, F. Davis, Miss N. Beresford.
Second Row—F. Watson, K. Gwynne.
Front Row—J. Phipps, A. Bockett, N. Davis, H. Thomas, K. Whittles, K. Shaw, L. Guiton, M. Goodwin.

The present M.P. for Leek and the Chairman of the L.U.D.C.
at the old British School some forty-five years ago

Teacher : Miss Atkinson.
Top Row : 1. W. Armitt, 2. W. Mollatt, 3. Not Known, 4. C. Noble, 5, C. Armitt.
Second Row : 1. H. Beech, 2. B. O. Wardle, 3, G. H. Sheldon, 4. H. Astbury. 5. Not Known.
Third Row : 1. Not Known, 2. A. Clark, 3. J. Cheetham, 4. Not Known, 5. J. Hampson, 6. A. Ratcliffe,
7. Not Known.
Front Row : 1 and 2 Not Known, 3. J. Hulme, 4. Not Known, 5. H, Clark.

Leek Cyclists' Club, Season 1898.

Front Row—J. P. Fellowes-Smith. W. Bowcock. G. Watson. W. E. Deakin. R. A. Crombie. F. Taylor. T. Oliver. A. Nadin
Second Row—W. Bott. S. Miller. G. V. Myatt. T. S. Myatt. W. T. Cook. T. Hawksworth. B. Holtham. B. Hill.
Third Row—E. Phillips. W. Overfield. A. Worthington. W. E. Brindley. E. Simpson. E. Flower. A. Clarke
W. H. Johnson. H. Moorhouse. J. N. Vass. J. Leese. T. Rigby. J. Hawksworth. T. Bould. W. Cox.
Back Row—W. Moorcroft C. Ward R. Manuell D. Cade J. Fogg C. Pickford W. Kinsey F. Coates J. Hudson

Old Photograph of Leek Fishing Club.

FRONT ROW—JOHN PICKFORD. MASTER HORNE. CHARLIE BOWCOCK. SAMUEL GOLDSTRAW. MASTER BOWCOCK.
2ND ROW—WILLIAM HALL. JAMES CREATHORNE. SAM CLARK. WILLIAM HORNE. ROBERT HILL. (EX. SEC.). TOM TAYLOR. JUN.. JOHN HURST. JOHN IND. HENRY PRIME AND SON.
3RD ROW—JOHN GOODWIN. JOHN ASTLES. JOHN RUSHTON. GUS BAYLEY. JOCK RIDER. ROLAND RIDER. (LATE SEC). ALBERT REX. TOM NIGHTINGALE. THOMAS TAYLOR. SENR.

IMAGES OF BYGONE LEEK: PART THREE
BEYOND THE VICTORIAN AND EDWARDIAN ERA

Offices of the Leek United and Midlands Building Society.

The tasteful decorations on this building for the Coronation Day were greatly admired by thousands of the inhabitants of Leek. The choice colourings made a wonderful show in the day time, and at night, the effect when floodlit was equally pleasing.

1937
HEAD OFFICE: 50 ST EDWARD STREET, LEEK.
DECORATED FOR THEIR MAJESTIES CORONATION ON THE 12TH MAY 1937.

BETWEEN THE TWO WORLD WARS

THE DEFINITIVE HISTORY OF TWENTIETH CENTURY LEEK is yet to be written, and it is not within the scope of this present book to fulfil this task. In the meantime, to take but a small step in this direction, we end as we began, with a few selected images from that period, to illustrate the continuing development of the town after the end of the First World War.

When the Leek Battery marched off to war in August 1914 nobody could predict the devastating effects the war would have on the nation and the town. The great cost to local families can be seen in the names of over 400 of Leek's fine young men recorded on the panels of the Nicholson War Memorial. The men of Leek who died in the conflicts are remembered on Armistice Sunday in November each year by the parade and ceremony at the Nicholson War Memorial, where poppy wreaths are laid by civic heads and representatives of other organisations, with the British Legion playing a leading role.

The Nicholson War Memorial, generally referred to by Leek people as the Monument, was given to the town by Sir Arthur and Lady Nicholson in memory of their son, Lieutenant Basil Lee Nicholson, and other local men killed in the First World War. The memorial, built of Portland stone, stands 90 feet high and was designed by Messrs Thomas Worthington and Sons of Manchester. The tablet was unveiled by Lieutenant-General Sir Charles Harrington (GOC Northern Command) and dedicated by the Bishop of Stafford on Thursday, 20 August 1925.

But there were many more whose names were not recorded, who returned from the war carrying the indelible scars of the conflict. The casualties of war included young men who had lost limbs, who were permanently crippled, who were blinded or gassed, who were suffering the after-effects of shellshock or whose minds had been shattered by their experiences. What would such men find in the so-called 'land fit for heroes'? And how did towns like Leek come to terms with the disillusion and despair, and begin to build for the future?

The euphoria of the Victorian era of enterprise, and the golden glow of the Edwardian summer (as recorded in previous chapters) were over for ever. The world had changed completely, and things would never be the same again. Many of the young men who would have taken their places as leaders in industry, trade and commerce, and in local government, were gone. How would Leek face the challenges of the post-war years? And would it find the resources to experience a new era of commercial growth and municipal expansion?

The great change in social conditions is reflected very noticeably in the fate of the halls and fine houses in and around Leek. Gentry families, who had formerly employed their little private armies of estate workers, gardeners, grooms and household servants, were faced with having to cut back drastically. The days of empire building were over. During a period of about thirty years or so, embracing the Second World War, great changes took place with halls and estates, as families could no longer afford to retain all their staff, and either died out or moved on, their once-cherished properties being devoted to other purposes.

Westwood became a Grammar School for girls. Ball Haye, following the demise of John Hall, was designated as the site for a brand new hospital, and became a base for American soldiers during the Second World War, its extensive gardens and duck pond having been taken to form part of Leek's public park - 'John Hall's Gardens'. Highfield failed to find a long-term permanent resident, but its grounds survived, thanks mainly to the efforts of Leek Cricket Club. Stockwell House was rebuilt by the Leek and Moorlands Building Society as its chief office. Woodcroft was pulled down for housing development, and Ashenhust was demolished for unknown reasons. Haregate and Greystones eventually reverted to flats, Nab Hill became the offices of a construction company. Pickwood and Ashcombe survived as private dwellings.

Most of the silk and textile factories still survived, more or less as they were, in the ownership of the families who had founded them in Victorian times. Large or small, the mills continued to find employment for many hundreds of workers, mainly female, for this was always a very labour-intensive industry. The era of man-made fibres and big take-overs (which would eventually be the hallmarks of the demise of the local industry) had not yet dawned. The industry was very resilient, for it survived a number of disastrous factory fires, a major hazard of the industry. A number of the mill owners, like their fathers before them, found time to serve in local government, as members of Leek Urban District Council. The industry had managed to survive the ravages of the First World War - it would not survive the next war for very long, but no-one could forsee this at the time.

On the leisure front, sport continued to thrive. The two cricket clubs, Leek and Leek Highfield, settled their differences after the First World War, and came together as one club. Each team having lost several of their star players in the war, the new Leek Cricket Club's survivors formed a strong team, and took several trophies during the 1920s. Junior football was doing well, with several successful teams. Rugby, hockey, tennis, golf, cycling and athletics all commanded a fair level of support and success. Hiking was a pastime which enjoyed an increasing measure of support, as increased leisure time enabled more and more people to escape into the countryside. Many areas of the moorlands that had hitherto been inaccessible were being opened up to walkers.

As in Victorian and Edwardian times, the amateur stage continued to thrive. The Leek Amateur Operatic Society, usually under the direction of William Warrington, a draper and town councillor, maintained the tradition of high standard productions of the Gilbert and Sullivan operettas and other musicals from the London stage. These usually took place at the Grand Theatre, then in

Dedication of the Nicholson War Memorial Thursday 20 August 1925.

A Club day procession in Derby Street, probably 1925 with Nicholson War Memorial under construction.

DURING the past few years, as the result of an agreement entered into between the Council and the Hospital Committee, Leek people have enjoyed the freedom of Ball Haye Gardens—a privilege that has been exercised and enjoyed to the full, and it would have been a thousand pities if those gardens had not been secured for the permanent enjoyment of the people of this district. Added to the Park they greatly enhance its attractiveness, and there is no doubt that their immense popularity has resulted in the Park itself being used far more than it would otherwise have been. The Council's decision to purchase the gardens and add them to the Park will therefore be acclaimed with unanimous enthusiasm and satisfaction. Subject to the consent of the Minister of Health to the borrowing of £2,000 the Council has decided to purchase 8.44 acres of land on the Ball Haye estate, including the ornamental gardens, lake, kitchen garden, glasshouses, and gardener's cottage. And subject to his consent to the borrowing of a further £1,200, also to purchase 4.60 acres of land adjoining the gardens. Although it is the Council that is taking up the loan for, and is making the purchase of, this additional 4.6 acres, it really amounts to a free gift from the Trustees of the Leek Town Lands, because, as a Commemoration of the Silver Jubilee of Their Majesties the King and Queen, the Trustees of the Town Lands, have very kindly offered to pay the amount of the annual instalments of both principal and interest on the necessary loan.

From Leek News

regular use as a cinema. The leading roles, formerly played by Kineton Parkes, were usually taken by A.D.Price, a physics master at Leek High School. The Leek Choral Society continued to flourish, and several amateur dramatic societies were formed. A number of churches had concert parties, giving traditional entertainment with limited resources. These amateur shows provided a great escape from the pressures of the times, when financial depression and the long-term effects of the war affected the lives of many ordinary townsfolk.

A Royal visit took place on Wednesday, 3 July 1931, when the visitor was Prince George, Duke of Kent. He was making a two-day tour of the industries of North Staffordshire, and visited Brough, Nicholson and Hall's factory, where he was welcomed by Col A. F. Nicholson. The oldest director, Mr A. H. Moore, recalled to his Royal Highness how he was one of those who showed the King and Queen through the Mill in July 1900 (when a mill recently added to the works was named the Royal York Mill by their permission) and again in April 1913.

Once again, the townspeople turned out in great numbers, the streets lined with people along the Prince's route out of Leek via Ball Haye Street, Stockwell Street, St Edward Street and Compton, at the end of a brief but memorable Royal visit.

Prince George made a second visit to Leek three years later, on Friday, 13 July 1934, during his tour of the district to inspect social service clubs and occupational centres. A huge crowd had assembled at the disused silk mill in Shoobridge Street, which was then the Occupational Centre for Leek unemployed, having been taken over and renovated by the Leek Town Unemployment Committee.

On his arrival, Prince George was welcomed by Councillor Fred Hill, Chairman of Leek Urban District Council, and also Chairman of the Leek Town Unemployment Committee, and Councillor W. Warrington (Chairman of the Centre Committee).

The Centre itself, under the guidance of Mr Lewis Everett, the organiser, had been made spick and span with exhibits of work produced. The Prince talked to some of the unemployed sat at their benches. At the end of his visit, he signed the Club book, shook hands with the officials and departed for Stoke by car. Many flag-waving Leek people lined the streets to cheer him on his way.

A CHRONICLE OF THE TIMES: 'LEEK NEWS'

Apart from the weekly reporting of events in the local newspapers, a great chronicler of the 1920s and 30s was the annual publication 'Leek News'. This was the brain-child of the Leek bookseller, stationer and printer, Fred Hill, who was also a local councillor. This was basically an advertising journal, published and freely distributed just before Christmas each year, from 1927 until the start of the Second World War. But it was much more than a mere string of advertisements, it contained a series of articles and photographs of great local interest, reflecting the contemporary scene as well as historical events. Fred Hill, with his many involvements in local affairs, was able to persuade a number of his contemporaries to give him an article. This led to an eclectic mix of items on a variety of subjects, and this was part of the charm of 'Leek News'. The journsl was printed at his own small printing works in Getliffe's Yard, and distrubuted freely around the town by an army of boys.

Such was the interest in the journal that many local people asked for extra copies to send to friends and families away, and to meet this demand a 'special edition' was produced, printed on better quality paper, for which a small charge was made. An attempt to produce a smaller edition on a monthly basis did not succeed due mainly to lack of advertising support.

The series of extracts from 'Leek News' which follow will serve to give a flavour of this unique publication, and at the same time, reflect some of the events of that period between the two world wars.

THE ROYAL VISIT

TO LEEK.

APRIL 23RD, 1913.

Processes to be shewn

at the MILLS of

Brough, Nicholson & Hall, Ltd.

FIRST ROOM.

The WINDING of SEWING MACHINE SILK and
OTHER SILKS on WOOD REELS, PAPER TUBES,
CONES, ROLLERS and CARDS.

SECOND ROOM.

KNITTING
of Silk and Artificial Silk
SCARVES, TIES, &c.,
KNITTED COATS.

THIRD ROOM.

The UTILISATION of SILK WASTE,
Waste Silk as received,
" " boiled off,
Dressing, Spreading, Drawing into threads,
and Spinning.

Prince George at Leek.

PRINCE GEORGE, COLONEL NICHOLSON & MR. MOORE

MR. J. HOWE HALL, MR. G. H. SHELDON, J.P., and MR. H. HENSHAW, the Town Clerk, can be seen in the background.

THE visit to Leek of His Royal Highness Prince George, on Wednesday, the 3rd July last, is far too outstanding an event not to be mentioned in an annual of this nature, and although the event is still fresh in the minds of the majority of the people that will see this article, there remain many to whom a copy of this annual will be sent, that will, I think, appreciate a brief note recording so interesting and important an occasion.

It was during a two-day's tour of the industries of North Staffordshire, arranged by the North Staffordshire Chamber of Trade, that the Prince graciously consented to visit Leek and inspect some of the processes connected with the staple industry of the town.

The town was *en fête* for the occasion and long before the scheduled time large crowds, including many farmers who delayed their return from the market in order to catch a glimpse of the Prince, assembled all along the route.

The Royal party journeyed to Leek from Tunstall where the Prince had been inspecting a large tile works. Entering Leek by Newcastle Road and Broad Street, the party proceeded via St. Edward Street, Sheep Market, Derby Street and Ashbourne Road to the entrance of Messrs. Brough, Nicholson and Hall's mill, at the entrance of which the Prince was warmly welcomed by Colonel A. F. Nicholson, T.D., J.P., D.L. On passing into the mill the party, which included Sir Francis Joseph, O.B.E., the Prince's Equerry, Major Humphrey Butler, and others, were met by Messrs. J. Howe Hall, B. R. Hall, P. Kiek, and A. H. Moore, directors of the firm. Mr. G. H. Sheldon, J.P., the chairman of the Leek Urban District Council, and Mr. H. Henshaw, the Clerk to the Council, were then presented to the Prince, and Mr. Sheldon asked His Royal Highness to convey to their Majesties the King and Queen and to all the members of the Royal Family the best wishes of the town of Leek.

The Prince's tour of the mill lasted approximately an hour, during which time he showed a keen and intelligent interest in the various processes of manufacture connected with the production of Leek goods.

Mr. Moore, who is the oldest Director and is also Chairman of the Leek Bench of Magistrates, recalled to his Royal Highness how he was one of those who showed the present King and Queen through the mill during their visits in July, 1900 (when a mill recently added to the works was named the Royal York Mill by their permission) and in April, 1913.

The route taken on leaving the town was Ball Haye Street, Stockwell Street, St. Edward Street and Compton, and throughout it was thickly populated, the townspeople, following upon their hearty welcome, giving him a wonderful "send-off."

In July 1931 Prince George made a tour of the industries of North Staffordshire. His itinerary included Leek where he was received by Colonel A F Nicholson at Brough, Nicholson and Hall.

MUNICIPAL DEVELOPMENT BETWEEN THE WARS

Much of the responsibility of planning the post-war 'land fit for heroes' at local level lay with the Leek Urban District Council. Like their predecessors, the Improvement Commissioners, the town councillors were mainly mill owners, professional men or tradesmen. Party politics were not usually an issue, although the councillors would, of course, have their own political affiliations.

The Local Government Act of 1894 superseded the Leek Improvement Act of 1855. Every householder was given the right to vote, or to be nominated as a councillor. The Leek Urban District Council had 24 members, and at the first election on December 17th, 1894 there were 53 candidates. A total of 2,268 of the electorate voted. This democratic system prevailed into the 20th century.

Leek is believed to be one of the first towns in Staffordshire to have its own water and gas works, cattle market, isolation hospital, public baths and public library, all of which were administered by the L.U.D.C. By 1901 the population had arisen to 14,224, and in 1931 it was 18,556. Between 1901 and 1931 the average age at death rose fom 38.8 to 54.1 years.

With the growth of the town and the increasing demand for water it became necessary to construct a new reservoir at Swainsmoor. In 1934 the council received a report that the borehole at Poolend could be developed to supply about a million gallons of water a day, and authority was given to construct a pumping station. Gas and electricity supplies were in the control of the council until after the Second World War. Street lighting was mainly by gas, the first gas lamps having been erected as long ago as 1828. The L.U.D.C. Gas Department showroom was in Derby Street, at the corner of Bath Street. This later moved to the Market Place, at the entrance to the Market Hall. The electricity showroom and service centre was on the opposite side of the entrance.

A local authority is only as strong as its officers, and the L.U.D.C. was fortunate to have a first-class surveyor who served for 34 years, from 1903 to 1937. He was William Ernest Beacham, and under his direction much progress was made in town planning and housing development. Under a succession of Housing Acts a total of 850 new houses was erected between 1919 and 1936. There were three major areas of development, the largest being the Abbotsville, Novi Lane and Haregate Housing Scheme. Other schemes under W.E. Beacham's direction were the Glebeville and Junction Road scheme and the Station Street and Morley Street scheme, which embraced Burton Street, The Walks and parts of West End Avenue. The public toilet at the top of Mill Street, known affectionately as 'Beacham's Pill', was another of his buildings.

Long-serving officers were the hallmark of the L.U.D.C. during the period between the wars. The Clerk to the Council from 1906 to 1946 was Harold Henshaw, and Frank Green served as Sanitary Inspector from 1905 to 1934. The Librarian from 1912 until 1951 was Arthur Vinen. These long-term appointments made for continuity and stability in the council's work during these difficult years.

Frank Green was evidently a very inventive man. In 1929 he addressed the problem of the removal and disposal of household refuse and invented a revolutionary new horse-drawn vehicle which he called the 'Economic Hygenic Non-tipping House Refuse Vehicle'. The principal of the vehicle was an easy and low loading level which would cut down on man-handling, prevent damage to bins and remain always covered. A system of tipping controls enabled the load to be discharged direct into the tip. He took out a patent for his invention, and commissioned local engineers Charles Leek and Sons to construct the vehicle. - but its long-term success is not known.

On the subject of health care, the Commissioners had purchased land off Ashbourne Road in 1880, where an isolation hospital was erected. A local voluntary hospital committee was responsible for the Leek Cottage Hospital. The hospital had been enlarged in 1909, to bring the accommodation to two male and two female wards, each containing 12 beds, plus four private wards. In 1921 the Leek Hospital and Convalescent Fund Committee installed much-needed X-Ray equipment. However, pressure on the hospital continued to grow, and during 1937 there were 506 X-Ray patients, and 366 ordinary patients, who were in hospital for 6301 days.

To meet the growing need, an ambitious plan for a purpose-built hospital was drawn up in the 1930s. The site was the environs of Ball Haye Hall, and annual carnivals were held to raise funds. A public appeal was launched - the estimated cost of the new hospital was £35,000 and there was a short-fall of £20,000. The hospital was to have a casualty department, maternity block and children's ward, as well as isolation wards, treatment rooms and operating theatre. Ball Haye Hall was designated as living accommodation for nursing staff. However, the war intervened, and the hospital was never built.

There was a Cripples' Clinic in Salisbury Street, built during the 1930s. This early orthopaedic clinic fulfilled a long-felt need in the town. The Medical Officer of Health from 1901 to 1940 was Dr. John Mountfort Johnson - another long-serving officer of the council.

The council celebrated 100 years of local government in Leek in 1955, and the great strides in municipal development during that time provided the spur to the council to apply for borough status for the town. A comprehensive document was drawn up to support the application, but it was not successful. Leek was destined to remain what it had always been - a town, but a town of history, character and achievement, justly fulfilling its title of 'Queen of the Moorlands'.

WESTWOOD PARK ESTATE.

PHOTOGRAPH BY JOHN MARTIN, LEEK.

AN INVITATION.

May we kindly offer you a cordial invitation to visit the Westwood Park Estate. We would like you to know that we can now offer a choice selection of sites on which to erect that House you have always desired.

We are pleased to inform you that of the Sixty houses already completed, only Two Houses remain available for immediate sale.

ALL SERVICES AVAILABLE.

The Town Services are available to all parts of the estate. Several roads are completed and others are now being extended.

HOUSE PURCHASE MADE EASY.

House Purchase is made easy by the service we offer you. Deposits are as low as £30 and repayments at 2/9 per £100 weekly.

CAREFUL PLANNING.

It is our intention to make the Westwood Estate worthy of its beautiful setting. The Layout Plan can be inspected by appointment by those who are interested and who desire to see the generous way in which the whole of the estate has been planned.

New Schools will adjoin the estate and new roads giving better access, are shortly to be constructed. Shopping facilities will also be available,

We have a selection of designs showing the full Plans for Houses at prices from £540. These can be submitted for your consideration, or Houses designed to meet your particular requirements can be built at inclusive prices. Our desire will be to give you entire satisfaction.

THE EFFECT OF CAREFUL PLANNING.

For two years we have been working on this estate, and something of its finished beauty is now coming to view. We sincerely hope that with the coming of the New Year, many more discerning home lovers will take the opportunity of choosing a charming site for a new home, amidst delightful surroundings, on the Westwood Park Estate.

F. M. NORTH & Co.

From Leek News

Housing Site at Nab Hill Avenue.

MR. BOWCOCK, in his official capacity as Secretary of the Leek United and Midlands Building Society and as an ex-town Councillor, has an almost unrivalled opportunity of acquiring an intimate and thorough knowledge of local housing problems.

Being ever a large-hearted and public-spirited man, keenly interested in all municipal and social problems, Mr. Bowcock has spared no effort in his endeavour thoroughly to study and ably to play his part in the solving of the acute and difficult problem of providing homes for the people.

His duties have naturally brought him into contact with many people vainly searching for houses in which to make their homes.

It was with a view to helping these and relieving the shortage of houses which was being so acutely felt in the town, that he decided, entirely on his own initiative and solely at his own personal risk, to purchase 9 acres of land at the West end of the Town and to build thereon a number of attractive houses of the most modern, convenient and healthy type, and at a price that would not be prohibitive to the man of only very moderate means.

Building operations were commenced in 1924 and have been in continuous progress until now. No less than 85 houses have been erected, all of which are occupied, most of the houses have, of course, been purchased by the occupiers.

THE CRESCENT.

L. U. D. Council Houses.

THE Housing question is still the all important one with us at Leek, and many families are in urgent need of more suitable Housing Accommodation.

It will be of interest to all our readers to know that the L.U.D. Council have since 1919 erected 304 houses for the people of Leek.

160 HOUSES IN 1926.

During the past 12 months some good progress has been made and 160 houses have been occupied. Of this number, the Council have erected 76, Mr. Solomon Bowcock 40, Mr. Grace, Builder, 18 and Mr. Overfield and others who have erected houses for their own accommodation, number about 27, bringing the total, in round figures to 160. These figures show that during the past 12 months great improvement has been achieved, when compared with production of Houses during the past few years.

Mr. Bowcock is now making good progress and he informs me that he intends to complete 35 more of these houses during the coming year. Mr. Bowcock, however, is hoping to erect 100 houses on the West End Estate before same is completed.

Councillor Wm. Provost, J.P., Chairman of the Housing Committee, together with his collegues on that Committee, are endeavouring to get more houses built as quickly as possible and a start has now been made on the Novi Lane Site, to erect 72 more houses, the same to be completed before the end of October, 1927.

The Council are also endeavouring to get possession of other suitable building sites, so we may look forward to a good supply of Houses in 1927.

From Leek News

The official party at the dedication of the Nicholson War Memorial, 20th August 1925.

The unveiling ceremony of the Memorial on Thursday 20th August 1925. The 'Monument' as it is commonly called, was presented to the Town by Sir Arthur and Lady Nicholson in memory of their son Lieutenant Basil Lee Nicholson and other local men killed in the First World War. The memorial, which is built of Portland stone and stands 90 feet high, was designed by Messrs. Thomas Worthington and Sons of Manchester. The tablet was unveiled by Lieutenant General Sir Charles Harrington, GBE, KCB, DSO, (GOC Northern Command) and dedicated by the Bishop of Stafford.

Shiny top hats in evidence in the annual Chairman's Sunday parade of 1932. The Chairman of Leek Urban District Council, J W Swindells, leads the procession to a service at the Congregational Church.

In the late 1920s and 1930s Leek's annual carnival was a popular event. They were fund raising efforts for Leek hospitals and other local charities. Money was raised to replace the Cottage Hospital (see p.230), but this never materialised. Many traders took part, and here the float mounted by Mutual Bargain Stores uses a lorry belonging to L Whittles & Son, corn mercahants.

In the same location as the previous photo - West Street, outside Goodwin and Tatton's factory - the Leek Fire Brigade is on parade. Later in the early 1940s, the fire brigade were here professionally when the factory was destroyed by fire.

A Co-operative Society coal lorry is seen with the decorations which won second prize in its class.

Leek Cricket Club won the North Staffs. District League championship for the fifth time in 1931.
The team, committee and officials is seen here with the Captain, Herbert Sedgwick, seated centre front row.

Works football teams abounded in local competitions. during the 1920s and 1930s. Wardle's Football Club played in the Tunstall and District League and won the Leek and Moorlands Cup in 1935. Front: A Johnson, H Peacock, G Hambleton, L Dean, R Billings. Back: H Notley, A Moss, R Rogers, G Lyons, L Hayward, R Dunkley, R Bollington, S Gosling.

LEEK NEWS.

LEEK CRICKET CLUB.

SECOND TEAM - Champions N. S. & District League, Season 1937.

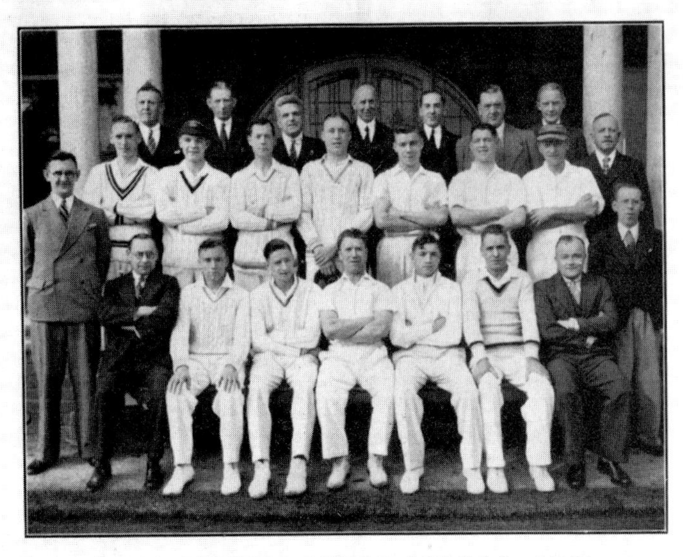

Back Row—E. Shires, H. Oliver, F. Hutchinson, H. Ball, B. Lees, S. Bould, W. C. Charnock, W. Dale.
Middle Row—Ron. Halton, T. H. Ball, F. W. V. Dale, H. Kidd, J. Bentley, L. Hall, J. G. Pointon, H. Alcock, N. Nott.
Front Row.—F. F. Furmston, P. Harrison, F. Boulton, J. Cotton (Capt), R. Stanyer, A Plant, T. Jones.

Last season was an eventful one for the Leek Cricket Club, in as much that the 2nd team won the Championship of the Junior "A" section for the second time and with a record total of 58 points. The "A" team won the League Championship and the Knock-out Cup of the Leek and District League.

For the 1st XI the first part of the season was most unfortunate, as only one match was won out of the first 14. Winning the Silverdale match by splendid bowling, put new heart into the players and six matches were then won in succession, two of them being won after looking hopeless.

The most encouraging part of the season has been the advance made by the younger players, particularly in the cases of Reg. Halton, E. Hayward, C. Bonsall, E. Hordern, R. Stanyer, F. Boulton, F. W. V. Dale and J. G. Pointon. In these young men the club has a number of most promising players, who should, if they are able to play regularly in the future and develop along normal lines, be good enough to win Leek the Championship of the Senior Division, which they have not won since 1931.

Of the more experienced players, Harold Birch showed a welcome return to form, not only winning the bowling cup, but also batting well and attractively on many occasions particularly so when runs were badly needed. As an all-rounder he is still one of the best in the league.

Mr. Charnock had a most unlucky time. He proved to be absolutely out of form for the first few matches and then during his great knock against Stone he was very unfortunate to break a bone in his hand, with the result he was unable to play again during the rest of the season. W. R. Rider however proved an able deputy and the form of the players during the latter part of the season must have given him great pleasure. He also batted stubbornly and saved his team from collapse on a number of occasions. Len Crump, in his second season as professional, played many useful innings and along with Eric Dale gave the team some good opening partnerships,

Probably the finest innings played for Leek last season, was hit by C. Bonsall, who scored a brilliant 51 against Porthill in about 25 minutes, enabling his team to win in the last over of the match. This player also scored 69 against Blythe and together with Ron Halton (52) saved the side from a very poor total, 5 wickets having fallen for 18 runs.

Reg Halton won the batting cup, scoring 364 runs for an average of 24'71, and by taking 35 wickets for 10'88 runs each, became one of the outstanding all-rounders in the league. His re-union with his old club was very welcome and it is to be hoped that this attractive player will be able to assist the club regularly next season.

"Johnny" Cotton must have been a proud man at the end of the season which was his first as captain of the second team. He moulded his young team together in a splendid way and the records show what an invincible side this second team became. They scored 2739 runs, with an average of 15'92 per wicket; while their opponents only scored 1617 runs, for an average of 7'77 runs per wicket, and only on 3 occasions did their opponents score more than 100 runs. In the match against Porthill, A. Plant did the "hat trick," all being stumped by P. Harrison, which must be unique in cricket history.

The "A" team went through the season unbeaten, a performance of exceptional merit and Harry Davis and his players are to be congratulated on this feat.

A matter worth recording is that a short broadcast was made of the Burslem v Leek match, the first ever having been given of a North Staffordshire League match.

In view of the possibility of having to move from Highfield to Beggars Lane at some future date, the Committee have made some progress towards putting the latter ground in a better condition so that if a removal is necessary, the ground will be of a sufficiently high standard on which to play North Staffordshire League Cricket.

The Leek News gave local sport good coverage in the 1930s. This is a comprehensive review of Leek Cricket Club's 1937 season.

LEEK . . .
AMATEUR
OPERA
SOCIETY

GRAND
THEATRE,
LEEK.

IOLANTHE

March 8th
TO
March 13th,
1926.

PRICE THREEPENCE.

"IOLANTHE"

(By permission of R. D'Oyly Carte, Esq.)

CAST.

The Lord Chancellor	A. D. PRICE / HAROLD GRACE
Earl of Mountararat...	LEONARD SALT
Earl Tolloller	GEORGE MASON
Private Willis (of the Grenadier Guards)	HARRY HUNT
Strephon (An Arcadian Shepherd)...	EDGAR BULL
Queen of the Fairies...	GLADYS BAINES
Iolanthe (a Fairy. Strephon's Mother)	EDITH RUSSELL BROWN
Celia (Fairies)	FLORENCE HALL
Leila (Fairies)	ETHELWYN GWYNNE
Fleta (Fairies)	NANCY TATTON
Phyllis (an Arcadian Shepherdess and Ward in Chancery) ...	DOROTHIE BULL

Mr. A. D. PRICE will appear in the part of "Lord Chancellor" on Monday, Wednesday, Thursday and Saturday Matinee, and Mr. H. GRACE will appear in the part of "Lord Chancellor" on Tuesday, Friday and Saturday Nights.

Miss May Poyser will appear as the "Queen" on Tuesday night.

CHORUS OF DUKES, MARQUISES, EARLS, VISCOUNTS, BARONS & FAIRIES:

Celia Bilton	Jessie Robinson	W. Earls	P. Poole
May Cope	Elsie Salt	Harry Foster	B. Sedgwick
Winifred Garner	Mabel Shute	Vincent Hall	Bert Sharpe
May Hawksworth	Kathleen Tomson	J. E. Morrow	Walter J. Turner
Violet Pearson		D. M. Newall	Albert Weston
May Poyser	Ida Wilson	Harry Owen	W. E. Wheeldon

ACT I. An Arcadian Landscape.
ACT II. Palace Yard, Westminster.
Date - - Between 1700 and 1882.

The Opera produced by Mr. W. Warrington.

Phyllis' and Gentlemen's Costumes by Messrs. B. J. Simmons and Co., Ltd., London. The Fairies' Dresses have been dyed by the Premier Dyeing Company and specially designed and made for the production.

Scenery by Messrs. C. E. Grantham, Leatherhead.

LEEK AMATEUR OPERA SOCIETY

FOUNDED 1909.

PREVIOUS PRODUCTIONS:
PATIENCE 1910.
MIKADO 1911.
THE YEOMEN OF THE GUARD 1912.
IOLANTHE 1913.

GONDOLIERS 1914.
IOLANTHE 1916.
GONDOLIERS 1920.
PATIENCE 1921.
MIKADO 1922.
THE YEOMEN OF THE GUARD 1923.
RUDDIGORE 1924.
PRINCESS IDA 1924.

GRAND PRODUCTION OF GILBERT AND SULLIVAN'S OPERA

IOLANTHE

By permission of R. D'Oyly Carte, Esq.

PRINCIPALS, CHORUS, AND ORCHESTRA OF SIXTY PERFORMERS.

LEEK AMATEUR OPERA SOCIETY.

PRESIDENT.

ADMIRAL SIR GUY GAUNT.

PAST PRESIDENTS.

W. E. CHALLINOR, PICKWOOD.
DR. J. M. JOHNSON, M.D., M.R.C.S.
H. J. JOHNSON, ESQ., J.P., Westwood Hall.

GENERAL COMMITTEE.

MR. W. E. BRINDLEY	MR. W. H. EATON	MR. H. J. JOHNSON
MR. N. CARR	MR. C. GELL	MR. G. MASON
MR. G. CARTLIDGE	MR. H. GRACE	MR. H. RICHES
MR. L. COPE	MR. H. HENSHAW	MR. W. WARRINGTON

HONORARY OFFICERS.

Acting Manager and Secretary	MR. SIDNEY STANNARD
Treasurer	MR. HAROLD HENSHAW
Conductor	MR. W H. EATON
Stage Manager and Producer	MR. W WARRINGTON
Property Master and Stage Steward	MR. W. NORMAN CARR
Auditor	MR. FRANCIS BILLING
Wardrobe Master	MR. H. RICHES
Wardrobe Mistress	MRS. W. NORMAN CARR
Accompanist	MRS. TERRY
Electrical Engineer	Mr. TULLOCK
Prompter	MR. W A FURMSTON
Assistant Secretary and Registrar	MR L. COPE
Deputy Conductor	MR. W. E. BRINDLEY
Deputy Accompanists	MISS SHUFFLEBOTHAM, L.L C M. Mrs. J ROBINSON

SOCIETY'S BANKERS - THE MANCHESTER & LIVERPOOL DISTRICT BANK, LEEK.

LEEK AMATEUR OPERA SOCIETY.

"The Gondoliers or The King of Barataria."

CAST.

The Duke of Plaza-Toro (a Grandee of Spain)		MR. A. D. PRICE
Luiz (his Attendant)		MR. CHARLES GELL
Don Alhambra del Bolero (the Grand Inquisitor)		MR. G. CARTLIDGE
Marco Palmieri	Venetian Gondoliers	MR. GEORGE MASON
Guiseppe Palmieri		MR. T. P. SPENCER
Antonio		MR. HARRY TATTON
Francesco		MR. PHILIP OWEN
Giorgio		MR. LANCE COPE
Annibale		MR. CYRIL BERMINGHAM
The Duchess of Plaza-Toro		MISS MARGARET BREALEY
Casilda (her Daughter)		MISS DOROTHY PEBWORTH
Gianetta	Contadine	MISS PHYLLIS BILTON
Tessa		MISS EDITH RUSSELL-BROWN
Fiametta		MISS DOROTHIE BULL
Vittoria		MRS. JAS. ROBINSON
Giulia		MISS ETHELWYN GWYNNE
Inez (the King's Foster-Mother)		MRS. WILLIAM SLATER
Drummer Boy		MASTER FRED CHELL

CHORUS OF GONDOLIERS AND CONTADINE, MEN-AT-ARMS, HERALDS AND PAGES.

Grace Bailey	Kathleen Hunt	Harry Bailey	Philip Owen
Lilian Booth	Dorothy Jackman	Cyril Bermingham	William Page
Dorothie Bull	Kathleen Parr	Reginald Brown	Leonard Salt
Loris Cartlidge	Jessie Robinson	Lance Cope	William Slater
Kathleen Conron	Kitty Slater	William O. Green	Harry Tatton
Elsie Grey	Marie Thompson	Robin Grey	Walter Turner
Ethelwyn Gwynne	Elsie Wilson	Vincent Hall	Walter Warburton
May Hawksworth	Elsie Wood	Arthur Halton	William Warburton

Pages. Dorothy Booth, Kathleen Henshaw, Winifred Sanders, Beatrice Sergison,

ACT I. The Piazetta, Venice. ACT II. Pavilion in the Palace of Barataria.

(An interval of three months is supposed to elapse between Act I. and II.)

Date 1750.

Scenery from the Savoy Theatre, London. Dresses by Messrs. Simmons, London.

The Opera produced by Mr. W. Warrington.

ILLUSTRATION OF THE NEW CLINIC FOR LEEK.

Leek and District Cripples' Aid Society.

THE Clinic was inaugurated in 1921 and has carried on its good work so far in Ball Haye Street Schools, and a room in the Cottage Hospital under rather trying conditions. The main object is to get into touch with all Orthopædic cases in the town and surrounding districts at the earliest possible moment. The sooner a case is treated the greater the hope of a permanent cure. Such cases as Club Foot can be entirely cured if the baby is treated in the first months of its existence and it is only by having a network of these clinics spread throughout the county that this becomes both practicable and possible. There have been 30,800 attendances and 32,700 treatments at the Leek Clinic since it was started.

The great good that is achieved is shewn by the Urban District Council, the Education Authority, the County Welfare Committee, the Guardians, and the Tuberculosis Authority, each and all contributing to the funds in payment for work done for sufferers under their respective jurisdictions. In addition the Hospital and Convalescent Fund also make a handsome contribution to the funds, and there are private donations and subscriptions. In this way enough money has so far been raised to meet the current expenses of the work undertaken. It has been decided that the time has now come to carry on the work in really suitable surroundings, specially built and adequately equipped. Land has been purchased in Salisbury Street, and Messrs. Longden and Venables have designed a building which in its exterior architecture will be a decided acquisition to the town's public buildings. It will contain waiting rooms, doctors' room, massage rooms, and a gymnasium, besides a large room which will be let to the T. B. authority and the Child Welfare Committee, so that they too can carry on their work in really suitable surroundings. Adjoining there will be a Shelter and Garden for open air sunlight treatment. It is hoped that the building will be ready for occupation in July next. The total cost will be somewhere about £7,500, and of this amount some £2,500 has been raised and the Committee are naturally anxious for further help both large and small so that the Clinic may be out of debt at the earliest moment

Any sums sent to Mr. F. Whitter, Building Fund Secretary, or to Williams Deacons Bank, Ltd., Derby Street, will be gratefully acknowledged.

H. B. C.

Municipal Development in Leek during 1930.

WHILST the Council has not launched out during the past year on any epoch-marking developments, considerable progress has been made in extending and improving some of the existing properties and undertakings, and although nothing of a spectacular nature has been undertaken, solid progress has been made in improving the general amenities of the town.

THE CEMETERY.

In 1912 the Council bought several acres of land adjoining the cemetery, at a cost of £1050, with a view to extending the burial ground. The work of laying out and enclosing this ground has been undertaken and completed during the present year at a cost of about £1,000.

CHEDDLETON ROAD IMPROVEMENT.

The work of widening Cheddleton road has been undertaken this year and work on this improvement has been in progress for some months. At present the contractors are engaged in widening the cutting from Broombank to Junction road, and considering the difficulties involved they have made remarkable progress with this part of the work. The widening of this road is estimated to cost £9,950. Toward this sum the Ministry of Transport has made a grant of £5,970, and as Cheddleton road is a county main road, the responsibility for providing the balance of £3,980 falls upon the County Council.

WATER SUPPLY.

Some time ago, with a view to improving the water supply in the higher parts of the town, the Council decided to construct a 1,000,000 gallon reservoir at Kniveden. The well known and highly respected local firm of Messrs. Thomas Grace & Sons were successful in securing the contract—the figure involved being £10,000, and the work is now being pressed forward as quickly as circumstances will allow. It will provide work for a number of local unemployed during the present winter, but should be completed towards the middle of next year.

The Council has been successful in obtaining financial assistance from the Unemployment Grants Committee in respect of this contract.

GAS AND ELECTRICITY DEPARTMENTS.

The new gas holder which is being erected at the gas works is now almost completed. It is to cost something like £6,000. A grant has been obtained from the Unemployment Grants Committee in respect to the interest charges on the necessary loans.

It is interesting to note that notwithstanding the slump in trade during the last twelve months the demand for electric supply has continuously increased. To meet this demand and to provide a margin for the future, the Lighting Committee have found it necessary during the year to make provision for additional plant. After due consideration the Committee decided to put down a mercury arc rectifer sub-station at the corner of Buxton road and Osborne street. This sub-station, which will have a total capacity of 400 kilowatts, will enable the present D.C. supply to be continued, and thus save the cost of laying an entirely new set of supply mains which a change over to A.C. supply would have made necessary. Further, as it is entirely automatic, it will save the cost of having to employ suitably qualified attendants to look after the sub-station, which expense would have been necessary if rotary or motor convertors had been adopted.

In considering this matter the Committee decided to look even further ahead, and in addition to this sub-station gave instructions to the department to supply and lay an 11,000 volt supply main from the power station in Station street to the Osborne street sub-station, and then on to a point situated on the Novi lane estate and there to erect a static sub-station suitable for supplying the whole of the Northern area of the town, together with further provision for continuing this 11,000 volt main at some future date, and as required by the demand, back by the new road along Junction road to the power station in Station street, thus forming a complete ring main round three parts of the town.

The Committee have not only been carefully looking after the needs of the electricity supply in Leek, but they have gone closely into the question of meeting the needs of districts immediately contiguous with Leek, and they decided to carry out the erection of a system of overhead supply mains in the village of Longsdon. This was completed in March last and a supply commenced, which we have reason to believe has proved of very considerable benefit to the inhabitants in that area. The demand for supply has continued to increase from the day the supply started, and this new venture of the Committee will, we feel sure, prove quite satisfactory financially and otherwise, and later become a valuable asset to the town.

HOUSING.

No new houses have been erected during the year. But a contract has been let for the development of a further portion of the Haregate estate, and it is hoped that when the estate is further developed, sites will be taken up and built upon by private enterprise.

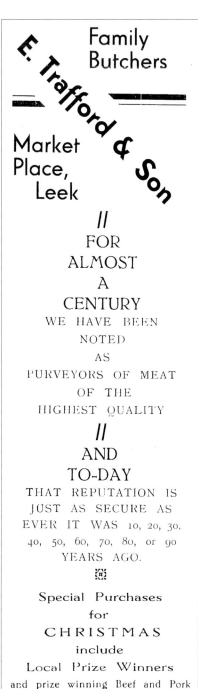

LOCAL EVENTS OF 1934.

:: A BRIEF REVIEW. ::

A BRIEF review of the chief local events of the year may interest a fair portion of the readers of this Journal who still reside in the town, and knowing, as I do, that many copies are sent to Leek people who have removed to other districts—some of them overseas—I feel that they especially will be interested to know something of what has been going on during the last twelve months.

I propose, therefore, to review very briefly a few of the chief events in which I have been called upon to take some part during the time I have had the honour of occupying the position of chairman of the Council.

I am writing these notes in hospital and am unable to give precise dates, but will do so as far as my memory serves.

The first public function in which I was called upon to take part was, of course, Chairman's Sunday. Favoured with a nice bright morning, a large gathering of friends and officials assembled and very kindly accompanied me to the Brunswick Methodist Chapel, where the Reverend W. E. Withers preached a most eloquent sermon—drawing upon incidents associated with the work of the Council to illustrate his points. It was a fine service, the singing was hearty, and Mr. Withers's sermon, which was one of the best I have heard on such an occasion, was thoroughly enjoyed and fully appreciated.

The gathering in the Town Hall after the service was a very happy affair. Councillor W. Provost, the father of the Council, made his customary speech of congratulation, and after mentioning that he and I had been acquainted since early boyhood, went on to allude to me in terms that I wish I could hope were as truthful as they were flattering. A man would be inhuman if he were not delighted and gratified with such a gathering, and it would be sheer false modesty for me not to admit quite frankly that the gathering of so many friends and the spirit which prevailed gave me the greatest pleasure.

Being now definitely launched on my way as Chairman of the Council I soon became involved in a multitude of duties, the first public one being to open the New Sewerage Scheme, on Thursday, May 10th. The proceedings on this occasion were opened by Colonel Worthington, the Chairman of the Health Committee, who had, of course, taken the lion's share of the work in connection with the inauguration of this scheme. Mr. Worthington pointed out the urgent necessity for such a scheme as was to be opened that day, and which although it had cost £80,000, and ought to be adequate to meet all demands likely to be made on it during the next fifty years, could not be considered any more ambitious than the circumstances warranted. Mr. W. E. Beacham, the Surveyor, who had borne the responsibility for the construction of the works then gave many interesting details of the undertaking and its working. Following which I declared the works open, and the company of from three to four [illegible] people who were present then made a tour of the works—the various units and processes being explained during the inspection.

EMPIRE DAY CELEBRATIONS.

Empire Day assumed a new significance for the Girl Guides and Scouts of Leek and District—this year, when they joined forces for the first united rally, which was held in the Town Hall, on Thursday, 24th May. The proceedings included a parade through the streets and I was honoured by being invited to take the salute as they marched along Market Street. A platform had been erected in front of the Town Hall, and I was accompanied on the platform by Captain Unwin, V.C., Mrs. H. Wardle (County Commissioner for the Guides), Mr. H. Henshaw, and Mr. E. Henshaw. Following this, the procession marched to the grounds adjoining Ladydale, very kindly lent for the occasion by Mrs. H Wardle. Here I had the pleasure of introducing Captain Unwin, V.C., to a large, enthusiastic, and appreciative audience. He made a fine manly speech, brimful of interest, and one that completely won the hearts of the Guides, Scouts, and adults alike. Having read "Smoke on the Horizon," in which here is a fine description of the glorious exploit by which Captain Unwin won his V.C., it was a great pleasure to meet him in person. He is a fine specimen of manhood, over six feet in height, and although over seventy years is still as straight as a poplar. He possesses a powerful personality, is a real "live" man of action, and is a fine example of the bull-dog breed. His address showed the great love he cherishes for England, and one felt that here was one of the nation's heroes that have played so great a part in the making of Britain and the Empire

L. U. D. C. ELECTION.

THE WARD SYSTEM.

Early this year the boundaries of the Urban District were extended to include certain portions of surrounding parishes. Simultaneously the town was divided into four wards, each ward electing six members, making a total of twenty-four, which was the number fixed when the Council took over from the old Commissioners thirty years ago.

The adoption of the Ward system occasioned an entire change in the method by which candidates had previously sought and secured election. Whereas previously a candidate had to appeal to the whole town with over 9,000 voters, he now appeals to only approximately a quarter of it, and of course a correspondingly smaller number of voters. Some of the members did not like the idea of the change, but with the extension of the franchise, and the continued growth of the town it had become a big and an expensive task to appeal to all the electorate, and some means by which the task could be made easier and less expensive for the candidate was quite due. Nevertheless, many of the members, if not all, felt they would much rather act as a representative of a complete and united community, rather than as the representative only of a separate unit, and this along with other reasons, may have accounted for the unusually large number of resignations which occurred at this year's election. Most of the resignations were by members of long [illegible] and proved ability, and as the following list of their names shows, were men whose services could ill be spared :—Mr. T. Birch, J.P., Mr. S. Bowcock, Mr. C. V. P. Cowlishaw, Mr. R. Eccles, Mr. A. Flower, Mr. A. Ratcliffe, M.P., and Mr. G. H. Sheldon, J.P.

As the election drew near there was much speculation as to what would happen under the new system, and it was thought not impossible that there might be a few surprises. But nothing very startling occurred. All the retiring Councillors were returned in honourable positions, and eight new members were elected. So that of this year's Council, a third of the members had not previously had any experience in Council work—that is except Council Harry Robinson who was an ex-member of the Council.

It is interesting to note that in North Ward No. 1, Councillors Provost and Shufflebotham tied for the top place—a very unusual event !

At this year's election, as I have already pointed out, each Ward elected six members—that was because the whole of the twenty-four members of the Council had been called upon to retire owing to the change over, but in subsequent years there will be only two retiring members in each of the four wards, and of course only two to be elected in each ward—making a total of eight—thus every member of the Council has to seek re-election every three years. But the electors will be able to vote for only two candidates—and not eight as before the the change over. Of course, in order to get the system working properly eight members will have to seek re-election next year, although they will have served only one year, and the following year another eight will have to seek re-election although they will have served only two years. After that the members will seek re-election every three years as already explained. The results of this year's election are as follows :

NORTH WARD No. 1.

Number of Electors—3319.

Percentage of Electors voted—54 %

Provost, William 1134
Shufflebotham, Harry 1134
Worthington, Lancelot Jukes 972
Hill, Fred 923
Cope, H. J. 910
Clowes, William 709

NORTH WARD No. 2.

Number of Electors—1877.

Percentage of Electors voted—59 %

Bayley, Joseph 652
Nicholson, Arthur Falkner... 613
Bloore, William Ratcliffe ... 520
Downes, Francis 470
Worthington, Andrew Yorke 465
Robinson, Henry 398

SOUTH WARD No. 1.

Number of Electors—2589.

Percentage of Electors voted—59 %

Furmston, William A. ... 989
Swindells, John W. 923
Skinner, John McPherson ... 892
White, Harry 711
Clowes, John 695
[illegible] ... [illegible]

SOUTH WARD No. 2.

Number of Electors—2001.

Percentage of Electors voted—55 %

Bullock, William L. ... 749
Rhead, James 638
Morton, Harry 553
Bowcock, Philip T. 531
Hine, Albert J. 493
Delaney, William 480

LEEK CYCLISTS' CLUB.

Group of members taken at the Peveril Hotel, Thorpe, on Sunday, 5th July, 1936—the Club's Diamond Jubilee Year.

FRONT ROW—F. Ferns, A. Shenton, H. Byrne, S. Counsell, P. K. Ager, E. Hall, E. Foster, C. Pegg, A. Goldstraw, A. Barlow, A. Burnett, K. Allen, P. Harrison, A. Fitch, G. Hall, W. Simcock

SECOND ROW—J. Hamilton, W. Keates, D. Keeling, E. Keates, T. Bestwick, T. Messham, B. Hill, W. T. Cook, A. Barnett, S. Godwin

THIRD ROW—E. Maycock, S. Cartwright, J. Frost, W. Frost, N. Foster, J. Beaumont, H. Byrne, J. Loxley, R. Chapman, J. P. Fellows-Smith, F. Bode, N. Keates, L. Wilshaw, J. Chambers, S. Hewitt, G. Fowler

BACK ROW—R. Binns, E. Hamilton, C. Counsell, R. Trafford, W. J. Ash, F. Allen, L. Smith.

IT will probably surprise many to learn that the Leek Cyclists' Club is believed to be the oldest active cyclists' club in England. It is a "toss up" between three clubs, one of which is the Pickwick, which, it is understood, has not been active for some years, and it seems as though the honour does definitely belong to Leek.

The club was founded in 1876 as the Leek and Moorlands Bicycle Club, the first meeting being held on the 3rd August, in the old Plough vaults.

The founders were :—

Mr. W. T. Cook, 17, King St. (Captain).
Mr. C. Clulow, Alsop's Bank, (Secretary).
Mr. J. Deakin, Sheephouse, Toll Gate,
Mr. W. H. Hambleton, Queen Street,
Mr. G. Watson, 80, West Street,
who formed the Committee and
Mr. J. Fisher, 5, Rose Bank.

Cycling in those days was very different, of course, from what it is today, and the club runs of 60 years ago may strike the cyclists of this generation as being equivalent to little more than half an hours "pottering about." Actually they were strenuous adventures. The primitive machines and the rough roads of the 'seventies, made cycling an adventurous pastime that demanded the expenditure of considerable energy and also involved not a little risk.

Those were pioneer days, and like all pioneers, the cyclist of 60 years ago had to be able to mix the rough with the smooth. The refinements of the modern cycle and the smooth hard surface of the modern road were beyond his rosiest dreams, and the club runs of the early days, though short, contained plenty of incident and excitement—probably more, in fact, than the 100 or 150 mile run of today.

It is not possible now to give much detail of the trials encountered or the pleasures enjoyed by the original members on their short runs. but the following brief description of the first few runs may be of interest.

The first run in the history of the club was to Congleton, the date being 19th August, 1876, when four members turned out. A week later three members ventured as far as Hanley, but the following week only two turned out—the run being to Kingsley, Froghall, Ipstones and Bottomhouse. The fourth run, which was to Cheadle, attracted seven members, but one turned back at Wetley Rocks, and one stayed at Cheadle. The 24th Sept. was a big day, three members cycled to Stockport and from there took train to Manchester, where, it is interesting to note, they walked round the principal places of interest "*in the rain*," so it seems it could rain in Manchester even in those days. On October 22nd, five members enjoyed a very interesting afternoon. Cycling to Werrington, they partook of refreshments at the Windmill Inn, then viewed the Reformatory, and later by courtesy of the miller were able to view the interior of the windmill from the top of which they got a magnificent view of the surrounding countryside.

Some idea of the state of the roads may be gauged from the fact that before the club had been in existence twelve months it was found necessary to pass a rule to the effect that "Any member riding on the footpath be cautioned by the captain, and if he still persists he shall be fined threepence." During the same year practice nights were instituted ; Tuesday and Thursday being set apart for practice, and in order to familiarise the members with the difficulties encountered on the various roads, each of the five main roads was taken in turn. During the winter months, practice nights were devoted to walking exercise.

In 1878 a wooden bicycle was acquired by the Club "to be hired out at so much per hour," and in the same year the first race was run. It was to Sutton Toll Gate (just this side Macclesfield) and back. Mr. E. Challinor (Compton) and Mr. C. Schofield acted as starter and judge.

On the 20th January, 1879, on the proposition of Mr. T. Alcock, seconded by Mr. J. Hawksworth, the name of the club was changed from the Leek and Moorlands Bicycle Club, to the Leek Bicycle Club. Nothing very notable is recorded during this year, but on the 4th October, there is a record of a run to Rudyard *after parading the town*. A company of cyclists parading the town in these days would not create much of a sensation, but in the 'seventies bicycles and bicyclists, were almost as uncommon a sight as areoplanes are today ; everywhere they were regarded with a mixture of awe and amusement. and no doubt this parade of Leek cyclists would be quite an event in the town.

In 1881 tricycles were admitted to the club and in the following year a uniform was adopted as "regulation." It was comprised Military Tunic, "braided moderately," with knickerbockers, and brown helmet and stockings to match. Two years later the name of the club was changed to the Leek Cyclists' Club.

The first President was Mr. William Challinor, of Pickwood, who, in 1892, presented a silver cup to be competed for over a five mile grass course ; this cup was eventually won by Mr. A. Dunwell. On his retirement from the office of President, Mr. Challinor gave a generous subscription towards another cup. The conditions for which were that it should be won three times in succession, or five times in all, and it was offered for competition annually until 1932, when it was won outright by Mr. J. Barlow.

The present cup was presented to the club in 1933 by Sir Enoch Hill, and according to the present conditions, the competitor who makes the best aggregate time in three races 25, 30 and 50 miles, receives a miniature cup and holds the Championship Cup for twelve months—the winners to date are :—

1933—W. Robey, 1934—H. Bourne.
1935—G. Ager. 1936—J. Frost.

Amongst prominent local people who have been connected with the club, mention may be made of the following :—
Mr. W. Challinor, Pickwood ; Mr. J. Challinor, Compton ; Mr. E. Challinor, Compton; Col. Bill, M.P. ; Capt. Byrom, the Abbey ; Mr. T. S. Myatt ; Mr. G. V. Myatt ; Mr. S. Prince ; Mr. V. Prince ; Mr. G. C. Wardle ; Mr. H. Davenport, Woodcroft ; Mr. S. Chesters Thompson, Rudyard ; Mr. R. S. Milner ; the Rev. W. H. Hopkins ; Mr. A. H. Moore, and Mrs. A. H. Moore, who was the first lady member.

Special mention should be made of Mr. W. T. Cook, the first captain, who has held office in one capacity or another ever since the club was founded over sixty years ago—a magnificent record of loyal and devoted service, that has been of invaluable benefit to the club.

LEEK POOLEND WATER SCHEME.

PUMPING STATION. PHOTO BY W. H. HORNE, LEEK.

WHEN the publisher of "Leek News" invited me to contribute a few notes on the above Scheme, I felt I must do so if only to show my appreciation of the keen interest he has taken as a member of the Water Committee in the development of the undertaking. It may be that interest was keener because as Chairman of the Fire Brigade and Baths Committee water is the great essential in both departments.

The Poolend Scheme is so certain to play a big part in the future welfare of the town that its inauguration must be looked upon as the great outstanding event in our municipal life during 1935.

The necessity for a greatly increased water supply has of course been brought about owing to the improved sanitary conditions now prevailing, the large number of new houses erected with baths, and also by additional demands for trade purposes.

For these reasons, coupled with the serious droughts during the past three summers, the difficulties of the Water Committee have become more and more acute year by year, until in order to prevent what might have proved a serious calamity to our town something definite had to be done.

It will be remembered that so far back as 1923 increased demand for water was such, that after months of discussion, the Council purchased land at Swainsmoor with the object of damming the river flowing through the Swainsmoor valley, and making a reservoir in order to augment the supply from the springs at Upperhulme. The estimated cost of that scheme, however, was about £150,000, and, as that sum was altogether in excess of what the town could face, it had to be abandoned.

Then in the year 1933 the Water Committee again gave the matter very serious consideration, and acting upon the advice of the eminent geologists, Messrs. Lapworth, Partners, of London, in conjunction with Mr. W. E. Beacham, our Water Engineer, the Council decided to purchase land at Poolend and boring was commenced.

Several months later, at a depth of 400 feet, water was reached.

As usually happens the supply at first was not quite satisfactory, but after continued pumping for several days the anxiety of the Water Committee and the Council was rewarded by a wonderful volume of water, beautifully soft, as clear as crystal and absolutely free from smell.

The fact that the natural condition of the water is soft means of course there will be no cost in providing a softening plant, and no expenditure for working and general upkeep in connection with softening processes.

The estimated output from Poolend is a million gallons per day, and that quantity, in addition to the 400,000 gallons per day under normal conditions from the springs at Upperhulme, will in all probability prove sufficient to satisfy the requirements of our town and district for many years to come.

The method of supply is by pumps driven by electricity to the reservoirs on Mount Pleasant and then back to the town by gravitation as from the springs at Upperhulme.

What the Council is now hoping for is a considerably increased demand for water for trading purposes, and for trades such as dyeing, bleaching and similar industries the supply offered is equal in quality to anything in the country.

Not only so, but a future important factor is that cheap rates are available for the purpose of encouraging new industries, especially trades employing male labour.

The exceptionally low Water Rate of fourpence in the £ on the rateable value of property is the charge made by the Council for domestic purposes.

The estimated cost of the Poolend scheme was about £20,000, but the actual cost will be considerably less than the estimate. The pipe line is laid for a distance of $2\frac{3}{4}$ miles.

We were favoured by a glorious afternoon for the opening ceremony, which took place at Poolend on October 13th in the presence of a great number of the leading and influential inhabitants of the town.

The people of Leek and District as owners of the water supply are to be congratulated upon the very pronounced success of the venture. Surely it will prove a great asset to the general prosperity of the town.

The following Councillors were members of the Water Committee during the development of the scheme:—Councillors S. Bowcock (Chairman 1933-34), J. W. Swindells (Chairman 1934-35), H. Morton (Ex-Officio 1934-35), J. Bayley, J. Clowes, W. Clowes, H. J. Cope (1933-34), F. Downes, A. Flower (1933-34), F. Hill, A. Ratcliffe, M.P., (1933-34), A. Y. Worthington, and Colonel L. J. Worthington.

With best wishes for a Happy and Prosperous New Year.

JOHN WM. SWINDELLS,
Chairman of the Water Committee.

The New Reservoir at Leek.

PROBABLY the biggest and most interesting municipal development in Leek during the past twelve months has been the construction of a new reservoir at Kniveden.

It is now six years since the Urban District Council obtained the necessary powers from Parliament to construct this Reservoir, and being commenced last year, it has recently been completed.

The necessary plans were prepared by Mr. W. E. Beacham, the Town Surveyor and Water Engineer, and it is satisfactory to know that the contract was placed locally with Mr. Thomas Grace, and Messrs. E. Phillips & Sons as sub-contractors. The accepted tender was £10,470, while a further £1,750 was spent on laying mains by direct labour, making a total cost of £12,220. The reservoir is 144 feet long by 100 feet 9 ins. wide and 12 feet deep and is divided into two equal compartments which can be used separately so as to permit of cleansing, and has a holding capacity of 1,000,000 gallons.

The top water level of the reservoir is 808 feet above Ordnance Datum and will give a static head in the town of 122 feet more than is given by the existing 2,000,000 gallons reservoir. This elevation will enable the town to be divided into low and high level zones. The low-level area with a consumption of 200,000 gallons per day being supplied from the existing reservoir, and the high-level area with a consumption of 300,000 gallons per day being supplied from the new reservoir.

This arrangement, when further extension of the mains have been carried out, will greatly improve the pressure in the town generally and will mean a more adequate supply in many high lying streets that in the past have not had a satisfactory water supply owing to lack of pressure on the mains.

The reservoir was formerly opened on Thursday, the 22nd October last.

Amongst those present were Mr. G. H. Sheldon, J.P., the chairman of the Council; Mr. H. J. Cope, chairman of the Water Committee, and other members of the Council with a number of officials, contractors and members of the public.

As a preliminary to the formal opening the company was invited to inspect the inside of the reservoir, and it was a somewhat strange and thrilling experience descending the iron ladder leading down to the floor of the reservoir. Despite the many brick pillars necessary to support the roof (as are seen in the above illustration) the inside of the reservoir presented the appearance of a very spacious chamber, the darkness of which was only pierced by the few glimmerings of light that came through the ventilators in the roof.

The ceremony was opened by Councillor Cope who briefly reviewed the considerations that had decided the Committee to recommend the construction of the reservoir, and said the Committee had taken every possible precaution to secure the greatest possible benefit for the town for the expense involved. He then called upon Councillor Sheldon formally to open the reservoir.

In a happy little speech Mr. Sheldon briefly expressed the pleasure and honour he felt in being asked to perform so important a duty, and then by opening the valve which allowed the water to pour into the reservoir, completed the formal opening.

We understand after being filled with water the reservoir was tested many times during the following two weeks, and it was pleasing to hear that in his report to the Committee, Mr. Beacham stated that the water in the reservoir had not decreased in the least during that time—it was in fact a thoroughly sound and satisfactory job in every way. A report which the contractor, Mr. Grace, and all concerned may well be proud.

Photograph of the Members of the Council, guests and officials at the inauguration of the 400 K.Ws. Vertical Tandem Generating Set at the Electricity Works in June, 1924.

The beautiful countryside around Leek

Left and below:

The Roches just north of Leek, Rock Hall and the Steps.

Near the steps is the "Queen's Chair", commemorating the visit to the Roches of the Duke and Duchess of Teck in 1872

THE ROCHES, NR. LEEK.

Left:
The old village of Upperhulme, sitting under the Roches, where William Tatton founded his first dyeworks in 1869

[illegible] UPPER HULME.

Solomons Hollow, on the main road from Leek to Buxton.

SOLOMONS HOLLOW, NR. LEEK.

Trade bills early 20th C

Telegraphic Address:
VALLEN, LEEK.
CHURNET VALLEY ENGINEERING Co.
HOPE FOUNDRY, LEEK,
May 27th 19
Bot. OF
DEC 4th 1905
EDDOWES
H. EDDOWES,
MILLINERY, GENERAL AND FANCY DRAPER.
DRESSES, GLOVES &c.
MANTLES,
5&7, SHEEP MARKET, LEEK.
32a, DERBY STR
LEEK,
DR. TO C. SIMISTER,
WHOLESALE & RETAIL SHOE MANUFACTURER.
TERMS:—5 per cent. charged on all overdu
TELEPHONE 29.
Strangman's Street.
Leek, Mch 31 1914
Bot. of L. Whittles & Son,
Millers & Corn Merchants.
AGENTS FOR IND. COOPE & Co's BURTON ALES, PORTER, ETC.
SACKS CHARGED 1/6 EACH.
5 PER CENT CHARGED ON OVERDUE ACCOUNTS.
TRADE MARK REGISTERED
No 207496
TRADE MARK REGISTERED
No 208333
MANUFACTURERS OF SEWIN
WEST ST MILL
AND CHORLEY MI
Staffordshire
1903
Memorandum From Wilcock & Co.
SILK MANUFACTURERS.

Transport in Leek

Leek was a busy railway station, as seen above and bottom of the page. There were also railway stations at Leekbrook, Rudyard, Ipstones and Wallgrange, seen right, next to the Caldon Canal at Longsdon.

Leek had the advantage of a canal connection into the national canal system from 1800.

It also had a railway connection from 1849 with lines to Macclesfield, Stoke, Waterhouses and Uttoxeter.

Right: Leek station.

Above:
The old Canal Basin behind Newcastle Road. The Churnet Valley Railway pub (now closed) is seen in the mid-background and the gasworks are seen to the right.
Right: the Leek branch of the Caldon canal that led to the canal basin .

After the First World War road transport inexorably grew in importance through the century. The Leek canal basin is now the site of Midco building supplies (previously Midlands Electricity Board). The railway station closed to passenger traffic in 1965. The site is now the Safeway store
Left: the Market Place with various forms of public transport c1930. The bus in the foreground is advertising a day-trip to Scarborough, fare 12 shillings.

BIBLIOGRAPHY

HISTORY OF THE ANCIENT PARISH OF LEEK: John Sleigh (First edition 1862) (Second, enlarged edition 1883)
OLDE LEEKE: M.H. Miller (1891); Vol. 2: M.H. Miller (1900)
FOOTBALL IN LEEK: Charles Diehl (1893)
LECTURES, VERSES, SPEECHES, REMINISCENCES etc: William Challinor (1891)
IN THE HIGHLANDS OF STAFFORDSHIRE: W.H. Nithsdale (1906)
LEEK PAST AND PRESENT: W.H. Nithsdale
A PEEP INTO THE PAST: Leek Moorlands Hospital: Percy Walton
OLD ST. EDWARD STREET: Beryl Johnson
COMPTON SCHOOL - A Century of Education: June Whitehead
80 YEARS OF LEEK CRICKET: Tom Tipper (1924)
150 YEARS OF LEEK CRICKET: Ray Poole (1994)
THE WARDLE STORY: Anne Jacques (1996)
HISTORY OF THE 2nd LEEK SCOUTS: Basil Turner (1997)
THE HAPPY HIGHWAYS: Ray Poole (1998)
OVER THERE - The Old Leek Battery 1908-1919: J.E. Blore
LEEK THIRTY YEARS AGO: Lindsey Porter (1991)
AROUND LEEK IN OLD PHOTOGRAPHS: Ray Poole (1994
IN NAME ONLY (Leek War Memorial): C.W. Sheldon (2000)
SPIRIT OF LEEK, Vols. 1 and 2: Cathryn Walton and Lindsey Porter (2001)
VICTORIA COUNTY HISTORY OF STAFFORDSHIRE Vol.VII: Leek & the Moorlands (1996)
A CERTAIN GROUP OF MEN: G.A. Lovenbury
AROUND LEEK IN CAMERA: Ray Poole (1990)
BONNIE PRINCE CHARLIE: Harold Bode
BRITANNIA BUILDING SOCIETY 1856-1985: R. Redden (1985)
CHRONICLES - Occasional journal of Leek Historical Society
COMMENTARIES AND RECOLLECTIONS: G.A.Lovenbury (1976)
DIEULACRES ABBEY: Michael Fisher (Revised edition 1989)
FRENCH CONNECTIONS: J. Bennett, C. Parrack, R. Poole, C. Walton (1995)
HISTORY OF LEEK HIGH SCHOOL: C.K.R. Pearce (1960)
IMAGES OF EDWARDIAN LEEK: Paul Anderton (1984)
LEEK IN OLD PICTURE POSTCARDS: Ray Poole (1984)
LEEK MARKET PLACE: G.A.Lovenbury (1981)
LEEK AND DISTRICT ROLL OF HONOUR 1914-1915
METHODISM IN LEEK AND THE MOORLANDS 1753-1943: J.W. Wardle (1943)
LEEK 50 YEARS AGO: M.H. Miller (1887)
LEEK - THE FORGOTTEN CENTURIES: Elizabeth Biddulph (1999)
LEEK CANAL AND RUYARD RESERVOIR: Harold Bode
LEEK IN 1861: Paul Anderton
LEEK REMEMBERED: V. Priestman (1980)
LEEK VOLUNTEERS: Paul Anderton and Cathryn Walton
PLACE NAMES IN THE MOORLANDS Harry Ball (1989)
MILL STREET: G.A. Lovenbury (1979)
THE NICHOLSON INSTITUTE: A Study of Middle Class Munificence. Pauline Smith (1984)
THE OLD LEEK SUNDAY SCHOOL 1797-1897 - A Centenary Record: Rev. T. Brigden
A BRIEF HISTORY OF THE RISE AND PROGRESS OF WESLEYAN METHODISM IN THE LEEK CIRCUIT: Rev J B. Dyson (1853)
RUDYARD LAKE 1797-1997: Basil Jeuda (1997)
RUDYARD REFLECTIONS: Basil Jeuda (2001)
THE CHURNET VALLEY RAILWAY Basil Jeuda (1999)
ST. EDWARD STREET AND BROAD STREET: G.A.Lovenbury (1990)
STAFFORDSHIRE (The King's England): Arthur Mee
STAFFORDSHIRE (The Buildings of England): Nicholas Pevsner
STAFFORDSHIRE MOORLANDS IN OLD PICTURE POSTCARDS Vol.1: George Short; Vol.2: G. Bowyer & R. Poole
SUGDENS OF LEEK: G.A. Lovenbury (1975)
THE CALDON CANAL AND RUDYARD RESERVOIR: Harold Bode (1971)
THE STAFFORDSHIRE MOORLANDS: Lindsey Porter (1983)
THE WASTED YEARS? Leek High School 1934-1949: Nancy Ramsey (1992)
THE WESTWOOD ESTATE: Marshall Boylan (1996)
VISITING LEEK 1 and 2: Harold Bode (1979 and 1984)
JAMES BRINDLEY: Harold Bode
JAMES BRINDLEY, CANAL ENGINEER - A new perpective: Kathleen M. Evans (1998)
WILLIAM TATTON & Co. CENTENARY 1869-1969
YESTERDAY'S TOWN - LEEK: Ray Poole (1988)
MONASTIC STAFFORDSHIRE: John L. Tomkinson (2000)
A VISION OF SPLENDOUR - Gothic Revival in Staffordshire 1840-1890: Michael Fisher
STAFFORDSHIRE MOORLANDS AND CHURNET VALLEY: L. Porter & C. Walton
THE STORY OF SILK: Dr. John Feltwell (1990)
FIFTY YEARS OF LOCAL GOVERNMENT IN LEEK 1855-1905
SOUVENIR HISTORY OF LEEK & MOORLANDS CO-OPERATIVE SOCIETY 1859-1909
LEEK METHODIST CIRCUIT YEAR BOOKS (Various years)
CHRONICLES - The occasional journal of Leek Historical Society
WHITE'S DIRECTORY OF STAFFORDSHIRE (1831 and 1851)
KELLY'S DIRECTORY OF STAFFORDSHIRE (Various years)

This list does not include many booklets, brochures, guide books, reports and commemorative items.